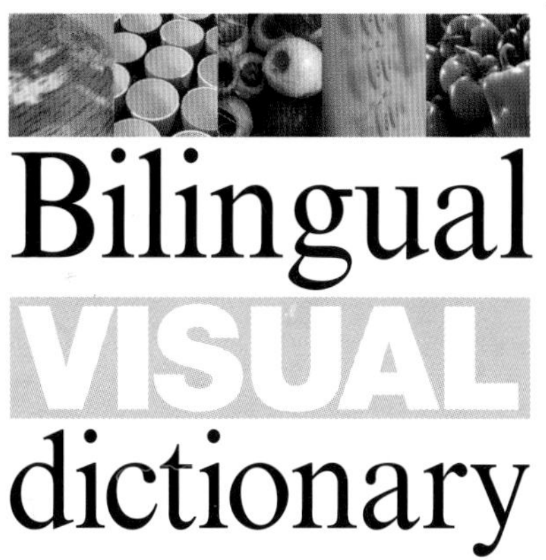
Bilingual
VISUAL
dictionary

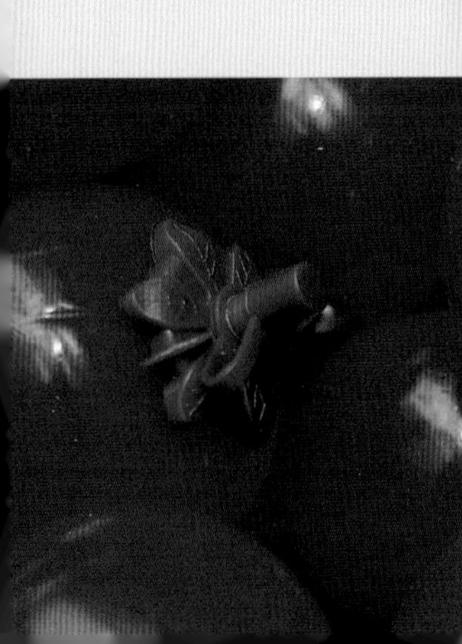

TOP-FLITE XL
Titleist

Bilingual VISUAL dictionary

Previously published as part of
5-Language Visual Dictionary

A DORLING KINDERSLEY BOOK

London, New York, Melbourne, Munich, Delhi

Senior Editor Angeles Gavira
Senior Art Editor Ina Stradins
DTP Designers Sunil Sharma, Balwant Singh, Harish Aggarwal, John Goldsmid, Ashwani Tyagi
DTP Coordinator Pankaj Sharma
Production Controller Liz Cherry
Picture Researcher Anna Grapes
Managing Editor Liz Wheeler
Managing Art Editor Phil Ormerod
Category Publisher Jonathan Metcalf

Designed for Dorling Kindersley by WaltonCreative.com
Art Editor Colin Walton, assisted by Tracy Musson
Designers Peter Radcliffe, Earl Neish, Ann Cannings
Picture Research Marissa Keating

Language content for Dorling Kindersley by g-and-w PUBLISHING
Managed by Jane Wightwick, assisted by Ana Bremón
Translation and editing by Ana Bremón
Additional input by Dr. Arturo Pretel, Martin Prill, Frédéric Monteil, Meinrad Prill, Mari Bremón, Oscar Bremón, Anunchi Bremón, Leila Gaafar

First American Edition, 2005
Published in the United States by
DK Publishing, 345 Hudson Street,
New York, New York 10014
20 19 18 17
061-BD219-Aug/2005

A Cataloging-in-Publication record for this book is available from the Library of Congress.
ISBN-13: 978-0-7566-1298-6

Color reproduction by Colourscan, Singapore
Printed and bound in China by L.Rex Printing Co., Ltd

Discover more at
www.dk.com

contenido
contents

42 **la salud**
health

146 **comer fuera**
eating out

252 **el ocio**
leisure

sobre el diccionario
about the dictionary

cómo utilizar este libro
how to use this book

la gente
people

el aspecto
appearance

la casa
home

los servicios
services

las compras
shopping

los alimentos
food

el estudio
study

el trabajo
work

el transporte
transport

los deportes
sports

el medio ambiente
environment

los datos
reference

índice
index

agradecimientos
acknowledgments

la gente • people

el cuerpo | body 12
la cara | face 14
la mano | hand 15
el pie | foot 15
los músculos | muscles 16
el esqueleto | skeleton 17
los órganos internos internal organs 18
los órganos reproductores reproductive organs 20
la familia | family 22
las relaciones relationships 24
las emociones | emotions 25
los acontecimientos de una vida | life events 26

el aspecto • appearance

la ropa de niño children's clothing 30
la ropa de caballero men's clothing 32
la ropa de dama (C la ropa de señora) | women's clothing 34
los accesorios | accessories 36
el pelo | hair 38
la belleza | beauty 40

la salud • health

la enfermedad | illness 44
el médico | doctor 45
la lesión | injury 46
los primeros auxilios first aid 47
el hospital | hospital 48
el dentista | dentist 50
el óptico | optometrist 51
el embarazo | pregnancy 52
el parto | childbirth 53
las terapias alternativas complementary therapy 54

la casa • home

la casa | house 58
las instalaciones internas internal systems 60
la sala (C el cuarto de estar) living room 62
el comedor | dining room 64
la cocina | kitchen 66
los utensilios de cocina kitchenware 68
el dormitorio | bedroom 70
el cuarto de baño bathroom 72
la habitación de los niños baby's room 74
la lavandería (C el lavadero) utility room 76
el taller | workshop 78
la caja de las herramientas toolbox 80
la decoración | decorating 82
el jardín | garden 84
las plantas de jardín garden plants 86
las herramientas de jardinería | garden tools 88
la jardinería | gardening 90

los servicios • services

los servicios de emergencia emergency services 94
el banco | bank 96
las comunicaciones communications 98
el hotel | hotel 100

las compras • shopping

el centro comercial shopping center 104
las tiendas departamentales (C los grandes almacenes) department store 105
el supermercado supermarket 106
la farmacia | pharmacy 108
la florería (C la floristería) florist 110
los tabacos y las revistas (C el vendedor de periódicos) newsstand 112
la dulcería (C el vendedor de golosinas) | confectionery 113
las otras tiendas other stores 114

los alimentos • food

la carne | meat 118
el pescado | fish 120
las verduras | vegetables 122
la fruta | fruit 126
los granos y las legumbres | grains and legumes 130
las hierbas y las especias herbs and spices 132
los alimentos embotellados bottled foods 134
los productos lácteos dairy produce 136
el pan y las harinas breads and flours 138
la repostería cakes and desserts 140
la charcutería | delicatessen 142
las bebidas | drinks 144

comer fuera • eating out

la cafeteria | café 148

el bar | bar 150

el restaurante | restaurant 152

la comida rápida | fast food 154

el desayuno | breakfast 156

la comida principal dinner 158

el estudio • study

la escuela ([C] **el colegio**) school 162

las matemáticas | math 164

las ciencias | science 166

la enseñanza superior college 168

el trabajo • work

la oficina | office 172

la computadora ([C] **el ordenador**) computer 176

los medios de comunicación | media 178

el derecho | law 180

la granja | farm 182

la construcción | construction 186

las profesiones | professions 188

el transporte • transportation

las carreteras | roads 194

el autobús | bus 196

el carro ([C] **el coche**) | car 198

la motocicleta | motorcycle 204

la bicicleta | bicycle 206

el tren | train 208

el avión | aircraft 210

el aeropuerto | airport 212

el barco | ship 214

el puerto | port 216

los deportes • sport

el fútbol americano football 220

el rugby | rugby 221

el fútbol | soccer 222

el hockey | hockey 224

el críquet | cricket 225

el baloncesto | basketball 226

el béisbol | baseball 228

el tenis | tennis 230

el golf | golf 232

el atletismo | track and field 234

los deportes de combate combat sports 236

la natación | swimming 238

la vela | sailing 240

la equitación | horse riding 242

la pesca | fishing 244

el esquí | skiing 246

los otros deportes other sports 248

la forma física | fitness 250

el ocio • leisure

el teatro | theater 254

la orquesta | orchestra 256

el concierto | concert 258

el turismo | sightseeing 260

las actividades al aire libre outdoor activities 262

la playa | beach 264

el camping | camping 266

el ocio en el hogar home entertainment 268

la fotografía | photography 270

los juegos | games 272

las manualidades arts and crafts 274

el medio ambiente • environment

el espacio | space 280

la Tierra | Earth 282

el paisaje | landscape 284

el tiempo | weather 286

las rocas | rocks 288

los minerales | minerals 289

los animales | animals 290

las plantas | plants 296

la ciudad | town 298

la arquitectura architecture 300

los datos • reference

el tiempo | time 304

el calendario ([C] **el almanaque**) | calendar 306

los números | numbers 308

los pesos y las medidas weights and measures 310

el mapamundi world map 312

partículas y antónimos particles and antonyms 320

frases útiles | useful phrases 322

sobre el diccionario

Está comprobado que el empleo de fotografías ayuda a la comprensión y a la retención de información. Basados en este principio, este diccionario bilíngüe y altamente ilustrado exhibe un amplio registro de vocabulario útil y actual en dos idiomas europeos.

El diccionario aparece dividido según su temática y abarca la mayoría de los aspectos del mundo cotidiano con detalle, desde el restaurante al gimnasio, la casa al lugar de trabajo, el espacio al reino animal. Encontrará también palabras y frases adicionales para su uso en conversación y para ampliar su vocabulario.

Este diccionario es un instrumento de referencia esencial para todo aquél que esté interesado en los idiomas; es práctico, estimulante y fácil de usar.

Algunos puntos a observar

Los dos idiomas se presentan siempre en el mismo orden: español (mejicano y castellano) e inglés. Cuando existen diferencias entre el castellano y el español mejicano, el mejicano aparece primero seguido por el castellano; este último entre paréntesis e indicado con una [C]: **la llave** ([C]**el grifo**).

En español, los sustantivos se muestran con sus artículos definidos reflejando el género (masculino o femenino) y el número (singular/plural):

la semilla	**las almendras**
seed	almonds

Los verbos se indican con una (v) después del inglés:

recolectar • harvest (v)

Cada idioma tiene su propio índice. Aquí podrá mirar una palabra en cualquiera de los dos idiomas y se le indicará el número de la página donde aparece. El género se indica utilizando las siguientes abreviaturas:

m = masculino f = femenino

about the dictionary

The use of pictures is proven to aid understanding and the retention of information. Working on this principle, this highly illustrated bilingual dictionary presents a large range of useful current vocabulary in two European languages.

The dictionary is divided thematically and covers most aspects of the everyday world in detail, from the restaurant to the gym, the home to the workplace, outer space to the animal kingdom. You will also find additional words and phrases for conversational use and for extending your vocabulary.

This is an essential reference tool for anyone interested in languages—practical, stimulating, and easy-to-use.

A few things to note

The two languages are always presented in the same order—Spanish (Mexican and Castilian) and English. Where a word or phrase is different in Castilian and Mexican Spanish, the Mexican appears first, followed by the Castilian; the latter in brackets and indicated by a [C]: **la llave** ([C]**el grifo**).

In Spanish, nouns are given with their definite articles reflecting the gender (masculine or feminine) and number (singular or plural), for example:

la semilla	**las almendras**
seed	almonds

Verbs are indicated by a (v) after the English, for example:

recolectar • harvest (v)

Each language also has its own index at the back of the book. Here you can look up a word in either of the two languages and be referred to the page number(s) where it appears. The gender is shown using the following abbreviations:

m = masculine f = feminine

cómo utilizar este libro

Ya se encuentre aprendiendo un idioma nuevo por motivos de trabajo, placer, o para preparar sus vacaciones al extranjero, o ya quiera ampliar su vocabulario en un idioma que ya conoce, este diccionario es un instrumento muy valioso que podrá utilizar de distintas maneras.

Cuando esté aprendiendo un idioma nuevo, busque palabras similares en distintos idiomas y palabras que parecen similares pero que poseen significados totalmente distintos. También podrá observar cómo los idiomas se influyen unos a otros. Por ejemplo, la lengua inglesa ha importado muchos términos de comida de otras lenguas pero, a cambio, ha exportado términos empleados en tecnología y cultura popular.

Actividades prácticas de aprendizaje

- Mientras se desplaza por su casa, lugar de trabajo o colegio, intente mirar las páginas que se refieren a ese lugar. Podrá entonces cerrar el libro, mirar a su alrededor y ver cuántos objetos o características puede nombrar.
- Desafíese a usted mismo a escribir una historia, carta o diálogo empleando tantos términos de una página concreta como le sea posible. Esto le ayudará a retener vocabulario y recordar la ortografía. Si quiere ir progresando para poder escribir un texto más largo, comience con frases que incorporen 2 ó 3 palabras.
- Si tiene buena memoria visual, intente dibujar o calcar objetos del libro; luego cierre el libro y escriba las palabras correspondientes debajo del dibujo.
- Cuando se sienta más seguro, escoja palabras del índice de uno de los idiomas y vea si sabe lo que significan antes de consultar la página correspondiente para comprobarlo.

how to use this book

Whether you are learning a new language for business, pleasure, or in preparation for an overseas vacation, or are hoping to extend your vocabulary in an already familiar language, this dictionary is a valuable learning tool that you can use in a number of different ways.

When learning a new language, look for cognates (words that are alike in different languages) and "false friends" (words that look alike but carry significantly different meanings). You can also see where the languages have influenced each other. For example, English has imported many terms for food from other European languages but, in turn, exported terms used in technology and popular culture.

Practical learning activities

- As you move around your home, workplace, or school, try looking at the pages which cover that setting. You could then close the book, look around you, and see how many of the objects and features you can name.
- Challenge yourself to write a story, letter, or dialogue using as many of the terms on a particular page as possible. This will help you retain the vocabulary and remember the spelling. If you want to build up to writing a longer text, start with sentences incorporating 2–3 words.
- If you have a very visual memory, try drawing or tracing items from the book onto a piece of paper, then closing the book and filling in the words below the picture.
- Once you are more confident, pick out words in a foreign-language index and see if you know what they mean before turning to the relevant page to see if you were right.

la gente
people

el cuerpo • body

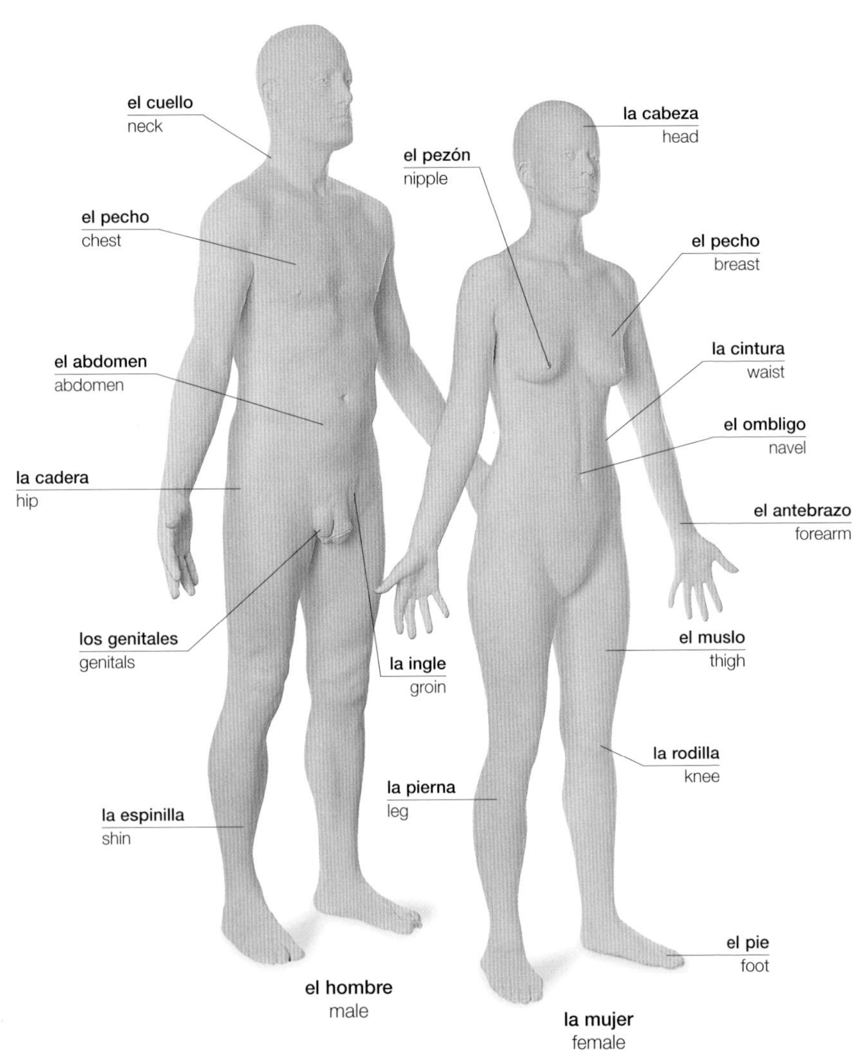

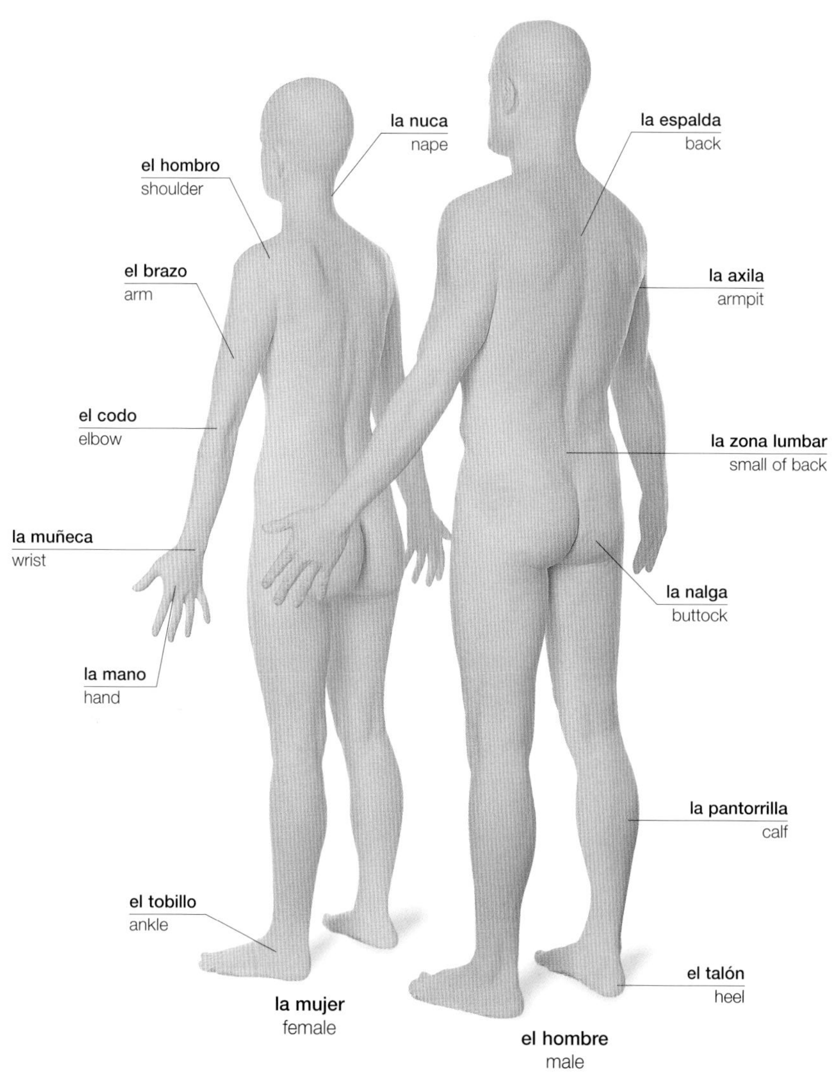
la nuca
nape
el hombro
shoulder
la espalda
back
el brazo
arm
la axila
armpit
el codo
elbow
la zona lumbar
small of back
la muñeca
wrist
la nalga
buttock
la mano
hand
la pantorrilla
calf
el tobillo
ankle
el talón
heel
la mujer
female
el hombre
male

la cara • face

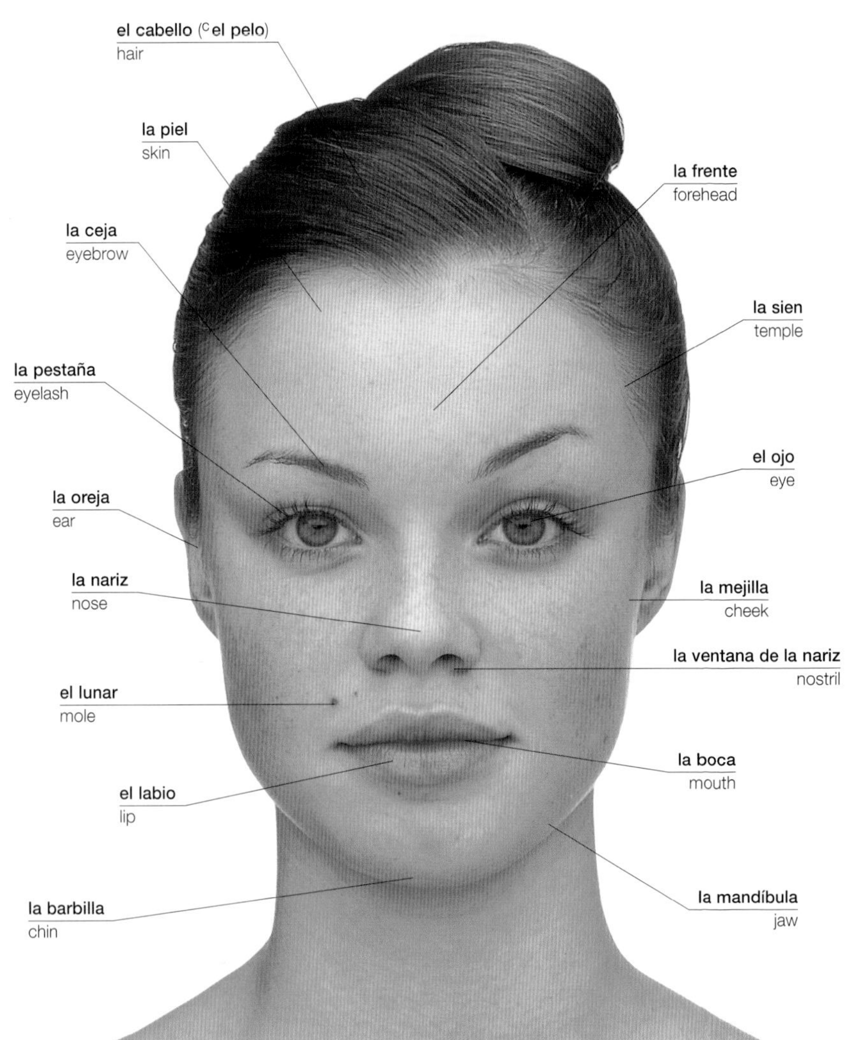
el cabello (C el pelo)
hair
la piel
skin
la frente
forehead
la ceja
eyebrow
la sien
temple
la pestaña
eyelash
el ojo
eye
la oreja
ear
la nariz
nose
la mejilla
cheek
la ventana de la nariz
nostril
el lunar
mole
la boca
mouth
el labio
lip
la mandíbula
jaw
la barbilla
chin

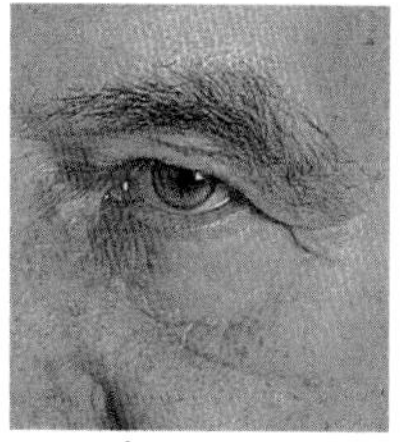

la arruga
wrinkle

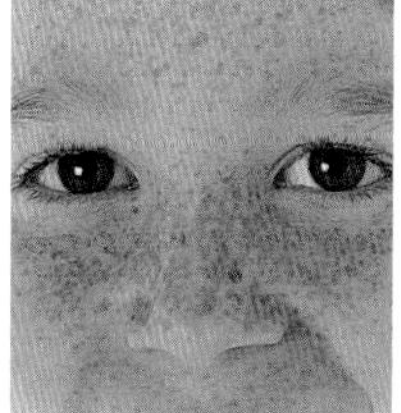

la peca
freckle

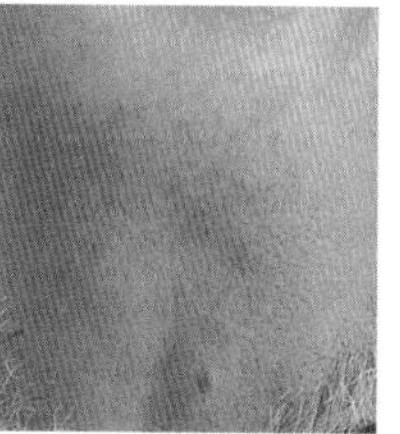

el poro
pore

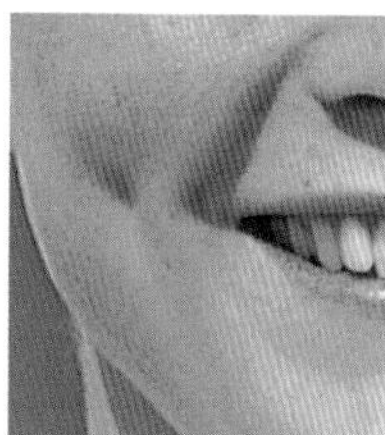

el hoyuelo
dimple

la mano • hand

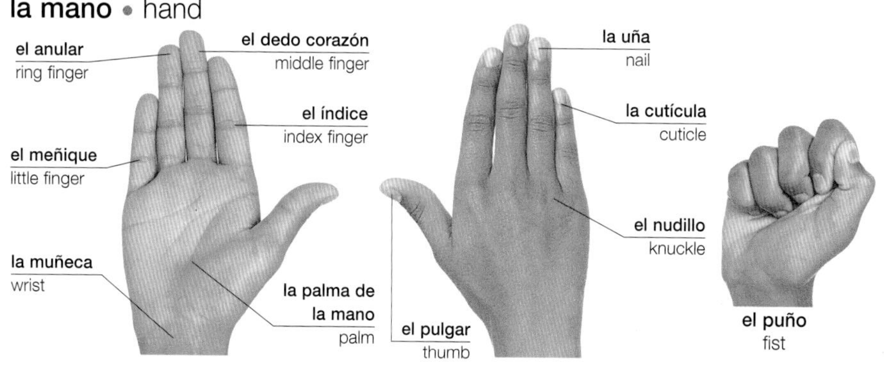

el pie • foot

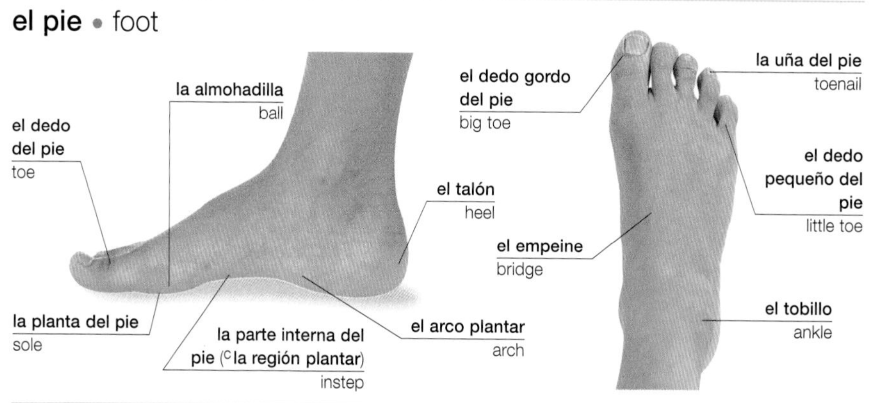

los músculos • muscles

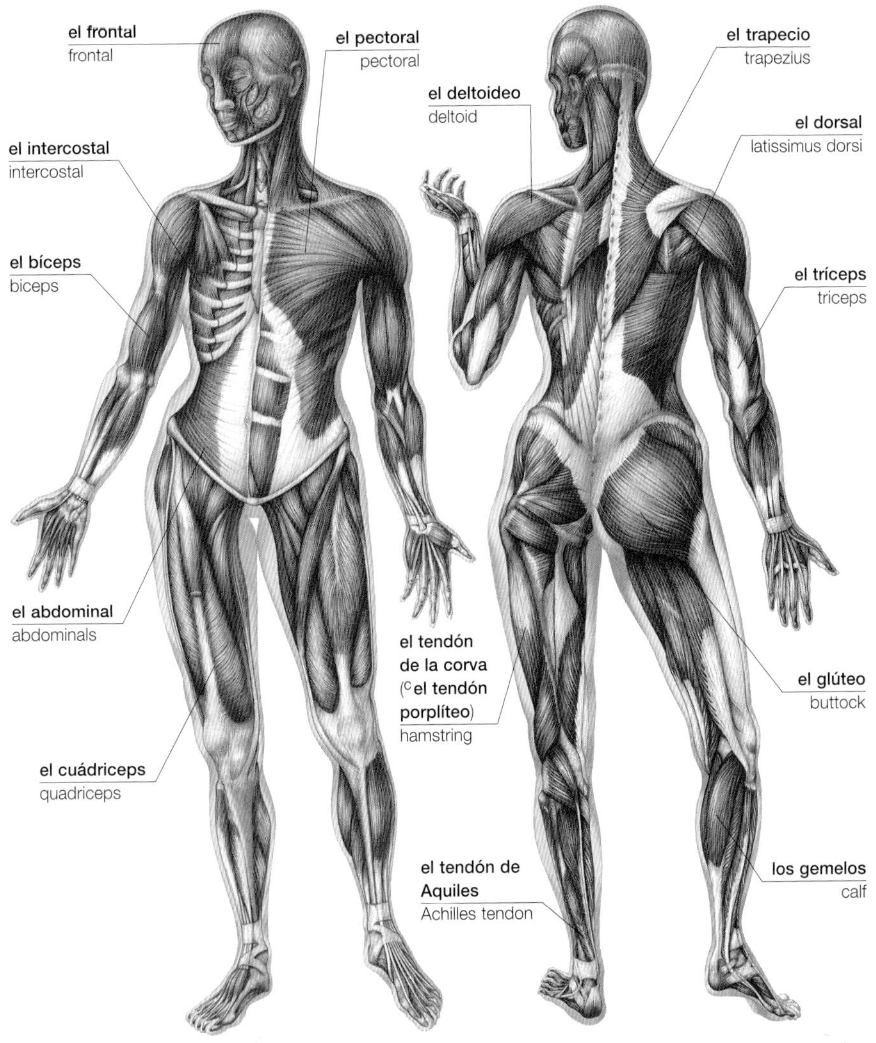

el esqueleto • skeleton

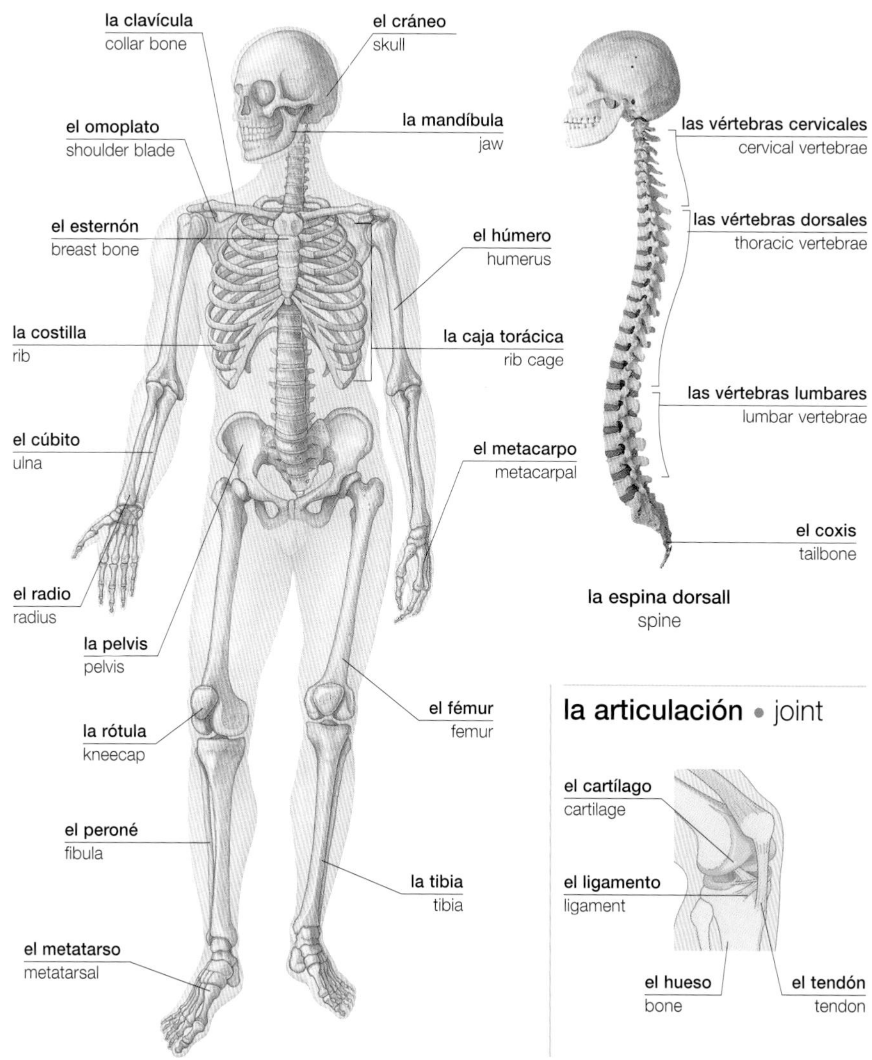

la articulación • joint

los órganos internos • internal organs

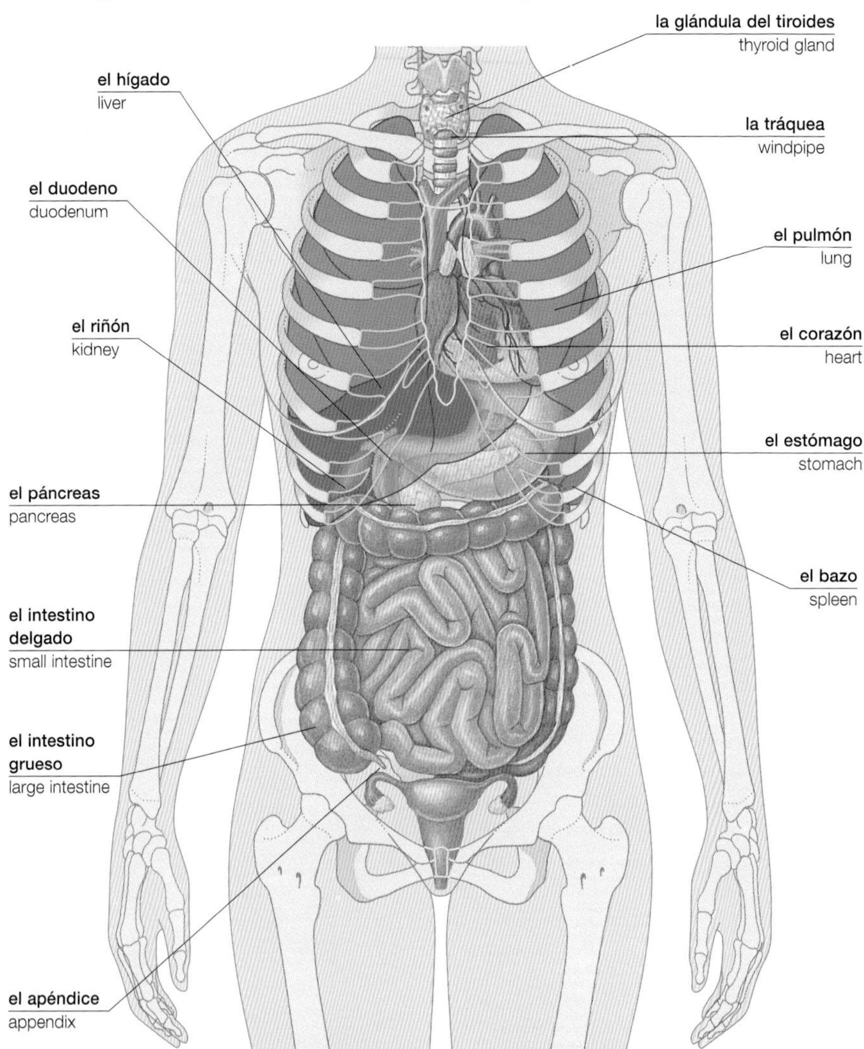

la cabeza • head

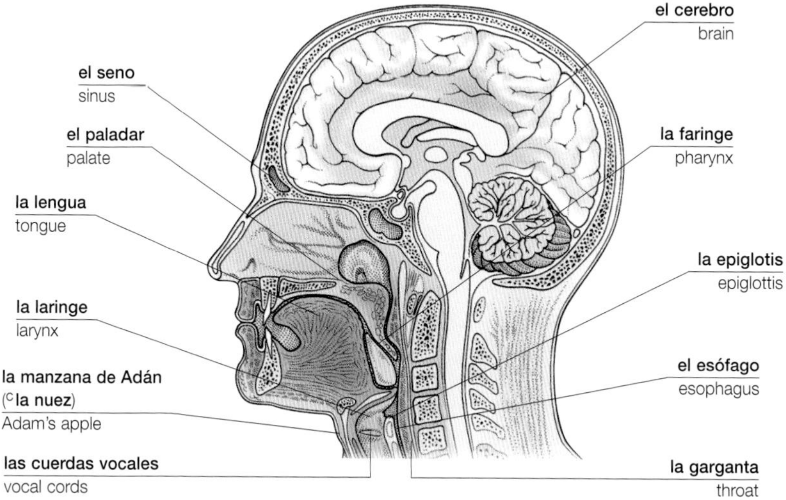

el cerebro
brain
el seno
sinus
el paladar
palate
la faringe
pharynx
la lengua
tongue
la epiglotis
epiglottis
la laringe
larynx
el esófago
esophagus
la manzana de Adán
(ᶜla nuez)
Adam's apple
las cuerdas vocales
vocal cords
la garganta
throat

los sistemas • body systems

el diafragma
diaphragm

respiratorio
respiratory

digestivo
digestive

la vena
vein
la arteria
artery

cardiovascular
cardiovascular

linfático
lymphatic

urinario
urinary

la glándula
gland

endocrino
endocrine

el nervio
nerve

nervioso
nervous

reproductor
reproductive

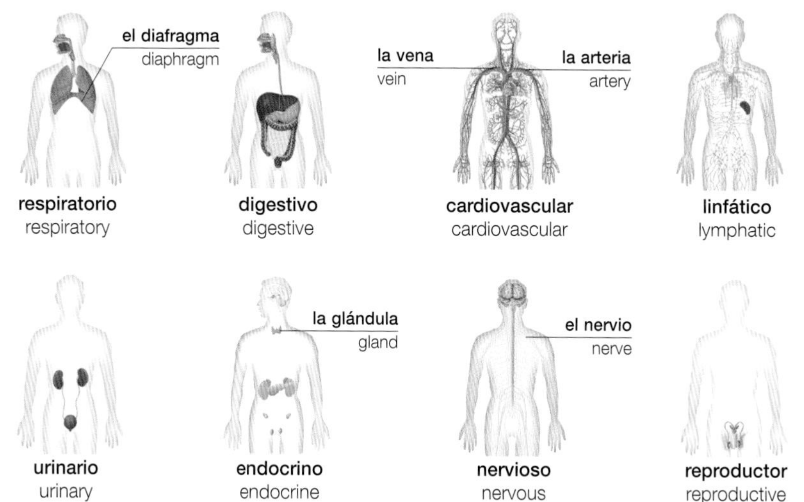

los órganos reproductores • reproductive organs

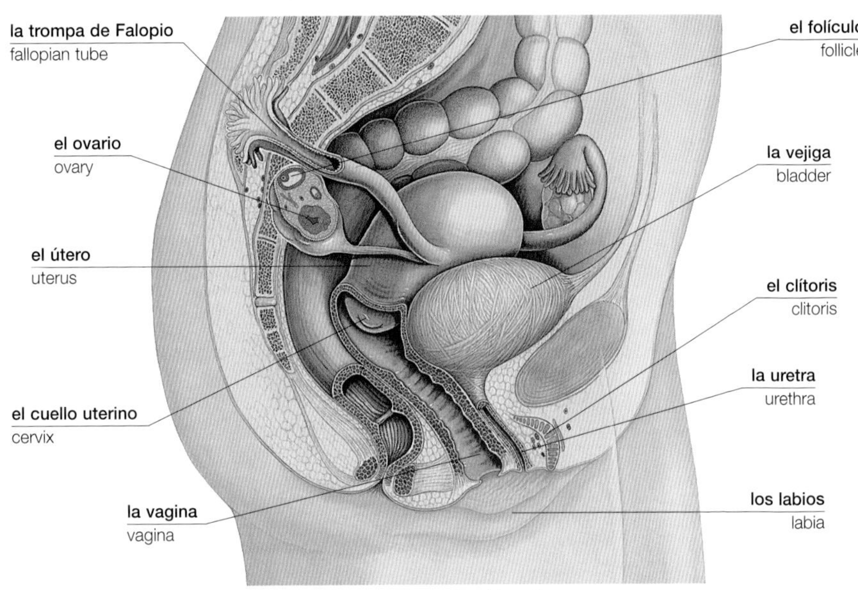

femenino | female

la reproducción • reproduction

el esperma
sperm

el óvulo
egg

la fertilización | fertilization

vocabulario • vocabulary

la hormona hormone	**impotente** impotent	**la menstruación** menstruation
la ovulación ovulation	**fértil** fertile	**el coito** intercourse
estéril infertile	**concebir** conceive	**la enfermedad de transmisión sexual** sexually transmitted disease

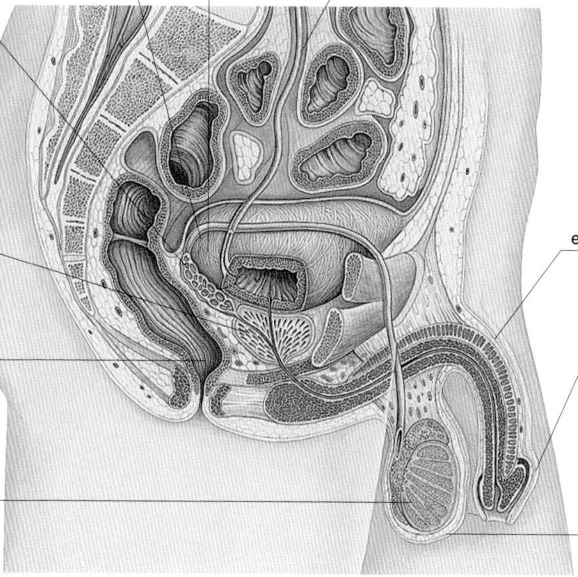

el conducto seminal
ejaculatory duct

el conducto deferente
vas deferens

el uréter
ureter

la vesícula seminal
seminal vesicle

la próstata
prostate

el pene
penis

el recto
rectum

el prepucio
foreskin

el testículo
testicle

el escroto
scrotum

masculino | male

la anticoncepción • contraception

el anillo cervical
cap

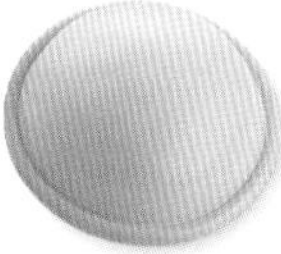

el diafragma
diaphragm

el condón
condom

el dispositivo intrauterino DIU
IUD

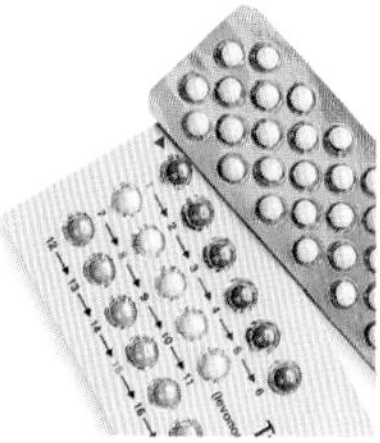

la pastilla (c**la píldora**)
pill

la familia • family

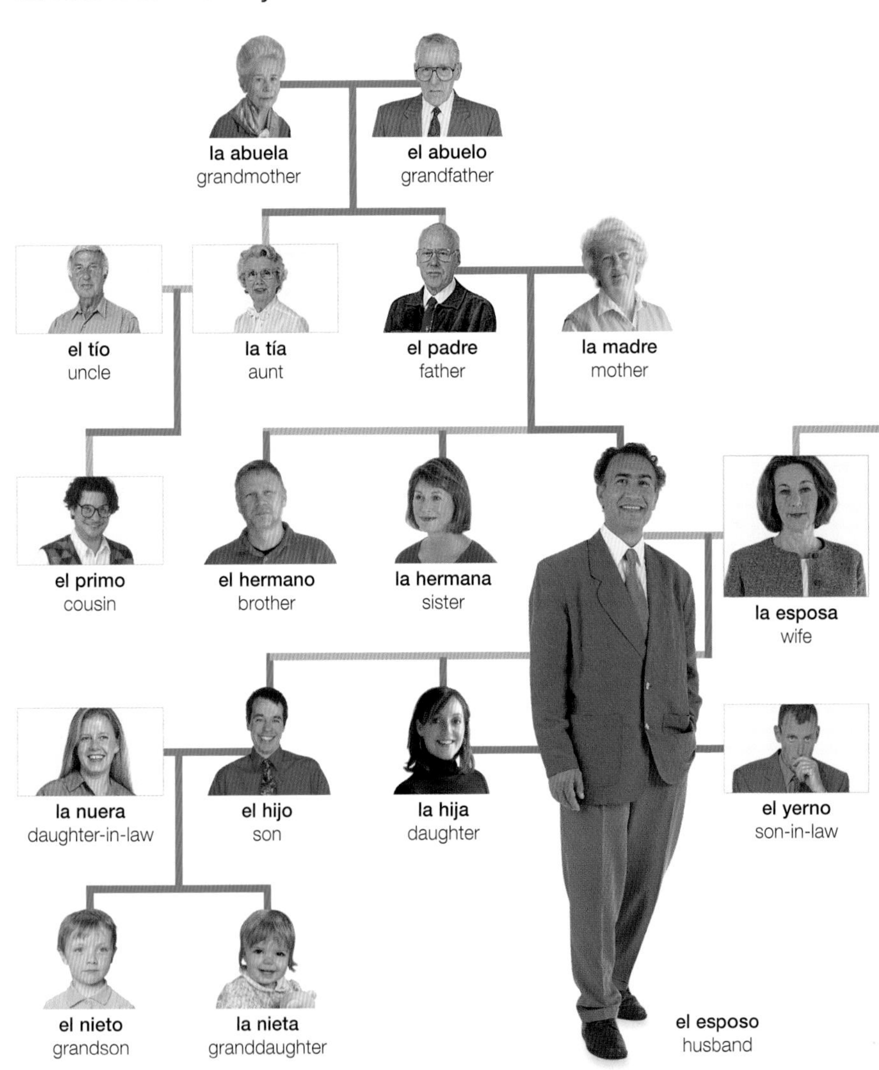

vocabulario • vocabulary

los parientes relatives	**los padres** parents	**los nietos** grandchildren	**la madrastra** stepmother	**el hijastro** stepson	**la generación** generation
los abuelos grandparents	**los niños** children	**el padrastro** stepfather	**la hijastra** stepdaughter	**el/la compañero/-a** partner	**los gemelos** twins

la suegra
mother-in-law

el suegro
father-in-law

el cuñado
brother-in-law

la cuñada
sister-in-law

la sobrina
niece

el sobrino
nephew

los tratamientos • titles

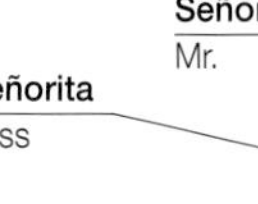

Señora
Mrs

Señor
Mr.

Señorita
Miss

las etapas • stages

el bebé
baby

el niño
child

el niño
boy

la niña
girl

la adolescente
teenager

el adulto
adult

el hombre
man

la mujer
woman

las relaciones • relationships

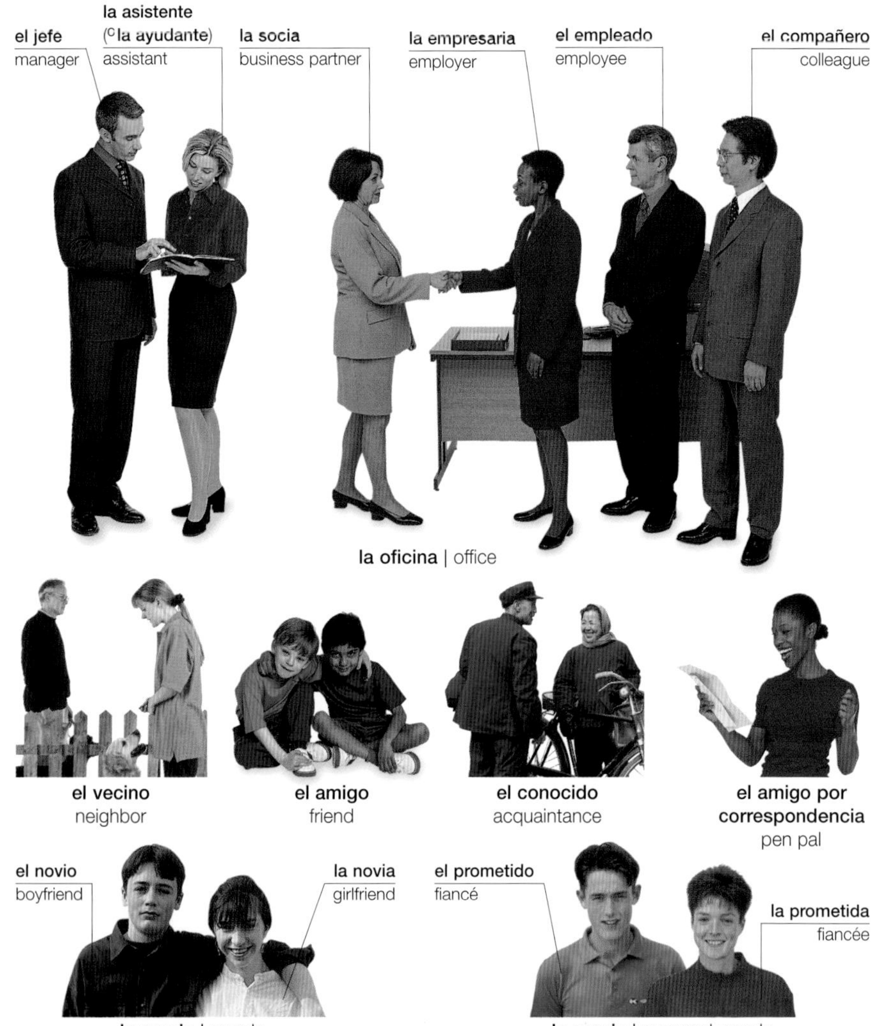

las emociones • emotions

contento
happy

triste
sad

entusiasmado
excited

aburrido
bored

sorprendido
surprised

asustado
scared

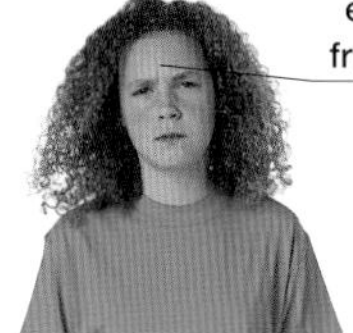

enfadado
angry

confuso
confused

preocupado
worried

nervioso
nervous

orgulloso
proud

seguro de sí mismo
confident

avergonzado
embarrassed

tímido
shy

vocabulario • vocabulary

triste upset	**reír** laugh (v)	**suspirar** sigh (v)	**gritar** shout (v)
horrorizado shocked	**llorar** cry (v)	**desmayarse** faint (v)	**bostezar** yawn (v)

los acontecimientos de una vida • life events

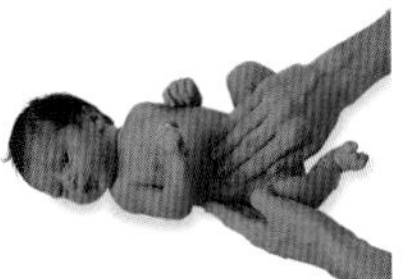

nacer
be born (v)

empezar el colegio
start school (v)

hacer amigos
make friends (v)

graduarse (C **licenciarse**)
graduate (v)

conseguir un trabajo
get a job (v)

enamorarse
fall in love (v)

casarse
get married (v)

tener un hijo
have a baby (v)

la boda | wedding

el divorcio
divorce

el funeral
funeral

vocabulario • vocabulary

el bautizo
christening

el bar mitzvah
bar mitzvah

el aniversario
anniversary

emigrar
emigrate (v)

retirarse
retire (v)

morir
die (v)

hacer testamento
make a will (v)

el banquete de boda
wedding reception

la luna de miel
honeymoon

el acta (C **la partida**) **de nacimiento**
birth certificate

las celebraciones • celebrations

la fiesta de cumpleaños
birthday party

la tarjeta
card

el regalo
present

el cumpleaños
birthday

la Navidad
Christmas

los festivales • festivals

la Pascua judía
Passover

el Año Nuevo
New Year

el carnaval
carnival

el desfile
procession

el Ramadán
Ramadan

la cinta
ribbon

el día de Acción de Gracias
Thanksgiving

la Pascua (ᶜla Semana Santa)
Easter

el día de Halloween
Halloween

el Diwali
Diwali

la apariencia
appearance

la ropa de niño • children's clothing

el bebé • baby

el traje de invierno (ᶜel buzo)
snowsuit

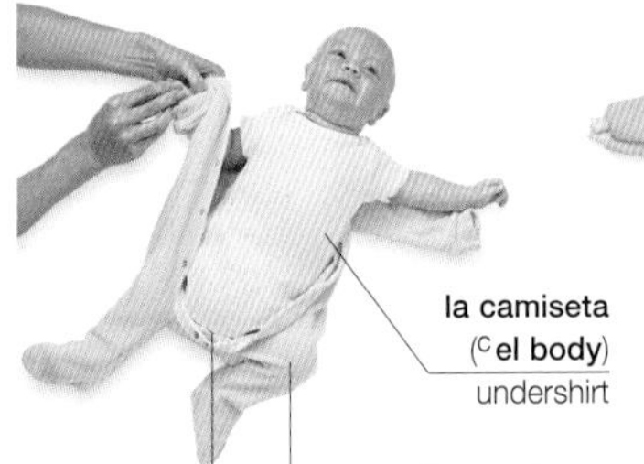

el mameluco (ᶜel pijama enterizo)
sleeper

el mameluco (ᶜel pelele) sin pies
romper suit

el babero
bib

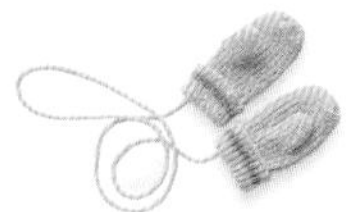

los guantes (ᶜlos manoplas)
mittens

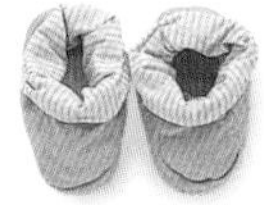

las botas (ᶜlos patucos)
booties

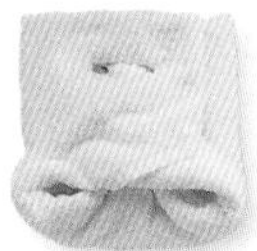

el pañal de felpa
cloth diaper

el pañal desechable
disposable diaper

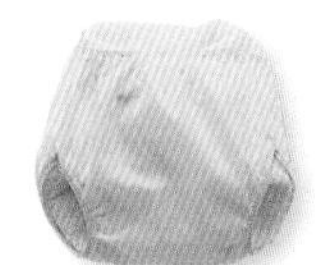

el calzón (ᶜlas braguitas) de plástico
plastic underpants

el niño pequeño • toddler

el gorro para el sol
sun bonnet

el delantal
apron

el niño • child

vocabulario • vocabulary

la fibra natural natural fiber	**¿Se puede lavar en lavadora?** Is it machine washable?
sintético synthetic	**¿Le quedará a un niño de dos años?** Will this fit a two-year-old?

la ropa de caballero • men's clothing

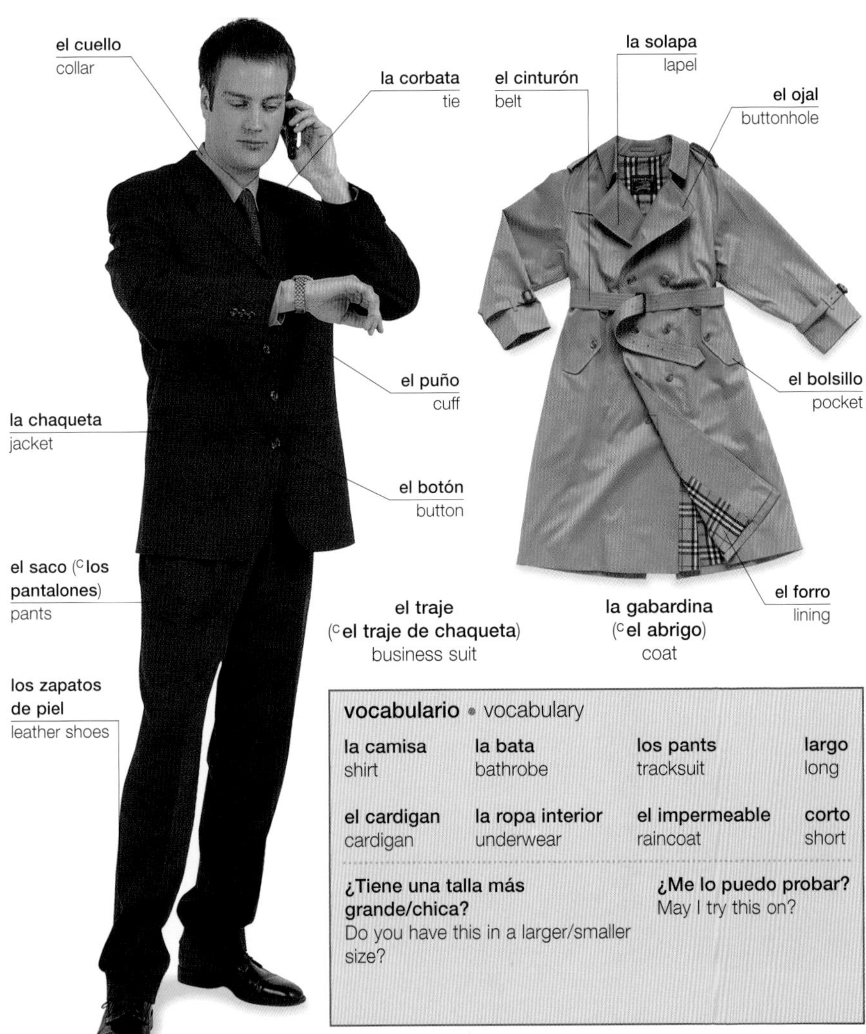

vocabulario • vocabulary

la camisa shirt	**la bata** bathrobe	**los pants** tracksuit	**largo** long
el cardigan cardigan	**la ropa interior** underwear	**el impermeable** raincoat	**corto** short

¿Tiene una talla más grande/chica?
Do you have this in a larger/smaller size?

¿Me lo puedo probar?
May I try this on?

los shorts ([c]**los pantalones cortos**) | shorts

los calzoncillos
briefs

los boxers ([c]**los calzoncillos de pata**) | boxer shorts

los calcetines
socks

la ropa de dama (c de señora) • women's clothing

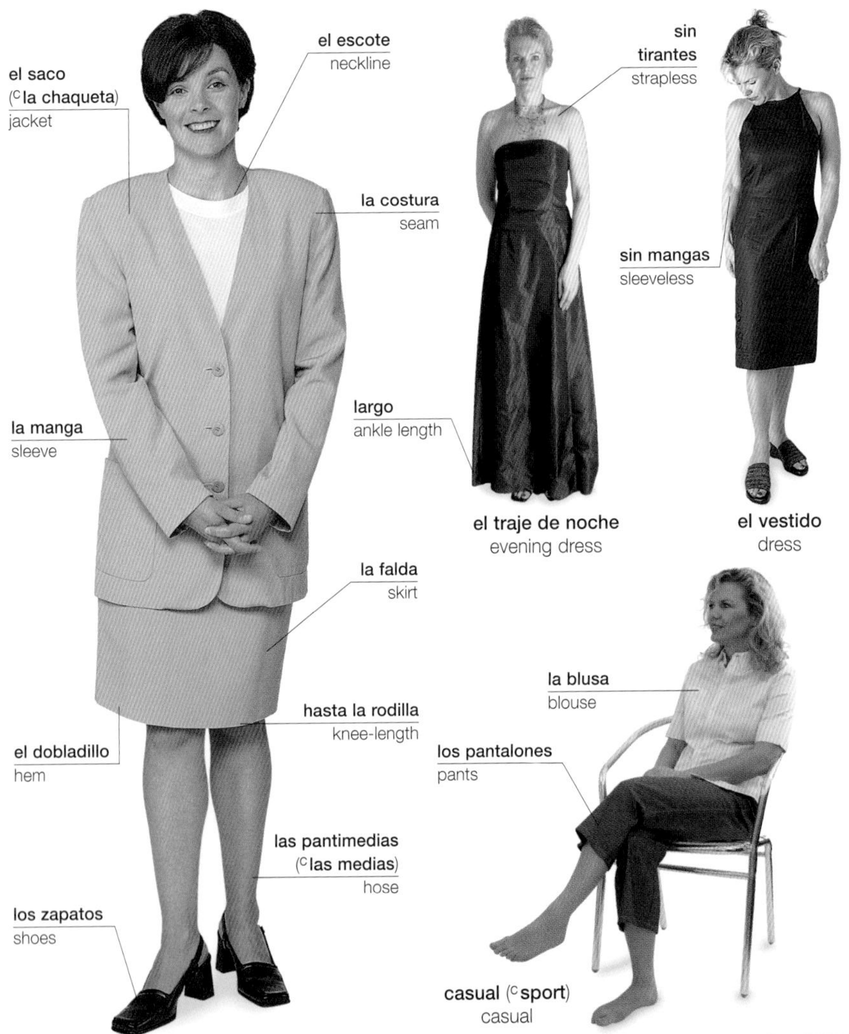

la lencería • lingerie

el negligé
([c]el salto de cama)
negligée

el fondo
([c]la combinación)
slip

la camisola
camisole

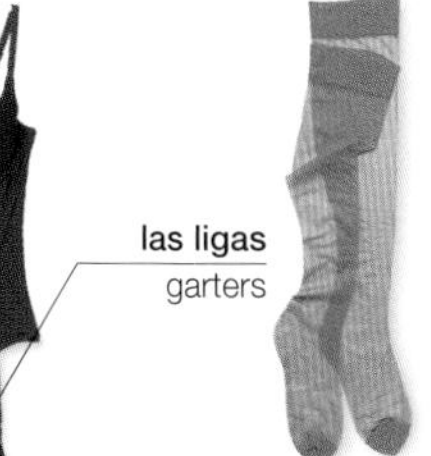

el corsé con liguero
bustier

las medias de liguero
stockings

las pantimedias
([c]las medias)
panty hose

el brassiere
([c]el sujetador)
bra

las pantaletas
([c]las bragas)
underpants

el camisón
nightgown

la boda • wedding

el vestido de novia
wedding dress

vocabulario • vocabulary

el corsé corset	**la liga** garter belt
el brassiere ([c]sujetador) deportivo sports bra	**entallado ([c]sastre)** tailored
la hombrera shoulder pad	**con varillas ([c]con aros)** underwire
la cinturilla waistband	**con los hombros al aire** halter neck

los accesorios • accessories

la gorra
cap

el sombrero
hat

la mascada
(ᶜ**el pañuelo**)
scarf

la hebilla
buckle

el cinturón
belt

el mango
(ᶜel asa)
handle
la punta
tip

el paraguas
umbrella

el pañuelo
handkerchief

el moño (ᶜ**la pajarita**)
bow tie

el alfiler de corbata
tiepin

los guantes
gloves

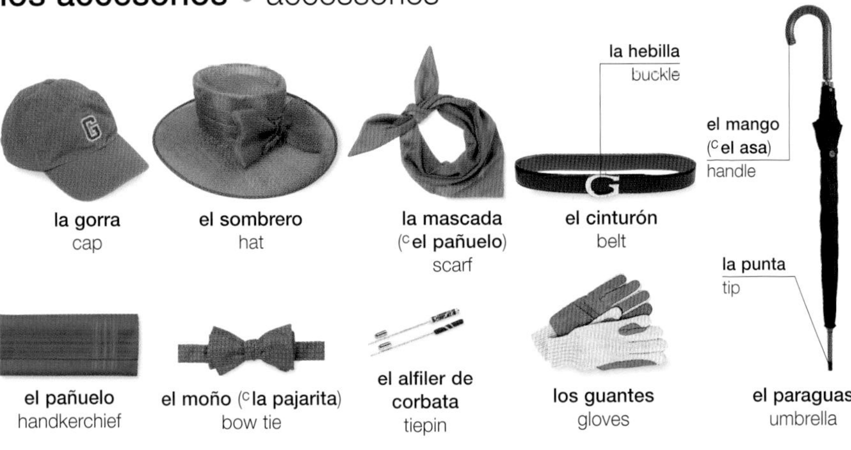

las joyas • jewelry

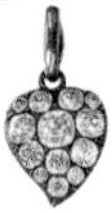

el colguije
(ᶜ**el colgante**)
pendant

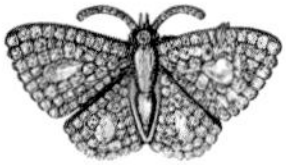

el prendedor
(ᶜ**el broche**)
brooch

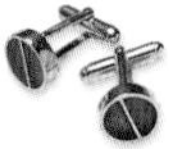

las mancuernillas
(ᶜ**el gemelo**)
cufflink

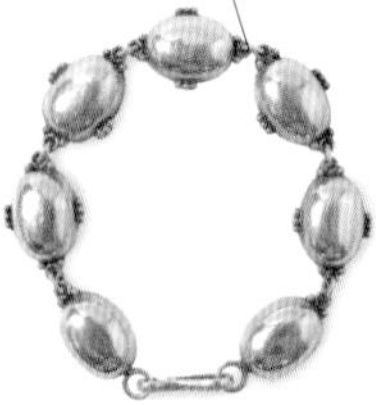
el eslabón
link

la pulsera
bracelet

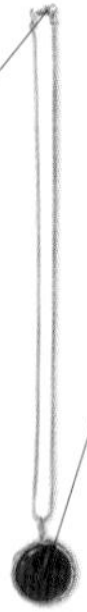
el broche
(ᶜel cierre)
clasp
la piedra
stone

la cadena
chain

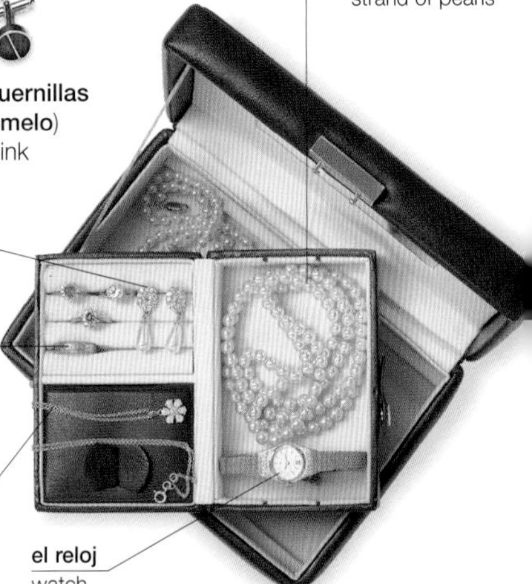
el collar de perlas
strand of pearls
el arete
(ᶜel pendiente)
earring
el anillo
ring
el collar
necklace
el reloj
watch

el joyero | jewelry box

las bolsas • bags

el cierre
clasp

la correa
shoulder strap

las asas
handles

la cartera
wallet

el monedero
change purse

la bolsa (c el bolso)
shoulder bag

la bolsa de viaje
duffle bag

el maletín
briefcase

la bolsa (c el bolso) de mano
handbag

la mochila
backpack

los zapatos • shoes

la agujeta (c la cordonera)
lace

la lengüeta
tongue

el ojal
eyelet

la suela
sole

el tacón
heel

el zapato de agujetas (c de cordoneras)
lace-up

la bota de trekking
walking boot

el tenis (c la zapatilla deportiva)
sneaker

el zapato de piel
leather shoe

la chancla
flip-flop

el zapato de tacón
high heel shoe

el zapato de plataforma
platform shoe

la sandalia
sandal

el mocasín
slip-on

el zapato de caballero
brogan

el cabello • hair

peinar
comb (v)

cepillar | brush (v)

lavar | wash (v)

enjuagar
rinse (v)

cortar
cut (v)

secar con la secadora
blowdry (v)

marcar
set (v)

los accesorios • accessories

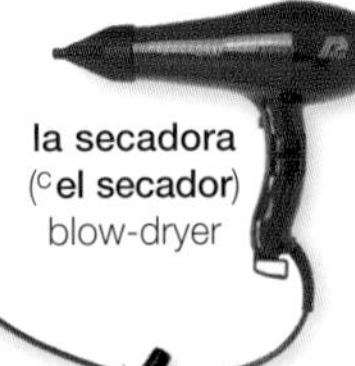

la secadora
(C **el secador**)
blow-dryer

el champú
shampoo

el acondicionador (C **el suavizante**) | conditioner

el gel
gel

la laca
hairspray

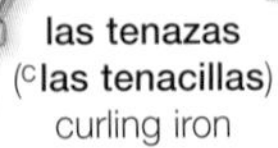

las tenazas
(C **las tenacillas**)
curling iron

las tijeras
scissors

la diadema
headband

el rulo
curler

el pasador (C **la horquilla**) | bobby pin

los estilos • styles

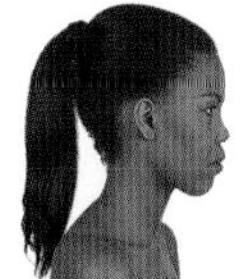
la cola de caballo
ponytail

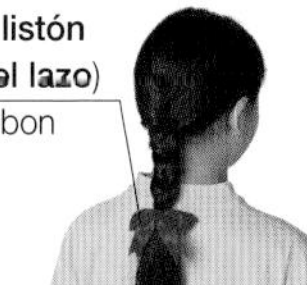
el listón (ᶜ**el lazo**)
ribbon

la trenza
braid

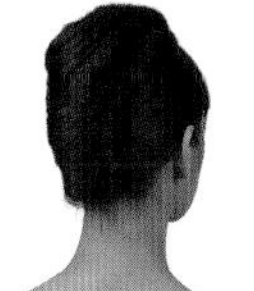
el chongo (ᶜ**el moño) francés**
French braid

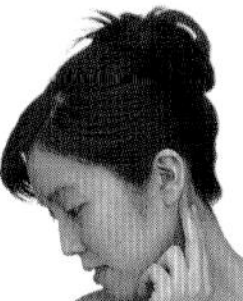
el chongo (ᶜ**el moño**)
bun

las coletas
pigtails

el príncipe valiente (ᶜ**la melena**) | bob

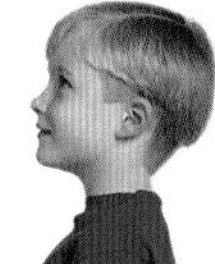
el pelo corto
crop

rizado
curly

la permanente
perm

lacio
straight

las raíces
roots

las luces (ᶜ**los reflejos**)
highlights

calvo
bald

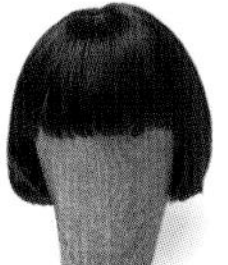
la peluca
wig

los colores • colours

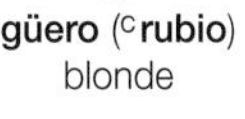
güero (ᶜ**rubio**)
blonde

castaño
brunette

rojizo
auburn

pelirrojo
pelirrojo

negro
black

gris
gray

blanco
white

teñido
dyed

vocabulario • vocabulary

la goma del pelo
hair band

despuntar (ᶜ**cortar las puntas**)
trim (v)

el peluquero (ᶜ**el barbero**)
barber

la caspa
dandruff

la orzuela (ᶜ**las puntas abiertas**)
split ends

graso
greasy

seco
dry

alaciar (ᶜ**alisar**)
straighten (v)

normal
normal

el cuero cabelludo
scalp

la belleza • beauty

el maquillaje • makeup

el lápiz de cejas
eyebrow pencil

el cepillo para las cejas
eyebrow brush

las pinzas
tweezers

el brillo de labios
lip gloss

el pincel de labios
lip brush

el lápiz de labios
lip liner

la brocha
brush

el lápiz corrector
concealer

el espejo
mirror

el maquillaje ([C]los polvos compactos)
face powder

la borla
powder puff

la polvera | compact

los tratamientos de belleza • beauty treatments

la mascarilla
face pack

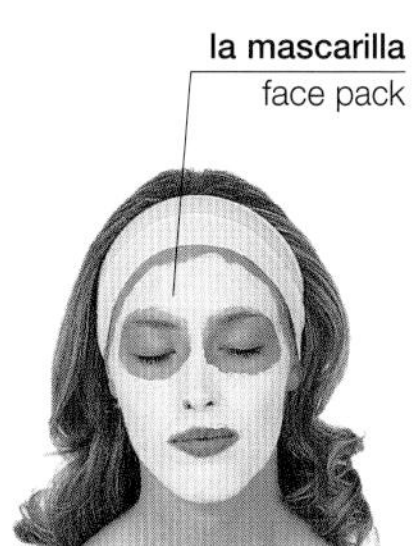

la limpieza de cutis
facial

la cama de rayos ultravioletas
sunbed

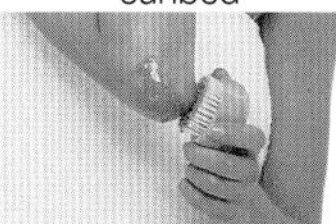

exfoliar
exfoliate (v)

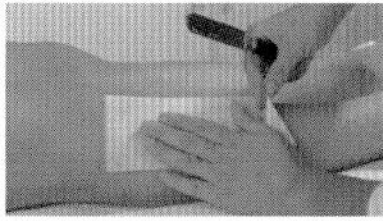

la depilación a la cera
wax

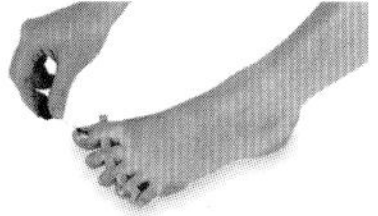

la pedicura
pedicure

la manicura • manicure

la lima de uñas
nail file

el quitaesmalte
nail polish remover

el esmalte de uñas
nail polish

las tijeras de uñas
nail scissors

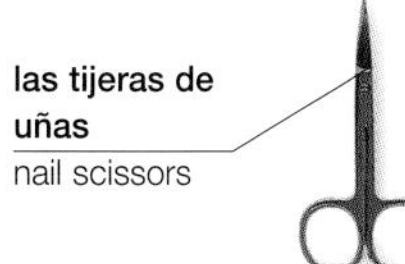

el cortaúñas
nail clippers

los artículos de tocador • toiletries

la crema limpiadora
cleanser

el tónico
toner

la crema hidratante
moisturizer

la crema bronceadora (C autobronceadora)
self-tanning lotion

el perfume
perfume

el agua de colonia
eau de toilette

vocabulario • vocabulary

el cutis complexion	**graso** oily	**el bronceado** tan
claro fair	**sensible** sensitive	**el tatuaje** tattoo
moreno dark	**hipoalergénico** hypoallergenic	**antiarrugas** antiwrinkle
seco dry	**el tono** shade	**las bolas de algodón** cotton balls

la salud
health

la enfermedad • illness

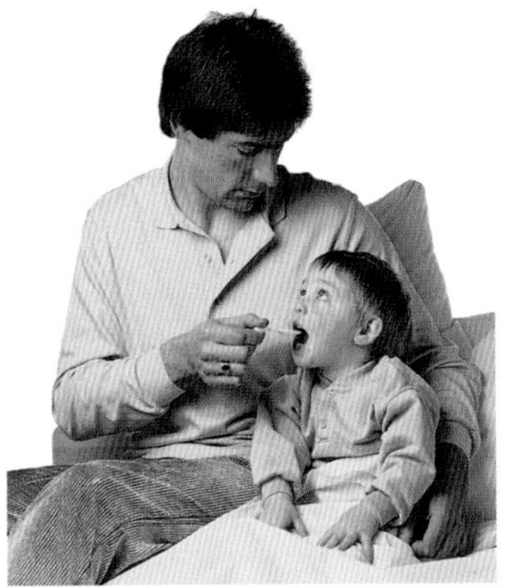

la fiebre | fever

el dolor de cabeza
headache

la hemorragia nasal
nosebleed

la tos
cough

el estornudo
sneeze

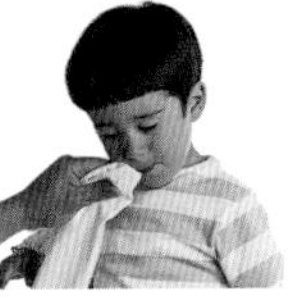

el resfriado
cold

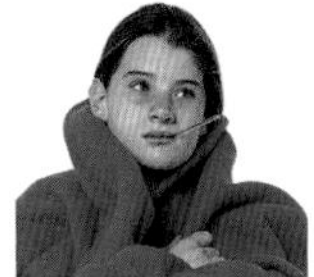

la gripe
the flu

el inhalador
inhaler

el asma
asthma

los calambres
cramps

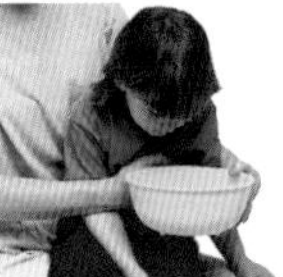

la náusea
nausea

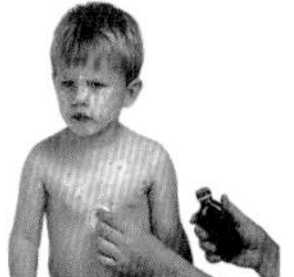

la varicela
the chickenpox

el sarpullido
rash

vocabulario • vocabulary

la aplopejía (C**el derrame cerebral**) stroke	**la fiebre del heno** hay fever	**la infección** infection	**el dolor de estómago** stomach ache	**la migraña** (C**la jaqueca**) migraine	**la diarrea** diarrhea
la diabetes diabetes	**la alergia** allergy	**el eccema** eczema	**el resfriado** chill	**vomitar** vomit (v)	**el sarampión** measles
el ataque cardiaco (C**el infarto de miocardio**) heart attack	**la presión arterial** (C**la tensión arterial**) blood pressure	**el virus** virus	**desmayarse** faint (v)	**la epilepsia** epilepsy	**las paperas** mumps

el doctor • doctor

la consulta • consultation

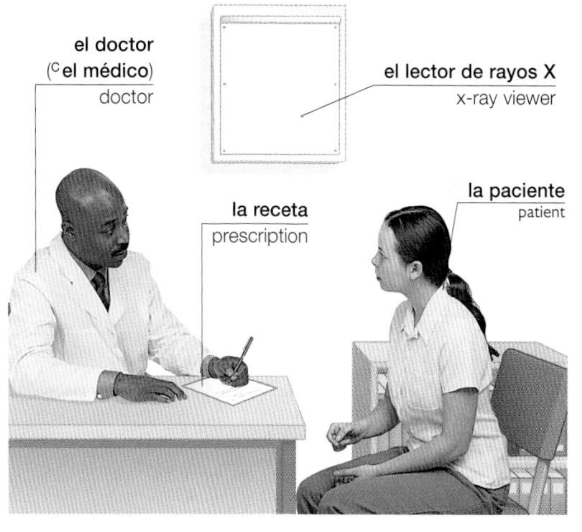

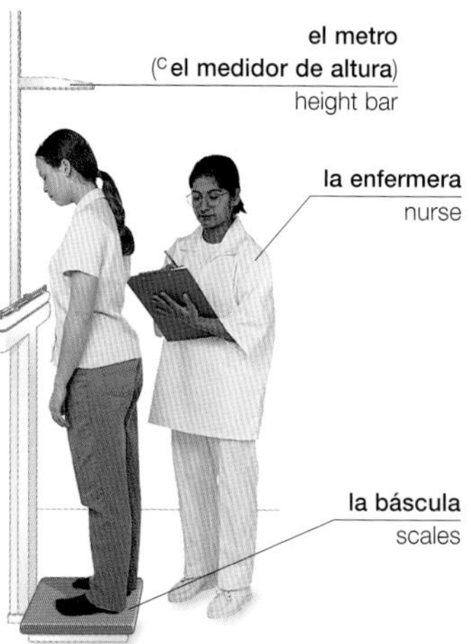

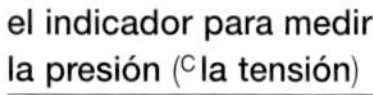

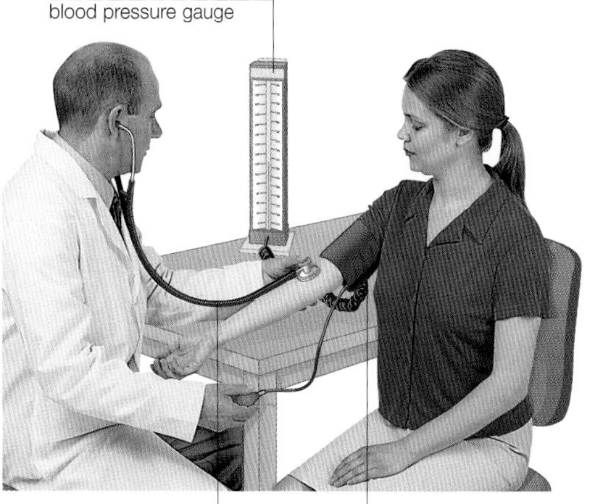

vocabulario • vocabulary

la cita appointment	**la inoculación** inoculation
la consulta doctor's office	**el termómetro** thermometer
la sala de espera waiting room	**el examen médico** medical examination

Necesito ver a un doctor.
I need to see a doctor.

Me duele aquí.
It hurts here.

la lesión • injury

la torcedura | sprain

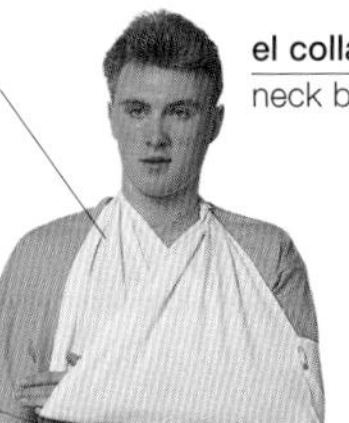

la fractura
fracture

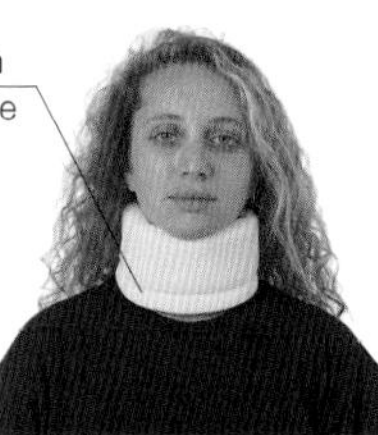

el tirón en el cuello
whiplash

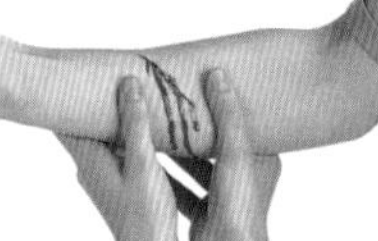

la cortada ([C]**el corte**)
cut

la raspada ([C]**el arañazo**)
graze

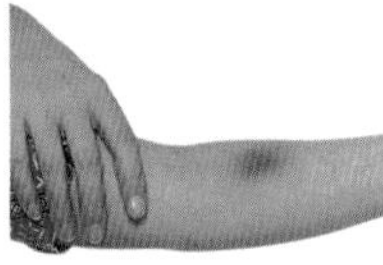

el moretón ([C]**el hematoma**)
bruise

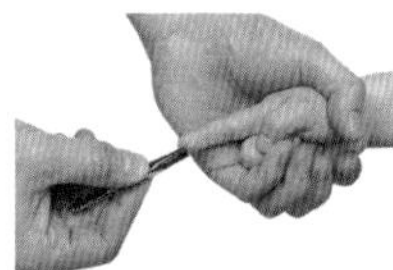

la astilla
splinter

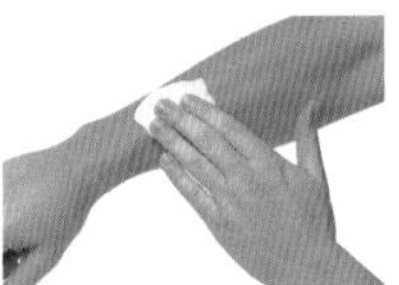

la ardida ([C]**la quemadura de sol**)
sunburn

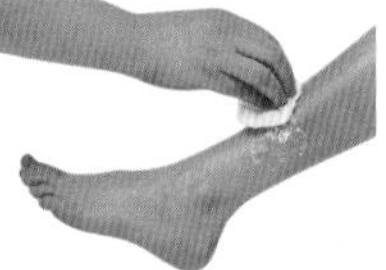

la quemadura
burn

el mordisco
bite

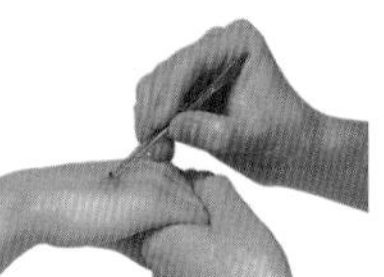

la picadura
sting

vocabulary • vocabulary

el accidente
accident

la herida
wound

la emergencia ([C]**la urgencia**)
emergency

la hemorragia
hemorrhage

la ampolla
blister

la lesión en la cabeza
head injury

la conmoción
concussion

el envenenamiento
poisoning

el shock eléctrico ([C]**la descarga eléctrica**)
electric shock

¿Se pondrá bien?
Will he/she be all right?

Por favor llame a una ambulancia.
Please call an ambulance.

¿Dónde le duele?
Where does it hurt?

los primeros auxilios • first aid

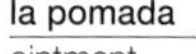

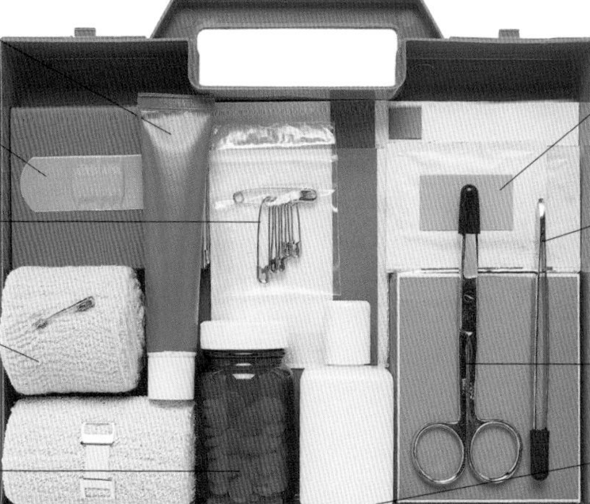

el botiquín | first aid kit

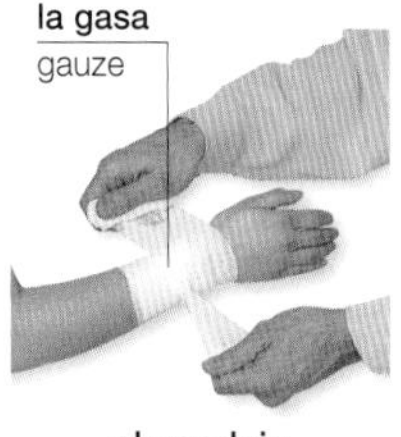

el vendaje
dressing

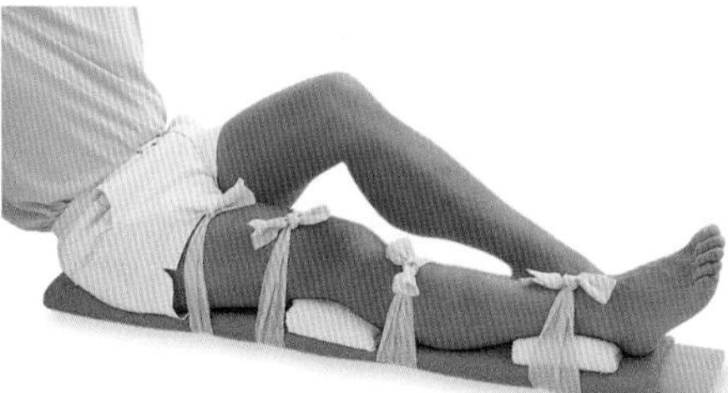

la tablilla | **splint**

la tela adhesiva
(C **el esparadrapo**)
adhesive tape

la reanimación
resuscitation

vocabulario • vocabulary

el shock shock	**el pulso** pulse	**ahogarse** choke (v)	**¿Me puede ayudar?** Can you help?
inconsciente unconscious	**la respiración** breathing	**estéril** sterile	**¿Sabe primeros auxilios?** Do you know first aid?

el hospital • hospital

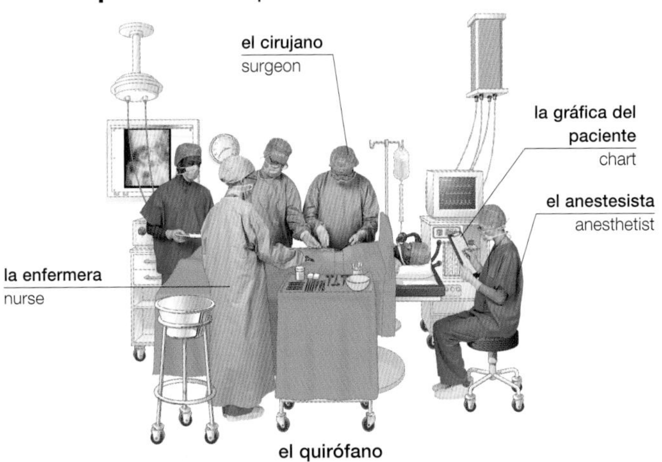

el quirófano
operating room

el análisis de sangre
blood test

la inyección
injection

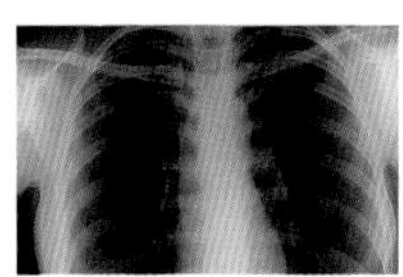

la radiografía
x-ray

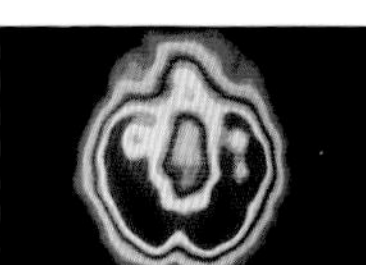

el ultrasonido
(ᶜ**la ecografía**)
scan

la camilla
gurney

la sala de urgencias
emergency room

la planta
ward

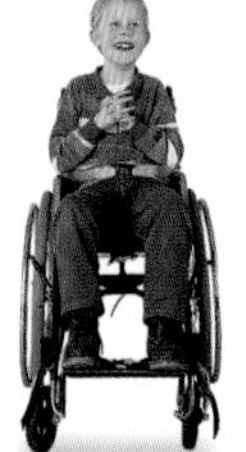

la silla de ruedas
wheelchair

vocabulario • vocabulary

la operación operation	**dado de alta** discharged	**las horas de visita** visiting hours	**la sala de maternidad** maternity ward	**la unidad de cuidados intensivos** intensive care unit
internado (C **ingresado**) admitted	**la clínica** clinic	**la sala de pediatría** children's ward	**la habitación privada** private room	**el paciente externo** outpatient

los servicios • departments

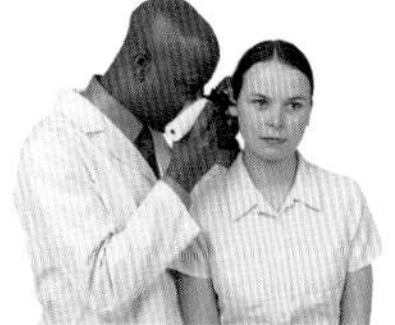
la otorrinonaringología
Ear, Nose, and Throat

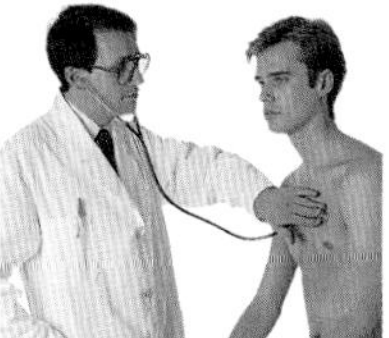
la cardiología
cardiology

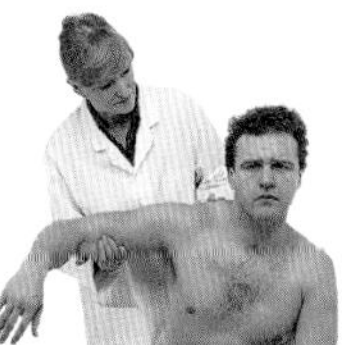
la ortopedia
orthopedics

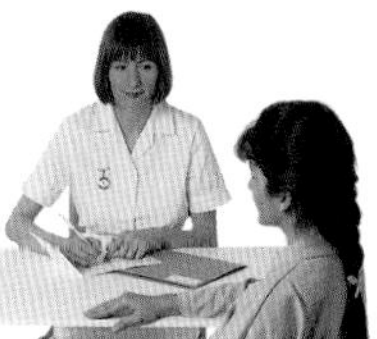
la ginecología
gynecology

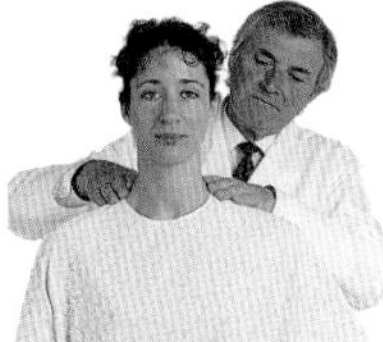
la fisioterapia
physiotherapy

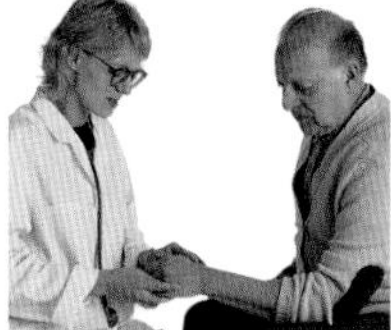
la dermatología
dermatology

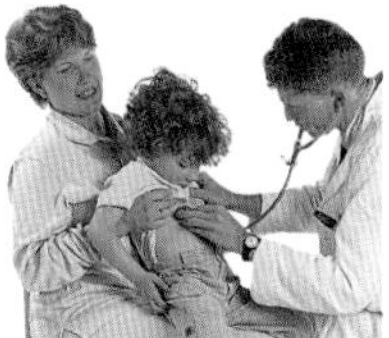
la pediatría
pediatrics

la radiología
radiology

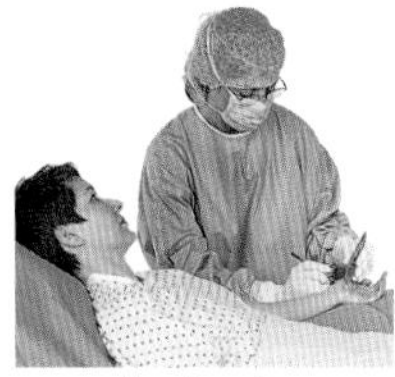
la cirugía
surgery

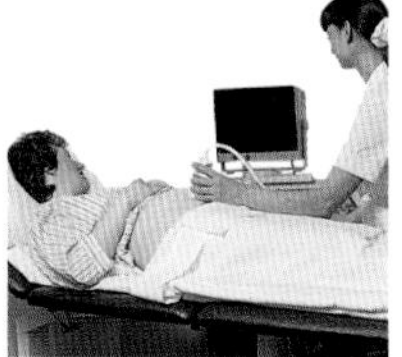
la maternidad
maternity

la psiquiatría
psychiatry

la oftalmología
ophthalmology

vocabulario • vocabulary

la neurología
neurology

la oncología
oncology

la urología
urology

la endocrinología
endocrinology

la cirugía plástica
plastic surgery

la referencia (C**el volante**)
referral

la patología
pathology

el análisis
test

el resultado
result

el especialista
consultant

el dentista • dentist

el diente • tooth

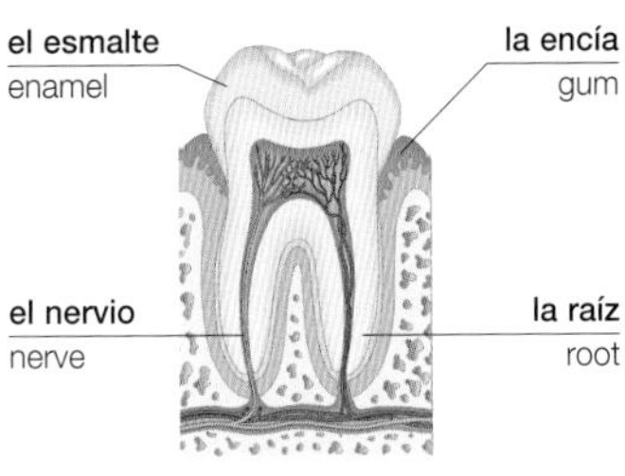

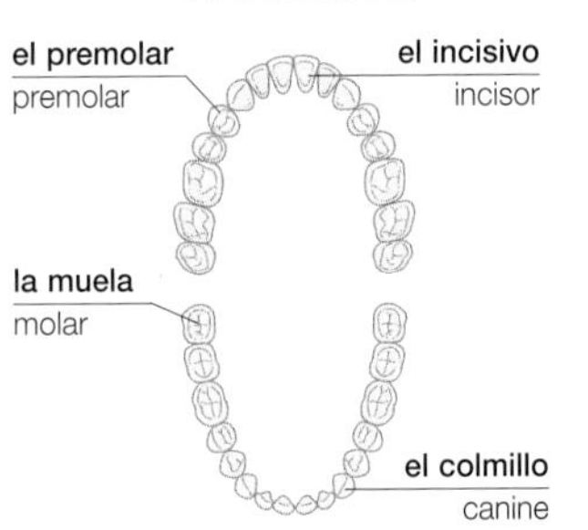

vocabulario • vocabulary

el dolor de muelas toothache	**el hilo dental** dental floss
la placa bacteriana plaque	**la extracción** extraction
la caries decay	**la corona** crown
el empaste filling	**el torno del dentista** drill

la revisión • check-up

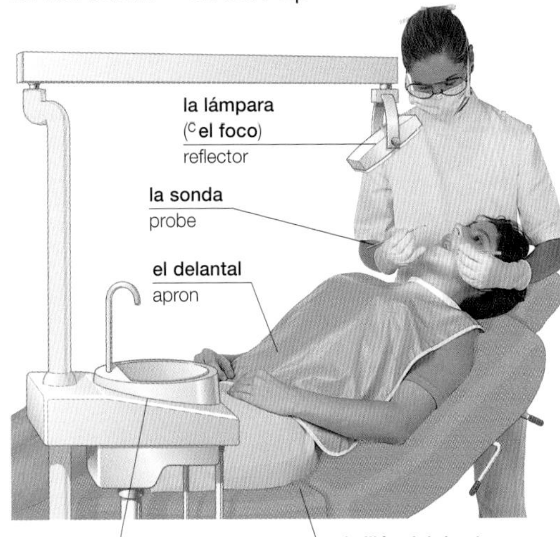

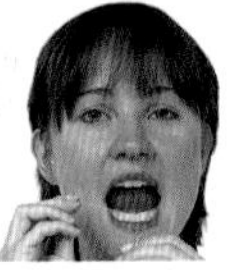

usar el hilo dental
floss (v)

cepillarse los dientes
brush (v)

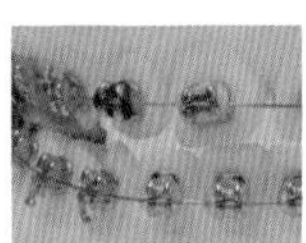

los frenos (^C **el aparato corrector**)
braces

los rayos x dentales
dental x-ray

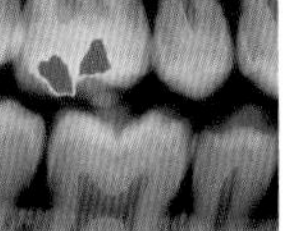

la radiografía
x-ray film

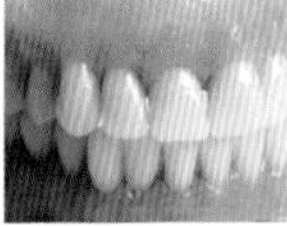

la dentadura postiza
dentures

el óptico • optician

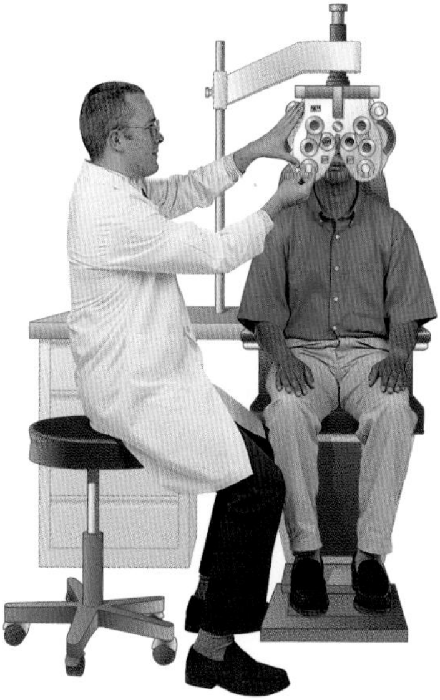

el examen de ojos | eye test

el estuche
(Cla funda)
case
el cristal
lens

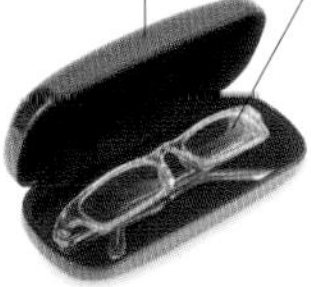

los lentes
glasses

la montura
frame

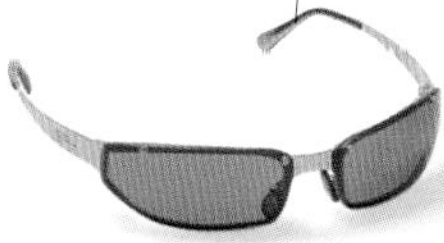

los lentes obscuros
(Clas gafas de sol)
sunglasses

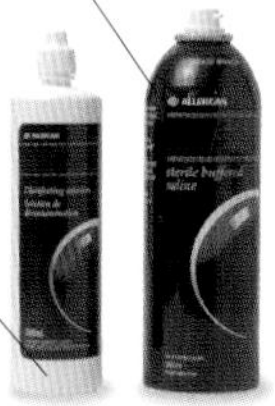

el líquido limpiador
cleaning fluid
la solución desinfectante
disinfectant solution

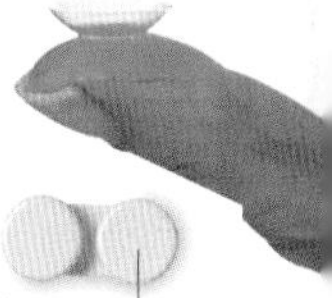

el estuche para los pupilentes
(Clas lentillas)
lens case

los pupilentes (Clas lentes de contacto) | contact lenses

el ojo • eye

la ceja
eyebrow
el párpado
eyelid
la pestaña
eyelash
la pupila
pupil
el iris
iris

la retina
retina
el cristalino
lens
el nervio óptico
optic nerve
la córnea
cornea

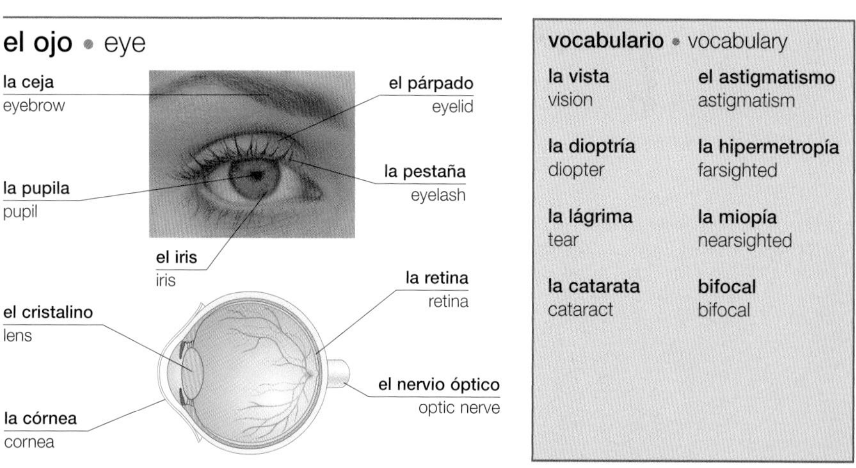

vocabulario • vocabulary

la vista vision	**el astigmatismo** astigmatism
la dioptría diopter	**la hipermetropía** farsighted
la lágrima tear	**la miopía** nearsighted
la catarata cataract	**bifocal** bifocal

el embarazo • pregnancy

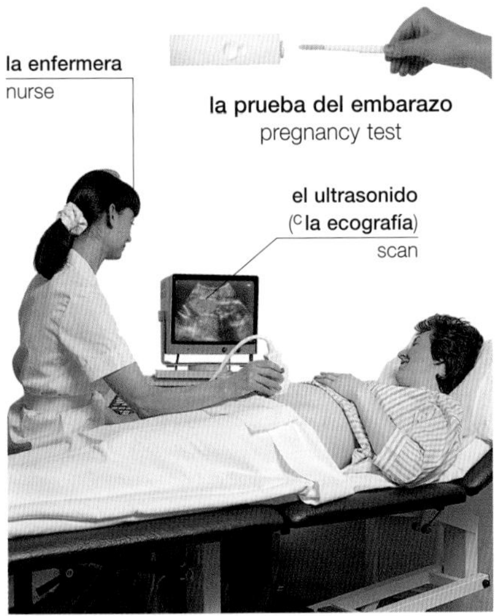

el ultrasonido | ultrasound

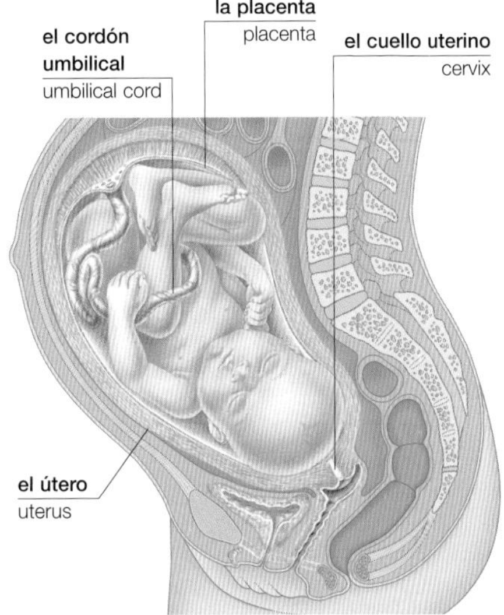

el feto | fetus

vocabulario • vocabulary

la ovulación
ovulation

la concepción
conception

embarazada
(C **encinta**)
expectant

embarazada
pregnant

prenatal
antenatal

el trimestre
trimester

el embrión
embryo

la matriz
womb

la contracción
contraction

romper aguas
break water (v)

el líquido amniótico
amniotic fluid

la amniocentesis
amniocentesis

la dilatación
dilation

la epidural
epidural

la cesárea
cesarean section

la episiotomía
episiotomy

el parto
delivery

el nacimiento
birth

el aborto espontáneo
miscarriage

las puntadas
(C **los puntos**)
stitches

prematuro
premature

el ginecólogo
gynecologist

el obstetra
(C **el tocólogo**)
obstetrician

de espaldas
(C **de nalgas**)
breech

el parto • childbirth

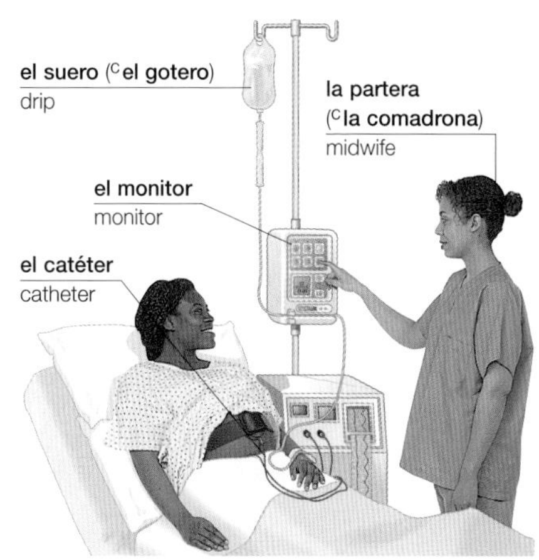

inducir el parto
induce labour (v)

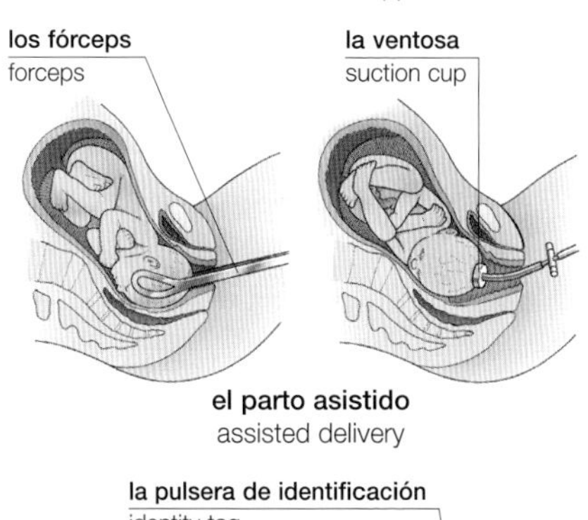

el parto asistido
assisted delivery

el recién nacido
newborn baby

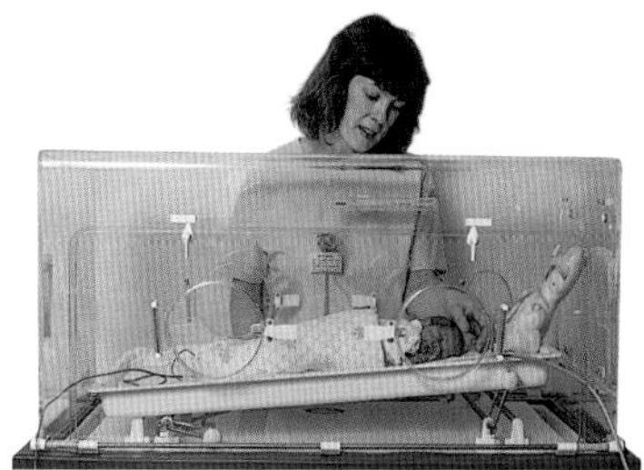

la incubadora | incubator

el peso al nacer | birth weight

la lactancia • nursing

el tiraleches (C el sacaleches)
breast pump

el brassiere (C el sujetador) para la lactancia
nursing bra

amamantar (C dar el pecho)
breastfeed (v)

los discos protectores
pads

las terapias alternativas • alternative therapy

el masaje
massage

el shiatsu
shiatsu

el yoga | yoga

la quiropráctica
chiropractic

la osteopatía
osteopathy

la reflexología
reflexology

la meditación
meditation

el terapeuta
counselor

la terapia de grupo
group therapy

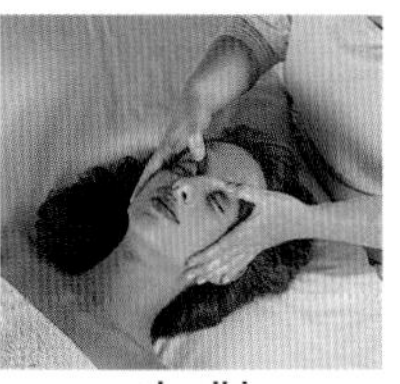

el reiki
reiki

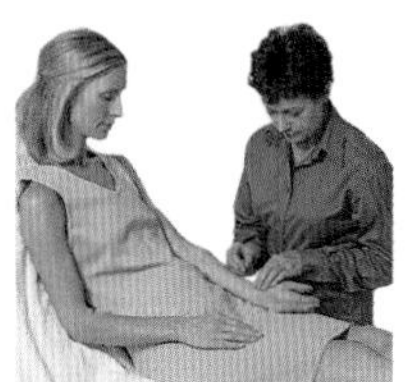

la acupuntura
acupuncture

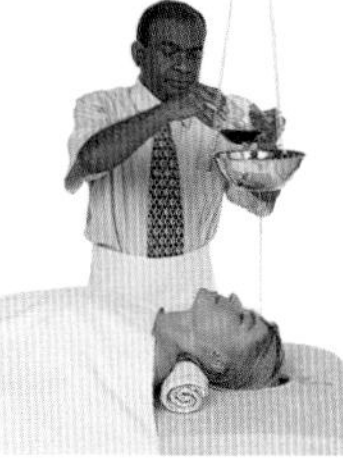

la ayurveda
ayurveda

la hipnoterapia
hypnotherapy

el herbolario
herbalism

los aceites esenciales
essential oils

la aromaterapia
aromatherapy

la homeopatía
homeopathy

la acupresión
acupressure

la terapeuta
therapist

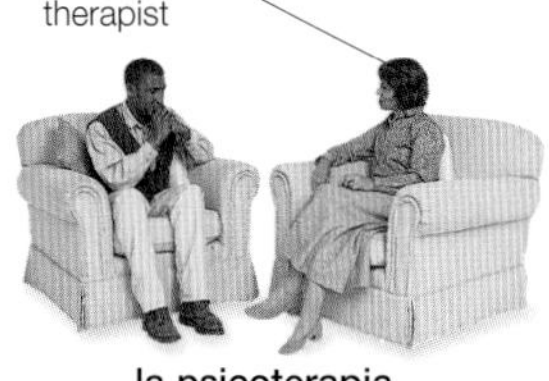

la psicoterapia
psychotherapy

vocabulario • vocabulary

la cristaloterapia crystal healing	**la naturopatía** naturopathy	**la relajación** relaxation	**la hierba** herb
la hidroterapia hydrotherapy	**el feng shui** feng shui	**el estrés** stress	**el suplemento** supplement

la casa
home

la casa • house

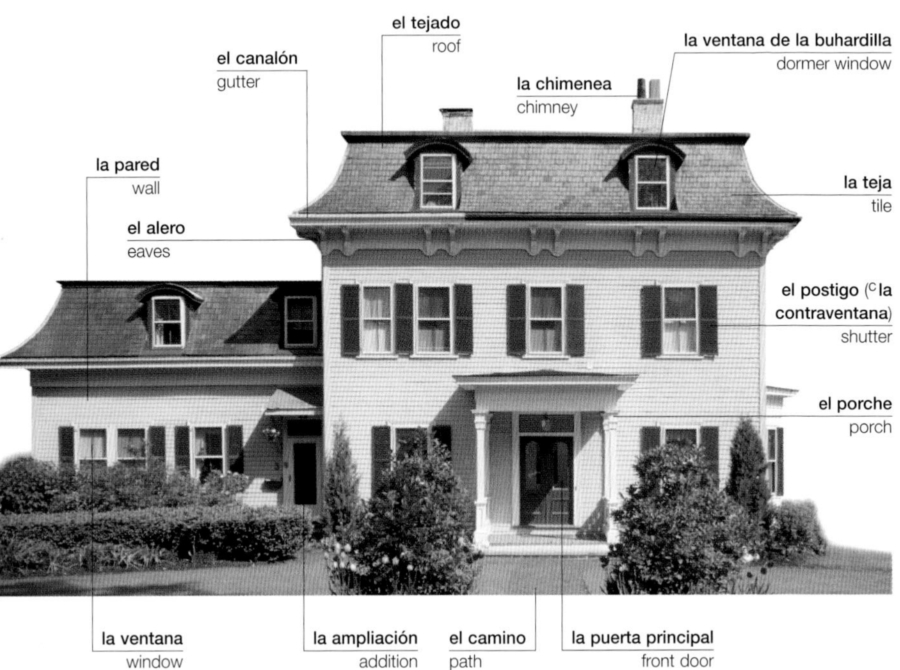

vocabulario • vocabulary

(condominio) horizontal row (house)	**la casa de la ciudad** townhouse	**la cochera** (C **el garaje**) garage	**la luz del porche** porch light	**la alarma antirrobo** burglar alarm	**rentar** (C **alquilar**) rent (v)
solo single-family	**el sótano** basement	**el ático** attic	**el piso** floor	**el buzón** mailbox	**el inquilino** tenant
dúplex duplex	**la vivienda de una planta** bungalow	**el cuarto** (C **la habitación**) room	**el patio** courtyard	**el propietario** landlord	**la renta** (C **el alquiler**) rent

la entrada • entrance

el vestíbulo
hallway

el timbre
doorbell

el tapete (C **el felpudo**)
doormat

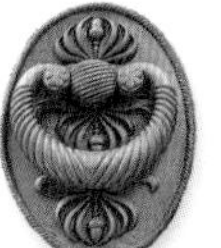

la aldaba
door knocker

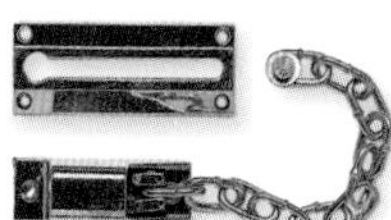

la cadena
door chain

la cerradura
lock

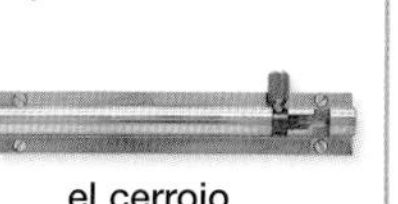

el cerrojo
bolt

el departamento (C el piso) • apartment

el edificio
apartment block

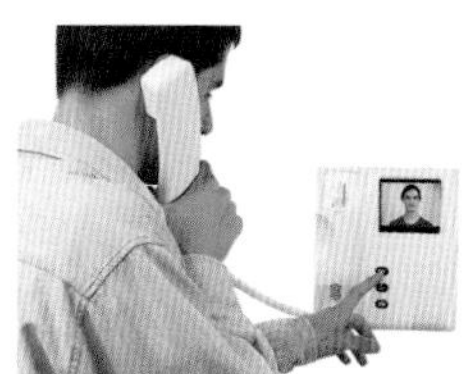

el interfono
intercom

el elevador (C **el ascensor**)
elevator

las instalaciones internas • internal systems

el radiador
radiator

el calentador (ᶜ**la estufa**)
space heater

el aspa
blade

el ventilador
fan

el calentador de convección
portable heater

la electricidad • electricity

el filamento
filament

el portalámparas
threads

el foco (ᶜ**la bombilla**)
light bulb

la toma de tierra
ground

la clavija
prong

el enchufe (**macho**)
plug

con corriente
hot

neutro
neutral

los cables
wires

vocabulario • vocabulary

el voltaje voltage	**el generador** generator	**el enchufe** (**hembra**) socket	**la corriente continua** direct current	**el transformador** transformer
el amperio amp	**el fusible** fuse	**el interruptor** switch	**el contador de la luz** electric meter	**el suministro de electricidad** household current
la corrriente eléctrica power	**la caja de los fusibles** fuse box	**la corriente alterna** alternating current	**el corte de luz** power outage	

la fontanería • plumbing

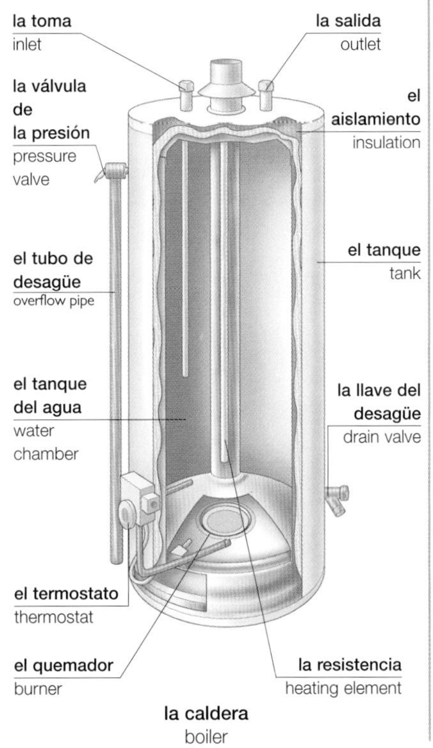

la caldera
boiler

el fregador • sink

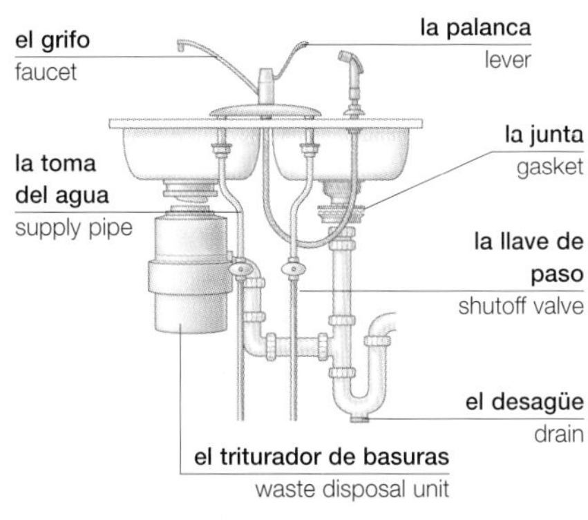

el retrete • toilet

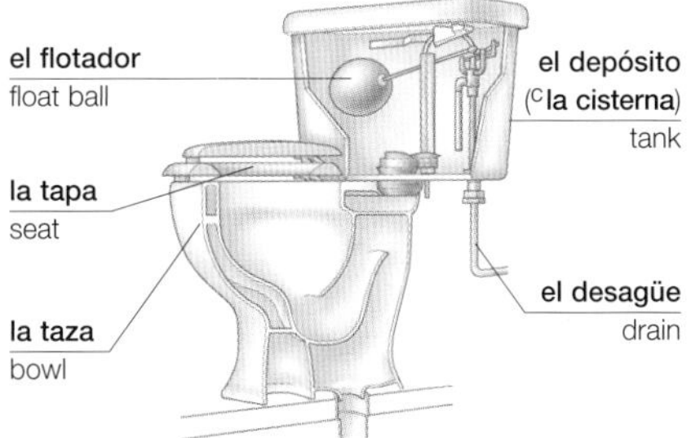

la eliminación de desechos • waste disposal

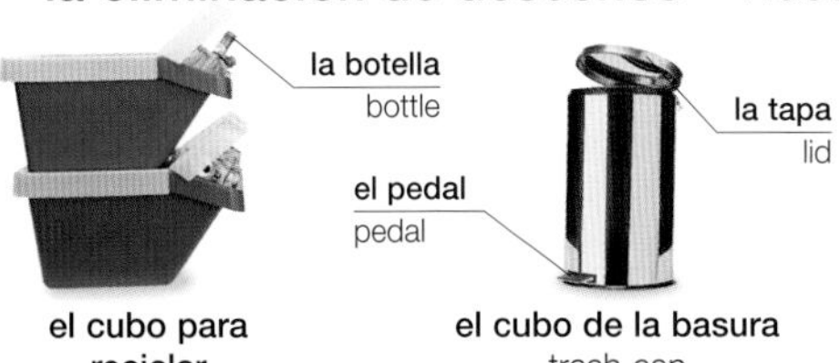

el cubo para reciclar
recycling bin

el cubo de la basura
trash can

el armario para clasificar la basura
sorting unit

los desperdicios orgánicos
organic waste

la sala (ᶜ el cuarto de estar) • living room

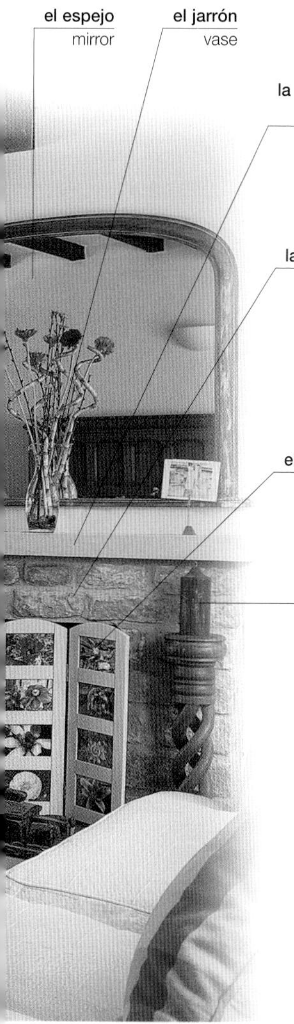

la cortina
curtain

el visillo
net curtain

la persiana (C **el estor de láminas**)
venetian blind

el estor
roller blind

el estudio (C **el despacho**) | study

el comedor • dining room

vocabulario • vocabulary

servir
serve (v)

comer
eat (v)

poner la mesa
set the table (v)

la comida
meal

el mantel
tablecloth

el mantel individual
place mat

el desayuno
breakfast

la comida
lunch

la cena
dinner

hambriento
hungry

lleno
full

la ración
portion

el anfitrión
host

la anfitriona
hostess

el invitado
guest

Estaba riquísimo.
(c **Estaba buenísimo.**)
That was delicious.

Estoy lleno, gracias.
I've had enough, thank you.

¿Puedo comer otro poco?
(c **¿Puedo repetir?**)
May I have some more?

la vajilla y los cubiertos • crockery and cutlery

la cocina • kitchen

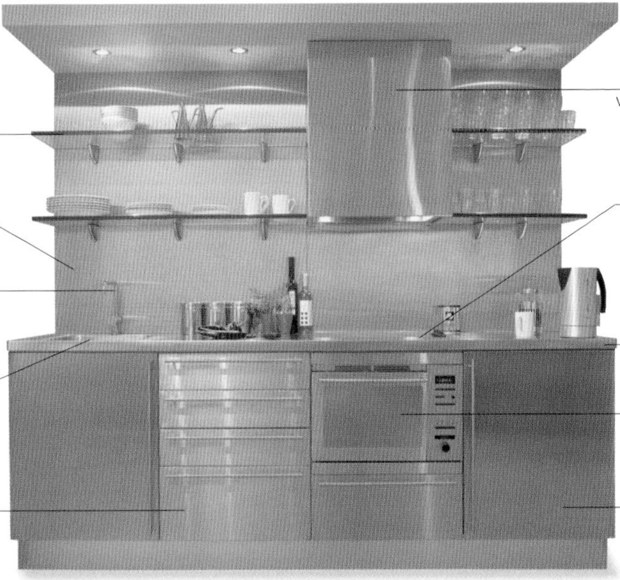

el extractor
ventilation hood

los estantes
shelves

la placa vitrocerámica
ceramic stovetop

el frente de la cocina
splashback

el grifo
faucet

la plancha (ᶜla encimera)
countertop

el fregadero
sink

el horno
oven

la gaveta (ᶜel armario)
cabinet

el cajón
drawer

los electrodomésticos • appliances

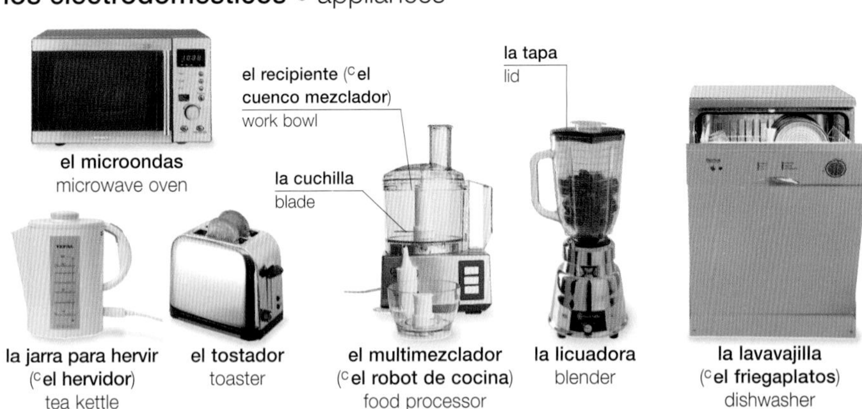

el microondas
microwave oven

el recipiente (ᶜel cuenco mezclador)
work bowl

la cuchilla
blade

la tapa
lid

la jarra para hervir (ᶜel hervidor)
tea kettle

el tostador
toaster

el multimezclador (ᶜel robot de cocina)
food processor

la licuadora
blender

la lavavajilla (ᶜel friegaplatos)
dishwasher

la máquina de los hielos
ice maker

el refrigerador (ᶜel frigorífico)
refrigerator

la charola (ᶜel estante)
shelf

el congelador
freezer

el cajón de las verduras
crisper

el refrigerador (ᶜfrigorífico) congelador | refrigerator-freezer

vocabulario • vocabulary

el escurridor draining board	**congelar** freeze (v)
el quemador burner	**descongelar** defrost (v)
el bote de basura garbage can	**cocer al vapor** steam (v)
la hornilla (ᶜla placa) stove	**saltear** sauté (v)

cocinar • cooking

pelar
peel (v)

cortar
slice (v)

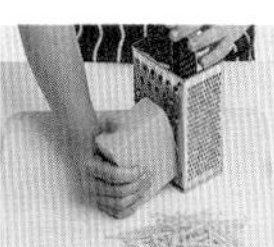

rallar
grate (v)

vaciar (ᶜechar)
pour (v)

mezclar
mix (v)

batir
whisk (v)

hervir
boil (v)

freír
fry (v)

amasar (ᶜextender) con el rodillo | roll (v)

remover
stir (v)

cocer a fuego lento
simmer (v)

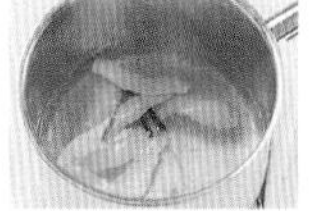

escalfar
poach (v)

hornear (ᶜcocer al horno)
bake (v)

asar
roast (v)

asar a la parrilla
grill (v)

los utensilios de cocina • kitchenware

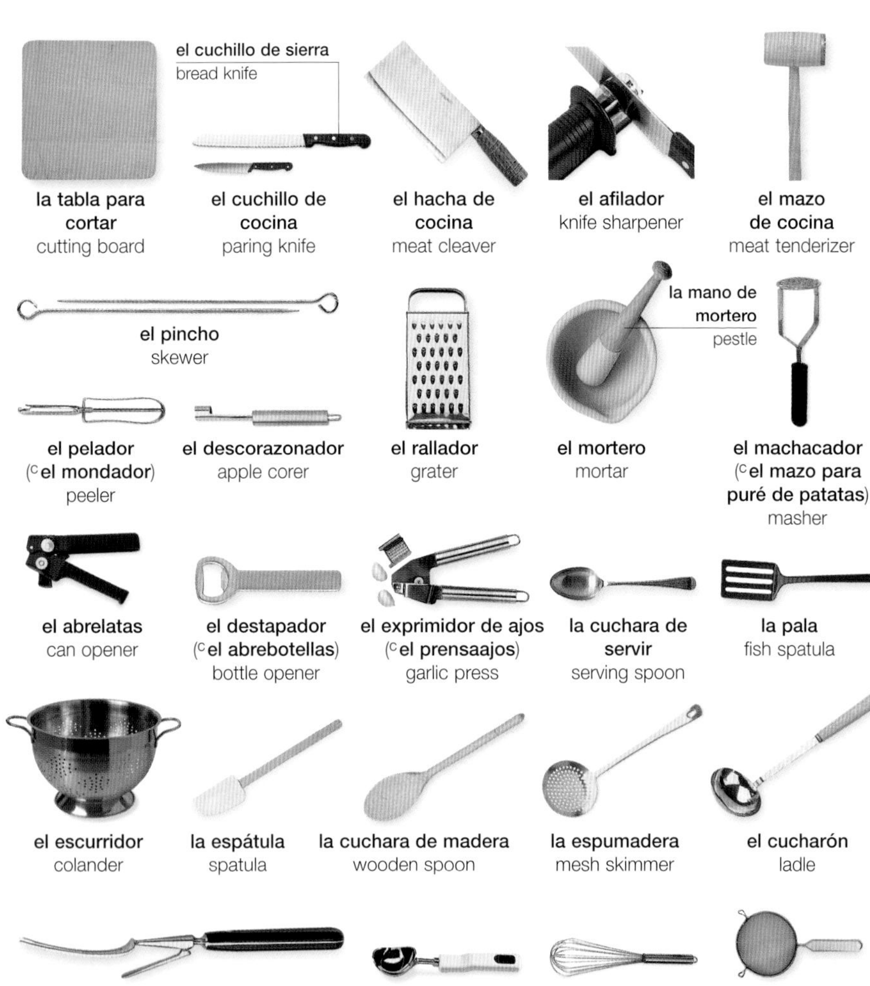

el trinche
(ᶜel tenedor para trinchar)
carving fork

la cuchara para helado
ice-cream scoop

el globo para batir
(ᶜel batidor de varillas)
whisk

el colador
strainer

la tapa
lid

antiadherente
nonstick

la sartén
frying pan

la cacerola ([C]el cazo)
saucepan

la parrilla
griddle

el wok
wok

la olla ([C]la cazuela) de barro
earthenware dish

de cristal
glass

resistente al horno
ovenproof

la ensaladera ([C]el cuenco)
mixing bowl

el molde para suflé
soufflé dish

la fuente para gratinar
gratin dish

el molde individual
ramekin

la cazuela
casserole dish

la repostería • baking cakes

la báscula de cocina
scales

la taza medidora ([C]la jarra graduada)
measuring cup

el molde para pastel ([C]bizcocho)
cake pan

el molde redondo
pie pan

la flanera
flan pan

la brocha de cocina
pastry brush

el rodillo de cocina
rolling pin

la dulla ([C]la manga pastelera)
piping bag

el molde para panqués ([C]magdalenas)
muffin pan

la charola ([C]la bandeja) de horno
cookie sheet

la rejilla
cooling rack

el guante ([C]la manopla) de cocina
oven mitt

el delantal
apron

la recámara • bedroom

el armario
wardrobe

la lámpara del buró ([C]de la mesilla)
bedside lamp

la cabecera ([C]el cabecero)
headboard

el buró ([C]la mesilla de noche)
nightstand

la cómoda
chest of drawers

el cajón
drawer

la cama
bed

el colchón
mattress

la colcha
bedspread

la almohada
pillow

la bolsa de agua caliente
hot-water bottle

la radio despertador
clock radio

el reloj despertador
alarm clock

la caja de pañuelos desechables
box of tissues

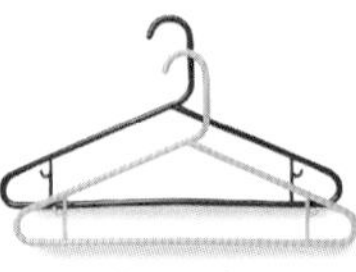

el gancho ([C]la percha)
coat hanger

el espejo
mirror

el tocador
vanity table

el suelo
floor

la ropa de cama • bed linen

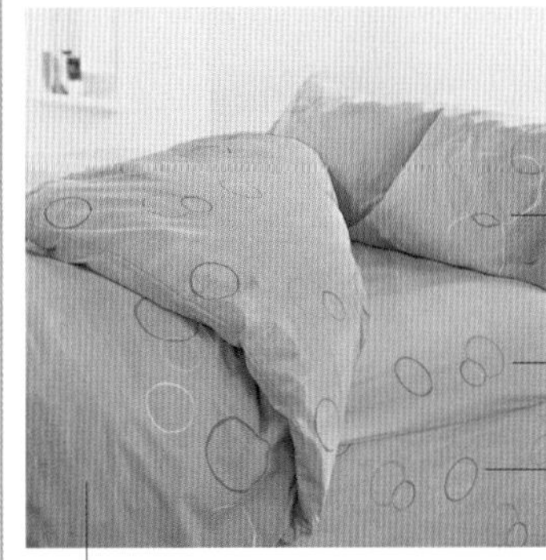

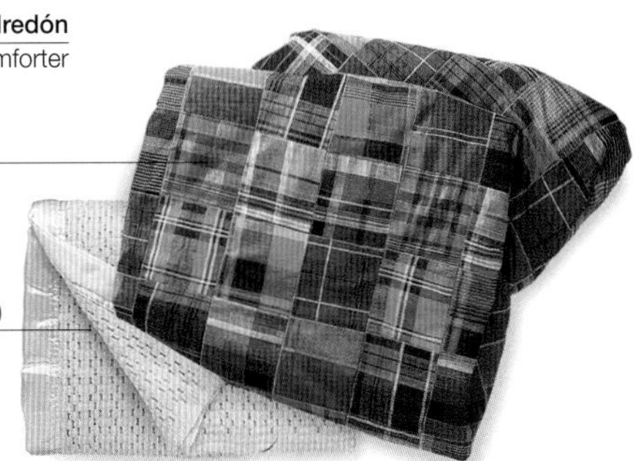

vocabulario • vocabulary

la cama individual
single bed

la cama matrimonial (c **de matrimonio**)
double bed

la cobija (c **la manta**) **eléctrica**
electric blanket

el pie de la cama (c **el estribo**)
footboard

el resorte (c **el muelle**)
box spring

el tapete (c **la moqueta**)
carpet

el insomnio
insomnia

acostarse
go to bed (v)

dormirse
go to sleep (v)

despertarse
wake up (v)

levantarse
get up (v)

hacer la cama
make the bed (v)

roncar
snore (v)

poner el despertador
set the alarm (v)

el armario empotrado
closet

el cuarto de baño • bathroom

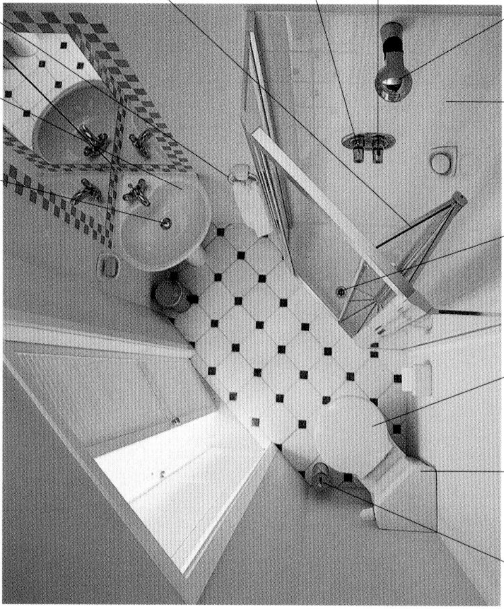
el toallero
towel rack
la puerta de la regadera (C ducha)
shower door
la llave (C el grifo) de agua fría
cold faucet
la llave (C el grifo) de agua caliente
hot faucet
la piña de la regadera (C la alcachofa de la ducha)
shower head
el lavabo
sink
la regadera (C la ducha)
shower
el tapón
stopper
el desagüe
drain
la tapa del excusado (C del wáter)
toilet seat
el excusado (C el wáter)
toilet
la escobilla del excusado (C del wáter)
toilet brush

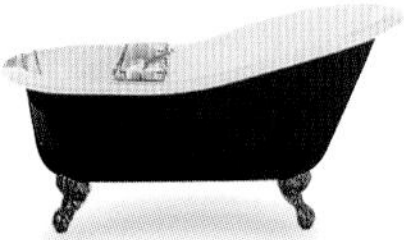

la tina (C **la bañera**)
bathtub

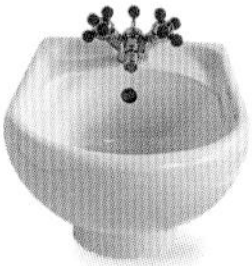

el bidé | bidet

vocabulario • vocabulary

el botiquín (C **el armario de las medicinas**) medicine cabinet	**el tapete** (C **la alfombrilla de baño**) bathmat
el rollo de papel higiénico toilet paper	**la cortina de la regadera** (C **de ducha**) shower curtain
bañarse (C **darse una ducha**) take a shower (v)	**darse un baño** take a bath (v)

la higiene dental • dental hygiene

el cepillo de dientes
toothbrush

la pasta de dientes
toothpaste

el hilo dental
dental floss

el enjuague bucal
mouthwash

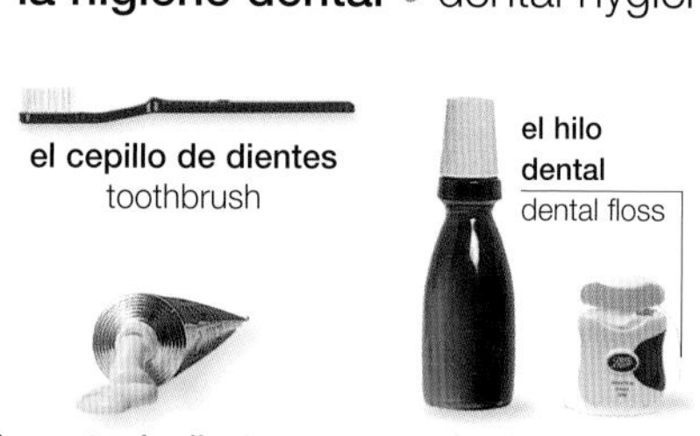

el zacate ([c]la esponja de luffa)
loofah

la esponja
sponge

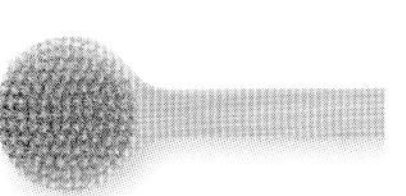

la piedra pómez
pumice stone

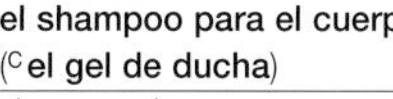

el cepillo para la espalda
back brush

el desodorante
deodorant

la jabonera
soap dish

el jabón
soap

el shampoo para el cuerpo ([c]el gel de ducha)
shower gel

la crema para la cara
face cream

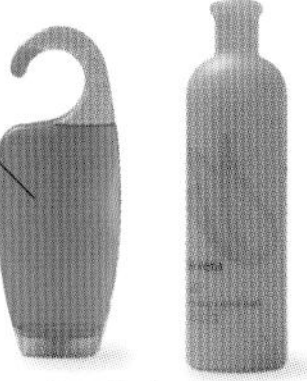

el gel de baño
bubble bath

la bata ([c]el albornoz)
bathrobe

la toalla de mano ([c]de lavabo)
hand towel

la toalla de baño
bath towel

las toallas
towels

la crema para el cuerpo ([c]la leche del cuerpo)
body lotion

el talco ([c]los polvos de talco)
talcum powder

el afeitado • shaving

la rasuradora
electric razor

la espuma de afeitar
shaving cream

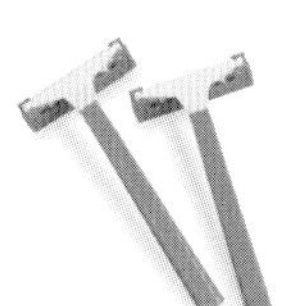

la navaja de afeitar desechable
disposable razor

la hoja de afeitar
razor blade

el aftershave
aftershave

la habitación de los niños • nursery

el cuidado del bebé • baby care

la hora de dormir • sleeping

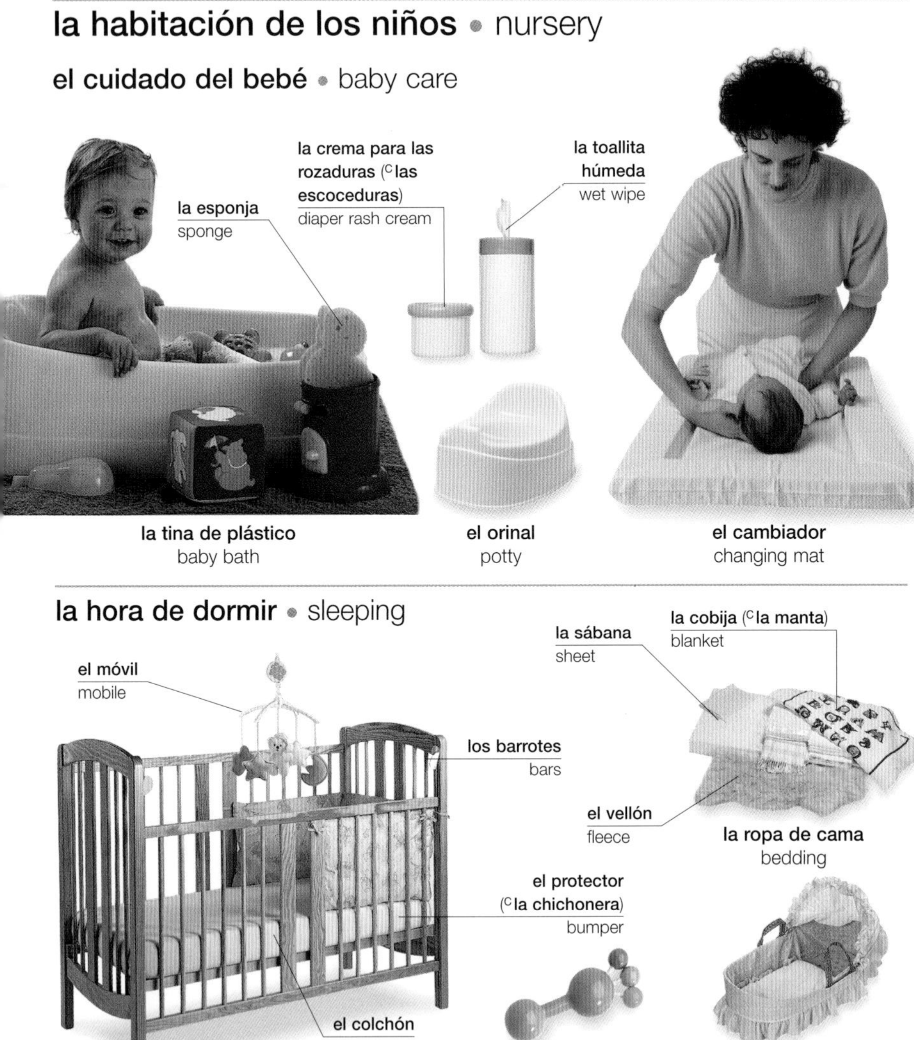

los juegos • playing

la muñeca
doll

el muñeco de peluche
stuffed toy

la casa de muñecas
dollhouse

la casa de juguete
playhouse

el oso de peluche
teddy bear

el juguete
toy

el cesto de los juguetes
toy basket

la pelota
ball

el corral ([c]**el parque**)
playpen

la seguridad • safety

el cierre de seguridad
child latches

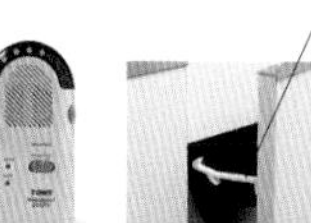

el intercomunicador
([c]**el escuchabebés**)
baby monitor

la barrera de seguridad
stair gate

la comida • eating

la periquera ([c]**la trona**)
high chair

el chupón
([c]**la tetina**)
nipple

la taza
drinking cup

la mamila ([c]**el biberón**)
bottle

el paseo • going out

la carriola
([c]**la silleta de paseo**)
stroller

la capota
hood

la carriola
([c]**el cochecito de niños**)
baby buggy

el bambineto
bassinet

el pañal
diaper

la pañalera
diaper bag

la cangurera ([c]**la mochila de bebé**) | front pack

la lavandería (C el lavadero) • utility room

la colada • laundry

la ropa sucia
dirty laundry

la ropa limpia
clean clothes

el cesto de la ropa sucia (C de la colada)
laundry basket

la lavadora
washing machine

la lavadora secadora
washer-dryer

la secadora
tumble dryer

el cesto de la ropa para planchar
linen basket

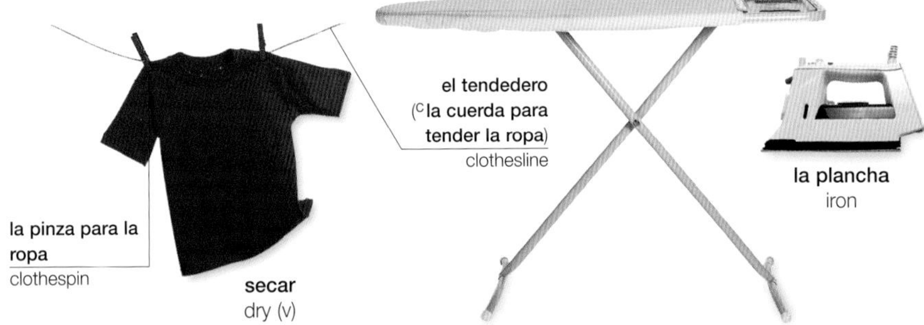

el tendedero (C la cuerda para tender la ropa)
clothesline

la plancha
iron

la pinza para la ropa
clothespin

secar
dry (v)

el burro (C la tabla) de la plancha | ironing board

vocabulario • vocabulary

cargar
load (v)

aclarar
rinse (v)

centrifugar
spin (v)

la centrífuga (C la centrifugadora)
spin dryer

planchar
iron (v)

el suavizante
fabric conditioner

¿Cómo funciona la lavadora?
How do I operate the washing machine?

¿Cuál es el programa para la ropa de color/blanca?
What is the setting for colors/whites?

el equipo de limpieza • cleaning equipment

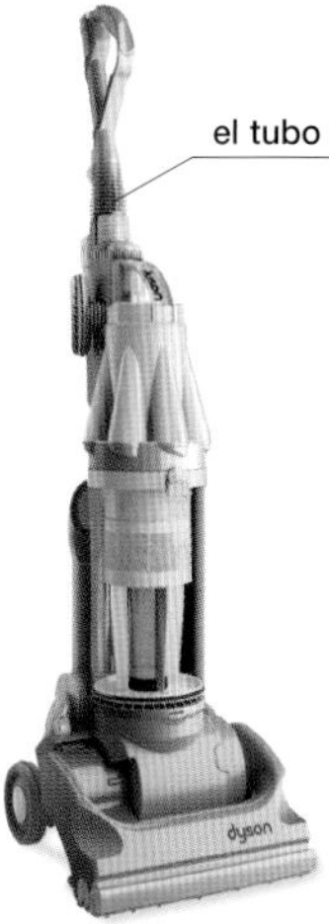

el tubo de la aspiradora
suction hose

la aspiradora
vacuum cleaner

el cubo
pail

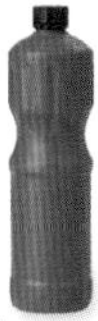

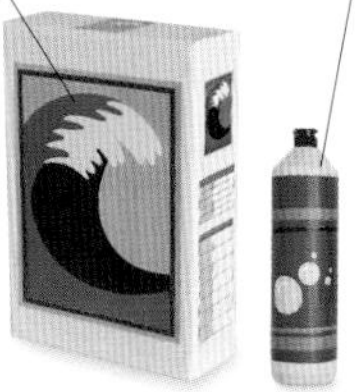

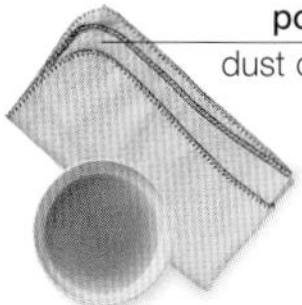

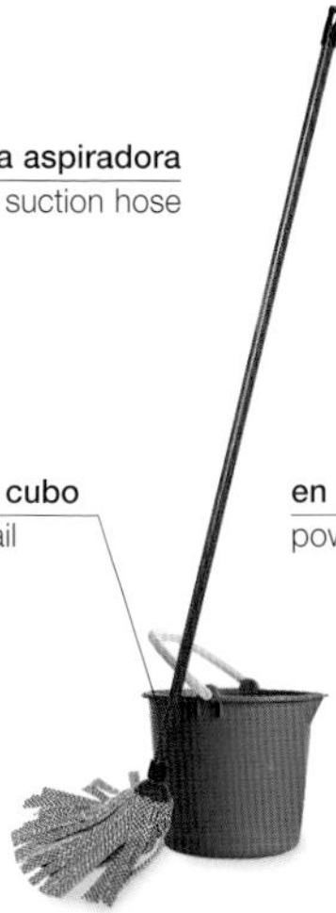

el trapeador ([c]**la fregona**)
mop

el cepillo
brush

el recogedor
dustpan

la lejía
bleach

en polvo
powder

líquido
liquid

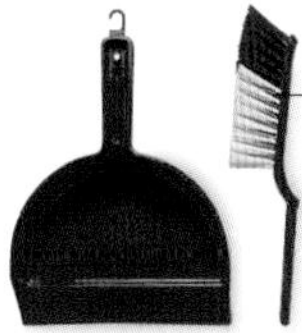

el detergente
detergent

el sacudidor ([c]el trapo del polvo)
dust cloth

la cera
polish

las acciones • activities

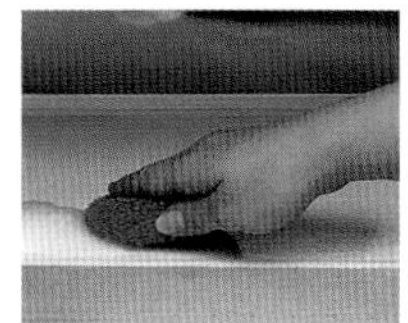

limpiar
clean (v)

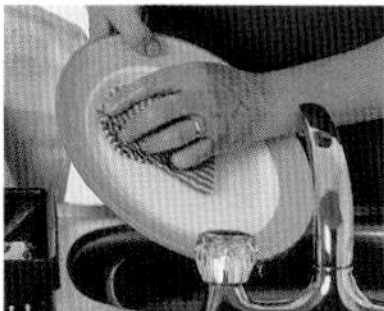

fregar
wash (v)

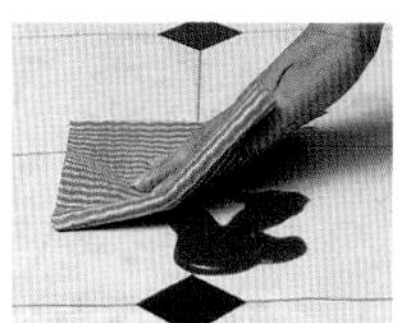

trapear ([c]**pasar la bayeta**)
wipe (v)

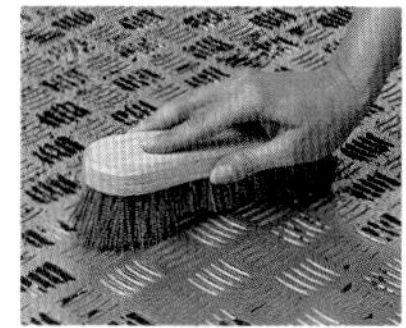

restregar
scrub (v)

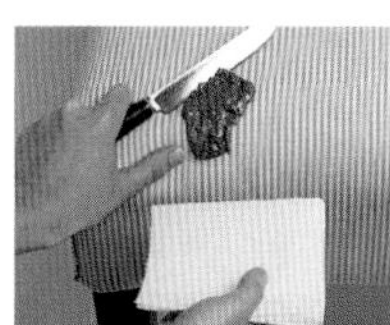

raspar
scrape (v)

la escoba
broom

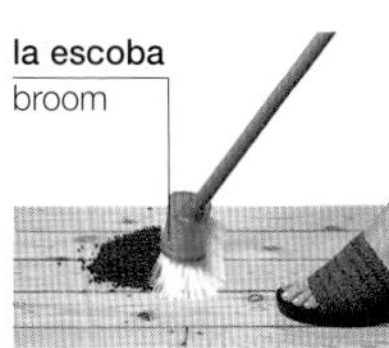

barrer
sweep (v)

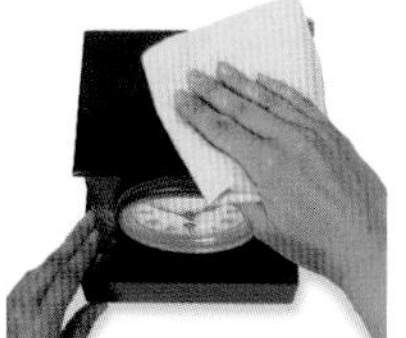

sacudir ([c]**limpiar el polvo**)
dust (v)

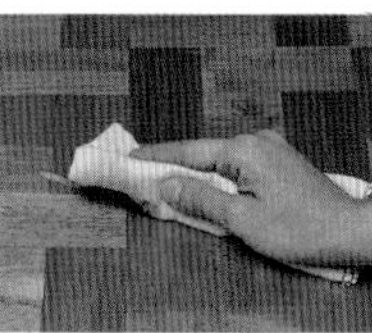

pulir ([c]**sacar brillo**)
polish (v)

el taller • workshop

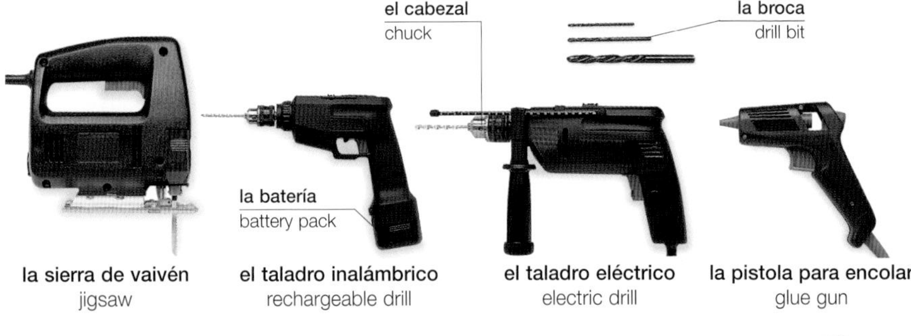

la sierra de vaivén
jigsaw

el taladro inalámbrico
rechargeable drill

el taladro eléctrico
electric drill

la pistola para encolar
glue gun

el tornillo (C **el torno**) **de banco** | vise

la lijadora
sander

la sierra circular
circular saw

el banco de trabajo
workbench

las técnicas • techniques

cortar
cut (v)

serrar
saw (v)

taladrar
drill (v)

clavar
hammer (v)

cepillar (C**alisar**)
plane (v)

tornear
turn (v)

tallar
carve (v)

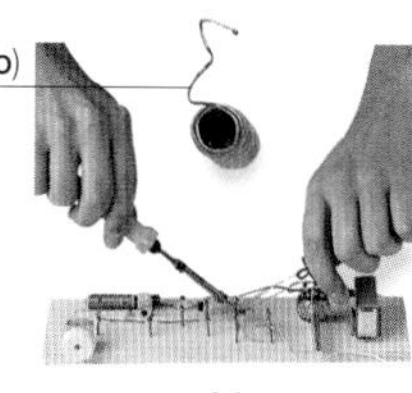

soldar
solder (v)

los materiales • materials

el tablero de densidad media
medium-density fiberboard

el contrachapado
plywood

el aglomerado
chipboard

el cartón madera
hardboard

la madera de pino
softwood

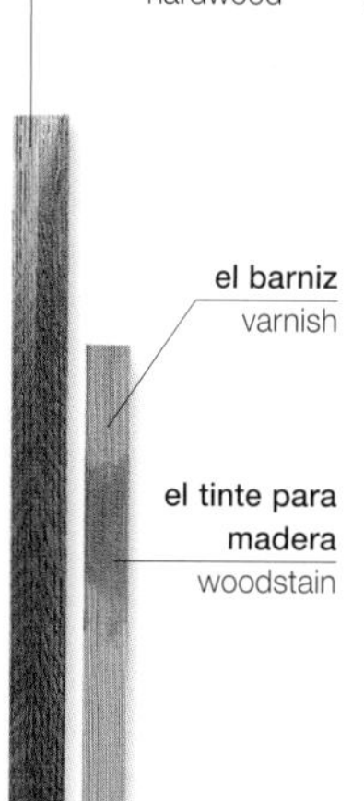

la madera | wood

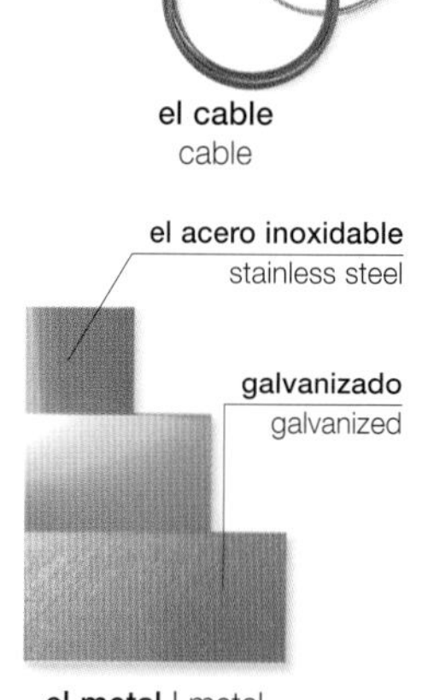

el metal | metal

la caja de las herramientas • toolbox

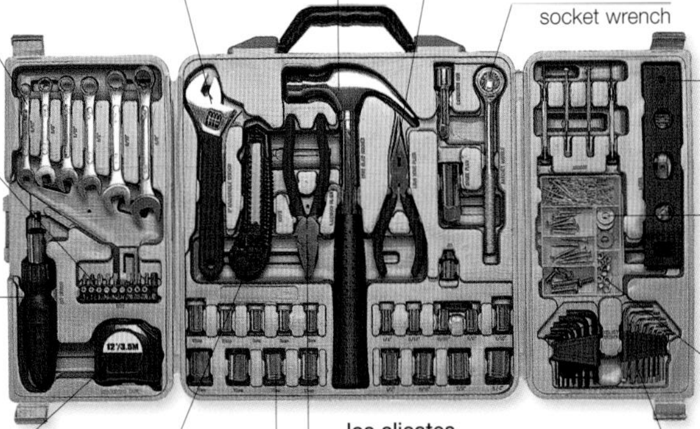

la llave de boca
wrench
la llave inglesa
adjustable wrench
el martillo
hammer
las pinzas (C las tenazas) de alambre
needle-nose pliers
la llave de tubo
socket wrench
el nivel
level
los cabezales de destornillador
screwdriver bits
la rondana (C la arandela)
washer
el destornillador
screwdriver
la tuerca
nut
los alicates
bull-nose pliers
la cinta métrica
tape measure
el cúter
utility knife
la llave
Allen wrench
el encaje
socket

las brocas • drill bits

la broca para metal
metal bit
la broca para madera
spade bit
el escariador
reamer
la broca de seguridad
security bit
las brocas para madera
wood bits
la broca de albañilería
masonry bit

el destornillador de cruz (C de estrella)
Phillips screwdriver

la cabeza
head

el clavo
nail

el tornillo
screw

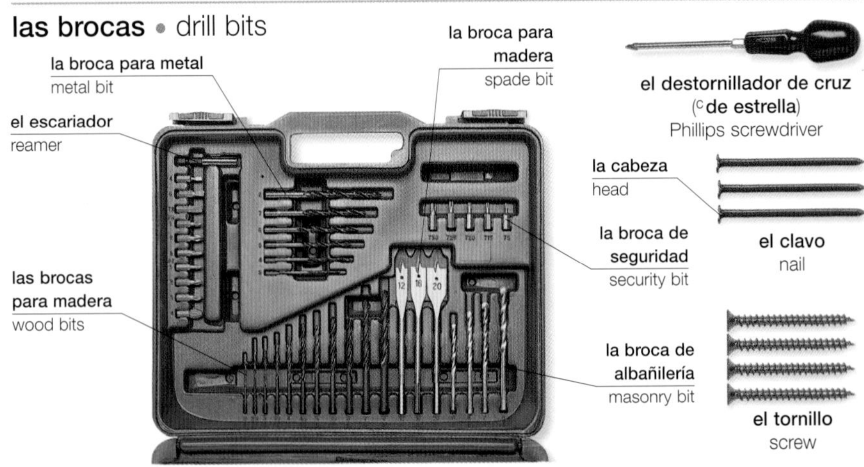

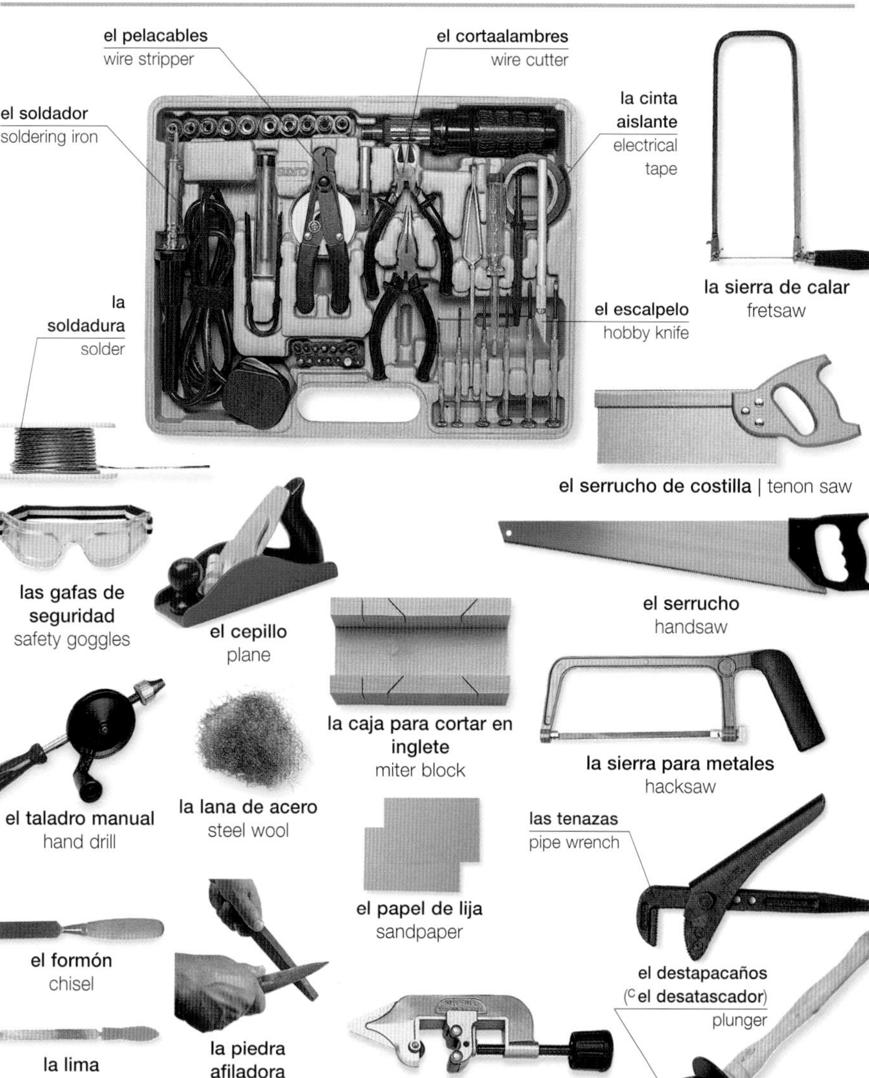

el pelacables
wire stripper
el cortaalambres
wire cutter
el soldador
soldering iron
la cinta aislante
electrical tape
la sierra de calar
fretsaw
la soldadura
solder
el escalpelo
hobby knife
el serrucho de costilla | tenon saw
las gafas de seguridad
safety goggles
el cepillo
plane
el serrucho
handsaw
la caja para cortar en inglete
miter block
la sierra para metales
hacksaw
el taladro manual
hand drill
la lana de acero
steel wool
las tenazas
pipe wrench
el papel de lija
sandpaper
el formón
chisel
el destapacaños
(C el desatascador)
plunger
la lima
file
la piedra afiladora
sharpening stone
el cortatuberías | pipe cutter

la decoración • decorating

tapizar (c **empapelar**) | wallpaper (v)

despegar (c **arrancar**)
strip (v)

rellenar
fill (v)

lijar
sand (v)

enyesar | plaster (v)

empapelar | hang (v)

poner azulejos (c **alicatar**) | tile (v)

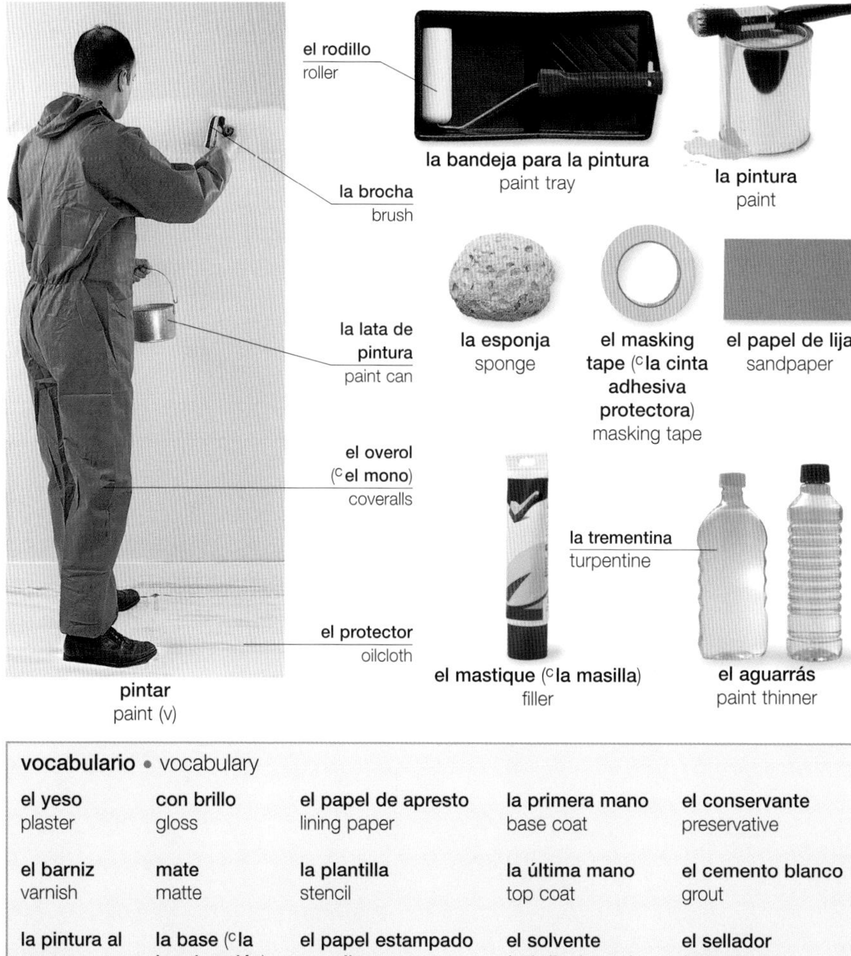

pintar
paint (v)

vocabulario • vocabulary

el yeso plaster	**con brillo** gloss	**el papel de apresto** lining paper	**la primera mano** base coat	**el conservante** preservative
el barniz varnish	**mate** matte	**la plantilla** stencil	**la última mano** top coat	**el cemento blanco** grout
la pintura al agua latex paint	**la base** (C **la imprimación**) primer	**el papel estampado en relieve** embossed paper	**el solvente** (C **el disolvente**) solvent	**el sellador** (C **el sellante**) sealant

el jardín • garden

los estilos de jardín • garden styles

el patio con jardín (c **la terraza ajardinada**)
patio garden

el jardín clásico | formal garden

el jardín campestre
English garden

el jardín de plantas herbáceas
herb garden

el jardín en la azotea
roof garden

la rocalla
rock garden

el patio
courtyard

el jardín acuático
water garden

los adornos para el jardín • garden features

la cesta colgante
hanging basket

la enredadera (c **la espaldera**) | trellis

la pérgola
arbor

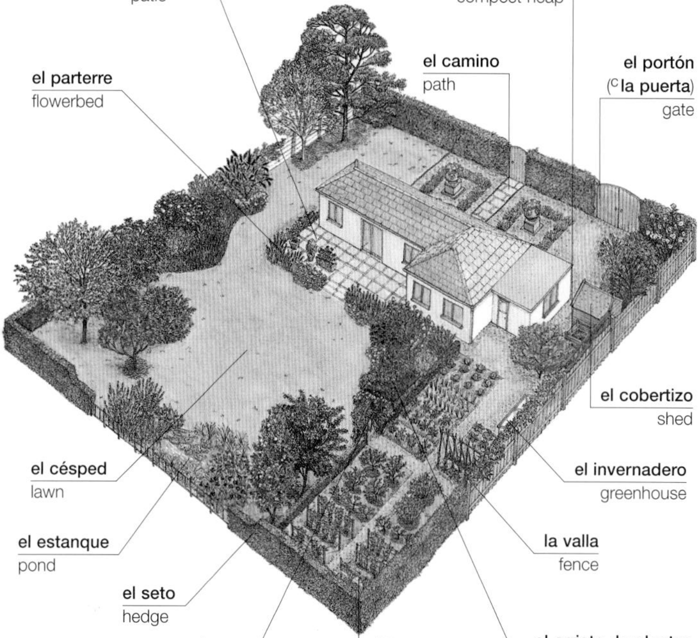

la terraza
patio

la composta
compost heap

el camino
path

el parterre
flowerbed

el portón
([c]**la puerta**)
gate

el cobertizo
shed

el invernadero
greenhouse

el césped
lawn

el estanque
pond

la valla
fence

el seto
hedge

el arco
arch

el huerto
vegetable garden

el arriate de plantas herbáceas
herbaceous border

el entarimado
deck

la fuente | fountain

la tierra • soil

la capa superior de la tierra
topsoil

la arena
sand

la creta
chalk

el cieno
silt

la arcilla
clay

las plantas de jardín • garden plants

los tipos de plantas • types of plants

anual
annual

bienal
biennial

perenne
perennial

el bulbo
bulb

el helecho
fern

el junco
cattail

el bambú
bamboo

las malas hierbas
weeds

la hierba
herb

la planta acuática
water plant

el árbol
tree

la palmera
palm

la conífera
conifer

de hoja perenne
evergreen

de hoja caduca
deciduous

as plantas podadas con formas
topiary

la planta alpestre
alpine

la planta suculenta
succulent

el cactus
cactus

la planta de maceta
potted plant

la planta de sombra
shade plant

la planta trepadora
climber

el arbusto de flor
flowering shrub

a planta para cubrir suelo
ground cover

la planta trepadora
creeper

ornamental
ornamental

el pasto ([C] el césped)
grass

las herramientas de jardinería • gardening tools

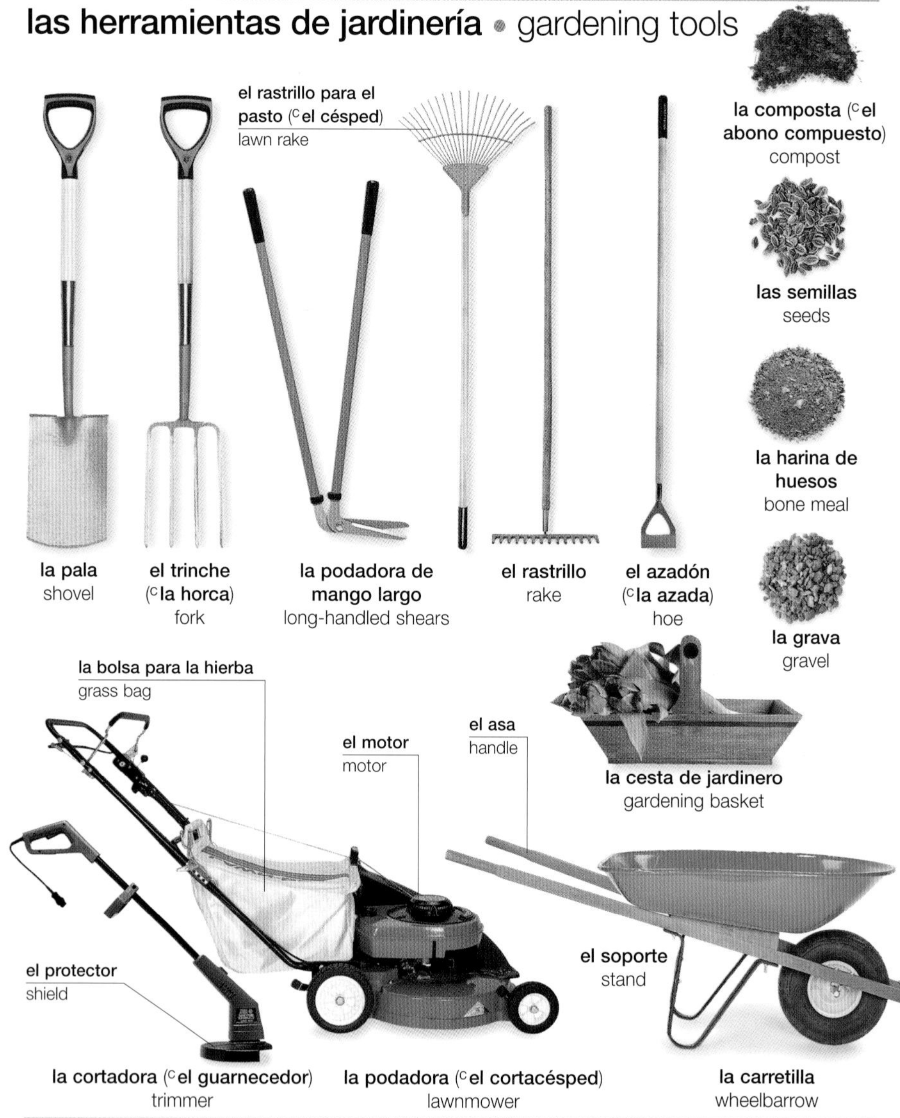

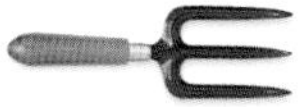

el trinche (ᶜ**la horquilla**)
hand fork

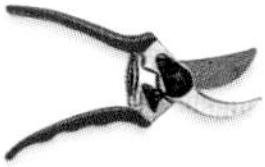

las podadoras (ᶜ**las tijeras de podar**)
pruning shears

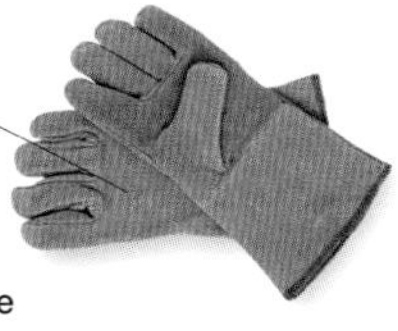

los guantes de jardín
gardening gloves

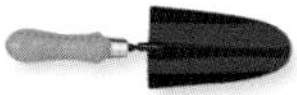

la pala pequeña
trowel

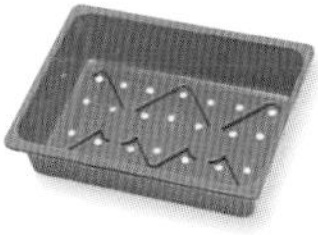

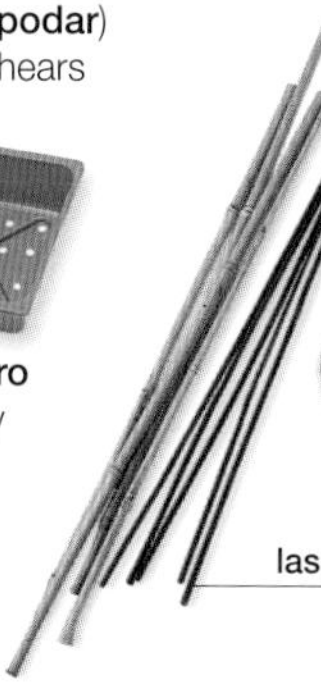

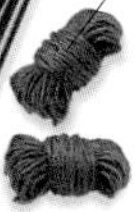

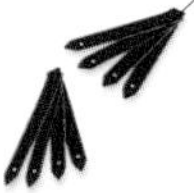

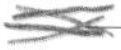

el semillero
seed tray

el hilo de bramante
twine

las etiquetas
labels

el alambre
twist ties

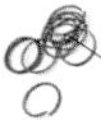

las anillas
ring ties

las cañas
canes

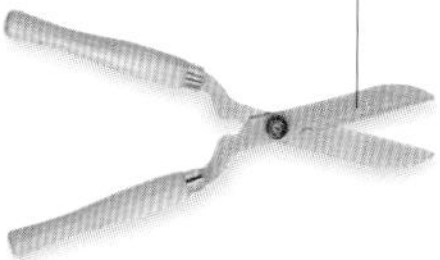

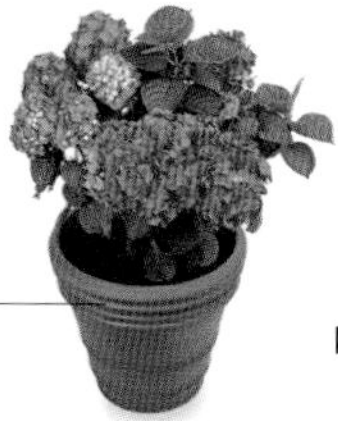

la hoja
blade

las tijeras (ᶜ**la cizalla**)
shears

la sierra de mano
hand saw

el pesticida
pesticide

la criba
sieve

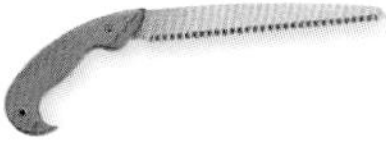

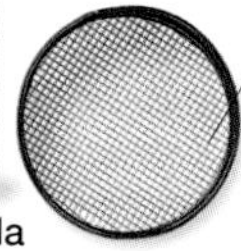

la maceta
plant pot

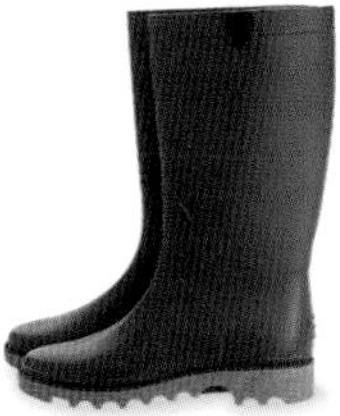

las botas de goma
rubber boots

el riego • watering

la regadera
watering can

la piña
(ᶜ**la alcachofa**)
rose

el pulverizador
spray gun

el aspersor
sprinkler

la boquilla
nozzle

la manguera
hose

el enrollador de manguera | hose reel

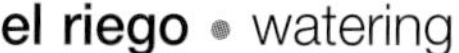

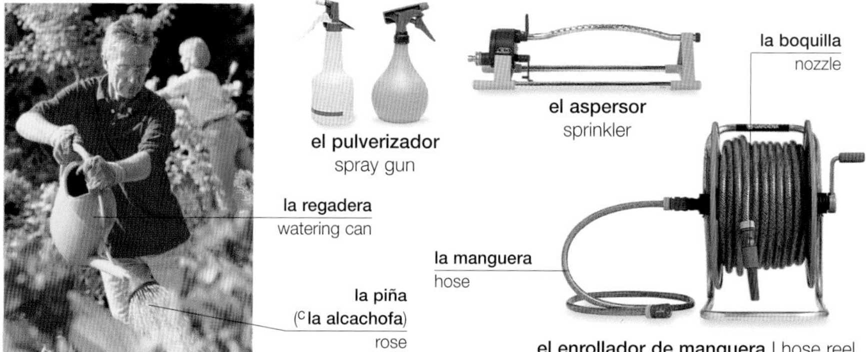

la jardinería • gardening

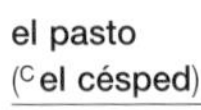

cortar el césped | mow (v)

poner césped
turf (v)

hacer agujeros con la trinche (C **la horquilla**)
spike (v)

rastrillar
rake (v)

podar
trim (v)

cavar
dig (v)

sembrar
sow (v)

abonar en la superficie
top dress (v)

regar
water (v)

guiar
train (v)

quitar las flores muertas
deadhead (v)

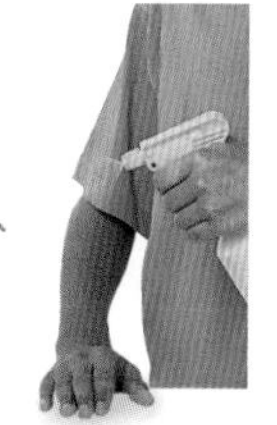

rociar
spray (v)

apuntalar
stake (v)

injertar
graft (v)

propagar
propagate (v)

podar
prune (v)

transplantar
transplant (v)

escardar
weed (v)

cubrir la tierra
mulch (v)

cosechar
harvest (v)

vocabulario • vocabulary

cultivar cultivate (v)	**diseñar** landscape (v)	**abonar** fertilize (v)	**cribar** sieve (v)	**el drenaje** drainage	**el plantón** seedling	**el subsuelo** subsoil
cuidar tend (v)	**plantar en tiesto** pot (v)	**coger** pick (v)	**airear** aerate (v)	**orgánico** (C **biológico**) organic	**el abono** fertilizer	**el herbicida** weedkiller

JKL
5
TUV
8
7
0

los servicios
services

los servicios de emergencia • emergency services

la ambulancia • ambulance

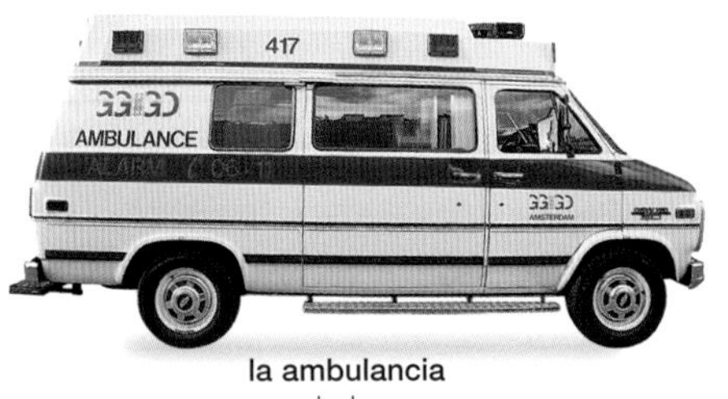

la ambulancia
ambulance

la camilla
stretcher

el paramédico ([c]el ambulancero)
paramedic

la policía • police

la placa
badge

el uniforme
uniform

la pistola
gun

la macana ([c]la porra)
nightstick

las esposas
handcuffs

el policía ([c]el agente de policía)
police officer

la sirena
siren

las luces
lights

la patrulla ([c]el coche de policía)
police car

la estación de policía
police station

vocabulario • vocabulary

el inspector captain	**el robo** burglary	**la denuncia** complaint	**el arresto** arrest
el detective detective	**la agresión** assault	**la investigación** investigation	**la celda** lockup
el crimen crime	**huella digital ([c]dactilar)** fingerprint	**el sospechoso** suspect	**el cargo** charge

los bomberos • fire department

los bomberos
firefighters

el incendio | fire

la estación ([c]el parque) de bomberos
fire station

la escalera ([c]la salida) de incendios
fire escape

el carro ([c]el coche) de bomberos
fire engine

el detector de humo
smoke alarm

la alarma contra incendios
fire alarm

el hacha
ax

el extintor
fire extinguisher

la bomba ([c]la boca) de agua
hydrant

Necesito la policía/los bomberos/una ambulancia.
I need the police/fire department/ambulance.

Hay un incendio en...
There's a fire at...

Ha habido un accidente.
There's been an accident.

¡Llame a la policía!
Call the police!

el banco • bank

el cliente
customer

la ventanilla
window

el cajero
teller

los folletos
brochures

el mostrador
counter

las fichas de depósito ([C] **las hojas de ingreso**)
deposit slips

la tarjeta de débito
debit card

la matriz
stub

el número de cuenta
account number

la firma
signature

la cantidad
amount

el gerente del banco ([C] **el director de banco**)
branch manager

la tarjeta de crédito
credit card

el talonario de cheques
checkbook

el cheque
check

vocabulario • vocabulary

los ahorros
savings

el sobregiro ([C] **el descubierto**)
line of credit

el préstamo
loan

la hipoteca
mortgage

la tasa ([C] **el tipo**) **de interés**
interest rate

los impuestos
tax

el pago
payment

la ficha de retiro
withdrawal slip

el débito directo ([C] **la domiciliación bancaria**)
automatic bill payment

depositar
deposit (v)

el pin
pin number

la transferencia bancaria
direct deposit

la cuenta corriente
checking account

la cuenta de ahorros
savings account

la comisión del banco
service charge

la moneda
coin

el billete
bill

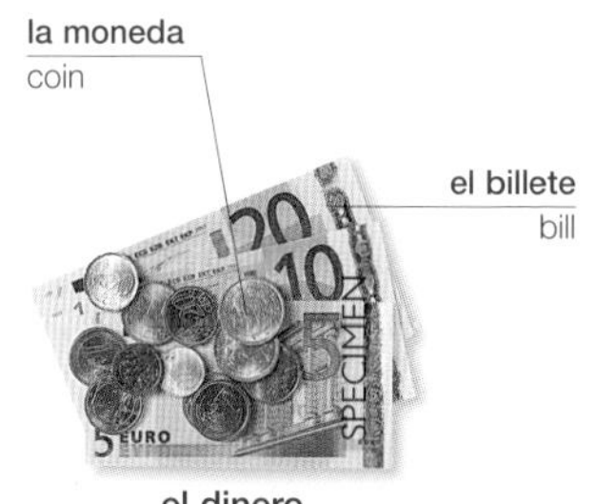

el dinero
money

la pantalla
screen

el teclado
keypad

la ranura de la tarjeta
card reader

el cajero automático
ATM

las divisas • foreign currency

la oficina de cambio
currency exchange

el cheque de viajero (ᶜde viaje)
traveler's check

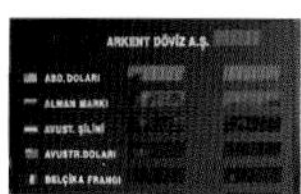

el tipo de cambio
exchange rate

las finanzas • finance

la asesora financiera
financial advisor

el valor de las acciones
stock price

el agente de bolsa
stockbroker

la bolsa de valores
stock exchange

vocabulario • vocabulary

cobrar
cash (v)

las acciones
stocks

la denominación (ᶜel valor nominal)
denomination

el contador (ᶜel contable)
accountant

la comisión
commission

los dividendos
dividends

la inversión
investment

la cartera
portfolio

las acciones
securities

el patrimonio neto
equity

¿Podría cambiar esto por favor?
Can I change this, please?

¿Cómo está el tipo de cambio hoy?
What's today's exchange rate?

las comunicaciones • communications

la oficina de correos | post office

el sobre | envelope

el cartero
mail carrier

vocabulario • vocabulary

la carta letter	**la firma** signature	**el reparto** delivery	**frágil** fragile	**no doblar** do not bend (v)
por avión by airmail	**la recogida** pickup	**el franqueo** postage	**el telegrama** telegram	**hacia arriba** this way up
el correo certificado registered mail	**el remitente** (ᶜ**el remite**) return address	**el giro postal** postal order	**la bolsa de correo** (ᶜ**la saca postal**) mailbag	**el fax** fax

el buzón
mailbox

el buzón
letter slot

el paquete
parcel

la mensajería
courier

el teléfono • telephone

el auricular
handset

la base
base station

la contestadora ([C]el contestador automático)
answering machine

el teléfono inalámbrico
cordless phone

el videoteléfono
video phone

la cabina telefónica
phone booth

el teclado
keypad

el celular
cellular phone

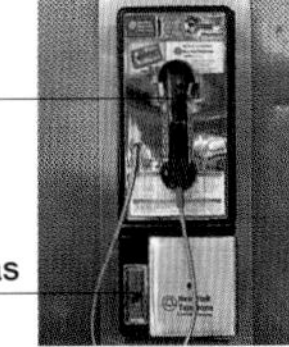

el auricular
receiver

las monedas devueltas
coin return

el teléfono de monedas
pay phone

el teléfono de tarjeta
card phone

vocabulario • vocabulary

la información telefónica directory assistance	**el mensaje de texto** text message	**ocupado ([C]comunicando)** busy
la llamada a por cobrar ([C]a cobro revertido) collect call	**el mensaje de voz** voice message	**desconectado ([C]apagado)** disconnected
marcar dial (v)	**contestar** answer (v)	**el operador** operator

¿Me podría dar el número de...?
Can you give me the number for...?

¿Cuál es el prefijo de larga distancia para llamar a...?
What is the area code for...?

el hotel • hotel

el lobby (cel vestíbulo) • lobby

el huésped
guest

la llave de la habitación
room key

los mensajes
messages

la casilla
pigeonhole

la recepcionista
receptionist

el registro
register

el mostrador
counter

la recepción | reception

el equipaje
luggage

el diablito (cel carrito)
luggage rack

el botones
porter

el elevador (cel ascensor)
escaltor

el número de la habitación
room number

los habitaciones • rooms

la habitación sencilla (cindividual)
single room

la habitación doble
double room

la habitación con dos camas individuales
twin room

el baño (cel cuarto de baño) privado
private bathroom

los servicios • services

el servicio de limpieza
maid service

el servicio de lavandería
laundry service

la charola ([C]la bandeja) del desayuno
breakfast tray

el servicio de habitaciones | room service

el minibar
minibar

el restaurante
restaurant

el gimnasio
gym

la piscina
swimming pool

vocabulario • vocabulary

la pensión completa
full board

la media pensión
half board

la habitación con desayuno incluido
bed and breakfast

¿Tiene alguna habitación libre?
Do you have any vacancies?

Tengo una reservación ([C]reserva).
I have a reservation.

Quiero una habitación sencilla ([C]individual).
I'd like a single room.

Quiero una habitación para tres días.
I'd like a room for three nights.

¿Cuánto cuesta la habitación por día?
What is the charge per night?

¿Cuándo tengo que dejar la habitación?
When do I have to vacate the room?

las compras
shopping

el centro comercial • shopping mall

vocabulario • vocabulary

el departamento (ᶜla sección) de zapatería
shoe department

el departamento (ᶜla sección) de niños
children's department

el departamento (ᶜla sección) de equipajes
luggage department

el servicio al cliente
customer services

el directorio
store directory

el vendedor (ᶜel dependiente)
sales clerk

el cuarto para cambiar a los bebés
baby changing room

los probadores
fitting rooms

los baños (ᶜlos aseos)
rest room

¿Cuánto cuesta esto?
How much is this?

¿Puedo cambiar esto?
May I exchange this?

las tiendas departamentales • department store

la ropa de caballero
menswear

la ropa de dama
(C **de señora**)
womenswear

la lencería
lingerie

la perfumería
perfumes

los cosméticos
(C **los productos de belleza**)
cosmetics

los blancos (C **la ropa de hogar**)
linens

el mobiliario para el hogar
home furnishings

la mercería
notions

los artículos de cocina
(C **el menaje de hogar**)
kitchenware

las vajillas
china

los aparatos eléctricos
electronics

la iluminación
lighting

los artículos deportivos
sportswear

la juguetería
toys

la papelería
stationery

los abarrotes
(C **el supermercado**)
groceries

el supermercado • supermarket

la panadería
bakery

los lácteos
dairy

los cereales
breakfast cereals

las conservas
canned goods

la dulcería
(C **la confitería**)
candies

la verdura
vegetables

la fruta
fruits

la carne y las aves
meat and poultry

el pescado
fish

la charcutería
deli

los congelados
frozen food

los platos preparados
prepared food

las bebidas
drinks

los productos de limpieza
household products

los artículos de aseo
toiletries

los artículos para el bebé
baby products

los electrodomésticos
electrical goods

la comida para animales
pet food

las revistas | magazines

la farmacia • chemist

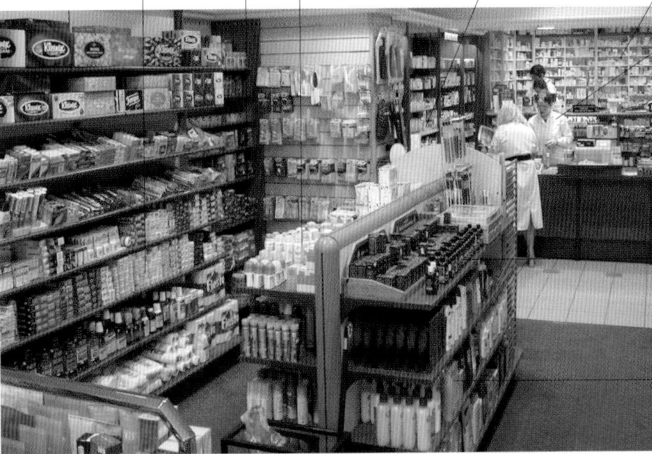

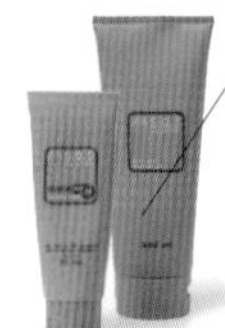

la crema protectora
sunscreen

la crema protectora total
sun block

el repelente de insectos
insect repellent

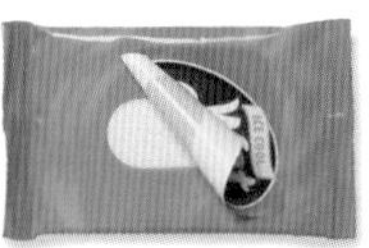

a toallita húmeda
wet wipe

el pañuelo desechable (C **de papel**)
tissue

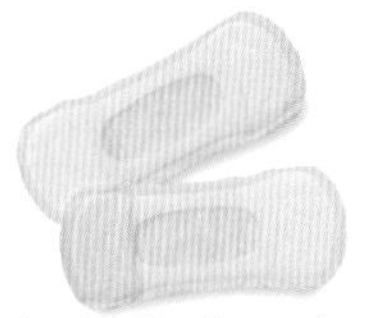

las toallas femeninas (C **la compresa**)
sanitary napkin

el tampón
tampon

el pantiprotector (C **el salvaslip**)
panty liner

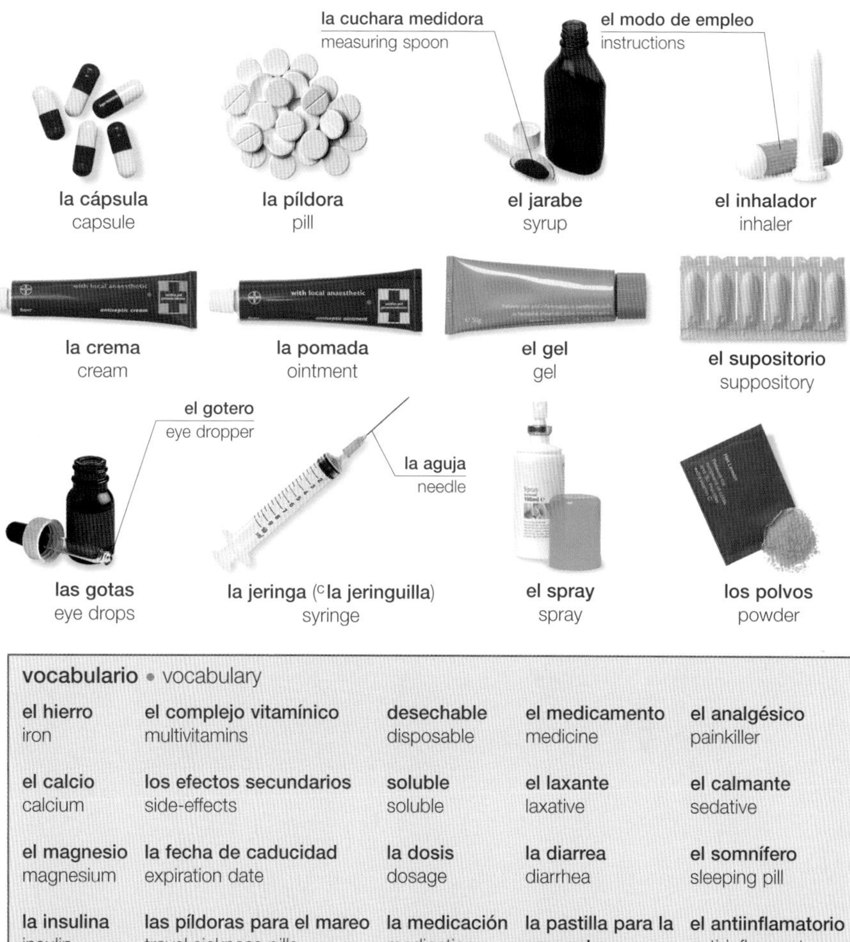

vocabulario • vocabulary

el hierro iron	**el complejo vitamínico** multivitamins	**desechable** disposable	**el medicamento** medicine	**el analgésico** painkiller
el calcio calcium	**los efectos secundarios** side-effects	**soluble** soluble	**el laxante** laxative	**el calmante** sedative
el magnesio magnesium	**la fecha de caducidad** expiration date	**la dosis** dosage	**la diarrea** diarrhea	**el somnífero** sleeping pill
la insulina insulin	**las píldoras para el mareo** travel sickness pills	**la medicación** medication	**la pastilla para la garganta** throat lozenge	**el antiinflamatorio** anti-inflammatory

la florería (ᶜla floristería) • florist

las flores
flowers

la azucena
lily

la acacia
acacia

el clavel
carnation

la maceta
potted plant

la gladiola
gladiolus

el iris
iris

la margarita
daisy

el crisantemo
chrysanthemum

la nube
(ᶜ**la gypsofila**)
gypsophila

el alhelí
stocks

la gerbera
gerbera

el follaje
foliage

la rosa
rose

la fresia
freesia

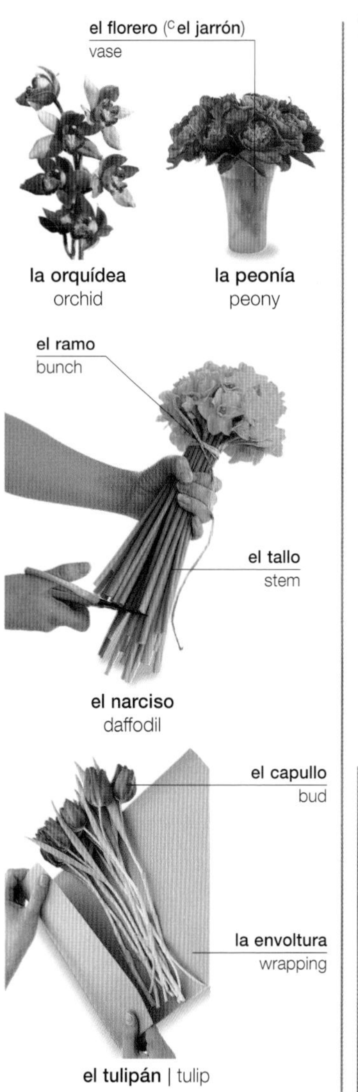

la orquídea orchid

la peonía peony

el narciso daffodil

el tulipán | tulip

los arreglos • arrangements

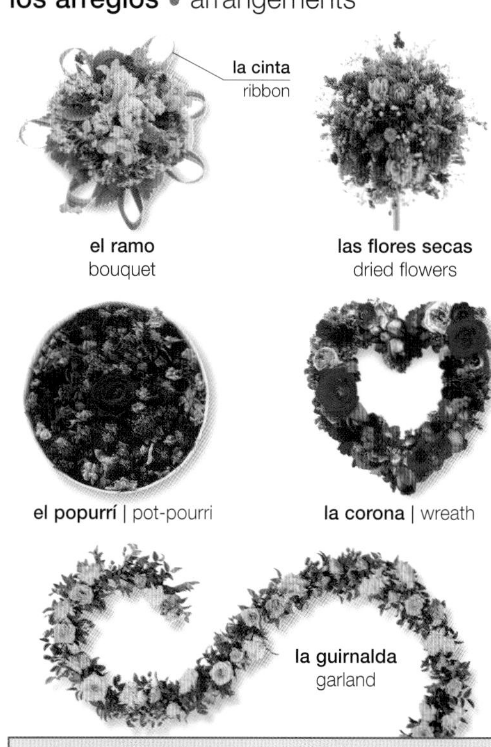

el ramo bouquet

las flores secas dried flowers

el popurrí | pot-pourri

la corona | wreath

la guirnalda garland

¿Me da un ramo de... por favor?
May I have a bunch of... please.

¿Me los puede envolver?
May I have them wrapped?

¿Puedo poner un mensaje?
May I attach a message?

¿Los puede enviar a...?
Would you send them to....?

¿Cuánto tiempo durarán éstos?
How long will these last?

¿Huelen?
Are they fragrant?

los tabacos y las revistas ([C]el vendedor de periódicos) • newsstand

los cigarros ([C]los cigarrillos)
cigarettes

la cajetilla de cigarros ([C]el paquete de tabaco)
pack of cigarettes

los cerillos ([C]las cerillas)
matches

los billetes de lotería
lottery tickets

los timbres ([C]los sellos)
stamps

la tarjeta postal
postcard

la historieta ([C]el tebeo)
comic

la revista
magazine

el periódico
newspaper

fumar • smoking

el tabaco
tobacco

el encendedor ([C]el mechero)
lighter

el tubo
stem

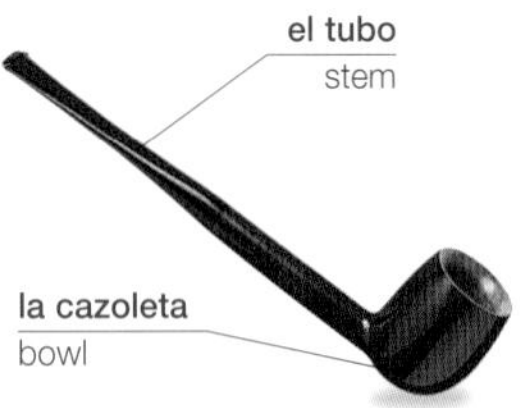

la cazoleta
bowl

la pipa
pipe

el puro
cigar

la dulcería • candy store

la caja de chocolates ([C] de bombones) box of chocolates

la barrita snack bar

las papas ([C] patatas) fritas potato chips

la dulcería ([C] la tienda de golosinas) | candy store

vocabulario • vocabulary

el chocolate de leche
milk chocolate

el chocolate negro
dark chocolate

el chocolate blanco
white chocolate

los dulces ([C] las golosinas) a granel
pick and mix

el caramelo
caramel

la trufa
truffle

la galleta
cookie

los caramelos duros
hard candy

los dulces ([C] las golosinas) • confectionery

el chocolate ([C] el bombón)
chocolate

la tablilla ([C] la tableta) de chocolate
chocolate bar

los caramelos duros
hard candy

la paleta ([C] la piruleta)
lollipop

el toffee
toffee

el turrón
nougat

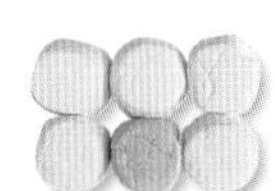
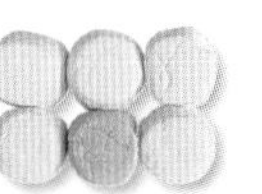

el malvarisco ([C] la nube)
marshmallow

la pastilla de menta
mint

el chicle
chewing gum

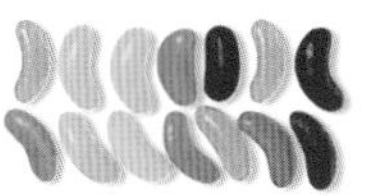

el caramelo blando
jellybean

la gomita ([C] la gominola)
gumdrop

el regaliz
licorice

las otras tiendas • other stores

la panadería
bakery

la confitería
cake shop

la carnicería
butcher shop

la pescadería
fish counter

la verdulería
produce stand

los abarrotes
([C] **el ultramarinos**)
grocery store

la zapatería
shoe store

la ferretería
hardware store

la tienda de antigüedades
antique store

la tienda de regalos
([C] **de artículos de regalo**)
gift store

la agencia de viajes
travel agency

la joyería
jewelry store

la librería
bookstore

la tienda de discos
record store

la tienda de licores
liquor store

la tienda de mascotas
(C **la pajarería**)
pet store

la mueblería
(C **la tienda de muebles**)
furniture store

la boutique
boutique

vocabulario • vocabulary

el vivero
garden center

la tienda naturista
(C **la herboristería**)
health food store

la lavandería
laundromat

la agencia inmobiliaria
realty office

la tienda de fotografía
camera store

la tienda de artículos usados
second-hand store

la tintorería
dry cleaner

la galería de arte
(C **la tienda de materiales de arte**)
art store

la sastrería
tailor shop

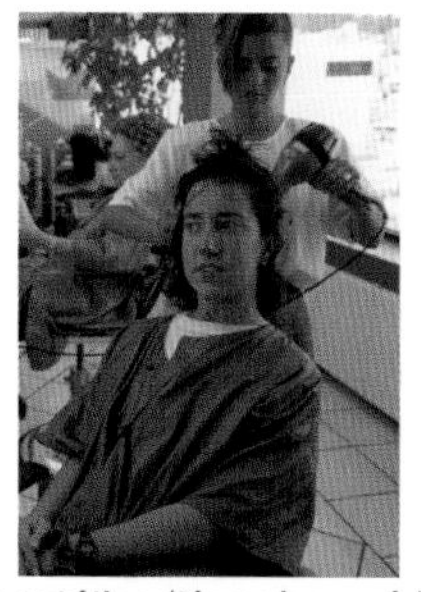
la estética (C **la peluquería**)
hair salon

el mercado | market

los alimentos
food

la carne • meat

vocabulario • vocabulary

el cerdo pork	**el venado** venison	**las asaduras** offal	**de granja** free range	**la carne roja** red meat
la vaca beef	**el conejo** rabbit	**curado** cured	**la carne blanca** white meat	**la carne magra** lean meat
la ternera veal	**la lengua** tongue	**ahumado** smoked	**orgánico** (C **biológico**) organic	**el fiambre** cooked meat

los cortes • cuts

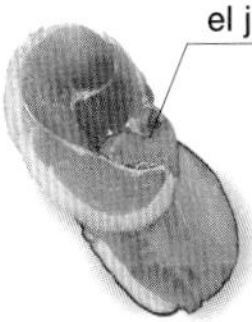

el jamón
ham

la corteza
rind

la rebanada (^c **la loncha**)
slice

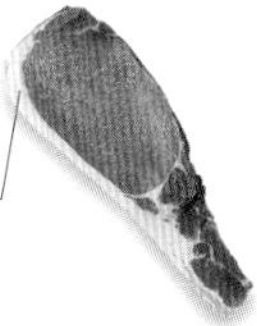

la rebanada (^c **la loncha**)
rasher

la carne molida (^c **picada**)
ground beef

el solomillo
fillet

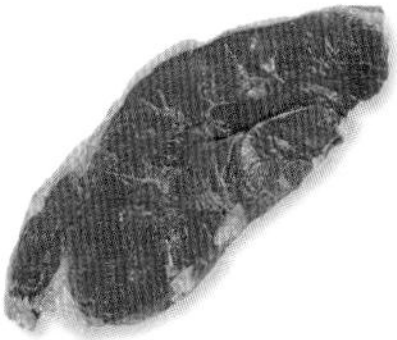

el filete de cadera
rump steak

el filete de lomo
sirloin steak

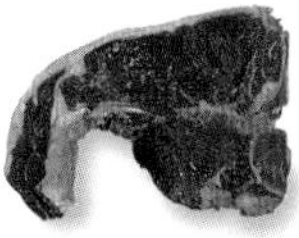

la costilla
rib

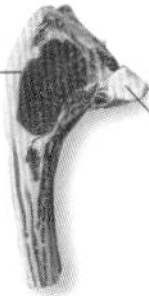

la grasa
fat

el hueso
bone

la chuleta
chop

el asado
joint

el riñón
kidney

el corazón
heart

las aves • poultry

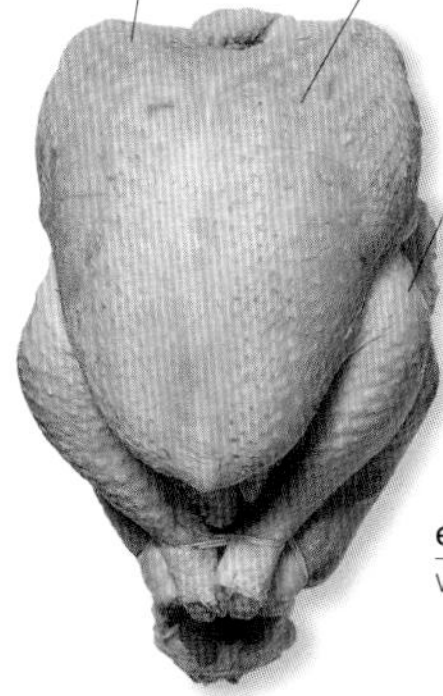

la piel
skin

la pechuga
breast

el muslo
thigh

el pavo
turkey

la carne de caza
game

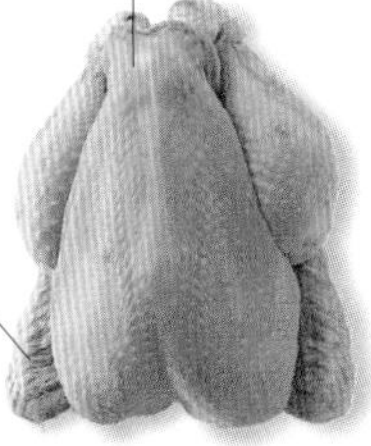

el pollo preparado
dressed chicken

el ala
wing

el pollo | chicken

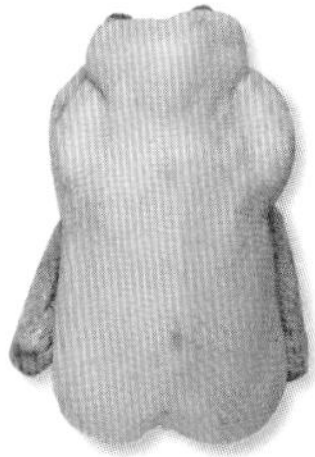

el faisán | pheasant

la pierna (^c la pata)
leg

la codorniz | quail

el pato | duck

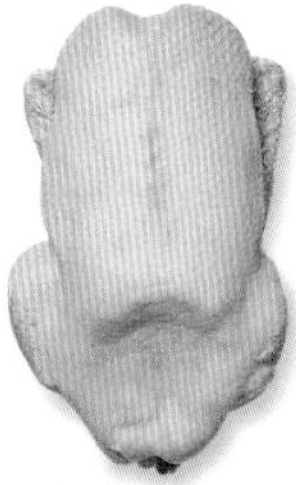

el ganso (^c **la oca**) | goose

el pescado • fish

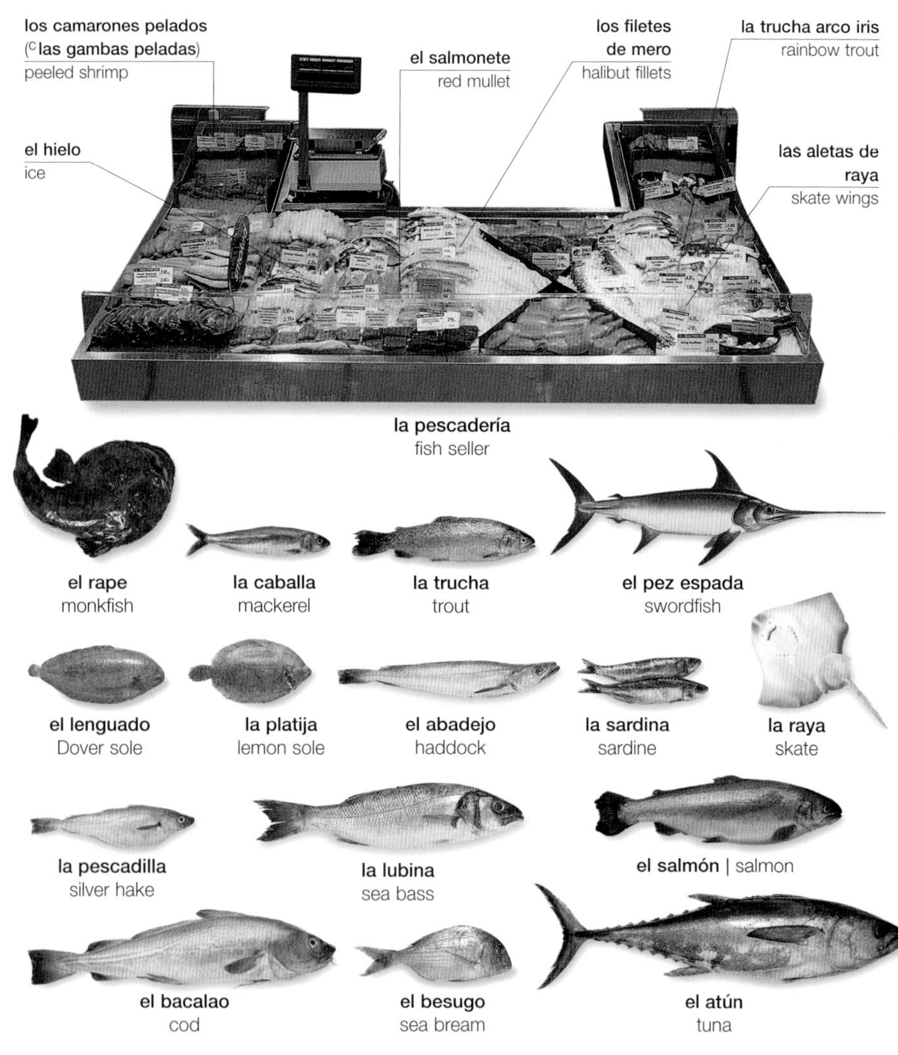

el marisco • seafood

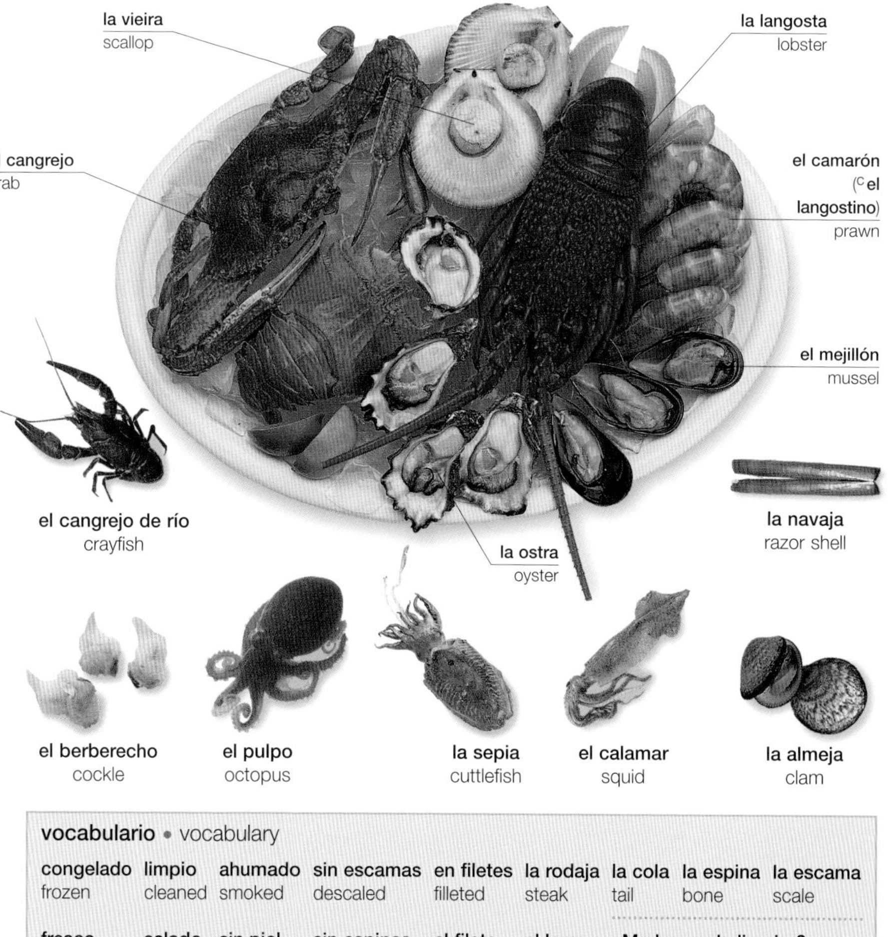

el berberecho
cockle

el pulpo
octopus

la sepia
cuttlefish

el calamar
squid

la almeja
clam

vocabulario • vocabulary

congelado frozen	**limpio** cleaned	**ahumado** smoked	**sin escamas** descaled	**en filetes** filleted	**la rodaja** steak	**la cola** tail	**la espina** bone	**la escama** scale
fresco fresh	**salado** salted	**sin piel** skinned	**sin espinas** boned	**el filete** fillet	**el lomo** loin	**¿Me lo puede limpiar?** Can you clean it for me?		

las verduras 1 • vegetables 1

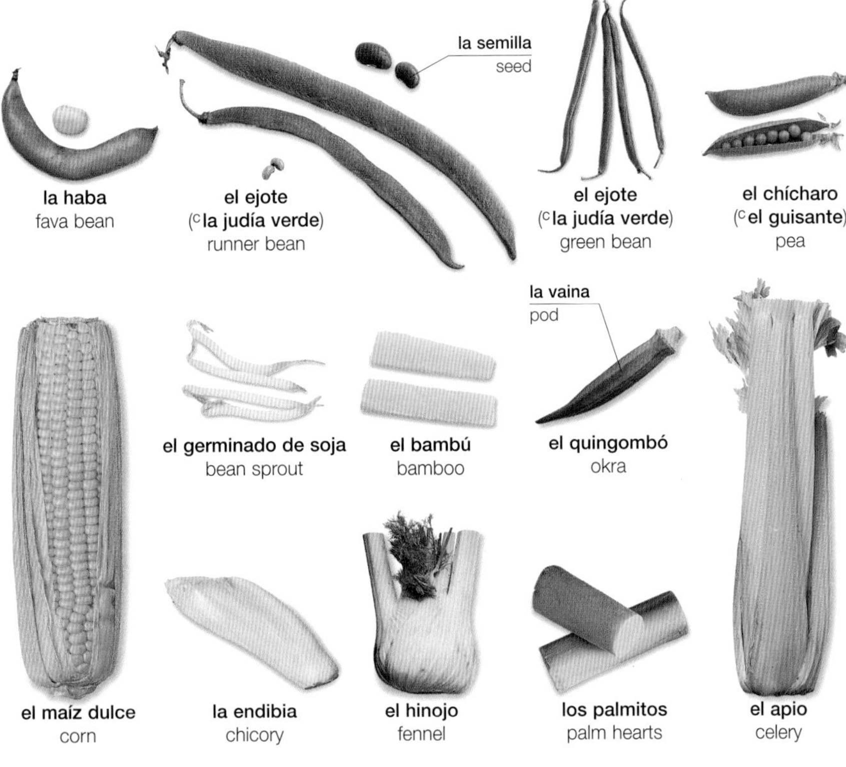

vocabulario • vocabulary

la hoja leaf	**la cabezuela** floret	**la punta** tip	**biológico** organic
el tallo stalk	**la almendra** kernel	**el corazón** (c **el centro**) heart	**la bolsa de plástico** plastic bag

¿Vende verduras orgánicas (c biológicas)?
Do you sell organic vegetables?

¿Son productos locales?
Are these grown locally?

la roqueta
arugula

el berro
watercress

el radicchio
radicchio

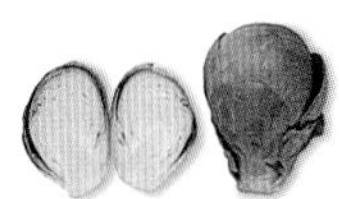
la col de bruselas
Brussels sprout

la acelga
swiss chard

la col rizada
kale

la acedera
sorrel

la escarola
endive

el diente de león
dandelion

la espinaca
spinach

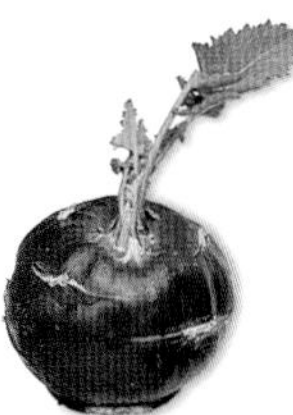
el colinabo
kohlrabi

la acelga china
bok choy

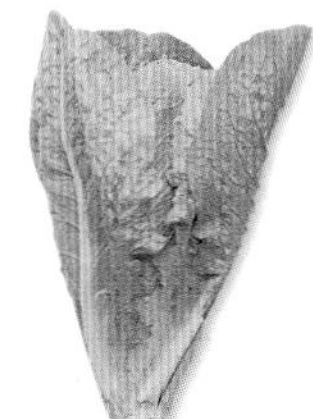
la lechuga
lettuce

el brócoli
broccoli

la col
cabbage

la berza
young cabbage

las verduras 2 • vegetables 2

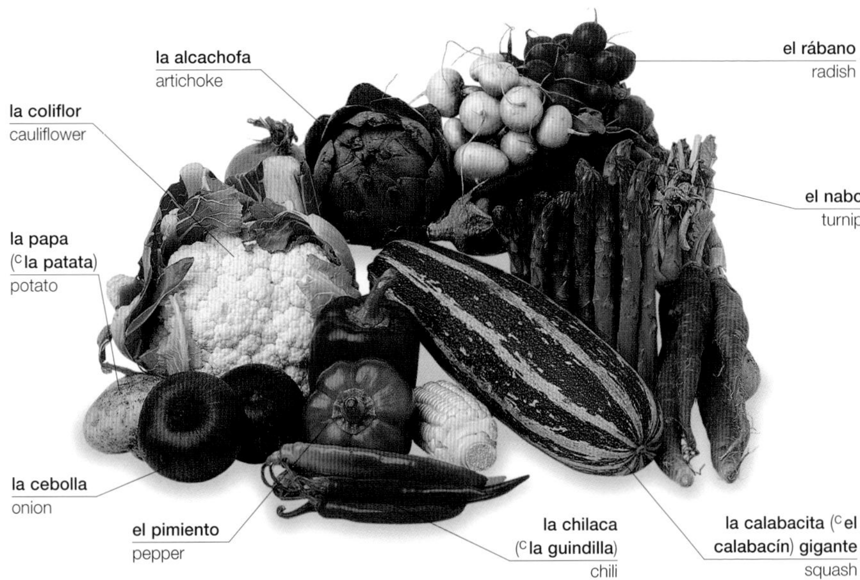

vocabulario • vocabulary

la mandioca
cassava

la zanahoria
carrot

el fruto del pan
breadfruit

la papa (C la patata) nueva
new potato

el apio-nabo
celeriac

la raíz del taro
taro root

la castaña de agua
water chestnut

el jitomate (C el tomate) cherry
cherry tomato

congelado
frozen

crudo
raw

picante
hot (spicy)

dulce
sweet

amargo
bitter

firme
firm

la pulpa
pulp

la raíz
root

¿Me da un kilo de papas (C patatas), por favor?
May I have one kilo of potatoes please?

¿Cuánto vale el kilo?
What's the price per kilo?

¿Cómo se llaman?
What are those called?

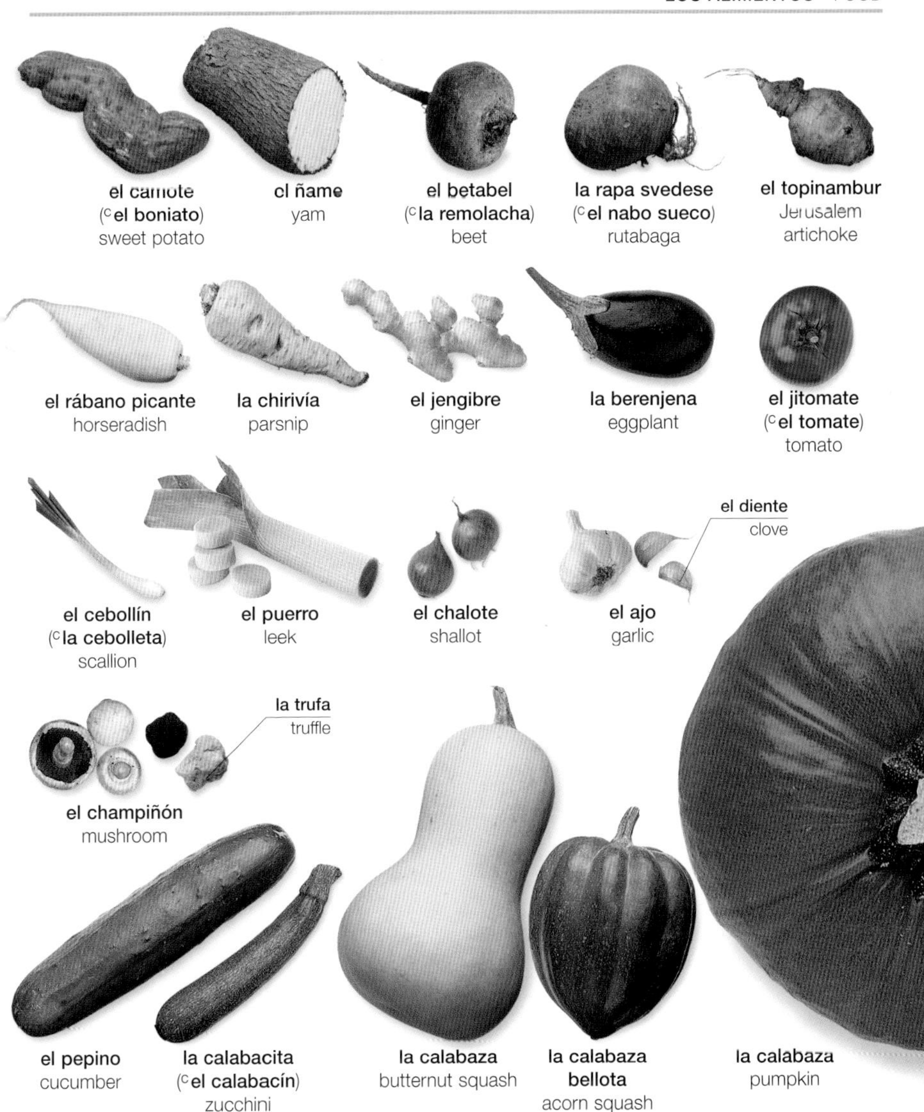
el camote
(C el boniato)
sweet potato
el ñame
yam
el betabel
(C la remolacha)
beet
la rapa svedese
(C el nabo sueco)
rutabaga
el topinambur
Jerusalem
artichoke
el rábano picante
horseradish
la chirivía
parsnip
el jengibre
ginger
la berenjena
eggplant
el jitomate
(C el tomate)
tomato
el cebollín
(C la cebolleta)
scallion
el puerro
leek
el chalote
shallot
el diente
clove
el ajo
garlic
la trufa
truffle
el champiñón
mushroom
el pepino
cucumber
la calabacita
(C el calabacín)
zucchini
la calabaza
butternut squash
la calabaza
bellota
acorn squash
la calabaza
pumpkin

la fruta 1 • fruit 1

los cítricos • citrus fruit

la naranja
orange

la mandarina clementina
clementine

el ugli
tangelo

la piel ([C]la médula)
pulp

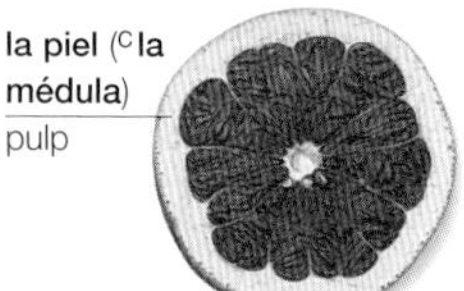

la toronja ([C]el pomelo)
grapefruit

la mandarina
tangerine

el gajo
segment

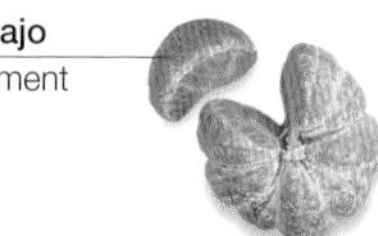

la mandarina satsuma
satsuma

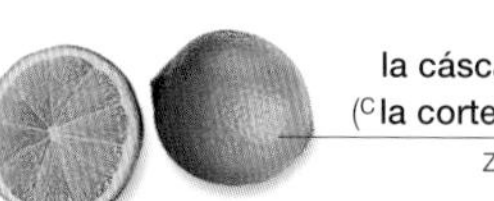

la cáscara ([C]la corteza)
zest

la lima
lime

el limón
lemon

la naranja china ([C]el kumquat)
kumquat

la fruta con hueso • stone fruit

el durazno ([C]el melocotón)
peach

la nectarina
nectarine

el chabacano ([C]el albaricoque)
apricot

la ciruela
plum

la cereza
cherry

la pera
pear

la manzana
apple

el frutero ([C]la cesta de fruta) | basket of fruit

las bayas y los melones • berries and melons

la fresa
strawberry

la frambuesa
raspberry

el melón
melon

la uva
grapes

la zarzamora (c **la mora**)
blackberry

la grosella
redcurrant

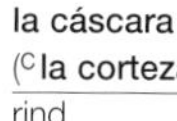
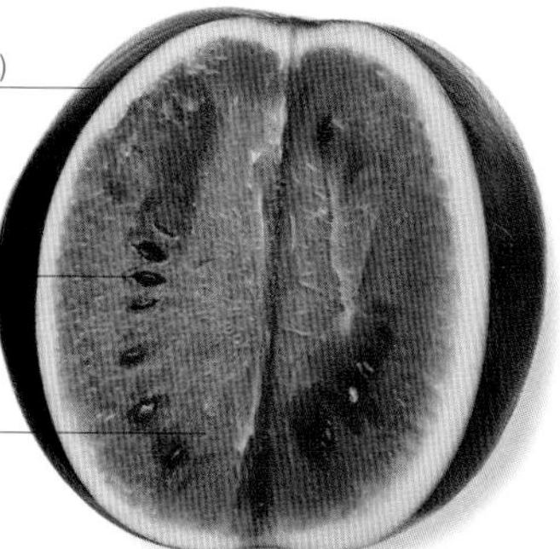

la sandía
watermelon

el arándano rojo
cranberry

la grosella negra
blackcurrant

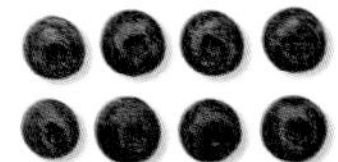

el arándano
blueberry

la grosella blanca
white currant

a frambuesa Logan
loganberry

el capulín
(c **la grosella espinosa**)
gooseberry

vocabulario • vocabulary

el ruibarbo rhubarb	**amargo** sour	**fresco** crisp	**el corazón** core	**¿Están maduros?** Are they ripe?
la fibra fiber	**fresco** fresh	**podrido** rotten	**la pulpa** pulp	**¿Puedo probar uno?** May I try one?
dulce sweet	**jugoso** juicy	**el jugo** (c **el zumo**) juice	**sin semillas** (c **pepitas**) seedless	**¿Hasta cuándo durarán?** How long will they keep?

la fruta 2 • fruit 2

el membrillo
quince

el maracuyá
passion fruit

el plátano
banana

la guayaba
guava

la granada
pomegranate

el caqui
persimmon

la feijoa
feijoa

la tuna
(C el higo chumbo)
prickly pear

la carambola
star fruit

el tomate de árbol
tamarillo

los frutos seco • nuts and dried fruit

el piñón
pine nut

el pistache
(c**el pistacho**)
pistachio

la nuez de la India
(c**el anacardo**)
cashew nut

el cacahuete
peanut

la avellana
hazelnut

la nuez de Brasil
Brazil nut

la nuez
(c**la pacana**)
pecan

la almendra
almond

la nuez de Castilla
(c**la nuez**) | walnut

la castaña
chestnut

la macadamia
macadamia

el higo
fig

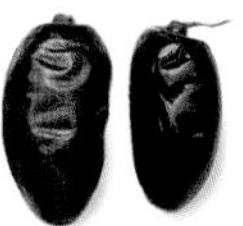
el dátil
date

la ciruela pasa
prune

la pasa sultana
sultana

la pasa
raisin

la pasa de Corinto
currant

el coco
coconut

vocabulario • vocabulary

verde green	**duro** hard	**la almendra** kernel	**salado** salted	**tostado** roasted	**las frutas tropicales** tropical fruit	**pelado** shelled
maduro ripe	**blando** soft	**desecado** dried	**crudo** raw	**de temporada** seasonal	**la fruta escarchada** candied fruit	**entero** whole

los granos y las legumbres • grains and pulses

los granos • grains

el trigo
wheat

la avena
oats

la cebada
barley

el mijo
millet

el maíz
corn

la quinoa
quinoa

vocabulario • vocabulary

la semilla seed	**fresco** fresh	**integral** whole-grain
la cáscara husk	**perfumado** fragranced	**largo** long-grain
el grano kernel	**los cereales** cereal	**corto** short-grain
seco dry	**poner a remojo** soak (v)	**de fácil cocción** easy-to-cook

el arroz • rice

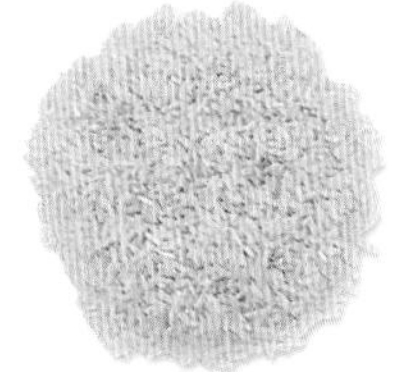
el arroz largo
white rice

el arroz integral
brown rice

el arroz salvaje
wild rice

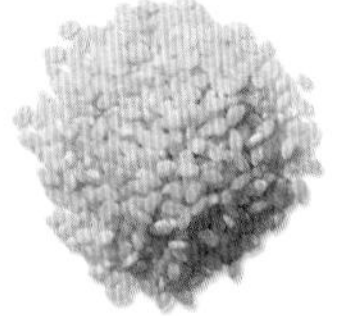
el arroz bomba
dessert rice

los granos procesados • processed grains

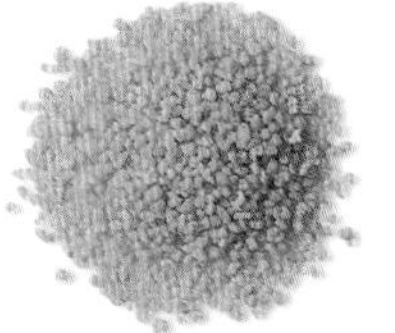
el cuscús
couscous

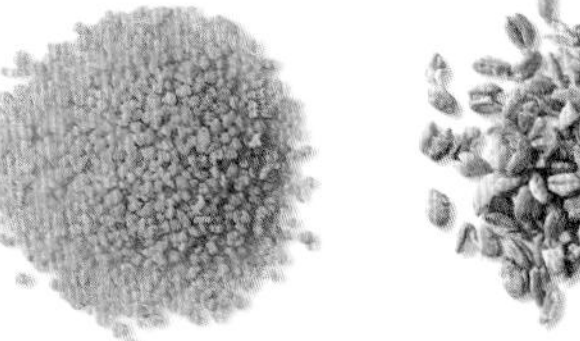
el trigo partido
cracked wheat

la sémola
semolina

el salvado
bran

los frijoles y los chícharos (c las alubias y los guisantes) • beans and peas

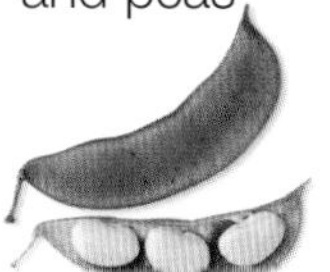

el frijol blanco (c la alubia blanca)
lima beans

el frijol blanco chico
navy beans

el frijol rojo (c la alubia roja)
kidney beans

el frijol morado (c la alubia morada)
aduki beans

las habas
fava beans

la semilla de soja
soybeans

el frijol (c la alubia) de ojo negro
black-eyed peas

el frijol pinto (c la alubia pinta)
pinto beans

el frijol mung (c la alubia mung)
mung beans

el frijol flageolet (c la alubia flageolet)
flageolet beans

la lenteja castellana
brown lentils

la lenteja roja
red lentils

los chícharos (c los guisantes tiernos)
peas

los garbanzos
chick peas

los chícharos secos (c los guisantes secos)
split peas

las semillas • seeds

la pepita (c la pipa) de calabaza
pumpkin seed

la semilla de mostaza (c la mostaza en grano)
mustard seed

el carvi
caraway

la semilla de sésamo
sesame seed

la semilla de girasol
sunflower seed

las hierbas y las especias • herbs and spices

las especias • spices

la vainilla
vanilla

la nuez moscada
nutmeg

la macis
mace

la cúrcuma
turmeric

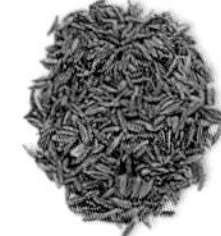
el comino
cumin

el ramillete aromático
bouquet garni

la pimienta de Jamaica
allspice

la pimienta en grano
peppercorn

el heno griego
fenugreek

el chile piquín (C **la guindilla**)
chili

el azafrán
saffron

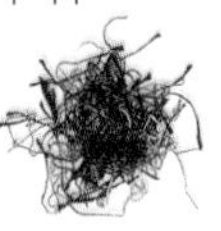
el cardamono
cardamom

el curry en polvo
curry powder

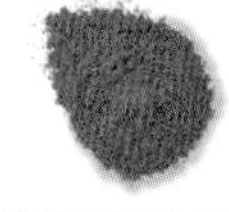

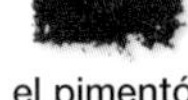
el pimentón
paprika

el ajo
garlic

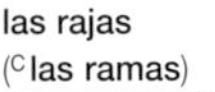

las rajas
(C las ramas)
sticks

la canela
cinnamon

la citronela
lemon grass

los clavos
cloves

el anís estrellado
star anise

el jengibre
ginger

las hierbas • herbs

el hinojo
fennel

las semillas de hinojo
fennel seeds

el laurel
bay leaf

el perejil
parsley

los cebollinos
chives

la menta
mint

el tomillo
thyme

la salvia
sage

el estragón
tarragon

la mejorana
marjoram

la albahaca
basil

el orégano
oregano

el cilantro
coriander

el eneldo
dill

el romero
rosemary

los alimentos embotellados • bottled foods

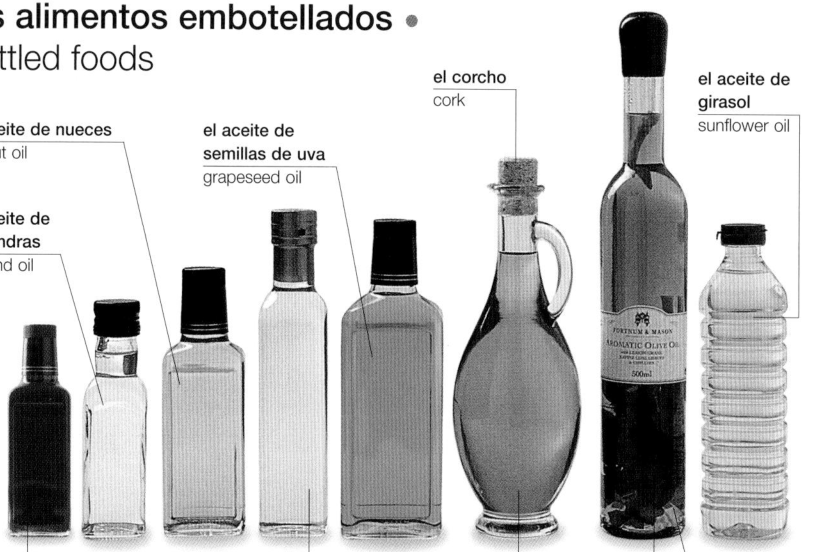
el aceite de nueces
walnut oil
el aceite de almendras
almond oil
el aceite de semillas de uva
grapeseed oil
el corcho
cork
el aceite de girasol
sunflower oil
FORTNUM & MASON
AROMATIC OLIVE OIL
500ml
el aceite de sésamo
sesame seed oil
el aceite de avellanas
hazelnut oil
el aceite de oliva
olive oil
las hierbas
herbs
el aceite aromatizado
flavored oil

los aceites
oils

las conservas dulces • sweet spreads

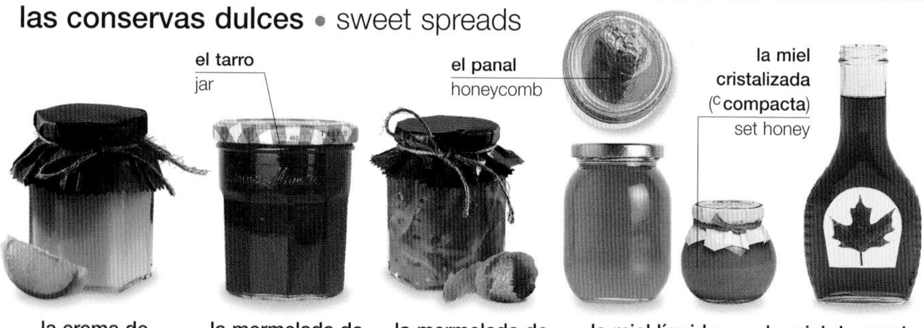

el tarro
jar
el panal
honeycomb
la miel cristalizada
(C compacta)
set honey
la crema de limón
lemon curd
la mermelada de frambuesa
raspberry jam
la mermelada de naranja
marmalade
la miel líquida
clear honey
la miel de maple
(C el jarabe de arce)
maple syrup

los condimentos • condiments and spreads

el vinagre de sidra
cider vinegar

el vinagre balsámico
balsamic vinegar

la mayonesa
mayonnaise

el chutney
chutney

el vinagre de malta
malt vinegar

el vinagre de vino
wine vinegar

el vinagre
vinegar

la botella
bottle

la catsup (*c* **el ketchup**)
ketchup

la salsa
sauce

la mostaza inglesa
English mustard

la mostaza francesa
French mustard

la mostaza en grano
wholegrain mustard

la crema de cacahuete
peanut butter

el tarro hermético
sealed jar

el chocolate para untar
chocolate spread

la fruta en conserva
preserved fruit

vocabulario • vocabulary

el aceite vegetal vegetable oil	**el aceite de colza** canola oil
el aceite de maíz corn oil	**el aceite de presión en frío** cold-pressed oil
el aceite de cacahuete peanut oil	

los productos lácteos • dairy products

el queso • cheese

la corteza
rind

el queso semicurado
semihard cheese

el queso rallado
grated cheese

el queso curado
hard cheese

el queso cremoso semicurado
semisoft cheese

el requesón
cottage cheese

el queso cremoso
cream cheese

el queso azul
blue cheese

el queso cremoso
soft cheese

el queso fresco | fresh cheese

la leche • milk

la mantequilla
butter

la margarina
margarine

la crema (ᶜ**la nata**)
cream

la crema (ᶜ**la nata**) **líquida**
half-and-half cream

la crema para batir (ᶜ**la nata para montar**)
whipping cream

la crema batida (ᶜ**la nata montada**)
whipped cream

la crema ácida (ᶜ**la nata agria**)
sour cream

el yogurt
yogurt

el helado
ice cream

los huevos • eggs

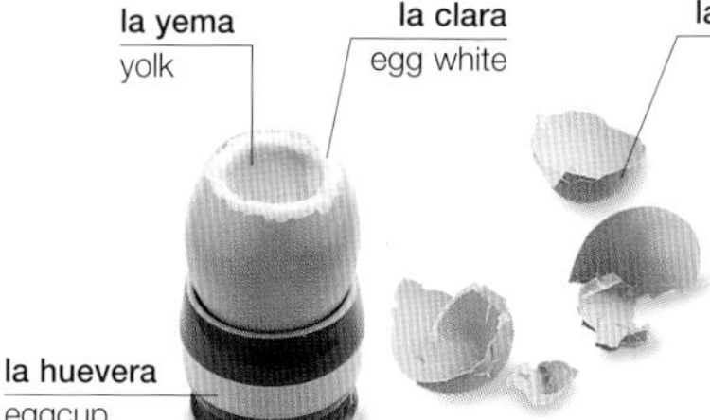

el huevo tibio (ᶜ**pasado por agua**)
soft-boiled egg

el huevo de gallina
hen's egg

el huevo de pato
duck egg

el huevo de ganso (ᶜ**de oca**)
goose egg

el huevo de codorniz
quail egg

vocabulario • vocabulary

pasteurizado pasteurized	**sin grasa** fat-free	**salado** salted	**la leche de oveja** sheep's milk	**homogeneizado** homogenized	**la lactosa** lactose
sin pasteurizar unpasteurized	**la leche en polvo** powdered milk	**sin sal** unsalted	**el suero de la leche** buttermilk	**la malteada** (ᶜ**el batido**) milkshake	**el yogurt helado** frozen yogurt

el pan y las harinas • breads and flours

el pan de caja ([C] de molde)
sliced bread

las semillas de amapola
poppy seeds

el pan de centeno
rye bread

la baguette
French bread

la panadería | bakery

haciendo pan • making bread

la harina blanca
white flour

la harina morena
whole-wheat flour

la harina integral
stone-ground flour

la levadura
yeast

cernir ([C] **cribar**) | sift (v)

mezclar | mix (v)

la masa
dough

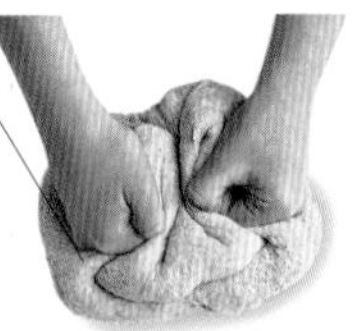

amasar | knead (v)

hornear | bake (v)

el pan blanco
white bread

el pan negro (ᶜmoreno)
brown bread

el pan integral
whole-wheat bread

el pan con grano
multigrain bread

el pan de maíz
corn bread

el pan al bicarbonato sódico
soda bread

el pan fermentado
sourdough bread

el pan sin levadura
flat bread

la dona (ᶜla rosquilla)
bagel

el bollo
bun

el panecillo
roll

el pan de frutas (ᶜel plumcake)
fruit bread

el pan con semillas
seeded bread

el naan
naan bread

la pita
pita bread

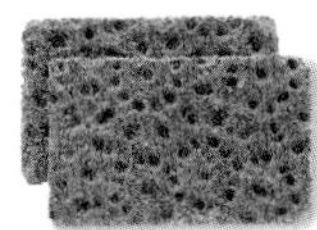

el pan danés (ᶜel biscote)
crispbread

vocabulario • vocabulary

la harina con levadura self-rising flour	**la harina blanca** all-purpose flour	**levar** prove (v)	**la barra** flute	**el rebanador** slicer
la harina para pan bread flour	**subir** rise (v)	**glasear** glaze (v)	**el pan molido** (ᶜ**rallado**) breadcrumbs	**el panadero** baker

la repostería • cakes and desserts

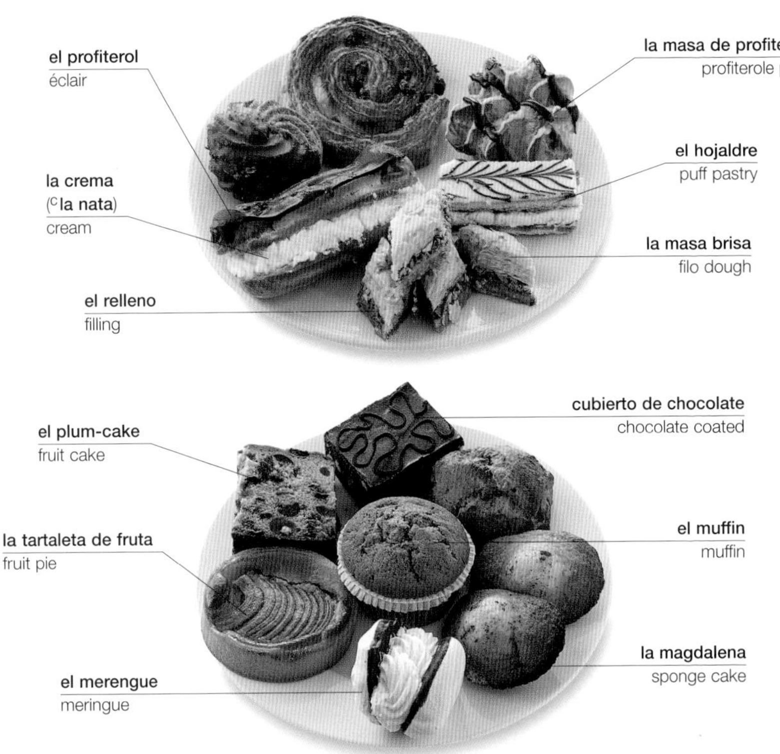

los pasteles | cakes

vocabulario • vocabulary

la crema pastelera
pastry cream

el pastel de chocolate
chocolate cake

el bollo
bun

las natillas
custard

la masa
pastry

la rebanada (C **el trozo**)
slice

la celebración
celebration

el arroz con leche
rice pudding

¿Puedo tomar una rebanada (C un trozo)?
May I have a slice please?

el postre de soletillas, gelatina de frutas y crema
trifle

las galletas | cookies

el mousse
mousse

el sorbete
sorbet

el pastel de crema (c nata)
custard pie

el flan
crème caramel

los pasteles para celebraciones • special occasion cakes

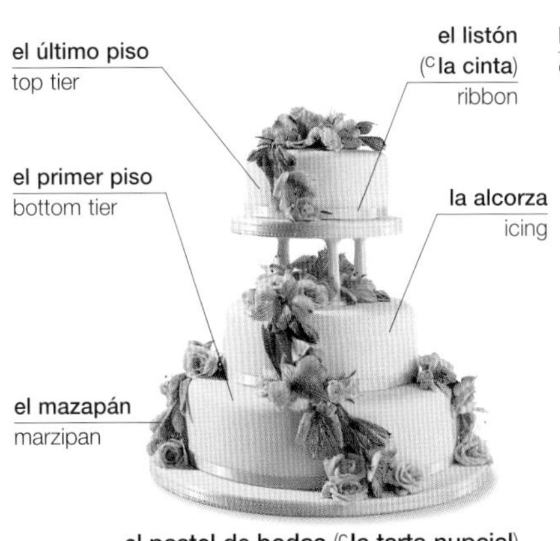

el pastel de bodas (c la tarta nupcial)
wedding cake

el pastel (c la tarta) de cumpleaños | birthday cake

la charcutería • delicatessen

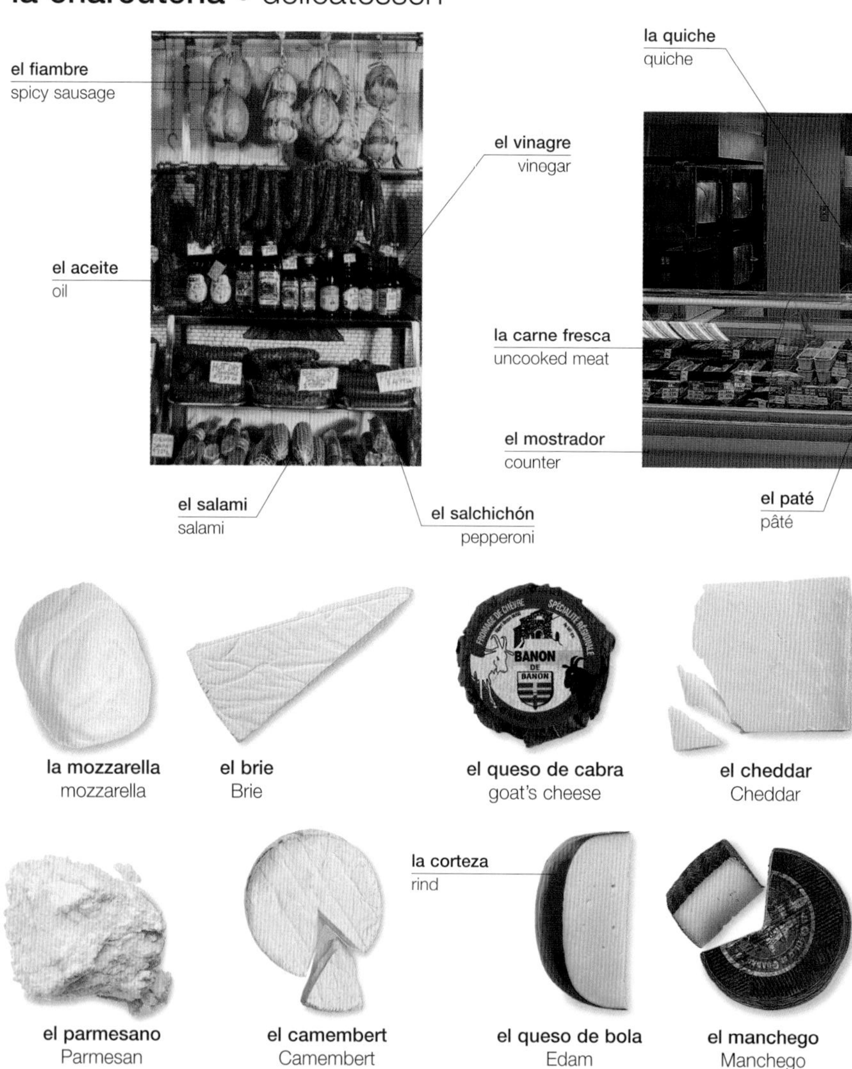

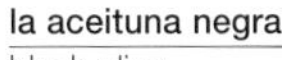

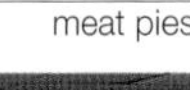

los pasteles de carne
meat pies

el panecillo
roll

el fiambre
cooked meat

el jamón
ham

la aceituna negra
black olive

el chile piquín (ᶜ**la guindilla**)
chili

la salsa
sauce

la aceituna verde
green olive

el mostrador de bocadillos
sandwich counter

el pescado ahumado
smoked fish

las alcaparras
capers

el chorizo
chorizo

el jamón serrano
prosciutto

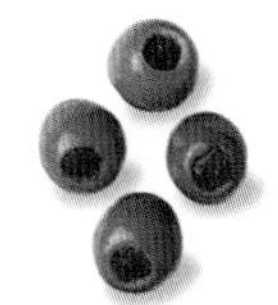

la aceituna rellena
stuffed olive

vocabulario • vocabulary

en aceite in oil	**salado** salted	**ahumado** smoked
en salmuera in brine	**marinado** (ᶜ**adobado**) marinated	**curado** cured

Tome un número, por favor.
Take a number, please.

¿Puedo probar un poco de eso?
Can I try some of that, please?

¿Me pone seis rebanadas (ᶜ**lonchas**) **de aquél?**
May I have six slices of that, please?

las bebidas • drinks

el agua • water

el agua mineral
mineral water

las bebidas calientes • hot drinks

el té
tea

el café
coffee

el chocolate caliente
hot chocolate

la bebida malteada
malted drink

los refrescos • soft drinks

el jugo (C el zumo) de tomate
tomato juice

el jugo (C el zumo) de uva
grape juice

el popote
(C la pajita)
straw

la limonada
lemonade

la naranjada
orangeade

la cola
cola

las bebidas alcohólicas • alcoholic drinks

la cerveza
beer

la sidra
hard cider

la cerveza amarga
bitter

la cerveza negra
stout

la ginebra
gin

el vodka
vodka

el whisky
whiskey

el ron
rum

el brandy (c **el coñac**)
brandy

el oporto
port

el vino de jerez
sherry

el campari
campari

el licor
liqueur

el tequila
tequila

el champán
champagne

el vino
wine

comer fuera
eating out

la cafetería • café

la sombrilla
umbrella

la terraza
terrace café

el toldo
awning

la carta
menu

la cafetería con mesas fuera | sidewalk café

el mesero (^C el camarero)
server

la máquina del café
coffee machine

la mesa
table

el bar | snack bar

el café • coffee

el café con leche
coffee with cream

el café solo
black coffee

el café de cafetera eléctrica
filter coffee

el expreso (^C el café solo)
espresso

la cocoa (^C el cacao en polvo)
cocoa powder

la espuma
froth

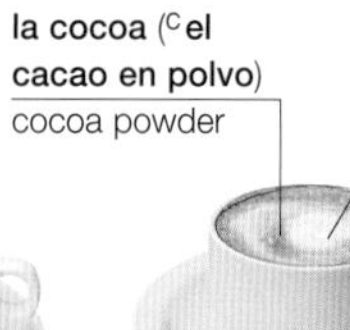

el cappuccino
cappuccino

el café con hielo
iced coffee

el té • tea

el té de hierbas (^C **la infusión**)
herbal tea

la manzanilla
camomile tea

el té verde
green tea

el té con leche
tea with milk

el té sólo
black tea

el té con limón
tea with lemon

la menta poleo
mint tea

el té con hielo
iced tea

los jugos y las malteadas (^C los zumos y los batidos) • juices and milkshakes

el jugo de naranja
orange juice

el jugo de manzana
apple juice

el jugo de piña
pineapple juice

el jugo de tomate
tomato juice

la malteada de chocolate
chocolate milkshake

la malteada de fresa
strawberry milkshake

la malteada de café
coffee milkshake

la comida • food

el pan integral
brown bread

el sandwich tostado
toasted sandwich

la ensalada
salad

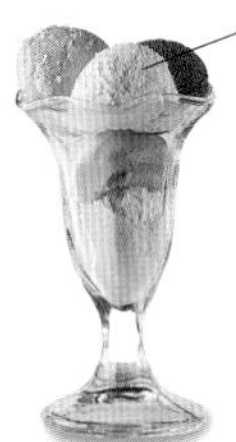

la bola
scoop

el helado
ice cream

el pan dulce (^C **el pastel**)
pastry

el bar • bar

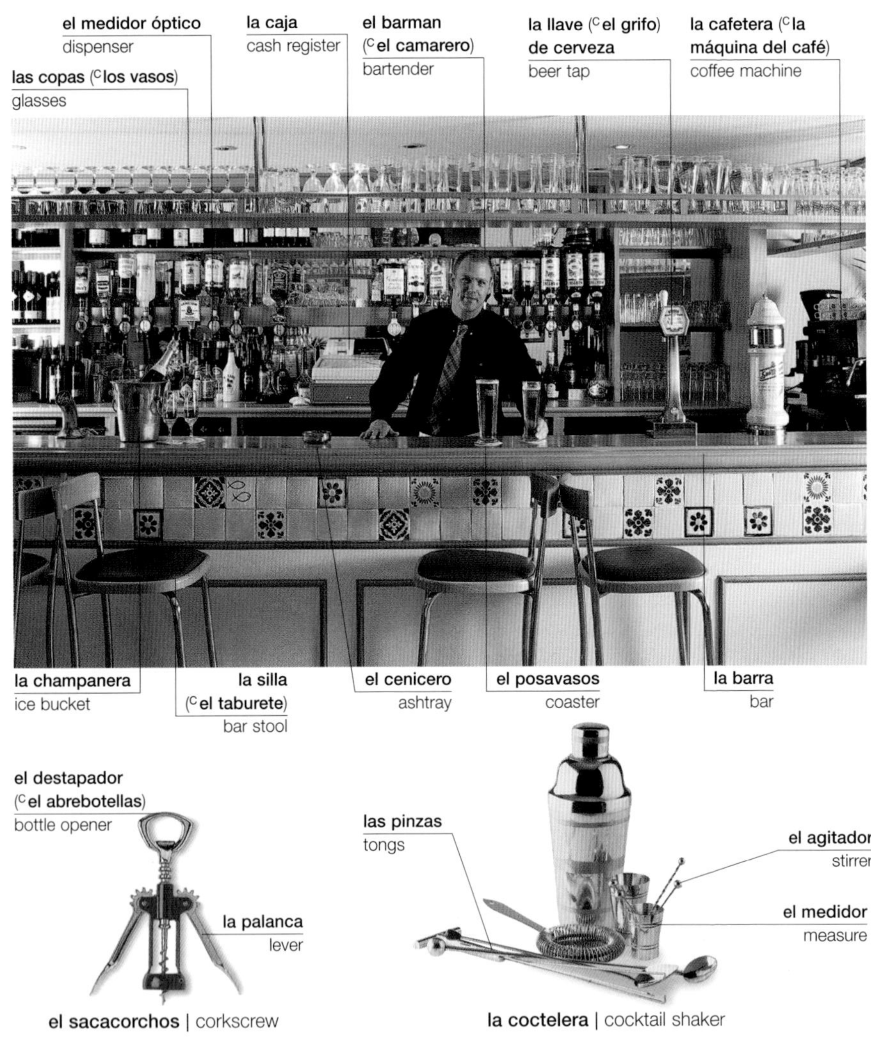
el medidor óptico
dispenser
las copas (C los vasos)
glasses
la caja
cash register
el barman
(C el camarero)
bartender
la llave (C el grifo) de cerveza
beer tap
la cafetera (C la máquina del café)
coffee machine
la champanera
ice bucket
la silla
(C el taburete)
bar stool
el cenicero
ashtray
el posavasos
coaster
la barra
bar
el destapador
(C el abrebotellas)
bottle opener
la palanca
lever
el sacacorchos | corkscrew
las pinzas
tongs
el agitador
stirrer
el medidor
measure
la coctelera | cocktail shaker

el gin tonic
gin and tonic

el whiskey escocés con agua
scotch and water

el cubito de hielo
ice cube

la cuba libre
(ᶜ**el ron con cola**)
rum and coke

el desarmador
(ᶜ**el vodka con naranja**)
vodka and orange

el martini
martini

el cóctel
cocktail

el vino
wine

la cerveza | beer

sencillo
single

doble
double

un trago
a shot

la medida
measure

sin hielo
without ice

con hielo y limón
ice and lemon

con hielo
with ice

la botana (ᶜ los aperitivos) • bar snacks

las papas (ᶜ**las patatas**) **fritas**
potato chips

los frutos secos | nuts

las aceitunas | olives

el restaurante • restaurant

la cocina
kitchen

el mesero (C el camarero)
server

vocabulario • vocabulary

la lista de vinos
wine list

el menú de la comida
lunch menu

el menú de la cena
dinner menu

a la carta
à la carte

el carrito de los postres
dessert cart

los platillos (C los platos) del día
specials

el precio
price

la cuenta
check

el recibo
receipt

la propina
tip

servicio incluido
service charge included

servicio no incluido
service charge not included

el buffet
buffet

el bar
bar

el área de fumar (C la zona de fumadores)
smoking section

el cliente
customer

la sal
la sal

la pimienta
pepper

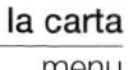

la carta
menu

el menú para niños
child's meal

ordenar (C **pedir**)
order (v)

pagar
pay (v)

los platos • courses

el aperitivo
apéritif

la entrada
(C **el entrante**)
appetizer

la sopa
soup

el plato principal
main course

el acompañamiento
side order

el tenedor
fork

el postre | dessert

la cucharilla de café
coffee spoon

el café | coffee

Una mesa para dos, por favor.
A table for two, please.

¿Podría ver la carta/lista de vinos, por favor?
Can I see the menu/wine list, please?

¿Hay menú del día?
Is there a prix fixe menu?

¿Tiene platos vegetarianos?
Do you have any vegetarian dishes?

¿Me podría traer la cuenta/un recibo?
Could I have the check/a receipt, please?

¿Podemos pagar por separado?
Can we pay separately?

¿Dónde están los baños (C **los servicios), por favor?**
Where are the rest rooms, please?

la comida rápida • fast food

el popote ([C]**la pajita**)
straw

la hamburguesa
burger

el refresco
soft drink

las papas fritas
([C]**las patatas fritas**)
French fries

la servilleta de papel
paper napkin

la charola
([C]**la bandeja**)
tray

la hamburguesa con papas fritas
burger meal

la pizza
pizza

la lista de precios
price list

el refresco en lata
([C]**la lata de bebida**)
canned drink

la entrega a domicilio
delivery

el puesto
hot-dog stand

vocabulario • vocabulary

la pizzería
pizzeria

el restaurant de hamburguesas
([C]**la hamburguesería**)
fast food restaurant

el menú
menu

para comer en el local
eat in

para llevar
carry out

recalentar
reheat (v)

la catsup ([C]**el ketchup**)
ketchup

¿Me lo pone para llevar?
Can I have that to go, please?

¿Entregan a domicilio?
Do you deliver?

la hamburguesa
hamburger

la hamburguesa de pollo
chicken burger

la hamburguesa vegetariana
veggie burger

el hot dog (ᶜ **el perrito caliente**) | hot dog

el bocadillo
sub

el club sandwich
club sandwich

el sandwich abierto
open-face sandwich

el taco
wrap

el alambre (ᶜ**el pincho moruno**)
kabob

los nuggets (ᶜ**las porciones**) **de pollo**
chicken nuggets

la crêpe | crepes

el pescado con papas fritas
fish and chips

las costillas
ribs

el pollo frito
fried chicken

la pizza
pizza

el desayuno • breakfast

la mesa del desayuno | breakfast table

las bebidas | drinks

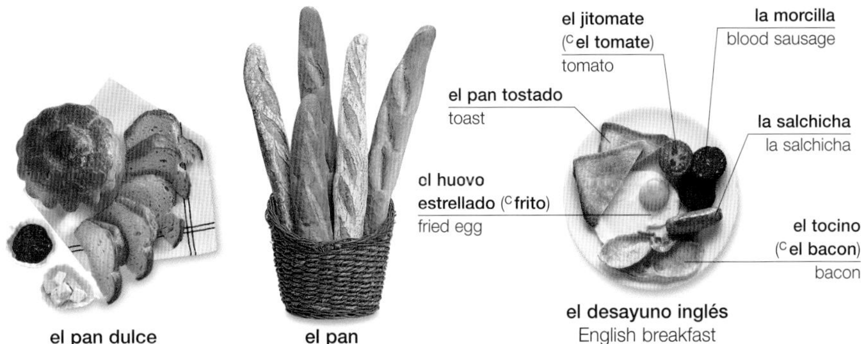

el pan dulce
brioche

el pan
bread

el desayuno inglés
English breakfast

los arenques ahumados
smoked herring

el pan francés (C la torrija)
French toast

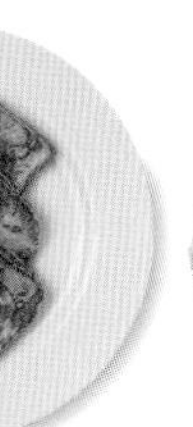

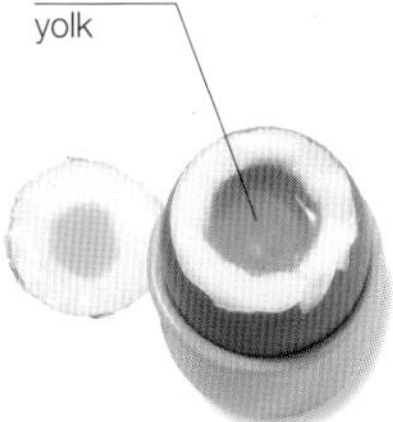

el huevo tibio (C pasado por agua)
soft-boiled egg

los huevos revueltos
scrambled eggs

los crepes
pancakes

los waffles (C los gofres)
waffles

la avena (C las gachas de avena)
oatmeal

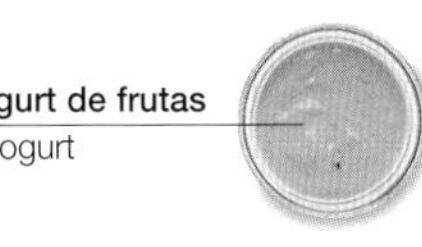

la fruta fresca
fresh fruit

la comida principal • dinner

la sopa | soup

el caldo | broth

el guiso | stew

el curry | curried lamb

el asado
roast

la empanada ([C]**el pastel**)
pie

el soufflé
soufflé

la brocheta ([C]**el pincho**)
kabob

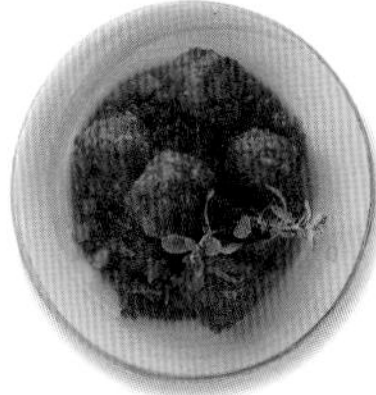
las albóndigas
meatballs

la omelette ([C]**la tortilla**)
omelette

el revuelto | stir fry

la pasta | pasta

el arroz
rice

la ensalada mixta
tossed salad

la ensalada verde
green salad

el aderezo ([C]**el aliño**)
dressing

las técnicas • techniques

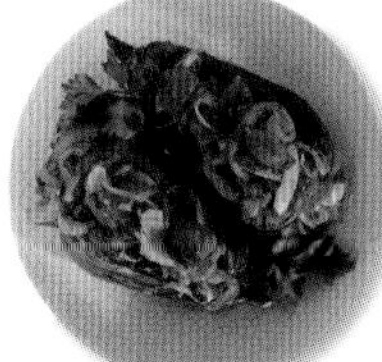

relleno | stuffed

en salsa | in sauce

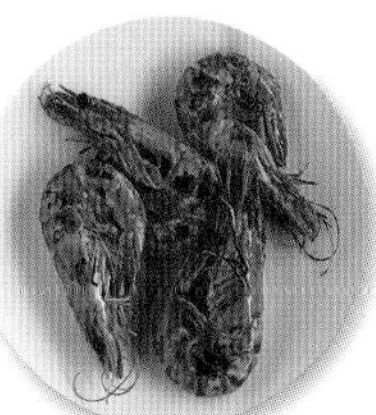

a la plancha | grilled

adobado | marinated

escalfado | poached

hecho puré | mashed

al horno ([c]**cocido en el horno**) | baked

frito con poco aceite
pan fried

frito
fried

en vinagre
pickled

ahumado
smoked

frito con mucho aceite
deep fried

en almíbar
in syrup

sazonado ([c]**aliñado**)
dressed

al vapor
steamed

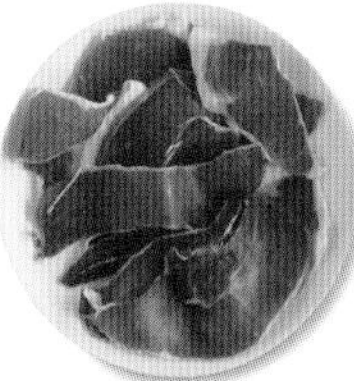

curado
cured

el estudio
study

la escuela • school

la maestra (ᶜla profesora)
teacher

el pizarrón (ᶜla pizarra)
chalkboard

el alumno
pupil

el pupitre
desk

el gis (ᶜla tiza)
chalk

el salón | classroom

el colegial
schoolboy

el uniforme
school uniform

la mochila (ᶜla cartera)
book bag

la colegiala
schoolgirl

vocabulario • vocabulary

la historia history	**el arte** art	**la física** physics
la literatura literature	**la música** music	**la química** chemistry
los idiomas languages	**la ciencia** science	**la biología** biology
la geografía geography	**las matemáticas** math	**la educación física** physical education

las actividades • activities

leer | read (v)

escribir | write (v)

deletrear
spell (v)

dibujar
draw (v)

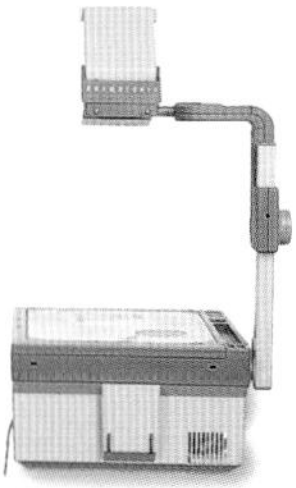

el proyector de acetatos
overhead projector

la punta
nib

la pluma
(C **el bolígrafo**)
pen

el color
(C **el lápiz de colores**)
colored pencil

el sacapuntas
pencil sharpener

el lápiz
pencil

la goma
eraser

el cuaderno
notebook

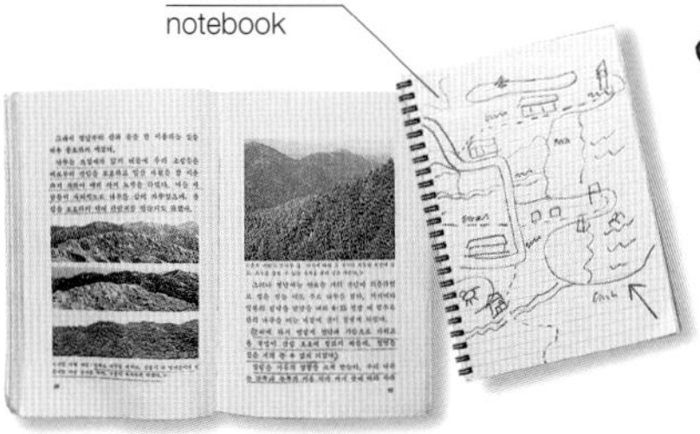

el libro de texto | textbook

el estuche
pencil case

la regla
ruler

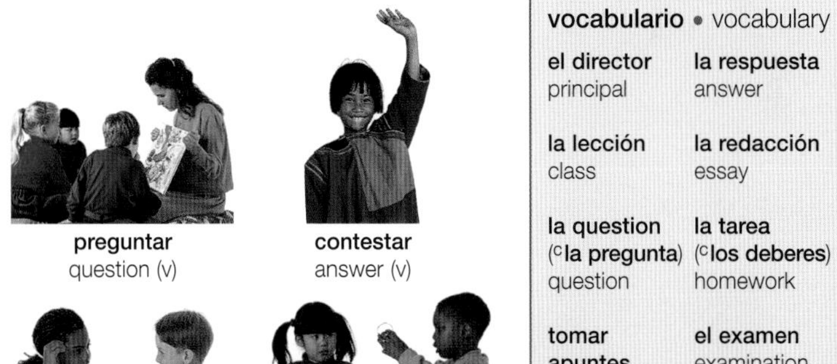

preguntar
question (v)

contestar
answer (v)

discutir
discuss (v)

aprender
learn (v)

vocabulario • vocabulary

el director principal	**la respuesta** answer	**el diccionario** dictionary
la lección class	**la redacción** essay	**la enciclopedia** encyclopedia
la question (C **la pregunta**) question	**la tarea** (C **los deberes**) homework	**la calificación** (C **la nota**) grade
tomar apuntes take notes (v)	**el examen** examination	**el año** (C **el curso**) year

las matemáticas • math

las formas • shapes

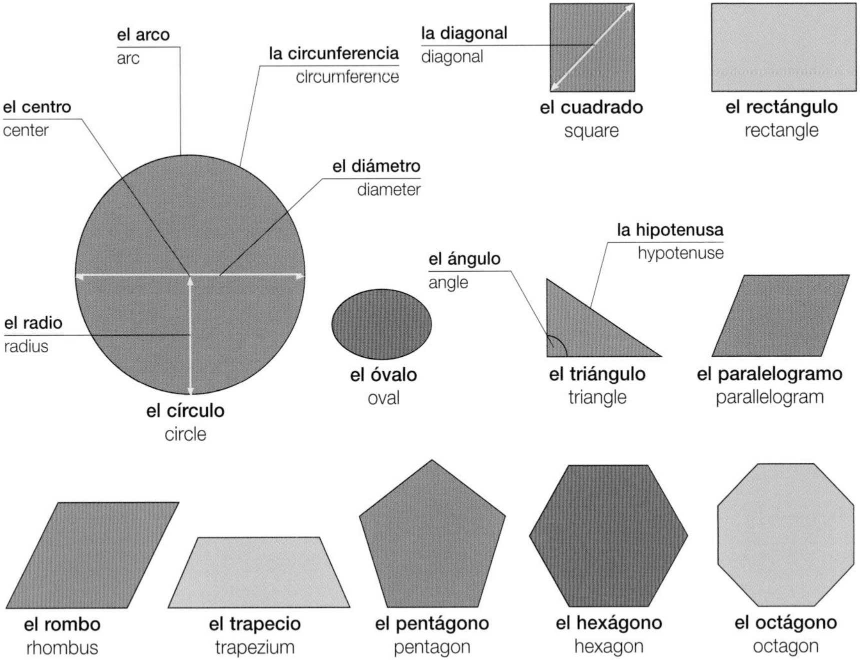

el arco
arc
la circunferencia
circumference
la diagonal
diagonal
el cuadrado
square
el rectángulo
rectangle
el centro
center
el diámetro
diameter
la hipotenusa
hypotenuse
el ángulo
angle
el radio
radius
el óvalo
oval
el triángulo
triangle
el paralelogramo
parallelogram
el círculo
circle
el rombo
rhombus
el trapecio
trapezium
el pentágono
pentagon
el hexágono
hexagon
el octágono
octagon

los cuerpos geométricos • solids

el lado
side
el ápice
apex
la base
base
el cono
cone
el cilindro
cylinder
el cubo
cube
la pirámide
pyramid
la esfera
sphere

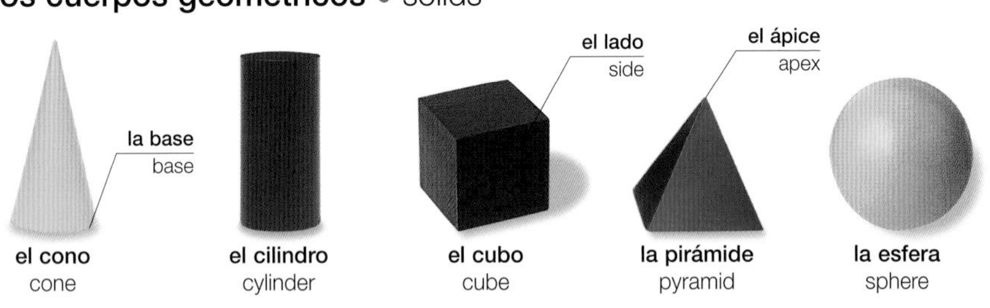

las líneas • lines

recto	paralelo	perpendicular	curvo
straight	parallel	perpendicular	curved

las medidas • measurements

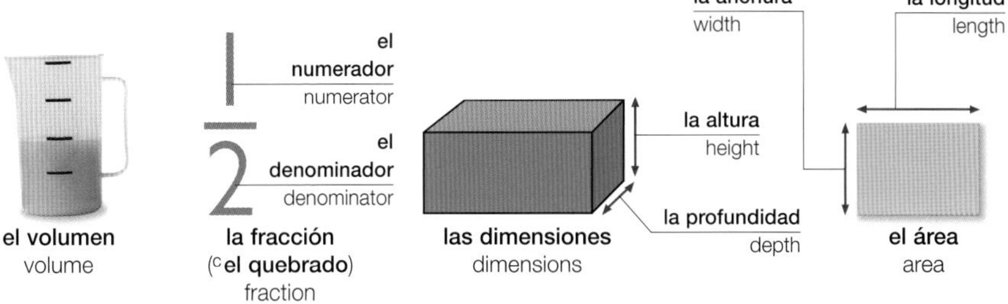

el volumen
volume

la fracción (c**el quebrado**)
fraction

las dimensiones
dimensions

el área
area

los materiales • equipment

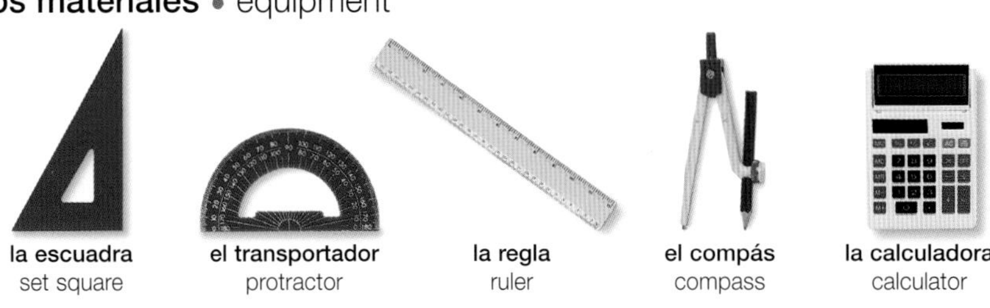

la escuadra	el transportador	la regla	el compás	la calculadora
set square	protractor	ruler	compass	calculator

vocabulario • vocabulary

la geometría geometry	**más** plus	**multiplicado por** times	**igual a** equals	**sumar** add (v)	**multiplicar** multiply (v)	**la ecuación** equation
la aritmética arithmetic	**menos** minus	**dividido entre** (c**dividido por**) divided by	**contar** count (v)	**restar** subtract (v)	**dividir** divide (v)	**el porcentaje** percentage

las ciencias • science

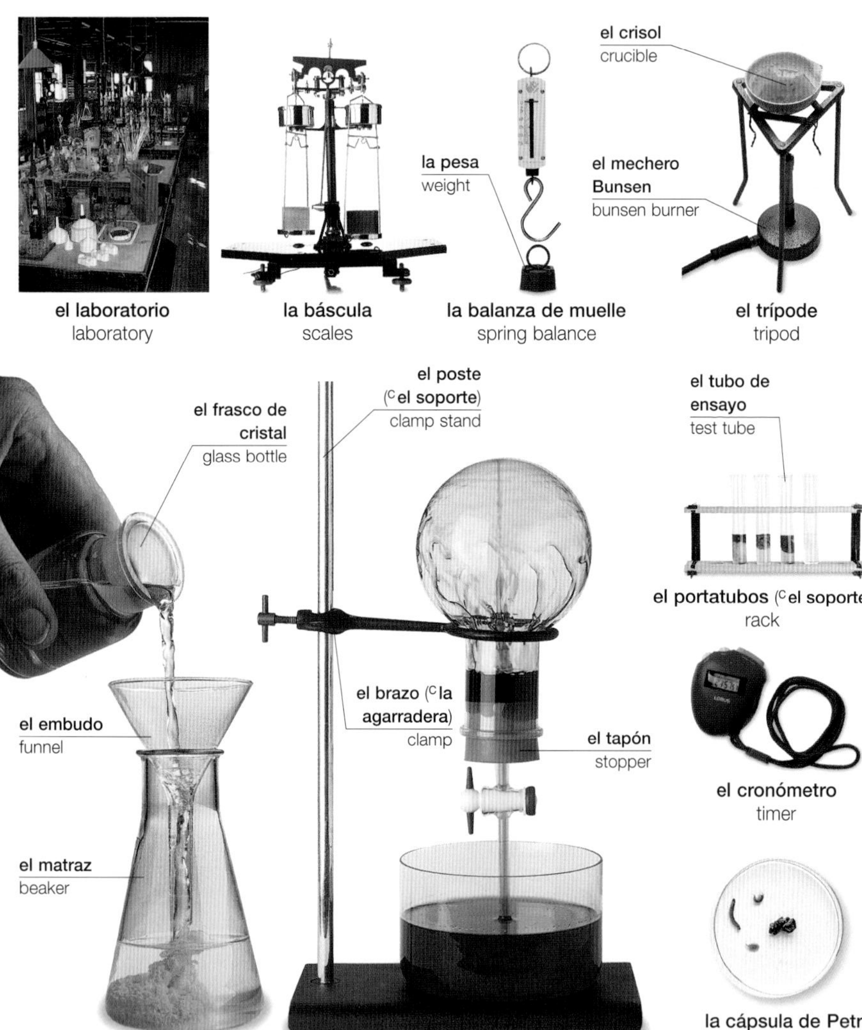

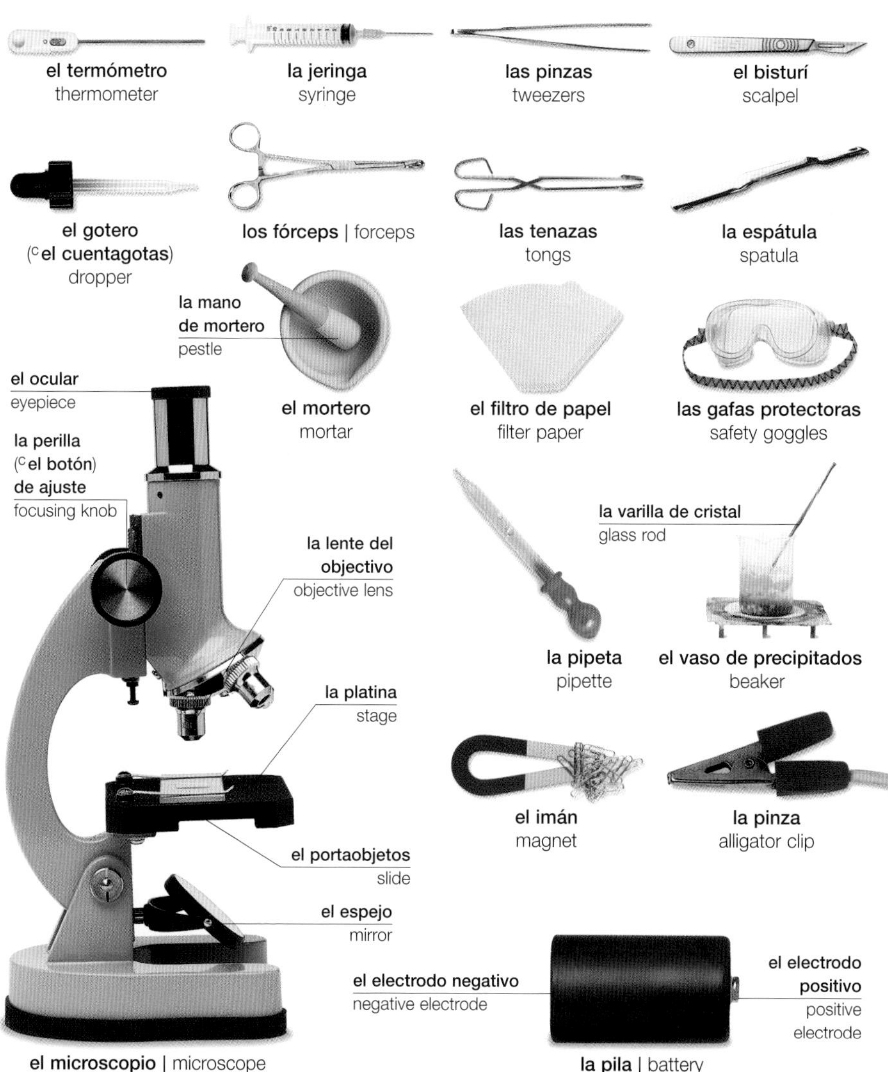
el termómetro
thermometer
la jeringa
syringe
las pinzas
tweezers
el bisturí
scalpel
el gotero
(C el cuentagotas)
dropper
los fórceps | forceps
las tenazas
tongs
la espátula
spatula
la mano
de mortero
pestle
el mortero
mortar
el filtro de papel
filter paper
las gafas protectoras
safety goggles
el ocular
eyepiece
la perilla
(C el botón)
de ajuste
focusing knob
la lente del
objectivo
objective lens
la platina
stage
el portaobjetos
slide
el espejo
mirror
el microscopio | microscope
la varilla de cristal
glass rod
la pipeta
pipette
el vaso de precipitados
beaker
el imán
magnet
la pinza
alligator clip
el electrodo negativo
negative electrode
el electrodo
positivo
positive
electrode
la pila | battery

la enseñanza superior • college

la secretaría
admissions office

el comedor (Cel refectorio)
dining room

el centro de salud
health center

el campo deportivo
playing field

la residencia estudiantil (Cel colegio mayor)
residence hall

el campus | campus

el catálogo
card catalogue

la bibliotecaria
librarian

el mostrador de préstamos
checkout desk

el librero (Cla estantería)
bookshelf

el periódico
periodical

la revista
journal

la biblioteca | library

vocabulario • vocabulary

el préstamo loan	**la información** inquiries	**renovar** renew (v)
reservar reserve (v)	**coger prestado** borrow (v)	**el libro** book
la lista de lecturas reading list	**la sala de lecturas** reading room	**el título** title
la fecha de devolución due date	**la credencial** (C**la tarjeta de la biblioteca**) library card	**el pasillo** aisle

el auditorio (ᶜel anfiteatro)
lecture hall

la ceremonia de graduación
graduation ceremony

las escuelas • schools

la escuela de Bellas Artes
art school

el conservatorio
music school

la academia de danza
dance school

vocabulario • vocabulary

la beca
scholarship

el diploma
diploma

la carrera
degree

posgrado
postgraduate

la investigación
research

el doctorado
doctorate

la tesis
thesis

la mestría (ᶜel máster)
master's degree

la tesina
dissertation

el departamento
department

el derecho
law

la ingeniería
engineering

la medicina
medicine

la zoología
zoology

la física
physics

la filosofía
philosophy

la política
political science

la literatura
literature

la historia del arte
art history

las ciencias económicas
economics

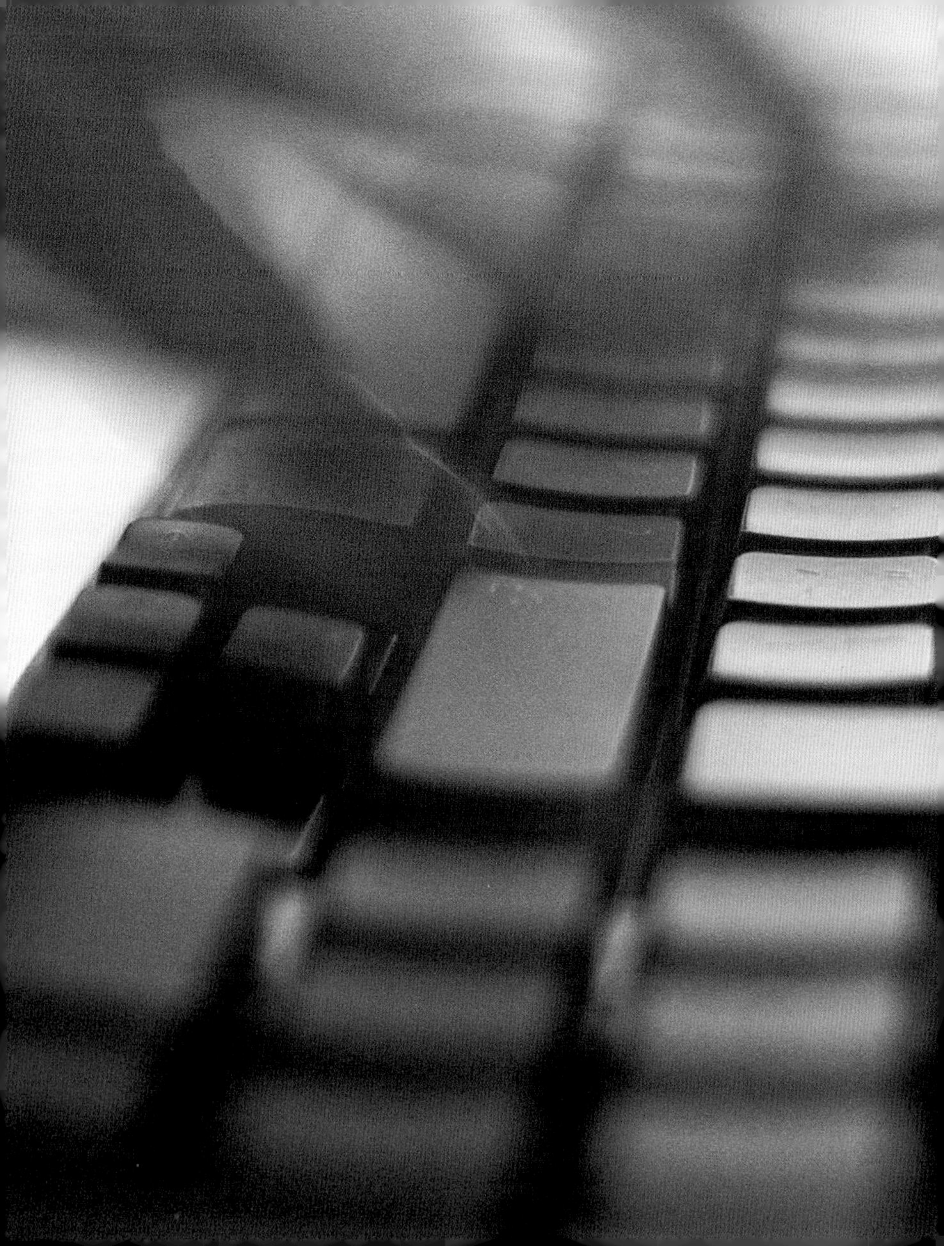

el trabajo
work

la oficina 1 • office 1

la oficina • office

la pantalla
monitor

el portaplumas
(C el portabolígrafos)
desktop organizer

la carpeta
file

la bandeja de entrada
in-tray

la computadora
(C el ordenador)
computer

la bandeja de salida
out-tray

el teclado
keyboard

el teléfono
telephone

el cuaderno
notebook

la etiqueta
label

el escritorio
desk

el cajón
drawer

el archivero
(C el archivador)
filing cabinet

el bote de basura
(C la papelera)
wastebasket

la silla giratoria
swivel chair

la cajonera
drawer unit

el equipo de oficina • office equipment

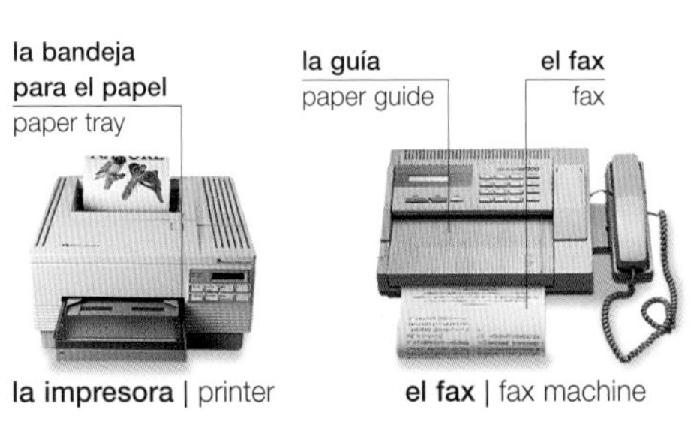

la impresora | printer

el fax | fax machine

vocabulario • vocabulary

imprimir
print (v)

ampliar
enlarge (v)

fotocopiar
copy (v)

reducir
reduce (v)

Necesito sacar (C hacer) unas copias.
I need to make some copies.

la papelería • office supplies

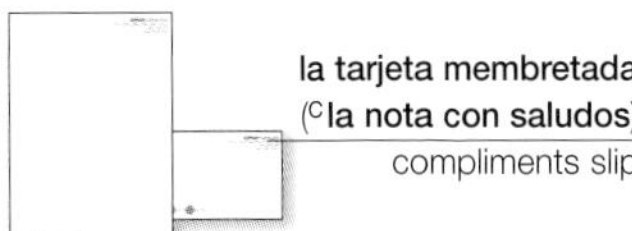

la tarjeta membretada (C la nota con saludos)
compliments slip

el membrete
letterhead

el sobre
envelope

la caja archivador
box file

el divisor
divider

el rótulo
tab

la tabla con portapapeles (C la tablilla con sujetapapeles)
clipboard

la libreta (C el bloc de apuntes)
notepad

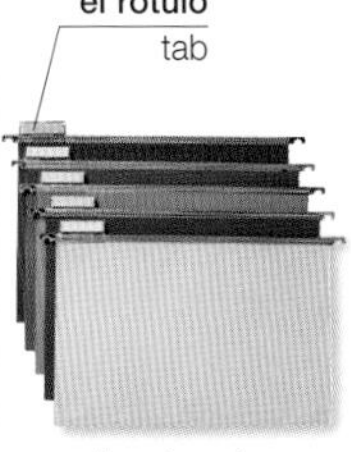

el colgante (C el archivador suspendido)
hanging file

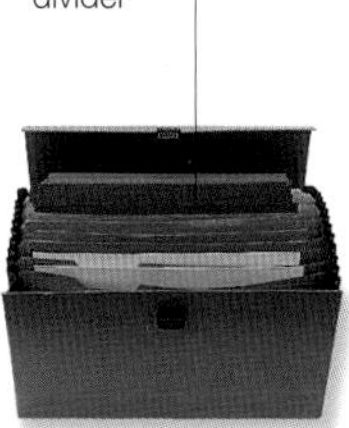

la carpeta de acordeón
accordion file

la carpeta de argollas (C de anillas)
binder file

las grapas
staples

la cinta scotch (C el papel celo)
adhesive tape

el cojín de la tinta
ink pad

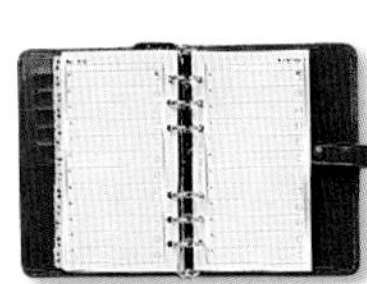

la agenda
personal organizer

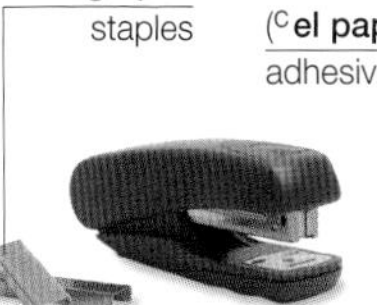

la engrapadora (C la grapadora)
stapler

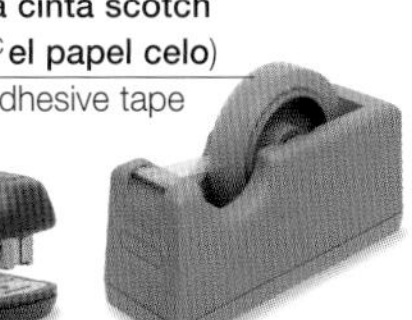

el portacinta (C el soporte del papel celo)
tape dispenser

la perforadora
hole punch

el sello
rubber stamp

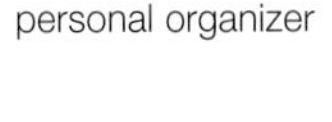

la liga (C la goma elástica)
rubber band

la pinza (C el clip)
bulldog clip

el clip (C el sujetapapeles)
paper clip

la chinche (C la chincheta)
thumbtack

el corcho | bulletin board

la oficina 2 • office 2

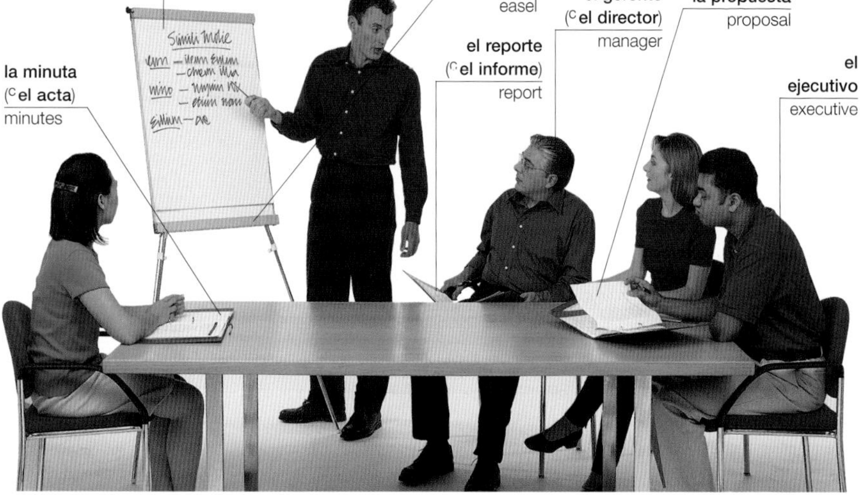
el pizarrón (c la pizarra)
flipchart
el caballete
easel
el gerente (c el director)
manager
la propuesta
proposal
la minuta (c el acta)
minutes
el reporte (c el informe)
report
el ejecutivo
executive

la junta (c la reunión) | meeting

vocabulario • vocabulary

el orden del día agenda	**asistir** attend (v)
la sala de juntas (c **reuniones**) meeting room	**presidir** chair (v)

¿A qué hora es la junta (c **la reunión**)**?**
What time is the meeting?

¿Cuál es su horario de oficina?
What are your office hours?

el proyector
projector
el orador
speaker

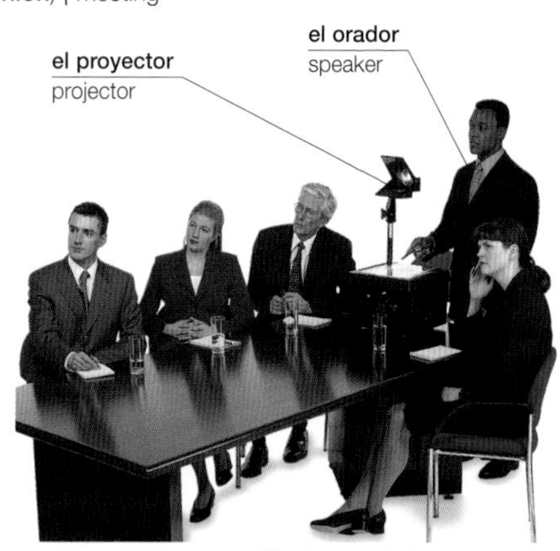

la presentación | presentation

los negocios • business

el laptop (C **el ordenador portátil**)
laptop

las notas (C **los apuntes**)
notes

la comida de negocios
business lunch

el hombre de negocios
businessman

la mujer de negocios
businesswoman

el viaje de negocios
business trip

la cita
appointment

la palmtop (C **el PDA**)
palmtop computer

la agenda | date book

el cliente
client

el director general
managing director

el trato
business deal

vocabulario • vocabulary

la empresa
company

la oficina central
head office

la sucursal
branch

el personal
staff

la nómina
payroll

el sueldo
salary

el departamento de ventas
sales department

el departamento de contabilidad
accounting department

el departamento de márketing
marketing department

el departamento legal
legal department

el departamento de atención al cliente
customer service department

el departamento de recursos humanos
human resources department

la computadora ([C]el ordenador) • computer

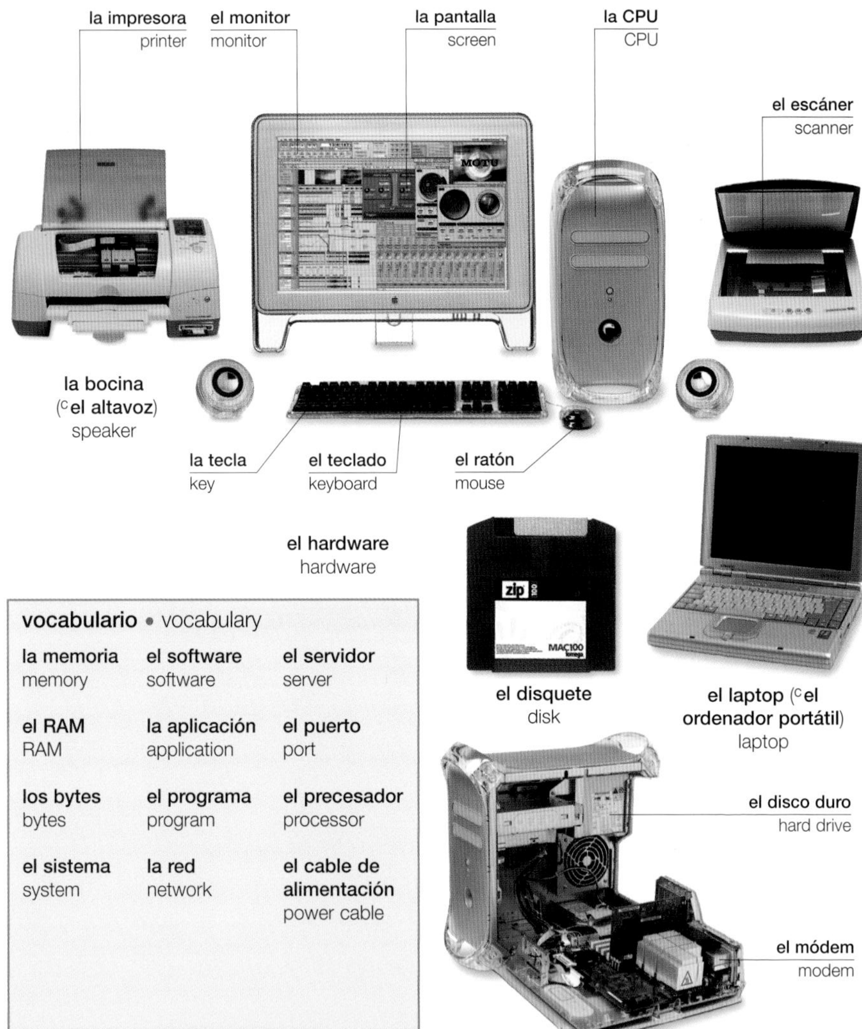

vocabulario • vocabulary

la memoria memory	**el software** software	**el servidor** server
el RAM RAM	**la aplicación** application	**el puerto** port
los bytes bytes	**el programa** program	**el precesador** processor
el sistema system	**la red** network	**el cable de alimentación** power cable

el escritorio • desktop

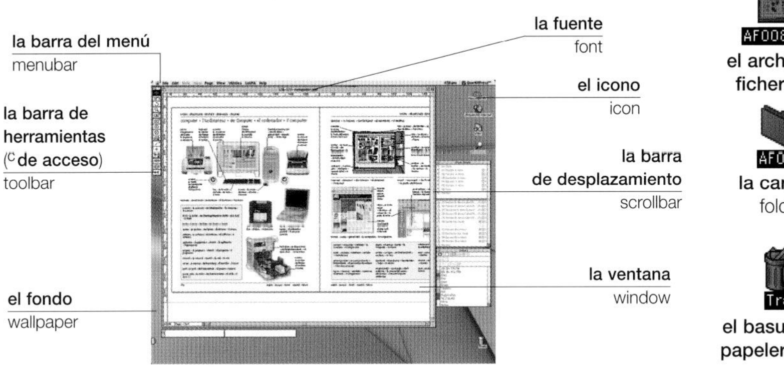

el archivo (^{C}**el fichero**) | file

la carpeta
folder

el basurero (^{C}**la papelera**) | trash

el internet • Internet

el correo electrónico • email

vocabulario • vocabulary

conectar
connect (v)

la cuenta de correo
email account

en línea
online

bajar
download (v)

enviar
send (v)

guardar
save (v)

instalar
install (v)

el proveedor de servicios
service provider

entrar en el sistema
log on (v)

el documento adjunto
attachment

recibir
receive (v)

buscar
search (v)

los medios de comunicación • media

el estudio de televisión • television studio

vocabulario • vocabulary

el canal channel	**el documental** documentary	**la prensa** press	**la telenovela** soap	**el concurso** game show	**en directo** live
la programación programming	**el noticiario** news	**la serie televisiva** television series	**transmitir** (C **emitir**) broadcast (v)	**las caricaturas** (C **los dibujos animados**) cartoon	**pregrabado** (C **en diferido**) prerecorded

el entrevistador
interviewer

la reportera
reporter

el teleprompter (C **el autocue**)
teleprompter

la presentadora de las noticias
anchor

los actores
actors

el micrófono de aire (C **la jirafa**) | sound boom

la pizarra (C **la claqueta**)
clapper board

el plató de rodaje
film set

la radio • radio

la consola (C **la mesa de mezclas**)
mixing desk

el micrófono
microphone

el técnico de sonido
sound technician

el estudio de grabación | recording studio

vocabulario • vocabulary

la estación de radio
radio station

el DJ (C **el pinchadiscos**)
DJ

la transmisión (C **la emisión**)
broadcast

la longitud de onda
wavelength

la onda larga
long wave

la onda corta
short wave

la onda media
medium wave

la frecuencia
frequency

el volumen
volume

sintonizar
tune (v)

el derecho • law

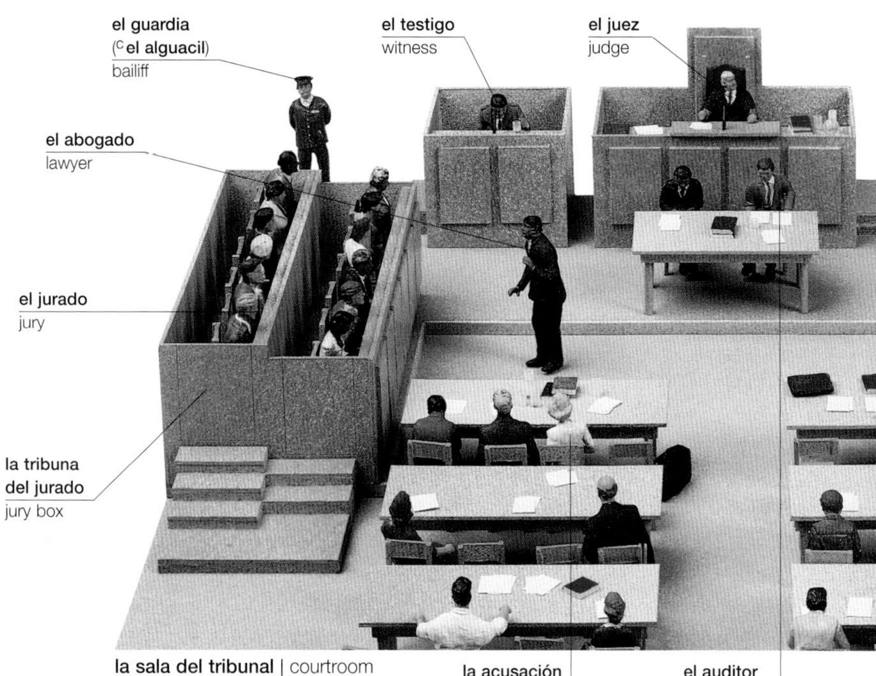

la sala del tribunal | courtroom

vocabulario • vocabulary

el bufete lawyer's office	**la citación** summons	**la orden judicial** writ	**el juicio** court case
la asesoría jurídica legal advice	**la declaración** statement	**la fecha del juicio** court date	**el cargo** charge
el cliente client	**la orden judicial** warrant	**cómo se declara el acusado** plea	**el acusado** accused

la taquígrafa
court reporter

el acusado
defendant

la defensa
defense

el sospechoso
suspect

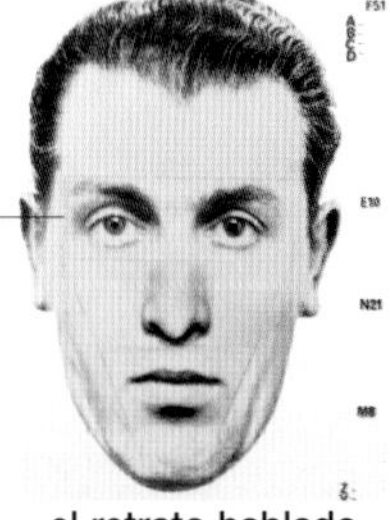

el retrato hablado (ᶜ**el retrato robot**)
facial composite

el criminal
criminal

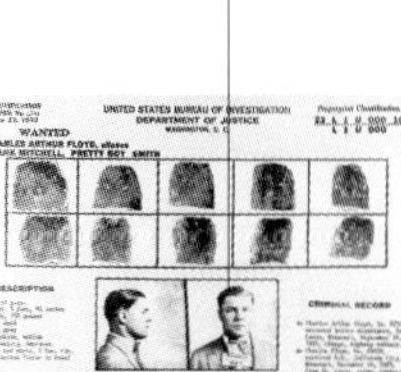

los antecedentes
criminal record

el celador (ᶜ**el funcionario de prisiones**)
prison guard

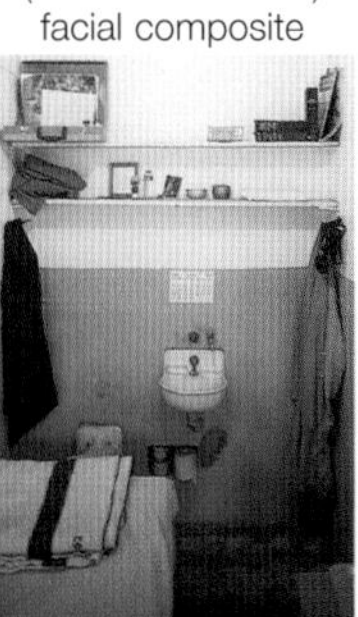

la celda
cell

la cárcel
prison

vocabulario • vocabulary

lel veredicto
verdict

inocente
innocent

culpable
guilty

absuelto
acquitted

la sentencia
sentence

la evidencia (ᶜ**la prueba**)
evidence

la fianza
bail

la apelación
appeal

la libertad condicional
parole

Quiero ver a un abogado.
I want to see a lawyer.

¿Dónde está el juzgado?
Where is the courthouse?

¿Puedo pagar la fianza?
Can I post bail?

la granja 1 • farm 1

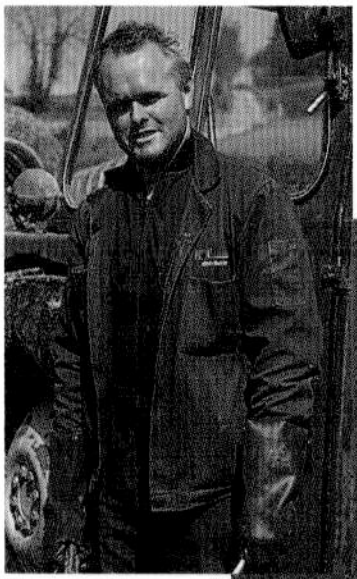
el granjero
farmer

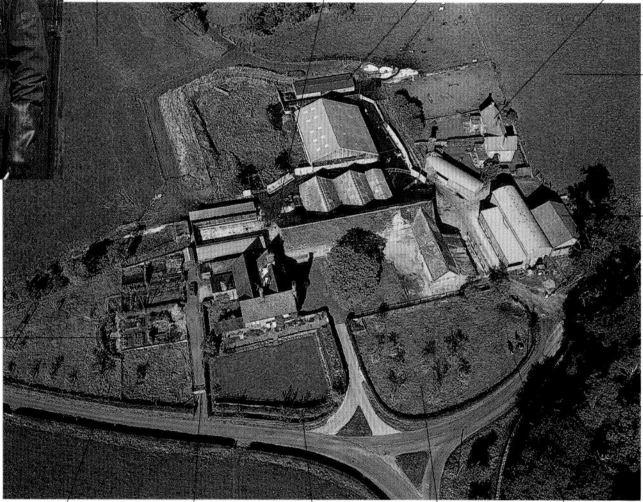
las tierras de labranza
farmland
el corral
farmyard
el cobertizo
outbuilding
la casa de labranza
farmhouse
el campo
field
el granero
barn
el huerto
vegetable garden
el seto
hedge
la puerta
gate
la cerca
fence
el pasto
pasture
el ganado
livestock

el cultivador
cultivator

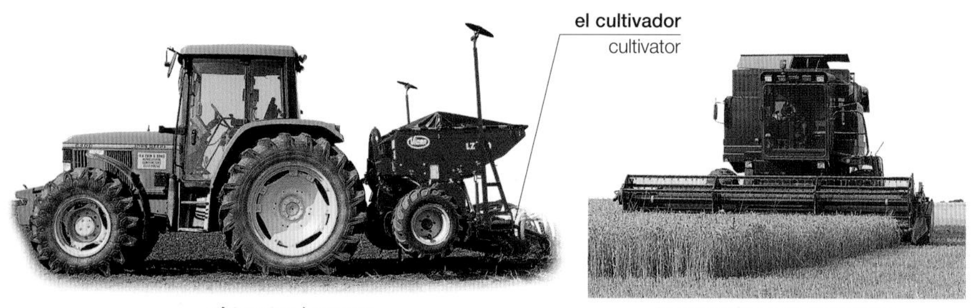

el tractor | tractor

la cosechadora | combine

los tipos de granja • types of farms

la granja de tierras cultivables
crop farm

la vaquería
dairy farm

la granja de ganado ovino
sheep farm

la granja avícola
poultry farm

la granja de ganado porcino
pig farm

el criadero de peces (C **la piscifactoría**)
fish farm

la granja de frutales
fruit farm

el viñedo
vineyard

las actividades • actions

arar
plow (v)

sembrar
sow (v)

ordeñar
milk (v)

alimentar (C **dar de comer**)
feed (v)

regar | water (v)

recolectar | harvest (v)

vocabulario • vocabulary

el herbicida herbicide	**la manada** herd	**el comedero** trough
el pesticida pesticide	**el silo** silo	**plantar** plant (v)

la granja 2 • farm 2

los cultivos • crops

el trigo
wheat

el maíz
corn

la cebada
barley

la colza
rapeseed

el girasol
sunflower

la paca
bale

el heno
hay

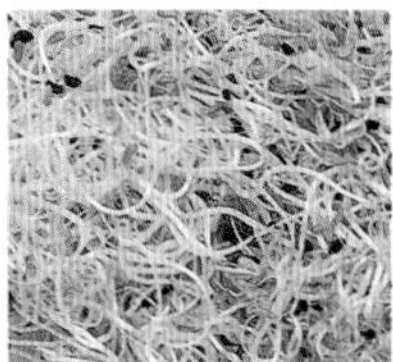
la alfalfa
alfalfa

el tabaco
tobacco

el arroz
rice

el té
tea

el café
coffee

el espantapájaros
scarecrow

el lino
flax

la caña de azúcar
sugarcane

el algodón
cotton

el ganado • livestock

el puerco ([C]el cerdo)
pig

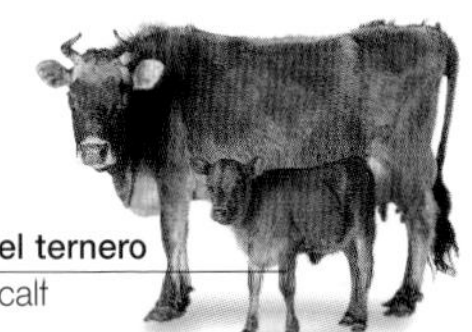

la vaca
cow

el toro
bull

la oveja
sheep

el cordero
lamb

la cabra
goat

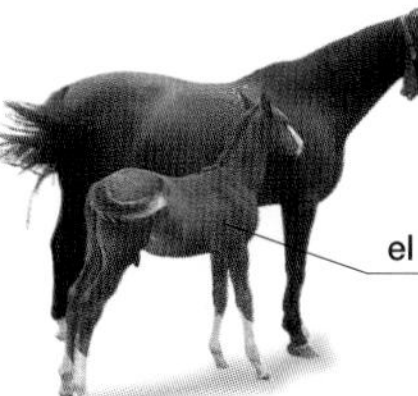

el caballo
horse

el burro
donkey

la gallina
chicken

el gallo
rooster

el guajolote ([C]el pavo)
turkey

el pato
duck

el establo
stable

el redil
pen

el gallinero
chicken coop

el chiquero ([C]la pocilga)
pigsty

la construcción • construction

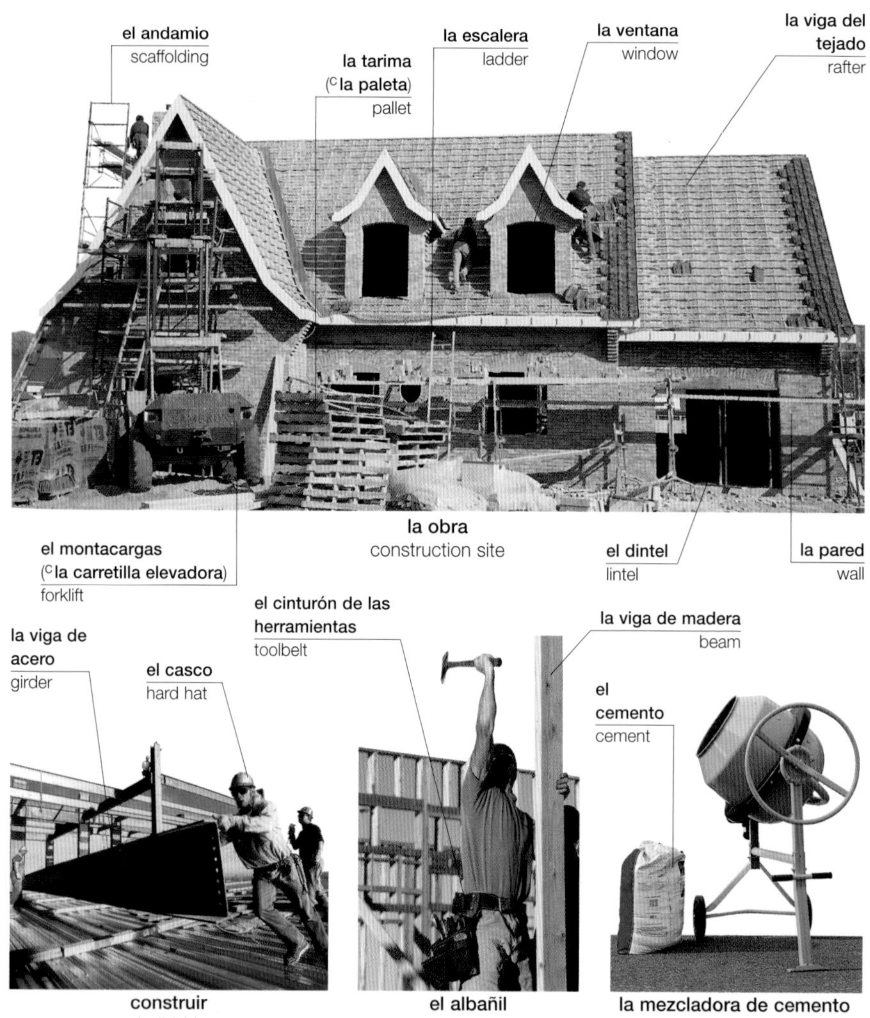

construir
build (v)

el albañil
construction worker

la mezcladora de cemento
(C **la hormigonera**)
cement mixer

los materiales • materials

el ladrillo
brick

la madera
timber

la teja
roof tile

el bloque de hormigón
cinder block

las herramientas • tools

la argamasa
mortar

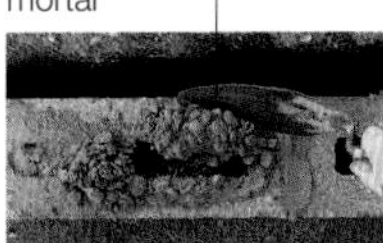
la paleta
trowel

el nivel
spirit level

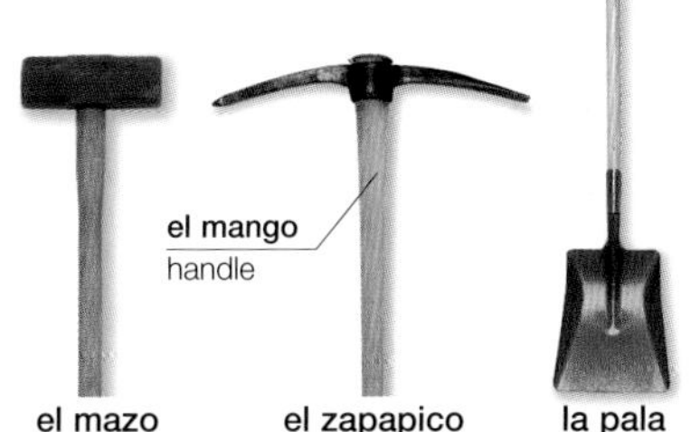
el mango
handle

el mazo
sledgehammer

el zapapico
(ᶜ**el pico**)
pickax

la pala
shovel

la maquinaria • machinery

la aplanadora
(ᶜ**la apisonadora**)
steam roller

el camión de volteo
(ᶜ**el camión volquete**)
dump truck

el soporte
support

el gancho
hook

la grúa | crane

las obras viales (ᶜlas obras) • roadwork

el martillo neumático
pneumatic drill

el asfalto
tarmac

el cono
cone

el revestimiento
resurfacing

la pala mecánica
(ᶜ**la excavadora mecánica**)
mechanical digger

los profesiones 1 • occupations 1

el carpintero
carpenter

el electricista
electrician

el plomero (C**el fontanero**)
plumber

el albañil
construction worker

el jardinero
gardener

la aspiradora
vacuum cleaner

el empleado de la limpieza
cleaner

el mecánico
mechanic

el carnicero
butcher

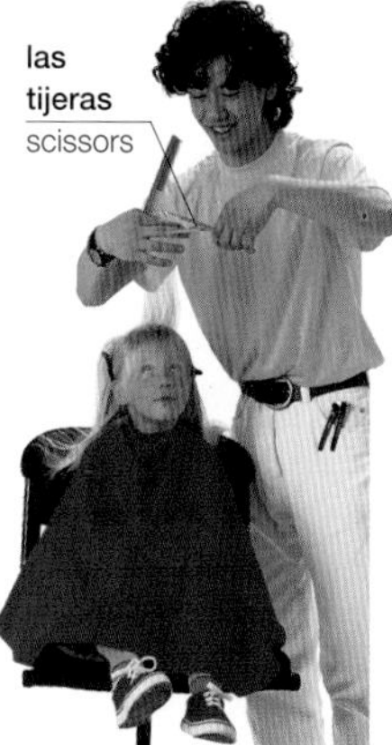
las tijeras
scissors

el estilista
(C**el peluquero**)
hairdresser

la pescadera
fishmonger

el frutero
greengrocer

la florista
florist

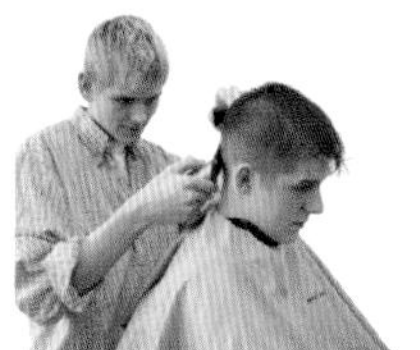
el peluquero
(C**el barbero**)
barber

el joyero
jeweler

la vendedora
sales assistant

la agente inmobiliario
estate agent

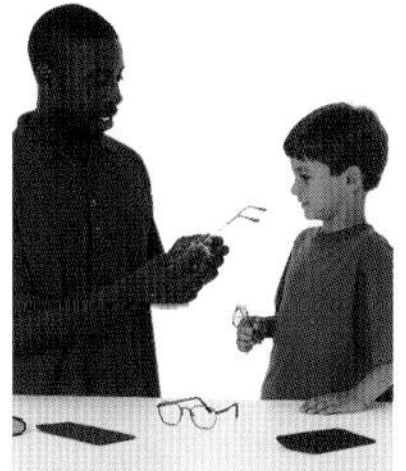

el optometrista
(ᶜ**el óptico**) | optician

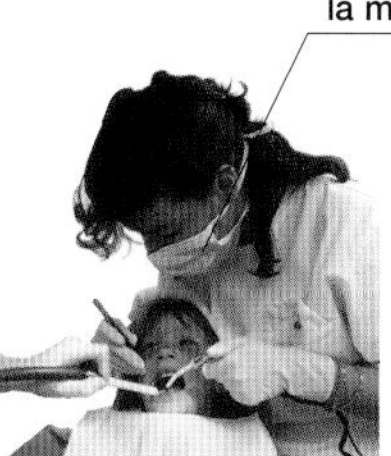

la mascarilla
mask

la dentista
dentist

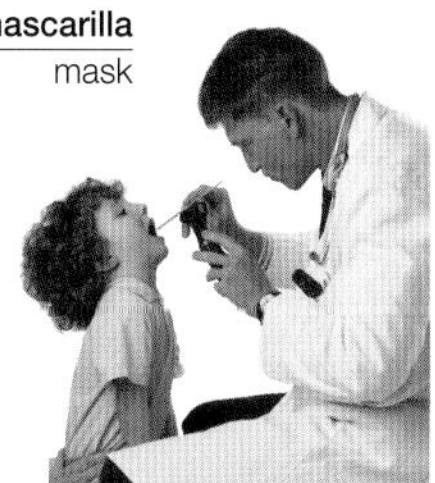

el médico
doctor

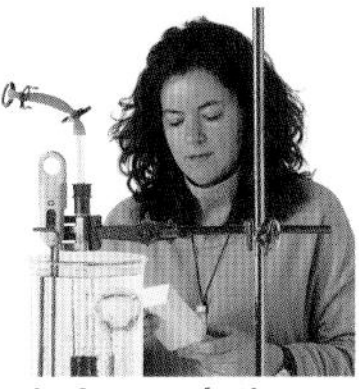

la farmacéutica
pharmacist

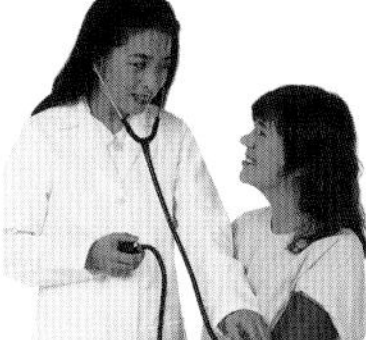

la enfermera
nurse

la veterinaria
vet

el agricultor
farmer

el pescador
fisherman

la metralleta
machine gun

el soldado
soldier

el uniforme
uniform

el policía
policeman

la placa de identificación
identity card

el guardia de seguridad
security guard

el marino
sailor

el bombero
fireman

las profesiones 2 • occupations 2

el abogado
lawyer

el contador ([C]**el contable**)
accountant

el arquitecto
architect

el científico
scientist

la maestra ([C]**el profesor**)
teacher

el bibliotecario
librarian

la recepcionista
receptionist

el cartero
mail carrier

el chófer
bus driver

el chófer
([C]**el camionero**)
truck driver

el taxista
taxi driver

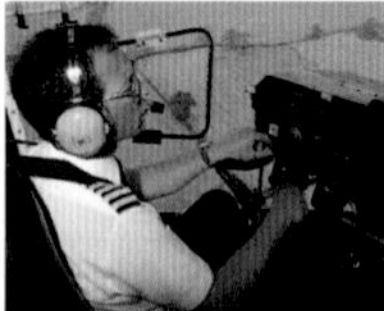
el piloto
pilot

la sobrecargo
([C]**la azafata**)
flight attendant

la agente de viajes
travel agent

el chef
chef

el tutú
tutu

el músico
musician

la bailarina
dancer

el actor
actor

la cantante
singer

la mesera
(c la camarera)
waitress

el barman
(c el camarero)
barman

el deportista
sportsman

el escultor
sculptor

la pintora
painter

el fotógrafo
photographer

el presentador
anchor

las notas
notes

el periodista
journalist

la redactora
editor

la diseñadora
designer

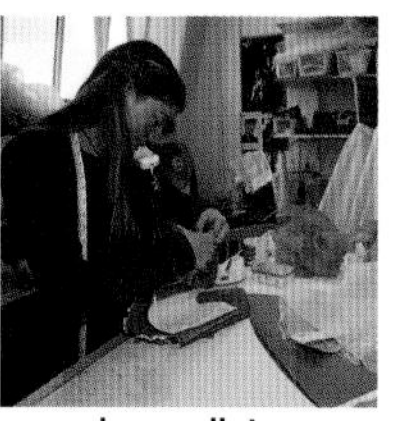
la modista
seamstress

el sastre
tailor

el transporte
transportation

las carreteras • roads

la autopista
highway

la caseta de cobro (C de peaje)
toll booth

las señales de piso (C las señales horizontales)
road markings

la entrada (C la vía de acceso)
entrance ramp

de sentido único
one-way

la línea divisoria
divider

el crucero (C la salida)
junction

el semáforo
traffic light

el camión
truck

el muro de división (C la mediana)
median strip

el carril de baja (C el carril para el tráfico lento)
inside lane

el carril central
middle lane

el carril izquierdo (C el carril de adelantamiento)
outside lane

la rampa de salida (C la vía de salida)
exit ramp

el tránsito (C el tráfico)
traffic

el puente (C el paso elevado)
overpass

el acotamiento (C el arcén)
hard shoulder

el paso a desnivel (C el paso subterráneo)
underpass

el paso de peatones
crosswalk

el teléfono de emergencia
emergency phone

el estacionamiento ([C] el aparcamiento) para minusválidos
disabled parking place

el tráfico ([C] el atasco de tráfico)
traffic jam

el mapa
map

el parquímetro
parking meter

el policía de tránsito ([C] el policía de tráfico)
traffic policeman

vocabulario • vocabulary

la desviación ([C] el desvío)
detour

estacionar ([C] aparcar)
park (v)

la glorieta
rotary

meter reversa ([C] dar marcha atrás)
reverse (v)

manejar ([C] conducir)
drive (v)

rebasar ([C] adelantar)
pass (v)

las obras
roadworks

el muro de contención ([C] la barrera de seguridad)
guardrail

remolcar
tow away (v)

la autovía
divided highway

¿Es ésta la carretera hacia...?
Is this the road to...?

¿Dónde me puedo estacionar ([C] aparcar)?
Where can I park?

las señales de tráqnsito • road signs

prohibido el paso
no entry

el límite de velocidad
speed limit

peligro
hazard

prohibido parar
no stopping

no dar vuelta ([C] no torcer) a la derecha
no right turn

el autobús • bus

el asiento del conductor
driver's seat

la barandilla
handrail

la puerta automática
automatic door

la rueda delantera
front wheel

el portaequipaje
luggage hold

la puerta | door

el autocar | bus

los tipos de autobuses • types of buses

el número de ruta
route number

el chófer
(ᶜ **el conductor**)
driver

el autobús de dos pisos
double-decker bus

el tranvía
tram

el trolebús
streetcar

el autobús escolar | school bus

la rueda trasera
rear wheel

la ventanilla ([C]la ventana)
window

el boleto ([C]el billete) de autobús
bus ticket

el botón de parada
stop button

el timbre
bell

la estación de autobuses
bus station

la parada de autobús
bus stop

vocabulario • vocabulary

la tarifa fare	**la marquesina** bus shelter
el horario timetable	**la rampa para sillas de ruedas** wheelchair access
¿Para usted en...? Do you stop at...?	**¿Qué autobús va a...?** Which bus goes to...?

el microbús
minibus

el autobús turístico | tourist bus

el autobús directo ([C]de enlace) | shuttle bus

el carro ([C]el coche) 1 • car 1

el exterior • exterior

la baca
roof rack

la puerta abatible ([C]la puerta del maletero)
tailgate

el cinturón de seguridad
seat belt

la silla para niños
child seat

los modelos • types

el compacto
subcompact

el carro (C el coche) de cinco puertas
hatchback

el carro familiar (C el turismo)
sedan

la camioneta (C el coche ranchera)
station wagon

el convertible (C el coche descapotable)
convertible

el carro deportivo
sports car

la minivan (C el monovolumen)
minivan

la doble tracción (C el todoterreno)
four-wheel drive

el auto (C el coche) de época
vintage

la limousine
limousine

la gasolinera • gas station

la bomba (C el surtidor)
gas pump

el precio
price

la zona de abastecimiento
forecourt

la bomba del aire
air hose

vocabulario • vocabulary

el aceite oil	**el diesel** diesel	**el anticongelante** antifreeze
la gasolina gasoline	**con plomo** leaded	**el auto-lavado (C el lavadero de coches)** car wash
sin plomo unleaded	**el taller** garage	**el líquido limpiaparabrisas** windshield wiper fluid

Llénelo (C Lleno) por favor.
Fill it up, please.

el carro (ᶜel coche) 2 • car 2

el interior • interior

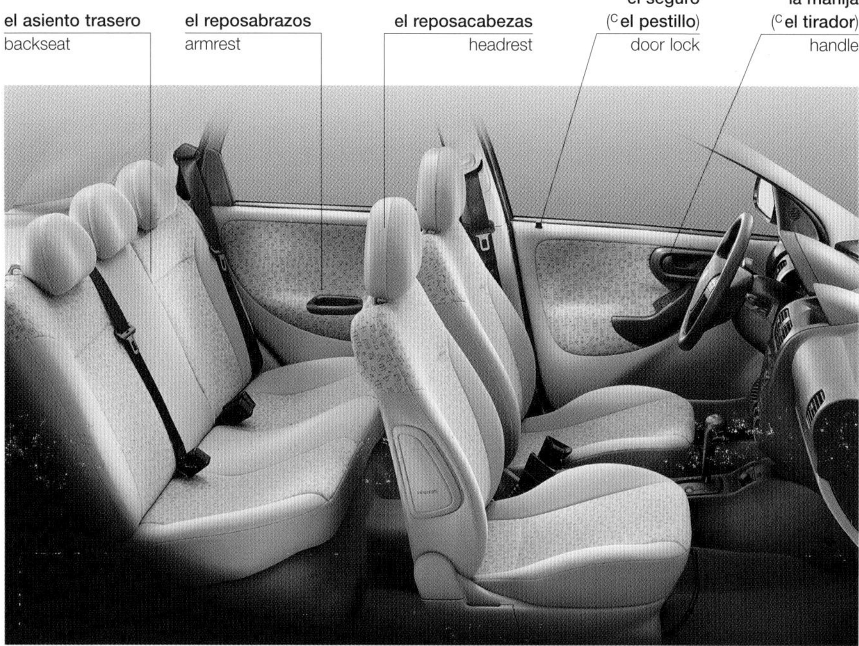

vocabulario • vocabulary

dos puertas two-door	**de cuatro puertas** four-door	**automático** automatic	**el freno** brake	**el acelerador** accelerator
de tres puertas three-door	**manual** manual	**el encendido** ignition	**el embrague** clutch	**el aire acondicionado** air-conditioning

¿Me puede decir cómo se va a...?
Can you tell me the way to...?

¿Dónde hay un estacionamiento (ᶜparking)?
Where is the parking lot?

¿Se puede estacionar (ᶜaparcar) aquí?
Can I park here?

los controles • controls

el volante
steering wheel

el claxon (C **la bocina**)
horn

el tablero (C **el salpicadero**)
dashboard

las luces de emergencia
hazard lights

la navegación por satélite
satellite navigation

el volante a la izquierda | left-hand drive

el indicador de temperatura
temperature gauge

el tacómetro (C **el cuentarrevoluciones**)
tachometer

el velocímetro (C **el indicador de velocidad**)
speedometer

el indicador de la gasolina
fuel gauge

la radio del coche
car stereo

la palanca (C **el conmutador**) **de luces**
light switch

la calefacción
heater controls

el odómetro (C **el cuentakilómetros**)
odometer

la palanca de velocidades (C **de cambios**)
gearshift

la bolsa de aire (C **el airbag**)
air bag

el volante a la derecha | right-hand drive

el carro (ᶜel coche) 3 • car 3

la mecánica • mechanics

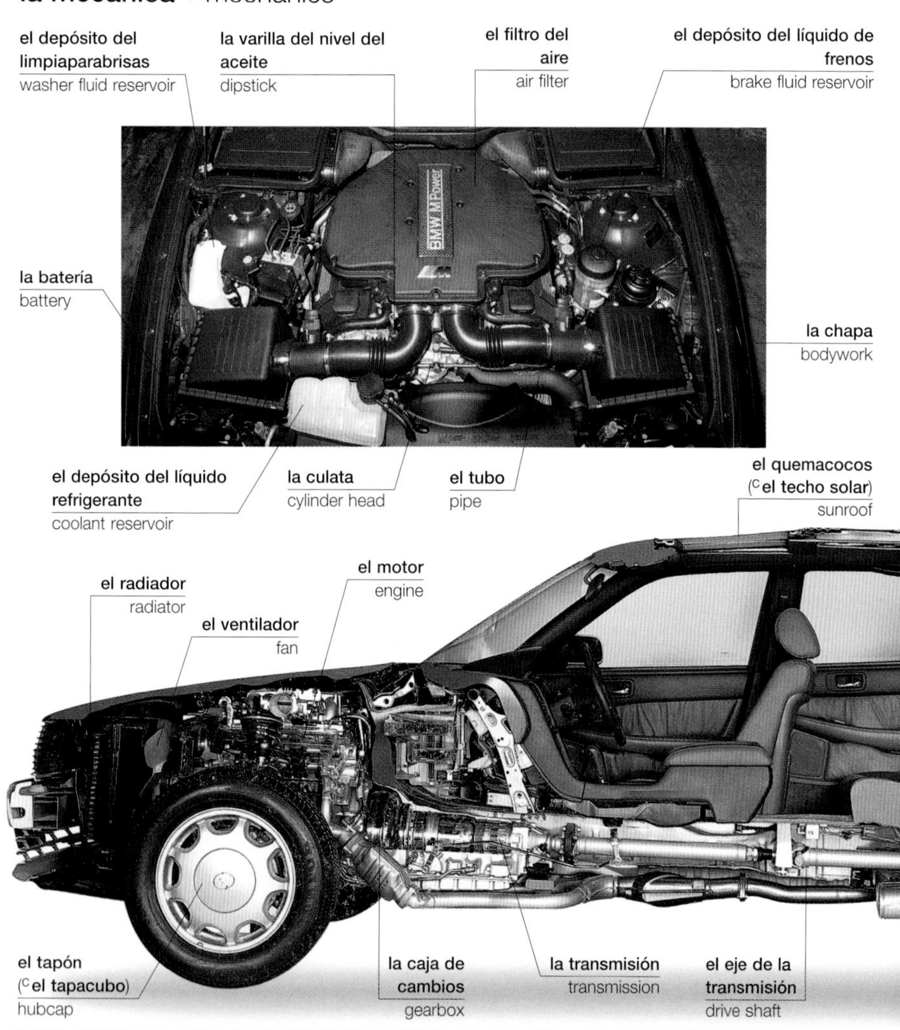

la ponchadura (ᶜel pinchazo) • flat tire

cambiar una llanta (ᶜuna rueda)
change a tire (v)

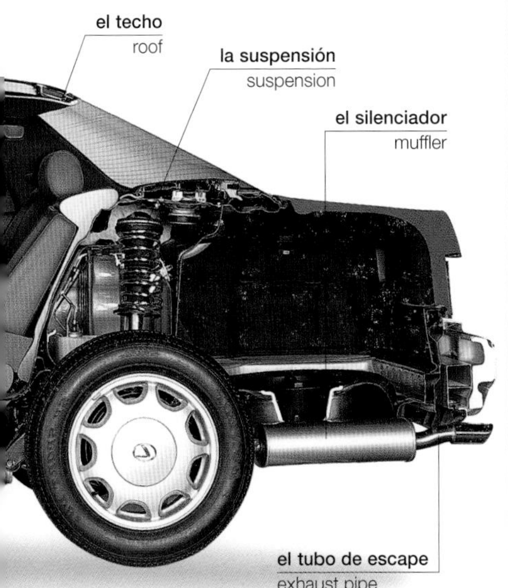

vocabulario • vocabulary

el accidente de carro car accident	**el tanque de la gasolina** petrol tank
la avería breakdown	**el turbo** turbocharger
el seguro insurance	**el distribuidor** distributor
la grúa tow truck	**el ralentí** timing
el mecánico mechanic	**el chasis** chassis
la presión del neumático tire pressure	**la banda del disco (ᶜla correa del disco)** cam belt
la caja de fusibles fuse box	**el freno de mano** parking brake
la bujía spark plug	**la banda del ventilador (ᶜla correa del ventilador)** fan belt
el alternador alternator	

Se descompuso el carro.
(ᶜMi coche se ha averiado.)
My car has broken down.

El carro no arranca.
(ᶜMi coche no arranca.)
My car won't start.

la motocicleta • motorcycle

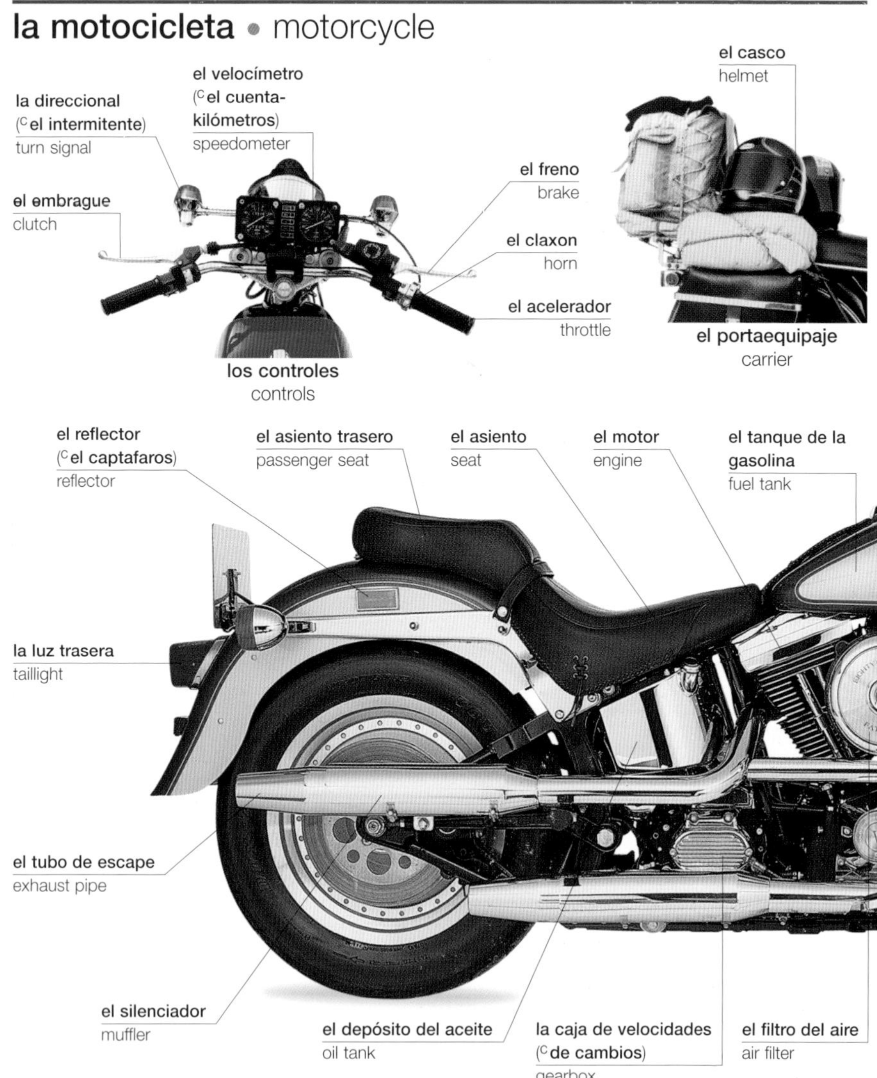

la visera
visor

el traje de cuero
leathers

la cinta reflectante
reflector strap

la rodillera
kneepad

el equipo | clothing

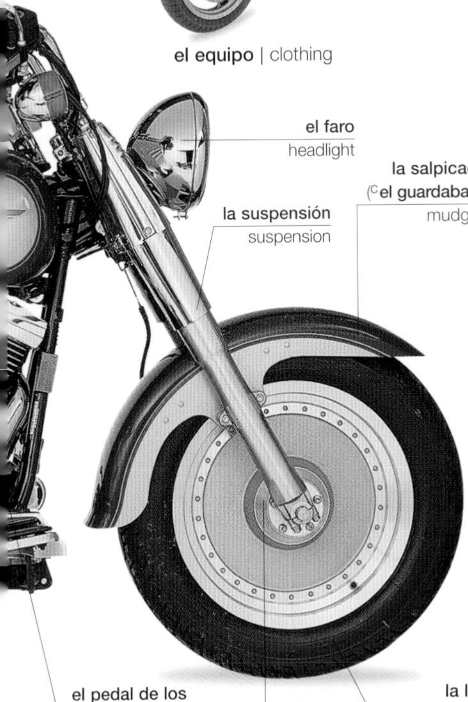

el faro
headlight

la salpicadera
(C el guardabarros)
mudguard

la suspensión
suspension

el pedal de los frenos
brake pedal

el eje
axle

la llanta
(C el neumático)
tire

los tipos • types

la moto de carreras | racing bike

el parabrisas
windshield

la moto de carretera | tourer

la motocross | dirt bike

el soporte
stand

la vespa | scooter

la bicicleta • bicycle

el tándem
tandem

la bicicleta de carreras
racing bike

la bicicleta de montaña
mountain bike

el asiento ([C]el sillín)
saddle

el poste del asiento ([C]el soporte del sillín)
seat post

la botella del agua
water bottle

el cuadro
frame

el freno
brake

el eje
hub

los cambios ([C]las marchas)
gears

el rin
rim

la llanta ([C]la cubierta)
tire

la cadena
chain

la estrella ([C]el diente de la rueda)
cog

el pedal
pedal

la bicicleta de paseo
touring bike

el casco
helmet

la bicicleta de pista ([C]de carretera)
road bike

el carril de bicicletas | cycle lane

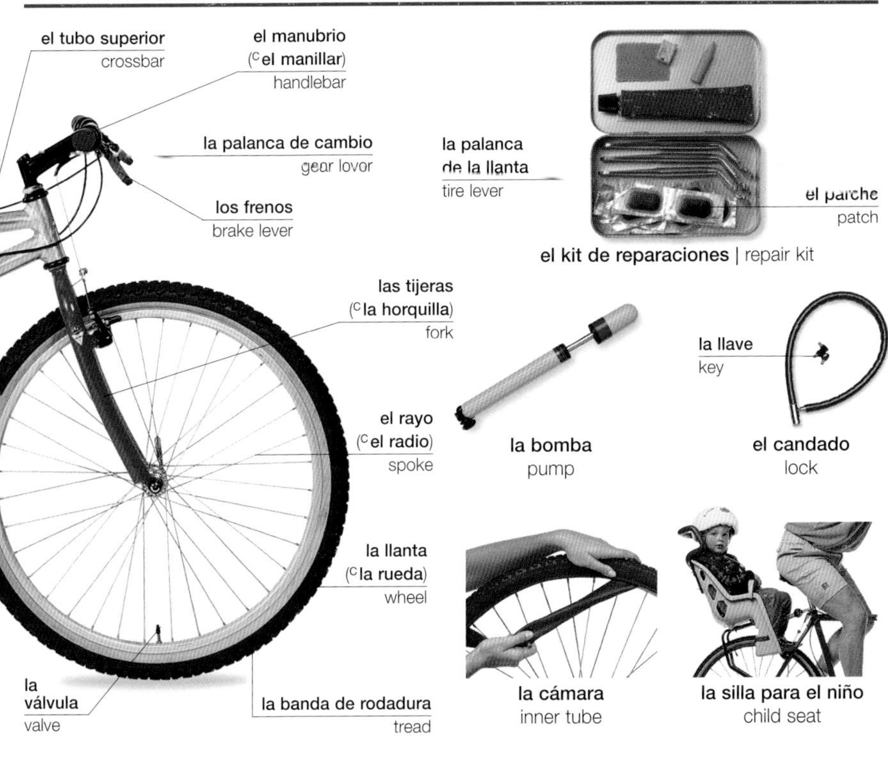

vocabulario • vocabulary

el faro
light

el faro trasero
rear light

la patilla de apoyo
kickstand

el cable
cable

el reflector ([C]el captafaros)
reflector

el rack ([C]la baca) para bicicletas
bike rack

el engrane ([C]el piñón)
sprocket

las ruedas de apoyo
stabilizers

la goma ([C]el taco) del freno
brake block

la dinamo
dynamo

la canastilla ([C]la cesta)
basket

la ponchadura ([C]el pinchazo)
flat tire

el calzapié
toe clip

la banda del calzapié ([C]la correa del calzapié)
toe strap

pedalear
pedal (v)

frenar
brake (v)

andar ([C]ir) en bicicleta
cycle (v)

cambiar de velocidad ([C]marcha)
change gear (v)

el tren • train

la estación de tren | train station

los tipos de tren • types of train

el tren de vapor
steam train

el tren diesel | diesel train

el tren eléctrico
electric train

el tren de alta velocidad
high-speed train

el monorriel (C el monorraíl)
monorail

el metro
underground train

el tranvía
streetcar

el tren de carga
(C el tren de mercancías)
freight train

el portaequipajes
luggage rack

la ventanilla
window

la puerta
door

el compartimento
compartment

la vía
track

la barrera
ticket barrier

el asiento
seat

el vagón restaurante | dining car

el altavoz ([C]el sistema de megafonía)
public address system

el horario
timetable

el boleto ([C]el billete)
ticket

el vestíbulo | concourse

el cochecama
sleeping compartment

vocabulario • vocabulary

la red ferroviaria railroad network	**el plano del metro** underground map	**la taquilla** ticket office	**el riel electrificado** live rail
el tren intercity inter-city train	**el retraso** delay	**cambiar** change (v)	**la señal** signal
la hora pico ([C]la hora punta) rush hour	**el precio** fare	**el checador ([C]el revisor)** ticket inspector	**la palanca de emergencia** emergency lever

el avión • aircraft

el avión de pasajeros • airliner

la nariz (C el morro) nose
la cabina de pilotaje cockpit
el motor engine
el fuselaje fuselage
el ala wing
la cola tail
el timón rudder
AIR CANADA
el tren delantero nosewheel
la salida exit
el tren de aterrizaje landing gear
el alerón aileron
la aleta fin
el estabilizador tailplane

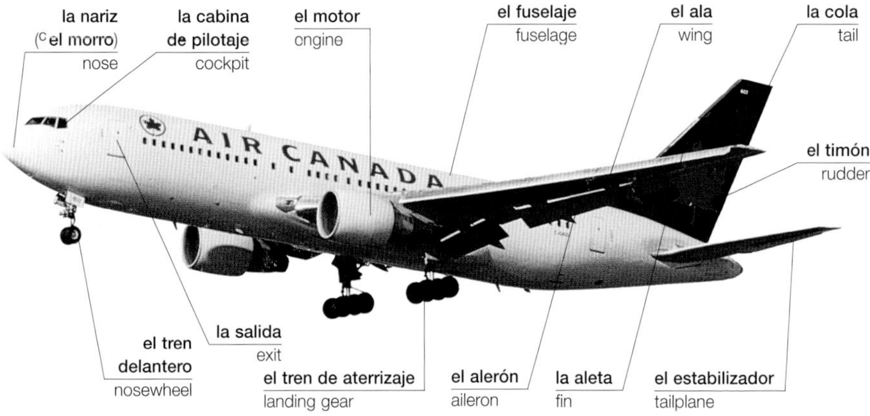

la cabina • cabin

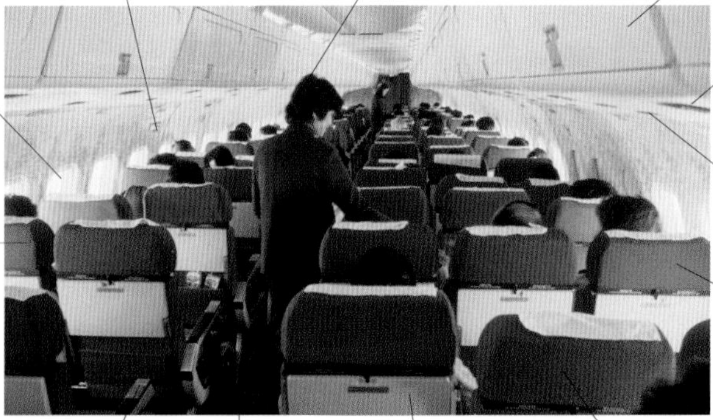

la salida de emergencia emergency exit
la sobrecargo (C la azafata de vuelo) flight attendant
el compartimento portaequipajes overhead bin
la ventanilla window
el ventilador air vent
la luz de lectura reading light
el asiento seat
la fila row
el descansabrazos (C el apoyabrazos) armrest
el pasillo aisle
la mesa plegable (C la bandeja) tray-table
el respaldo seat back

el globo aerostático
hot-air balloon

el ultraligero
ultralight

el planeador
glider

el biplano
biplane

la hélice
propeller

la avioneta
light aircraft

el hidroavión
seaplane

el jet privado
private jet

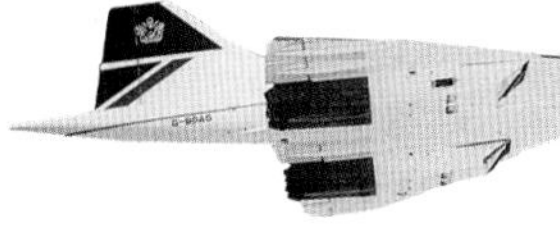

el avión supersónico
supersonic jet

el aspa
rotor blade

el helicóptero
helicopter

el avión de bombardeo
bomber

el misil
missile

el caza
fighter plane

vocabulario • vocabulary

el piloto pilot	**despegar** take off (v)	**aterrizar** land (v)	**la clase turista** economy class	**el equipaje de mano** carry-on luggage
el copiloto copilot	**voler** fly (v)	**la altitud** altitude	**la clase preferente** business class	**el cinturón de seguridad** seatbelt

el aeropuerto • airport

vocabulario • vocabulary

la pista runway	**la aduana** customs	**la seguridad** security	**las vacaciones** vacation
el vuelo internacional international flight	**el número de vuelo** flight number	**la banda transportadora** (C**la cinta de equipajes**) baggage carousel	**reservar un vuelo** make a flight reservation (v)
el vuelo nacional domestic flight	**inmigración** immigration	**la máquina de rayos x** X-ray machine	**la torre de control** control tower
la conexión connection	**el exceso de equipaje** excess baggage	**el folleto de viajes** travel brochure	**hacer check-in** (C**facturar**) check in (v)

el equipaje de mano
carry-on luggage

el equipaje
luggage

el carrito
(^C el carro)
cart

el mostrador de check-in
check-in desk

la visa
(^C el visado)
visa

el pasaporte | passport

el control de pasaportes
passport control

la tarjeta de embarque
boarding pass

el boleto (^C el billete)
ticket

el número de puerta de embarque
gate number

la sala de embarque
departure lounge

el destino
destination

las llegadas
arrivals

las salidas
departures

la pantalla informativa
information screen

el duty-free (^C la tienda libre de impuestos)
duty-free store

la recogida de equipajes
baggage claim

el sitio de taxis
(^C la parada de taxis)
taxi stand

la renta de carros
(^C el alquiler de coches)
car rental

el barco • ship

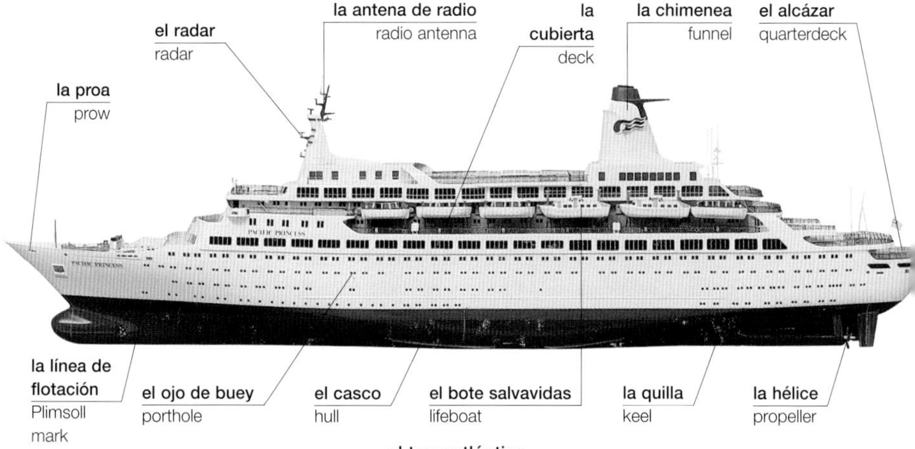

la proa
prow

el radar
radar

la antena de radio
radio antenna

la cubierta
deck

la chimenea
funnel

el alcázar
quarterdeck

la línea de flotación
Plimsoll mark

el ojo de buey
porthole

el casco
hull

el bote salvavidas
lifeboat

la quilla
keel

la hélice
propeller

el transatlántico
ocean liner

el puente
bridge

la sala de máquinas
engine room

el camarote
cabin

la cocina
galley

vocabulario • vocabulary

el muelle dock	**el cabrestante** windlass
el puerto port	**el capitán** captain
la pasarela gangway	**la lancha de motor** el capitán
el ancla anchor	**la barca de remos** rowboat
el noray bollard	**la piragua** canoe

otras embarcaciones • other ships

el ferry
ferryboat

la zodiac
inflatable dinghy

el hidrodeslizador
hydrofoil

el yate
yacht

el catamarán
catamaran

el remolcador
tugboat

el aerodeslizador
hovercraft

el barco carguero (C**el buque portacontenedores**)
container ship

el barco de vela
sailboat

el buque de carga
freighter

el buque tanque
(C**el petrolero**)
oil tanker

el portaaviones
aircraft carrier

el barco de guerra
battleship

el submarino
submarine

el puerto • port

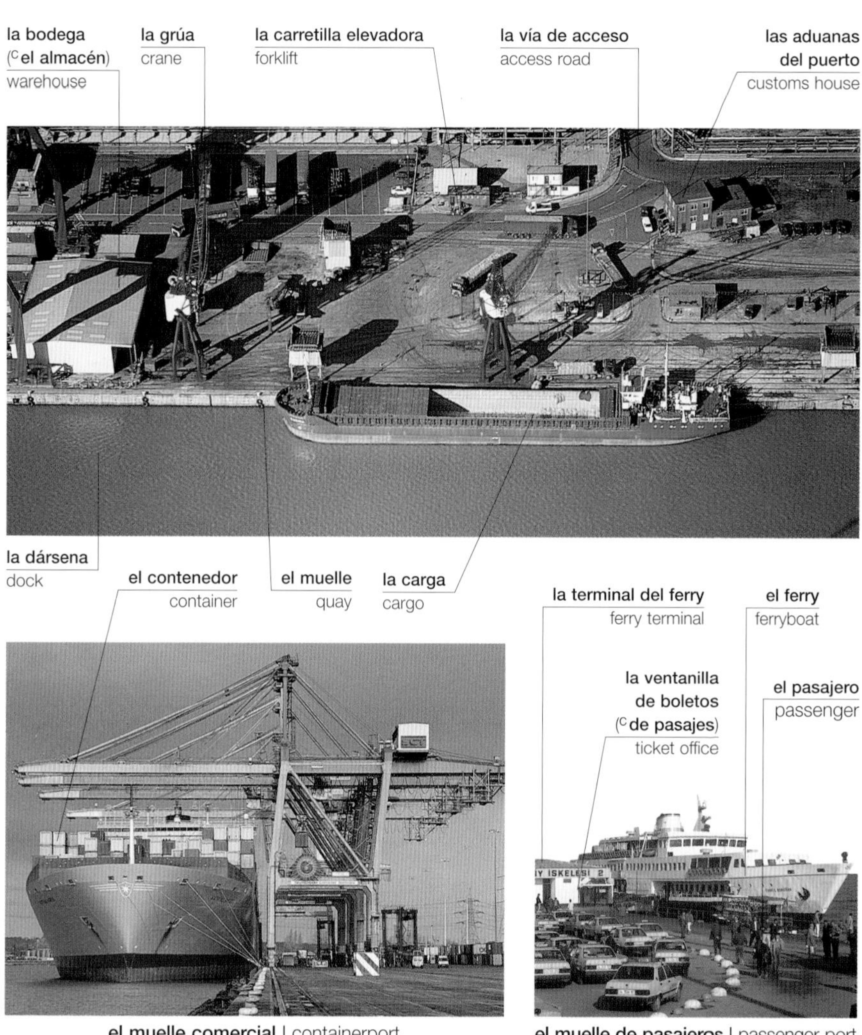

el muelle comercial | containerport

el muelle de pasajeros | passenger port

la red
net

el barco pesquero (**ᶜel barco de pesca**)
fishing boat

el punto de amarre
mooring

el puerto deportivo
marina

el puerto pesquero (**ᶜel puerto de pesca**)
fishing port

el puerto
harbor

el embarcadero
pier

el espigón
jetty

el astillero
shipyard

la lámpara
lantern

el faro
lighthouse

la boya
buoy

vocabulario • vocabulary

el guardacostas coast guard	**el dique seco** dry dock	**embarcar** board (v)
el capitán del puerto harbormaster	**amarrar** moor (v)	**desembarcar** disembark (v)
anclar (**ᶜfondear**) drop anchor (v)	**atracar** dock (v)	**zarpar** set sail (v)

ULTRA
3
DUNLOP
DDH
4
DUNLOP
MOLITOR
TOUR
EDITION
1
ProStaff
4
BANFF SPRINGS
GOLF CLUB
TOP-FLITE
HOT XL
4
ProStaff
4
RAM TOUR
1
MAXFLI
TOP-FLITE
STRATA
3
DISTANCE

los deportes
sports

el fútbol americano • football

el poste de la portería
goalpost

la línea de banda
sideline

el juez de línea
referee

la línea de gol
goal line

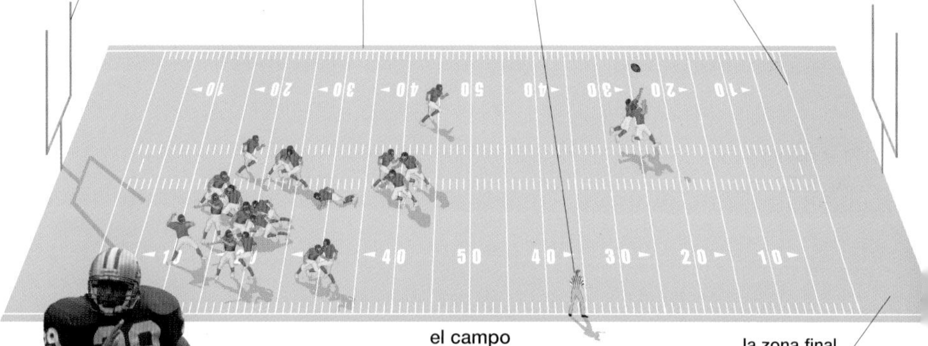

el campo
football field

la zona final
end zone

el balón
football

las rodilleras
pads

el casco
helmet

los tenis (c la bota)
cleat

el jugador
football player

taclear (c placar)
tackle (v)

pasar
pass (v)

atrapar (c coger)
catch (v)

vocabulario • vocabulary

el tiempo fuera time out	**el equipo** team	**la defensa** defense	**el intento** touchdown	**¿Cómo van?** What is the score?
el balón perdido fumble	**el ataque** attack	**la puntuación** score	**la porrista** (c **la animadora**) cheerleader	**¿Quién va ganando?** Who is winning?

el rugby • rugby

el fútbol • soccer

el balón
soccer ball

el delantero
forward

el árbitro
referee

el círculo central
center circle

el portero
goalkeeper

el uniforme
soccer uniform

el futbolista
soccer player

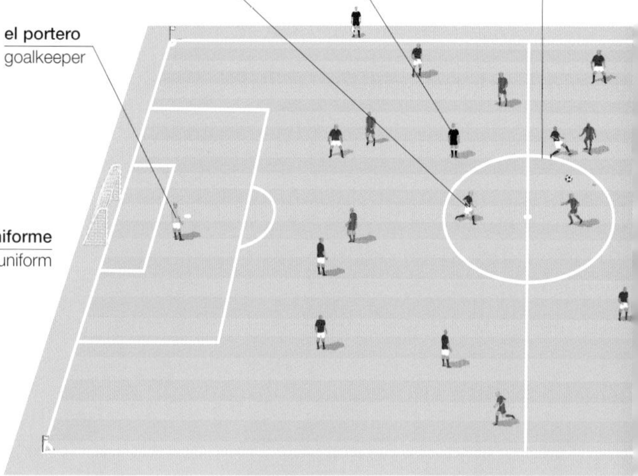

el campo de fútbol
soccer field

el poste
goalpost

la red
net

el larguero
crossbar

el gol | goal

regatear | dribble (v)

cabecear (ᶜ**tirar de cabeza**) | head (v)

la barrera
wall

el tiro libre | free kick

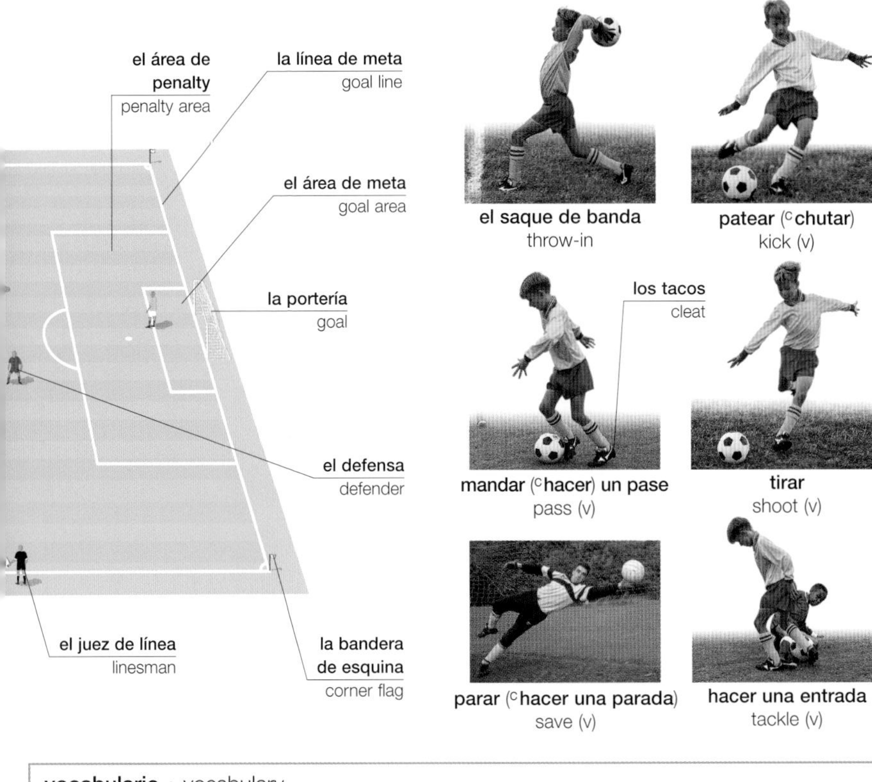

el saque de banda
throw-in

patear (ᶜchutar)
kick (v)

mandar (ᶜhacer) un pase
pass (v)

tirar
shoot (v)

parar (ᶜhacer una parada)
save (v)

hacer una entrada
tackle (v)

vocabulario • vocabulary

el estadio
stadium

marcar un gol
score a goal (v)

el penalty
penalty

la tarjeta amarilla
yellow card

la tarjeta roja
red card

el tiro de esquina (ᶜel córner)
corner

la falta
foul

el fuera de juego
offside

la expulsión
send off

la liga
league

el empate
draw

el descanso
halftime

el reserva
substitute

el cambio
substitution

el tiempo extra (ᶜla prórroga)
extra time

el hockey • hockey

el hockey sobre hielo • ice hockey

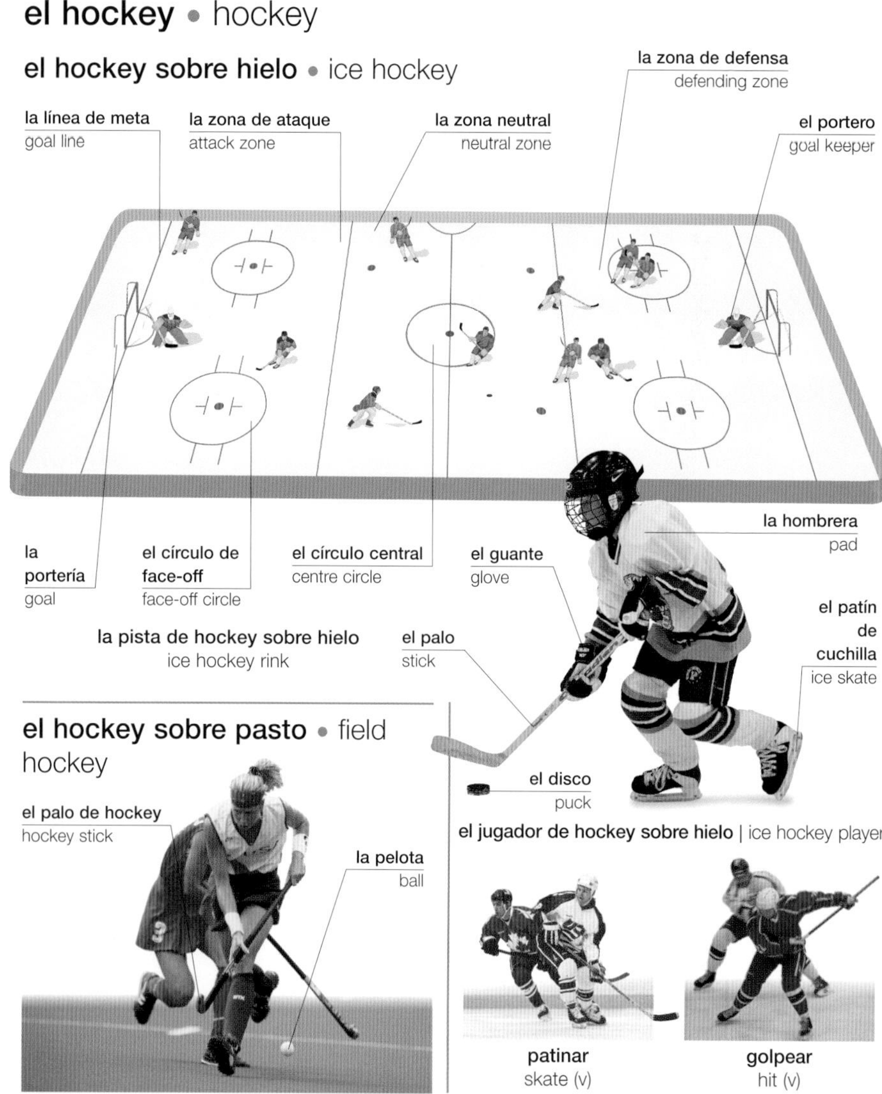

el hockey sobre pasto • field hockey

el críquet • cricket

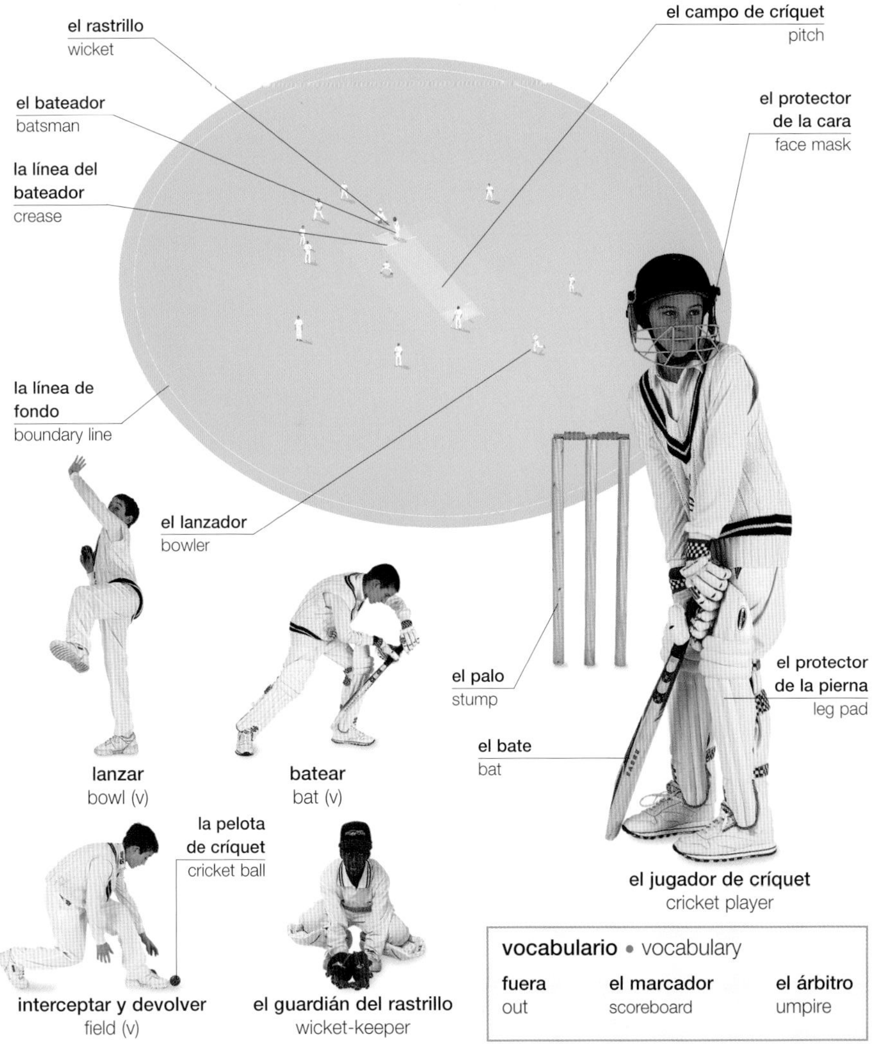

lanzar
bowl (v)

batear
bat (v)

interceptar y devolver
field (v)

el guardián del rastrillo
wicket-keeper

el jugador de críquet
cricket player

vocabulario • vocabulary

fuera	el marcador	el árbitro
out	scoreboard	umpire

el baloncesto • basketball

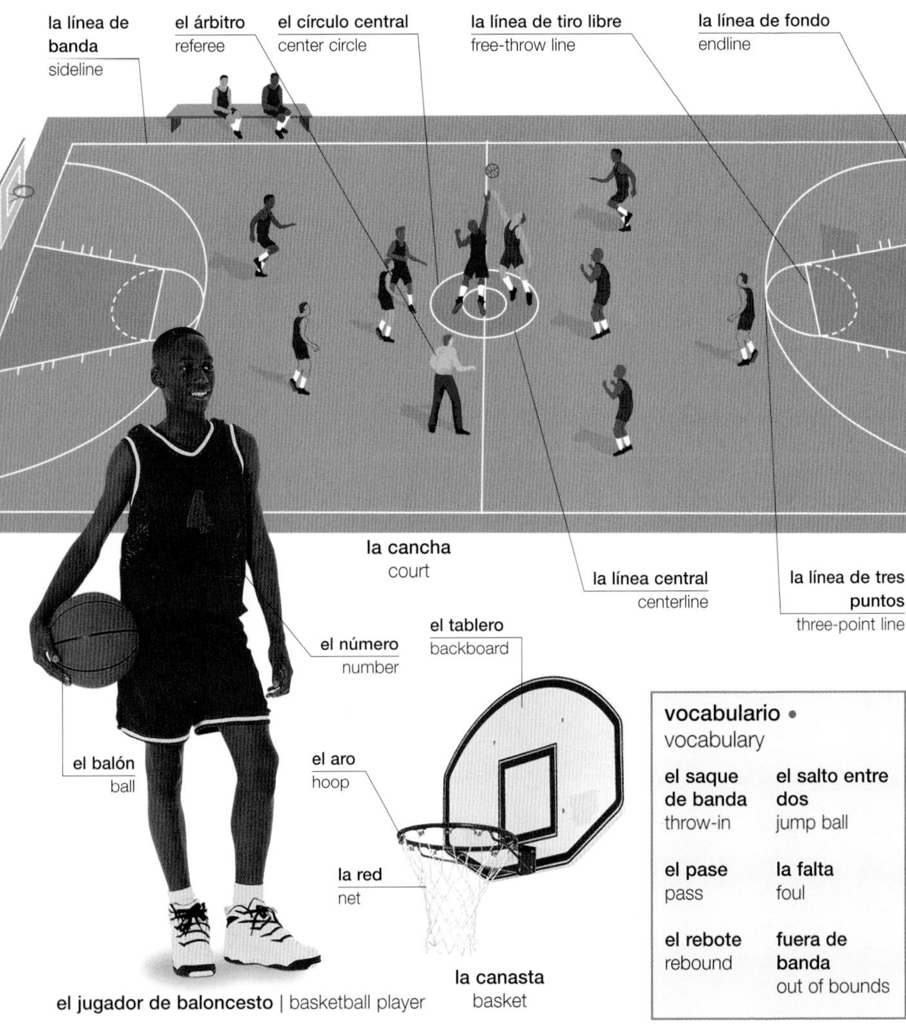

vocabulario • vocabulary

el saque de banda throw-in	**el salto entre dos** jump ball
el pase pass	**la falta** foul
el rebote rebound	**fuera de banda** out of bounds

las acciones • actions

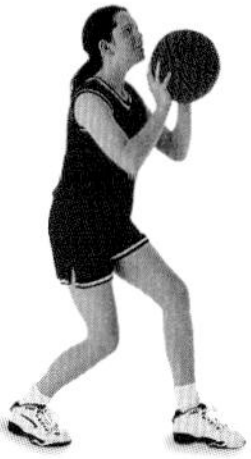

lanzar
throw (v)

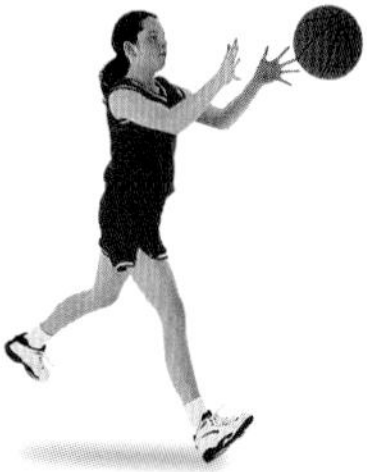

cachar (ᶜ**coger**)
catch (v)

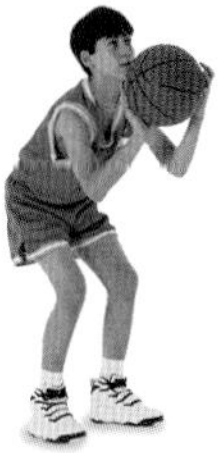

tirar
shoot (v)

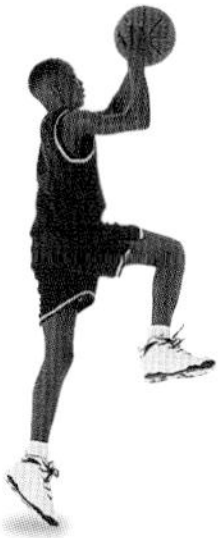

saltar
jump (v)

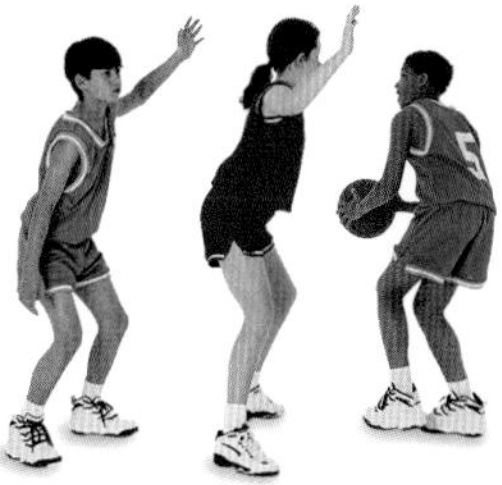

marcar
cover (v)

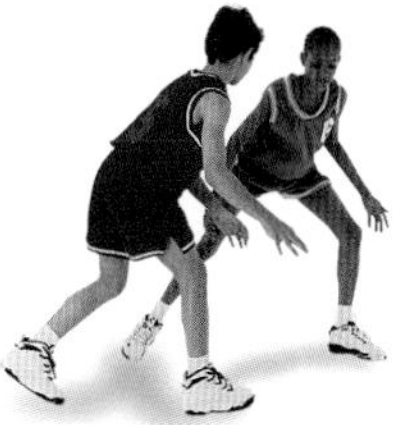

bloquear
block (v)

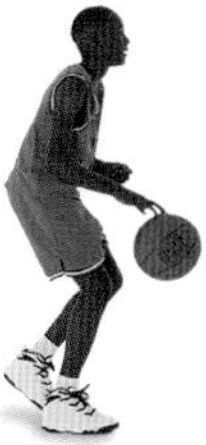

botar
dribble (v)

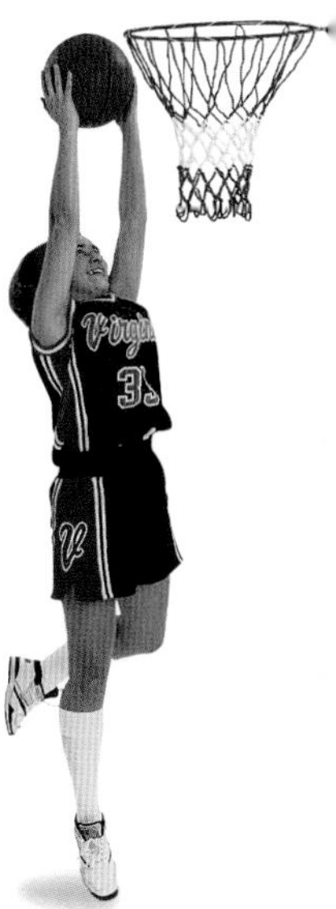

marcar
dunk (v)

el vóleibol (ᶜel balonvolea) • volleyball

bloquear
block (v)

la red
net

recibir
dig (v)

el árbitro
referee

la rodillera
knee support

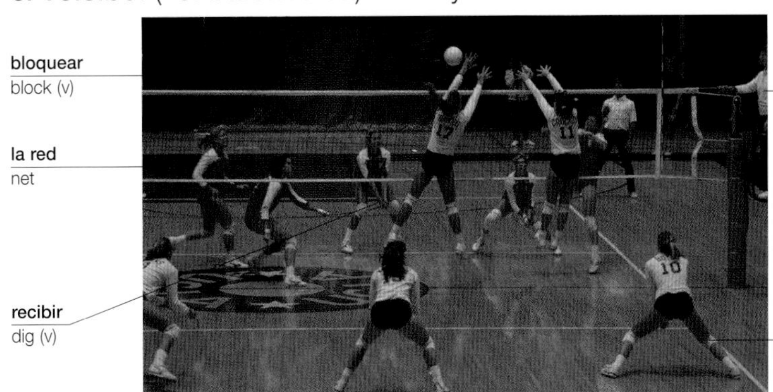

la cancha | court

el béisbol • baseball

el campo • field

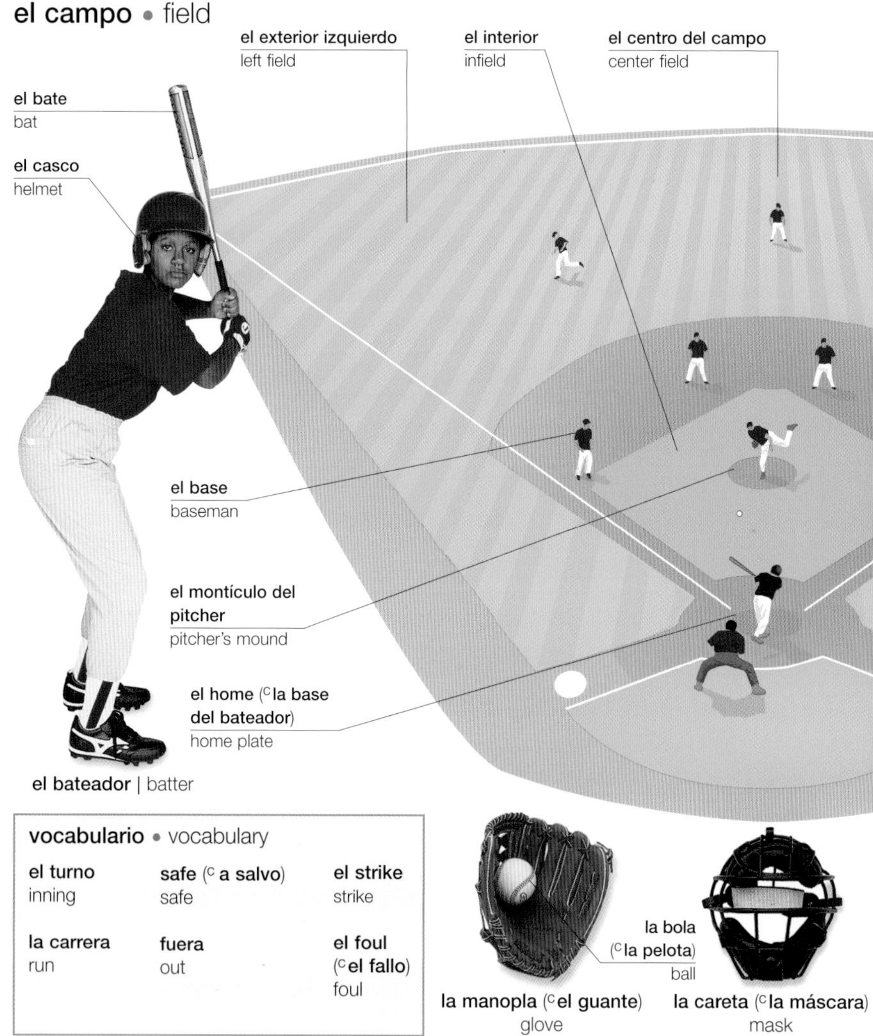

vocabulario • vocabulary

el turno inning	**safe ([C] a salvo)** safe	**el strike** strike
la carrera run	**fuera** out	**el foul ([C] el fallo)** foul

las acciones • actions

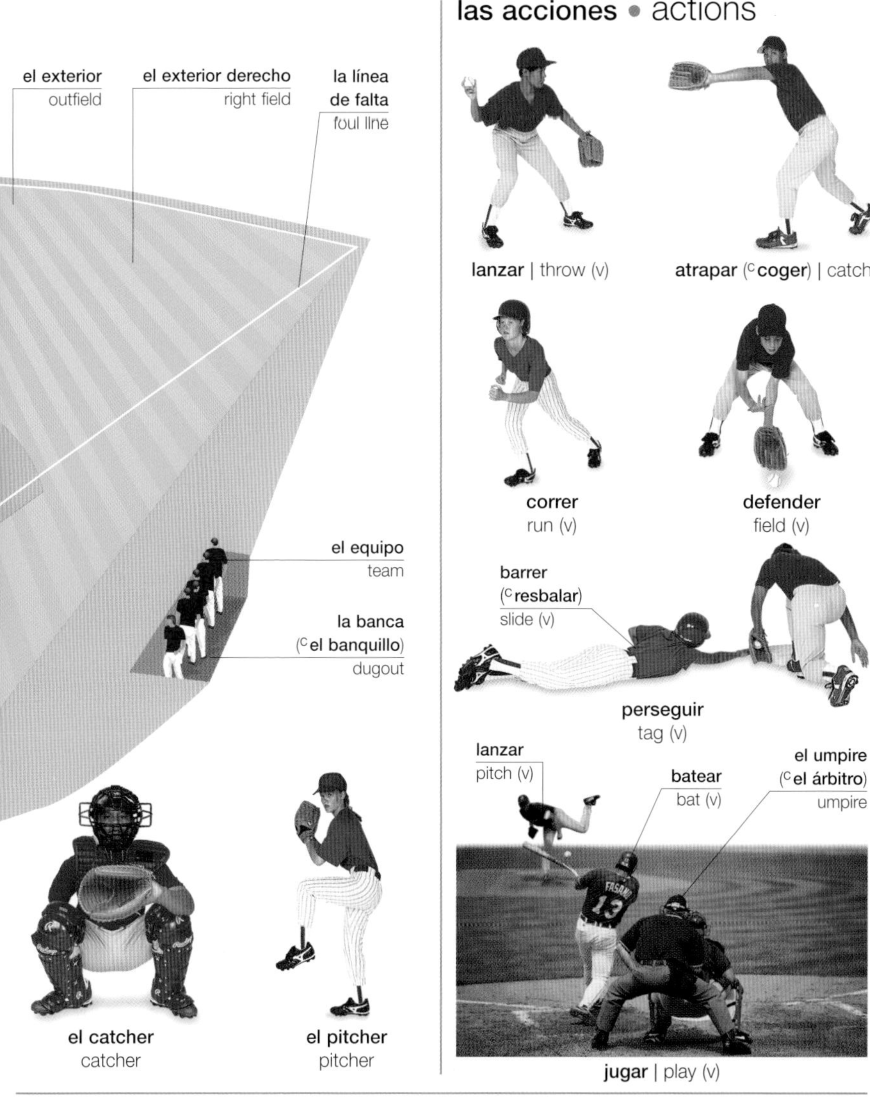

el tenis • tennis

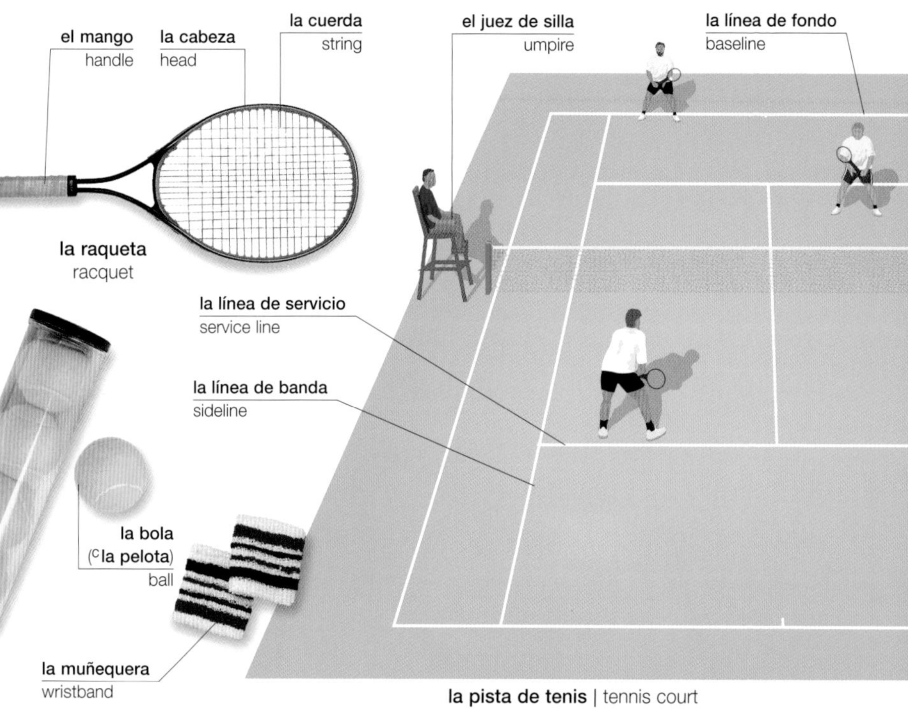

la pista de tenis | tennis court

vocabulario • vocabulary

el juego game	**el set** set	**nada** love	**la falta** fault	**el peloteo** rally	**el efecto** spin
los dobles doubles	**el partido** match	**la ventaja** advantage	**el as** ace	**¡red!** let!	**el juez de línea** linesman
el singles (C **el individual**) singles	**el tiebreak** tiebreaker	**cuarenta iguales** deuce	**la dejada** dropshot	**el tiro con efecto** slice	**el campeonato** championship

el jugador
player

los golpes • strokes

los juegos de raqueta • racquet games

el bádminton
badminton

el ping-pong
table tennis

el squash
squash

el racketball
racquetball

el golf • golf

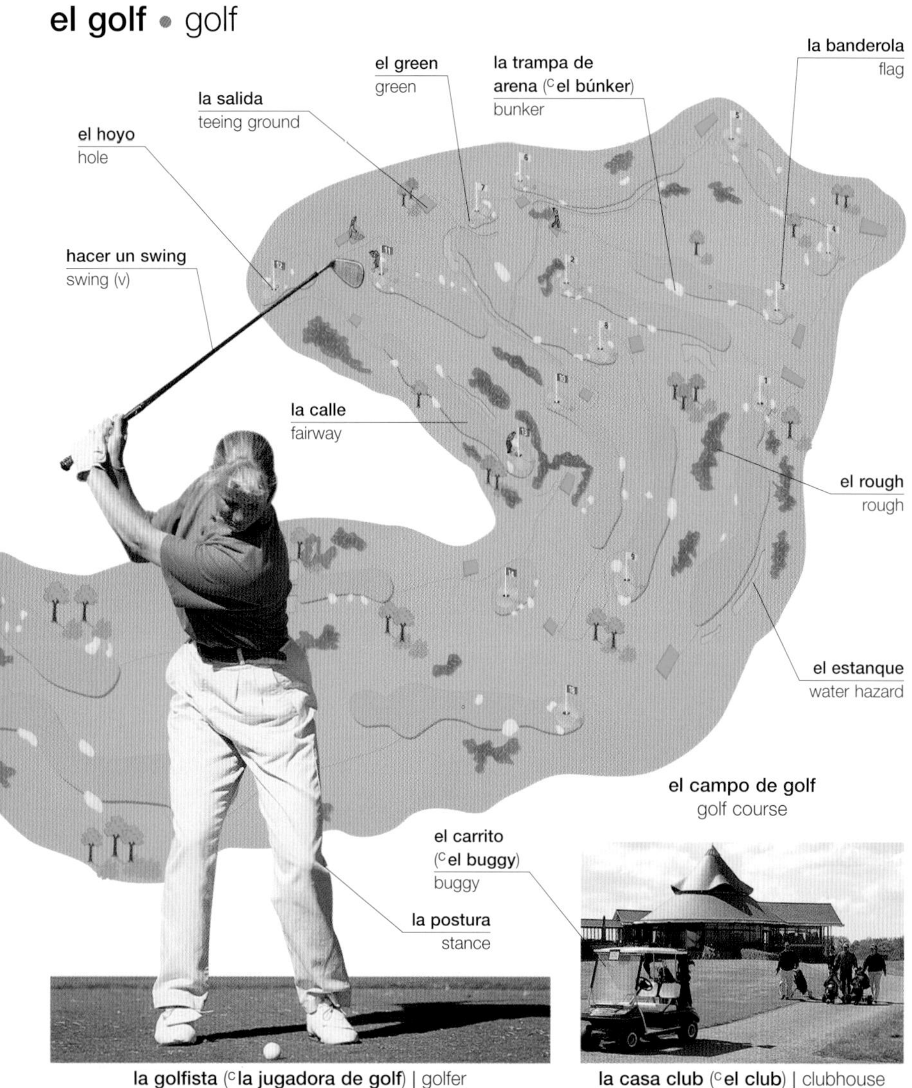

la golfista (C la jugadora de golf) | golfer

la casa club (C el club) | clubhouse

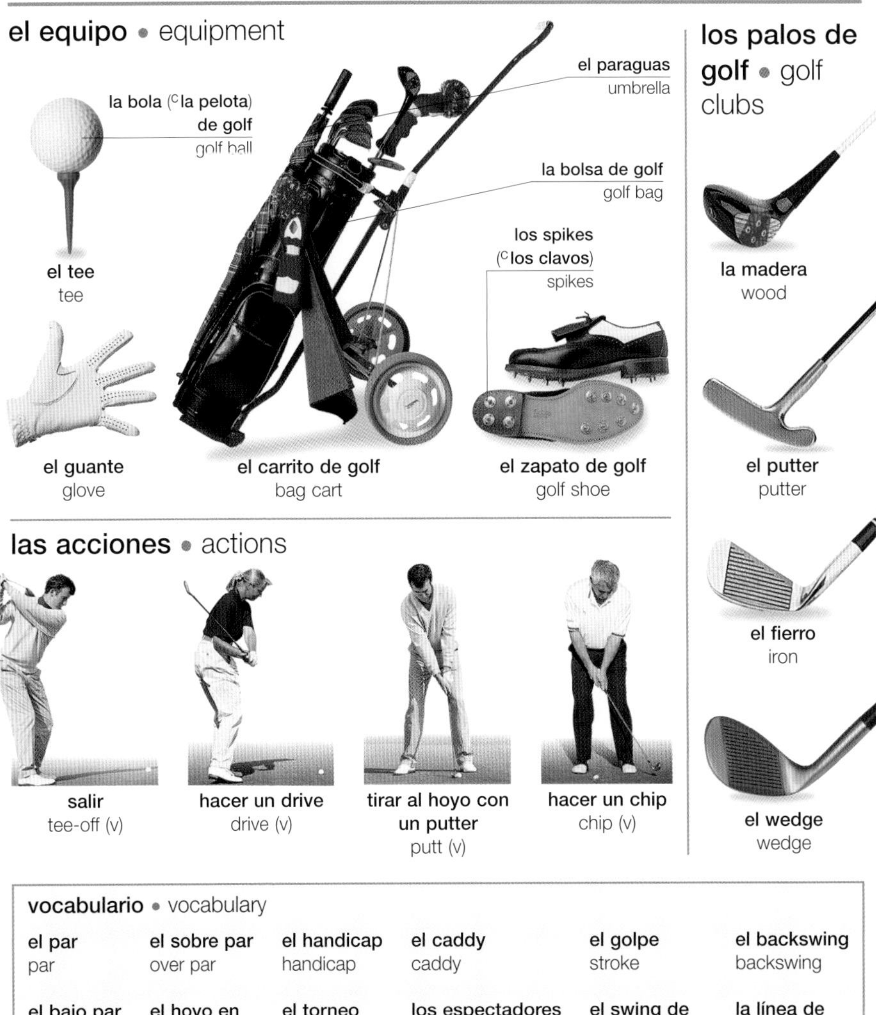

el equipo • equipment

la bola (^Cla pelota) de golf
golf ball

el tee
tee

el paraguas
umbrella

la bolsa de golf
golf bag

los spikes ([C] los clavos)
spikes

el guante
glove

el carrito de golf
bag cart

el zapato de golf
golf shoe

las acciones • actions

salir
tee-off (v)

hacer un drive
drive (v)

tirar al hoyo con un putter
putt (v)

hacer un chip
chip (v)

los palos de golf • golf clubs

la madera
wood

el putter
putter

el fierro
iron

el wedge
wedge

vocabulario • vocabulary

el par par	**el sobre par** over par	**el handicap** handicap	**el caddy** caddy	**el golpe** stroke	**el backswing** backswing
el bajo par under par	**el hoyo en uno** hole in one	**el torneo** tournament	**los espectadores** spectators	**el swing de práctica** practice swing	**la línea de juego** line of play

el atletismo • track and field

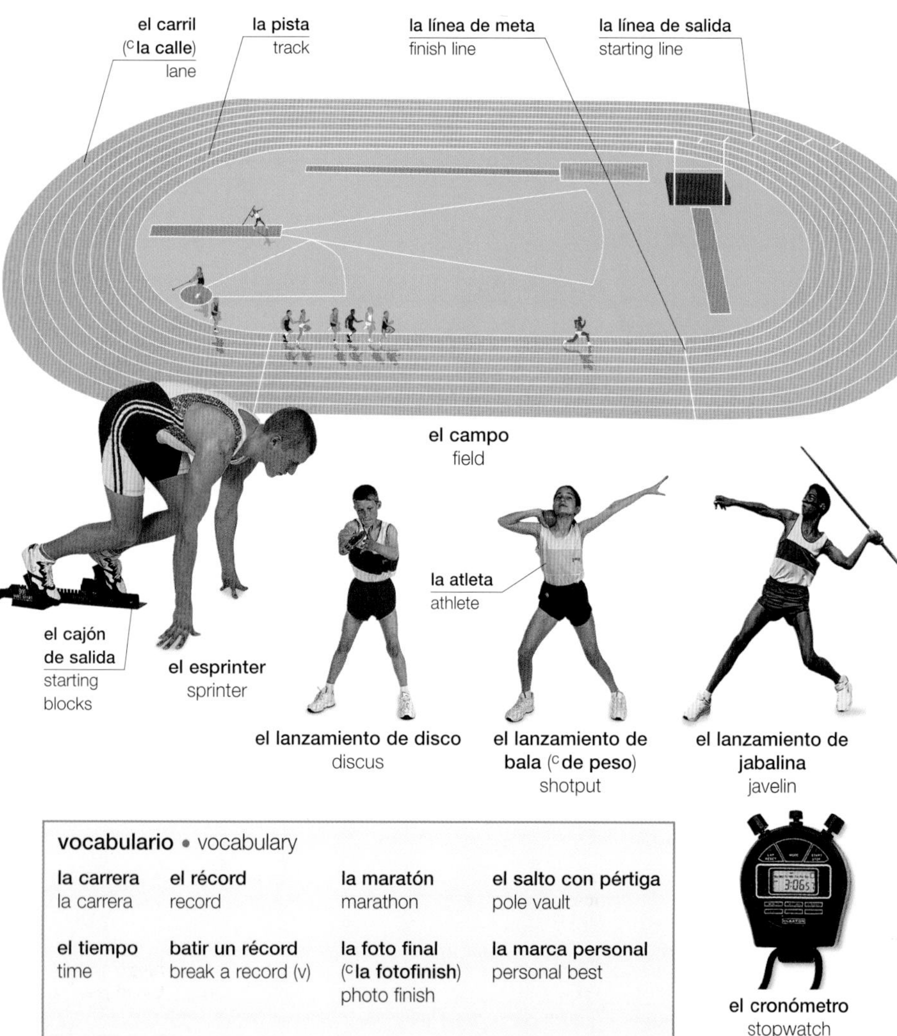

vocabulario • vocabulary

la carrera la carrera	**el récord** record	**la maratón** marathon	**el salto con pértiga** pole vault
el tiempo time	**batir un récord** break a record (v)	**la foto final** (c **la fotofinish**) photo finish	**la marca personal** personal best

el cronómetro
stopwatch

la carrera de relevos
relay race

el salto de altura
high jump

el salto de longitud
long jump

la carrera de vallas
hurdles

la gimnasia • gymnastics

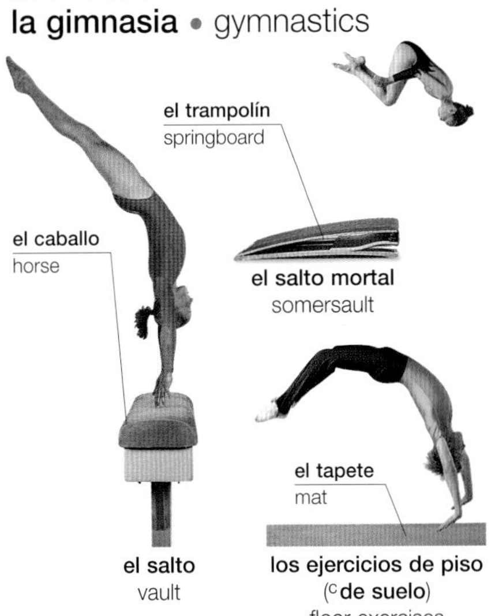

el salto mortal
somersault

el salto
vault

los ejercicios de piso (ᶜde suelo)
floor exercises

la viga (ᶜla barra) de equilibrio
beam

la voltereta
cartwheel

la gimnasia rítmica
rhythmic gymnastics

vocabulario • vocabulary

las barras paralelas (ᶜlas paralelas)
parallel bars

la barra fija
horizontal bar

las barras asimétricas
asymmetric bars

el caballo con arcos
pommel horse

las argollas (ᶜlas anillas)
rings

el podio
podium

las medallas
medals

el oro
gold

la plata
silver

el bronce
bronze

los deportes de combate • combat sports

el taekwondo
tae kwon do

el karate
karate

el judo
judo

el aikido
aikido

el kendo
kendo

el kung fu
kung fu

el full contact
kickboxing

la lucha libre
wrestling

el boxeo
boxing

los movimientos • actions

la caída
fall

el agarre
hold

el derribo
throw

la inmovilización
pin

la patada
kick

el puñetazo
punch

el golpe
strike

el golpe
chop

el salto
jump

el bloqueo ([C]**la parada**)
block

vocabulario • vocabulary

el ring
boxing ring

los guantes de boxeo
boxing gloves

el protegedientes
mouth guard

el combate
bout

el round ([C]**el asalto**)
round

el entrenamiento
sparring

el puño
fist

el K.O.
knockout

el saco de arena
punching bag

el cinturón negro
black belt

la defensa personal
self-defense

las artes marciales
martial arts

la capoeira
capoeira

el sumo
sumo wrestling

el tai-chi
tai-chi

la natación • swimming

el equipo • equipment

los estilos • styles

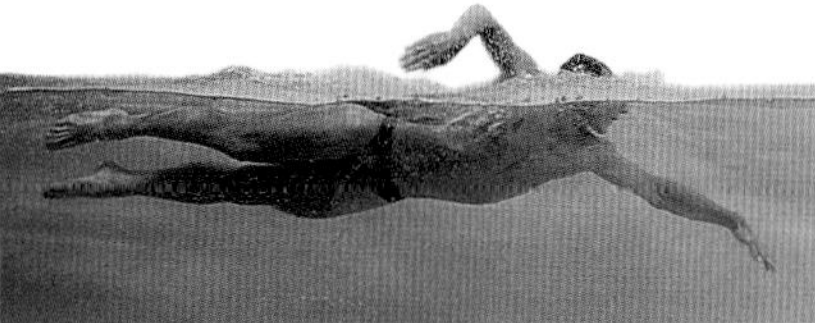

el crol
front crawl

el pecho ([c]**la braza**)
breaststroke

el dorso ([c]**la espalda**) | backstroke

la mariposa | butterfly

el buceo • scuba diving

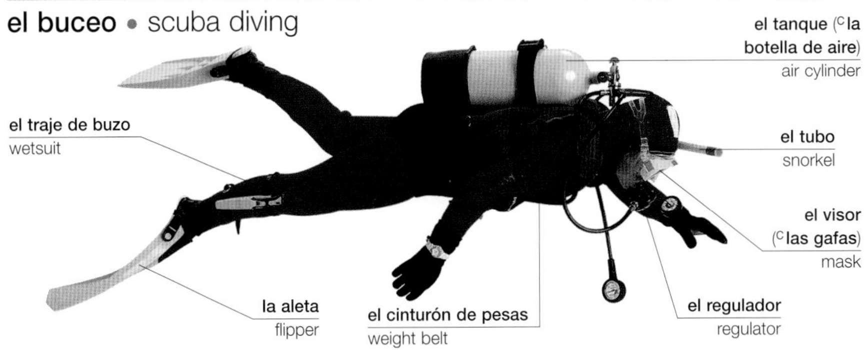

vocabulario • vocabulary

el clavado ([c]**el salto**)
dive

el clavado ([c]**el salto**) **alto**
high dive

hacer agua
tread water (v)

el clavado ([c]**el salto**) **de salida**
racing dive

el salvavidas ([c]**el socorrista**)
lifeguard

las taquillas
lockers

la zona profunda
deep end

el waterpolo
water polo

la zona poco profunda
shallow end

el nado sincronizado
synchronized swimming

el calambre ([c]**el tirón**)
cramp

ahogarse
drown (v)

la vela • sailing

la brújula
compass

el ancla
anchor

el mástil
mast

las jarcias
rigging

la vela mayor
mainsail

el foque
headsail

la escotera
cleat

la cubierta
sidedeck

la botavara
boom

la proa
bow

la popa
stern

la caña del timón
tiller

el casco
hull

navegar | navigate (v)

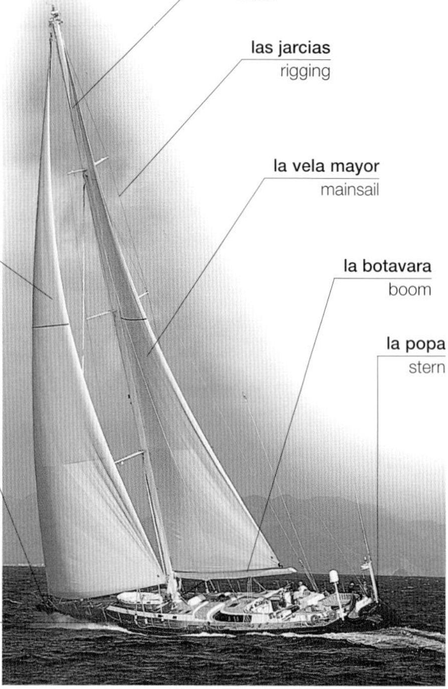

el yate | yacht

la seguridad • safety

la bengala
flare

el salvavidas
life preserver

el chaleco salvavidas
life jacket

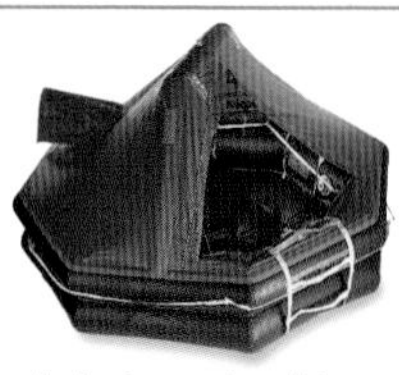

la balsa salvavidas
life raft

los deportes acuáticos • watersports

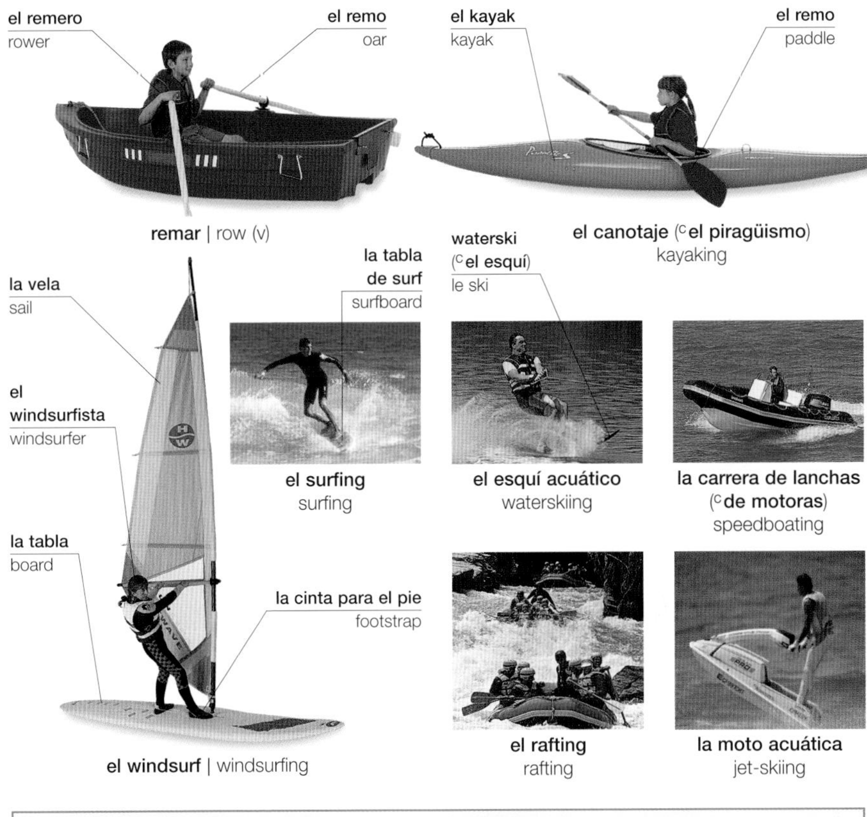

remar | row (v)

el canotaje (C **el piragüismo**)
kayaking

el surfing
surfing

el esquí acuático
waterskiing

la carrera de lanchas (C **de motoras**)
speedboating

el windsurf | windsurfing

el rafting
rafting

la moto acuática
jet-skiing

vocabulario • vocabulary

el surfista surfer	**la tripulación** crew	**el viento** wind	**la rompiente** surf	**la escota** sheet	**la orza** centerboard
el esquiador acuático waterskier	**virar** tack (v)	**la ola** wave	**los rápidos** rapids	**el timón** rudder	**volcar** capsize (v)

la equitación • horseback riding

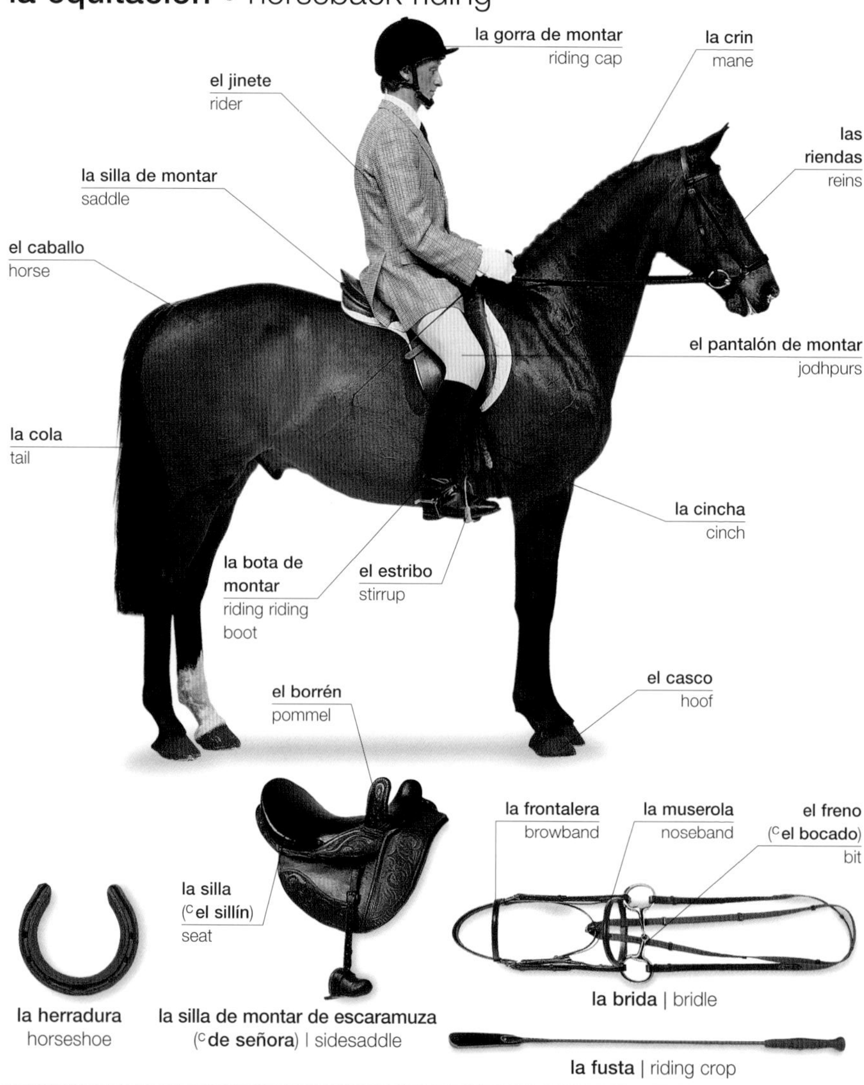

la herradura
horseshoe

la silla de montar de escaramuza (ᶜde señora) | sidesaddle

la brida | bridle

la fusta | riding crop

las modalidades • events

la carrera de caballos
horse race

la carrera de obstáculos
steeplechase

la carrera al trote
harness race

el rodeo
rodeo

el concurso de saltos
show jumping

la carrera de carrozas
carriage race

el paseo
trekking

la doma y monta
dressage

el polo
polo

vocabulario • vocabulary

el paso walk	**el medio galope** canter	**el salto** jump	**el cabestro** halter	**el cercado** paddock	**el hipódromo** racecourse
el trote trot	**el galope** gallop	**el mozo de cuadra** groom	**la cuadra** stable	**el ruedo** arena	**la carrera sin obstáculos** flat race

la pesca • fishing

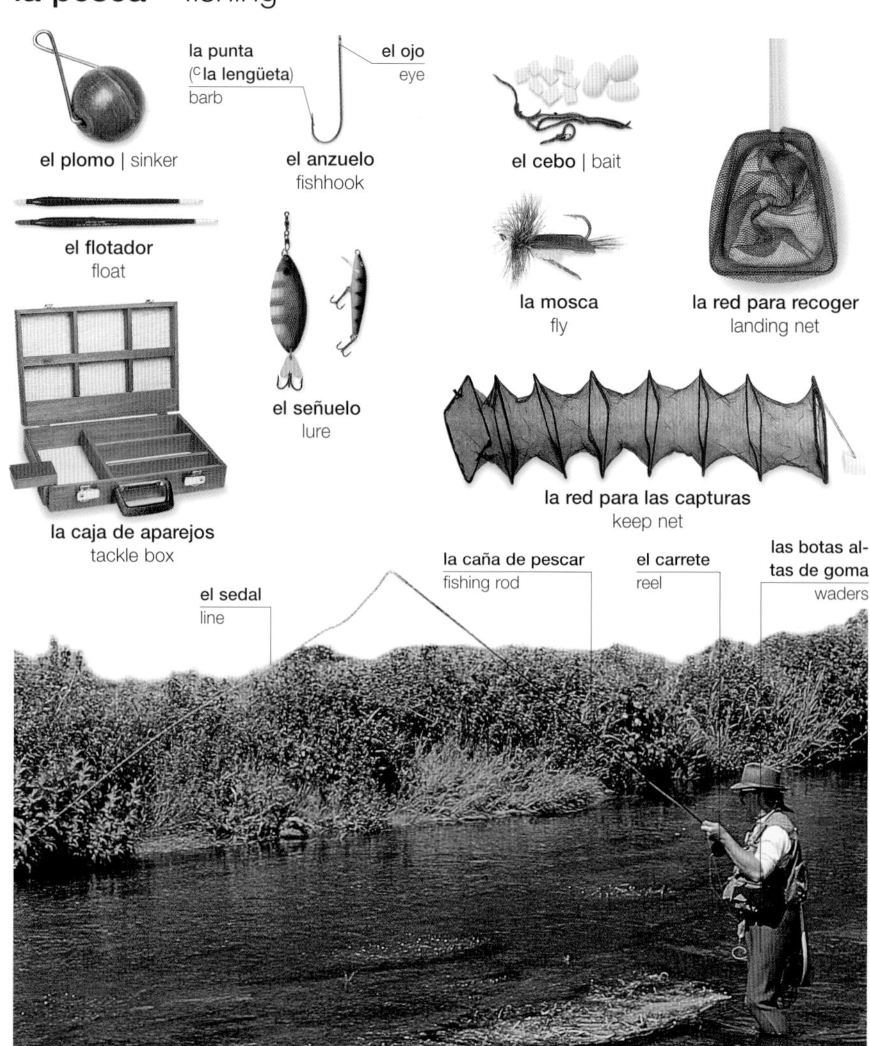

el pescador de caña | fisherman

los tipos de pesca • types of fishing

la pesca en agua dulce
freshwater fishing

la pesca con mosca
fly fishing

la pesca en la orilla
surfcasting

la pesca deportiva
sport fishing

la pesca de altura
deep sea fishing

las acciones • activities

lanzar
cast (v)

atrapar (ᶜ**coger**)
catch (v)

recoger
reel in (v)

atrapar (ᶜ**coger**) **con la red**
net (v)

soltar
release (v)

vocabulario • vocabulary

cebar bait (v)	**los aparejos** tackle	**la ropa impermeable** rain clothes	**la licencia de pesca** fishing license	**la nasa** creel
picar bite (v)	**el carrete** spool	**la pértiga** pole	**la pesca en alta mar** marine fishing	**la pesca con arpón** spearfishing

el esquí • skiing

las modalidades • events

el descenso
downhill skiing

el slálom
slalom

el salto
ski jump

el esquí de fondo
cross-country skiing

los deportes de invierno • winter sports

la escalada en hielo
ice climbing

el patinaje sobre hielo
ice skating

el patinaje artístico
figure skating

el snowboarding
snowboarding

el bobsleigh
bobsled

el luge
luge

la moto de nieve
snowmobile

tirarse en trineo
sledding

vocabulario • vocabulary

el esquí alpino
alpine skiing

el slálom gigante
giant slalom

fuera de pista
off-piste

el curling
curling

el trineo con perros
dogsledding

el biatlón
biathlon

la avalancha
avalanche

el patinaje de velocidad
speed skating

los otros deportes • other sports

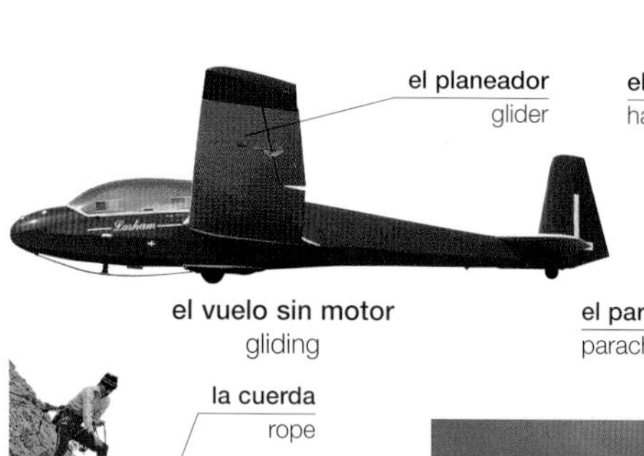

el vuelo sin motor
gliding

el vuelo con ala delta
hang-gliding

la escalada
rock climbing

el paracaidismo
parachuting

el parapente
parasailing

el paracaidismo en caída libre
skydiving

el rappel
abseiling

el salto bungee ([c]el puenting)
bungee jumping

el rally
rally driving

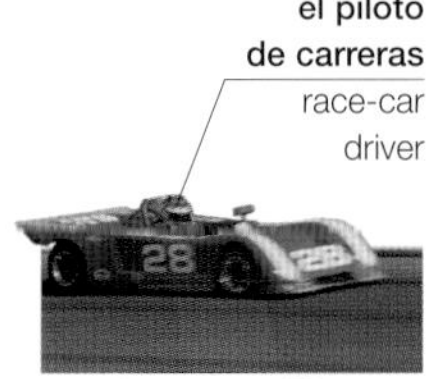

el automovilismo
auto racing

el motocross
motocross

el motociclismo
motorbike racing

andar en patineta (C montar en monopatín)
skateboarding

el patinaje
roller skating

el lacrosse
lacrosse

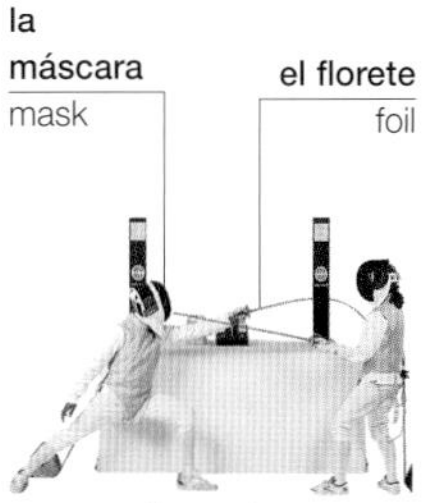

el esgrima
fencing

el boliche (C los bolos)
bowling

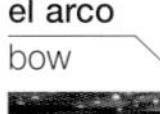

el tiro con arco
archery

el tiro
target shooting

el pool (C el billar americano) | pool

el billar
snooker

la forma física • fitness

la bicicleta
exercise bike

la máquina de ejercicios
gym machine

el banco
bench

las pesas
free weights

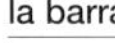

la barra
bar

el gimasio
gym

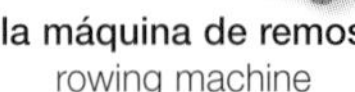

la máquina de remos
rowing machine

la banda caminadora
treadmill

la máquina de cross
elliptical trainer

la entrenadora personal
personal trainer

la máquina de step
step machine

la alberca
(ᶜla piscina)
swimming pool

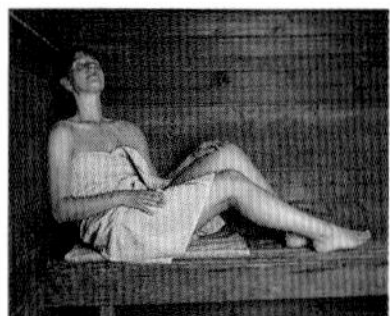

el sauna
sauna

los ejercicios • exercises

el estiramiento
stretch

la flexión con estiramiento
lunge

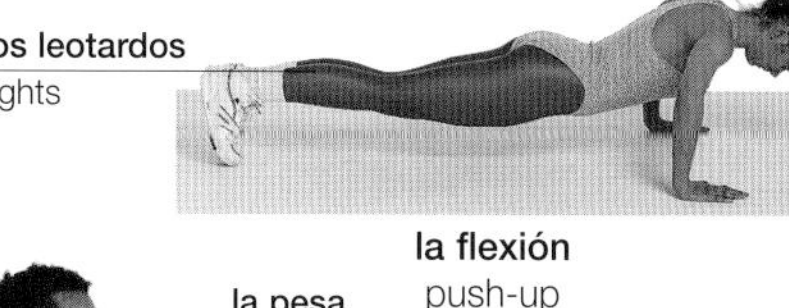

la flexión
push-up

ponerse en cuclillas
squat

el abdominal
sit-up

el ejercicio de bíceps
bicep curl

los ejercicios de piernas
leg press

los ejercicios pectorales
chest press

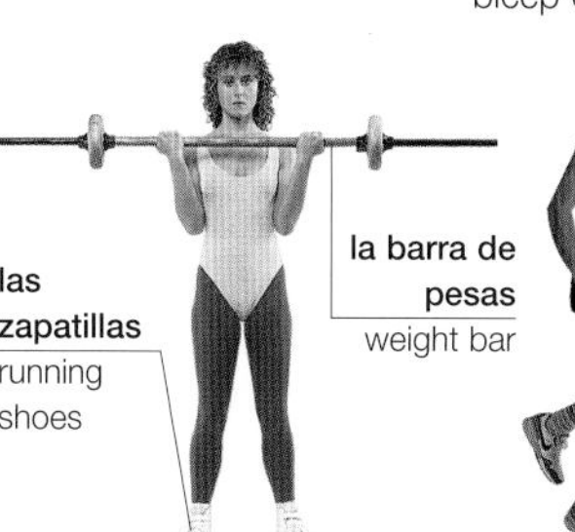

el levantamiento de pesas
weight training

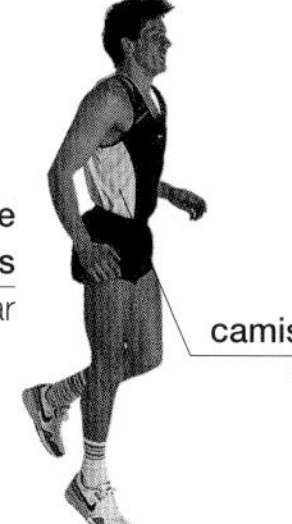

el jogging
(C **el footing**)
jogging

los aerobics
(C **el aerobic**)
aerobics

vocabulario • vocabulary

entrenar train (v)	**correr en parada** jog in place (v)	**estirar** extend (v)	**el pilates** Pilates	**la tabla de gimnasia** circuit training
calentar warm up (v)	**flexionar** flex (v)	**levantar** pull up (v)	**la gimnasia prepugilística** boxercise	**saltar a la comba** jumping rope

el ocio
leisure

el teatro • theater

el escenario | stage

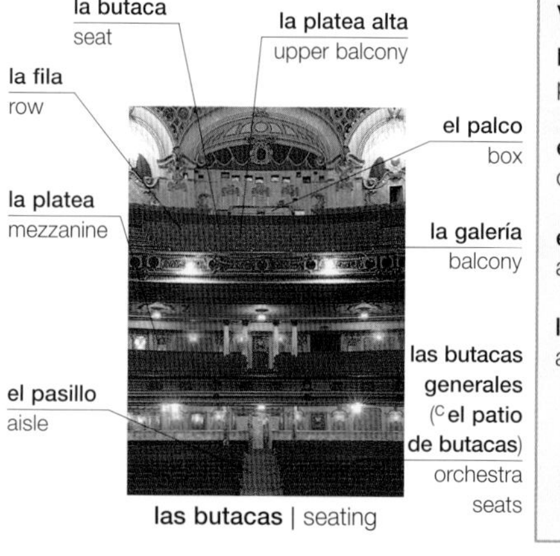

las butacas | seating

vocabulario • vocabulary

la obra
play

el reparto
cast

el actor
actor

la actriz
actress

el director
director

el productor
producer

el guión
script

el telón de fondo
backdrop

el estreno
opening night

el programa
program

el foso de la orquesta
orchestra pit

el entreacto
(C **el descanso**)
intermission

el concierto
concert

el musical
musical

el vestuario (C **el traje**)
costume

el ballet
ballet

la ópera
opera

vocabulario • vocabulary

el acomodador usher	**la banda sonora** soundtrack
la música clásica classical music	**aplaudir** applaud (v)
la partitura musical score	**el bis** encore

Quisiera dos entradas para la sesión de esta noche.
I'd like two tickets for tonight's performance.

¿A qué hora empieza?
What time does it start?

el cine • movies

las palomitas
popcorn

la taquilla
box office

el vestíbulo
lobby

el póster
poster

el cine
movie theater

la pantalla
screen

vocabulario • vocabulary

la comedia comedy	**la película romántica** romance
la película de suspenso thriller	**la película de ciencia ficción** science fiction movie
la película de miedo horror movie	**la película de aventuras** adventure
la película de vaqueros (C **del oeste**) Western	**la película de dibujos animados** animated movie

la orquesta • orchestra

la cuerda • strings

el piano | piano

la notación | notation

vocabulario • vocabulary

la obertura overture	**la sonata** sonata	**la pausa** rest	**sostenido** sharp	**natural** natural	**la escala** scale
la sinfonía symphony	**los instrumentos** instruments	**el tono** pitch	**bemol** flat	**la barra** bar	**la batura** baton

el viento-madera • woodwind

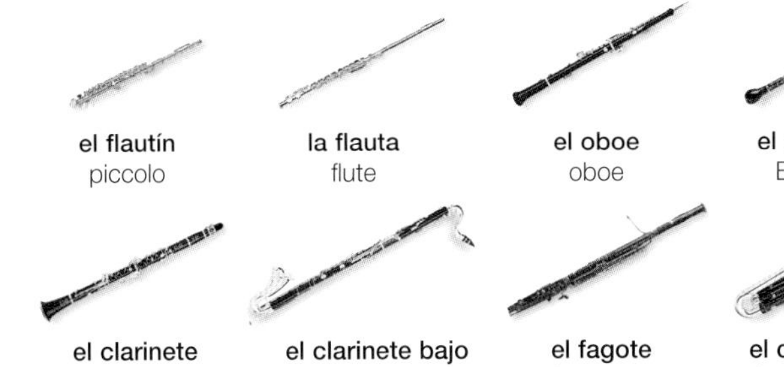

el flautín
piccolo

la flauta
flute

el oboe
oboe

el corno inglés
English horn

el clarinete
clarinet

el clarinete bajo
bass clarinet

el fagote
bassoon

el contrafagote
double bassoon

el saxofón
saxophone

la percusión • percussion

el timbal
kettledrum

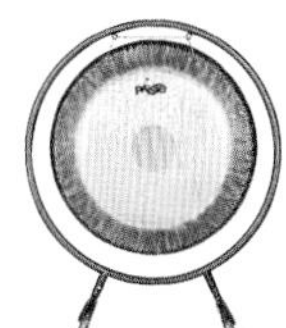

el gong
gong

los bongos
bongos

el tambor pequeño
snare drum

los platillos
cymbals

el pandero
([c]**la pandereta**)
tambourine

la marimba ([c]**el vibráfono**)
vibraphone

el triángulo
triangle

las maracas
maracas

el viento-metal • brass

la trompeta
trumpet

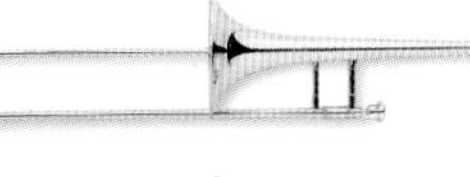

el trombón de varas
trombone

el corno de caza
French horn

la tuba
tuba

el concierto • concert

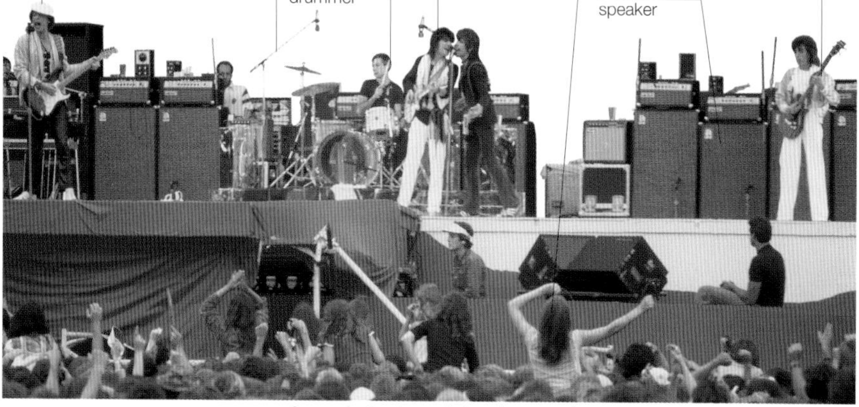

el micrófono
microphone
el vocalista ([C]el cantante)
lead singer
el baterista ([C]el batería)
drummer
el guitarrista
guitarist
los fans
fans
la bocina ([C]el altavoz)
speaker
el bajista ([C]el bajo)
bass guitarist

el concierto de rock | rock concert

los instrumentos • instruments

la pastilla
pickup
el mástil
neck

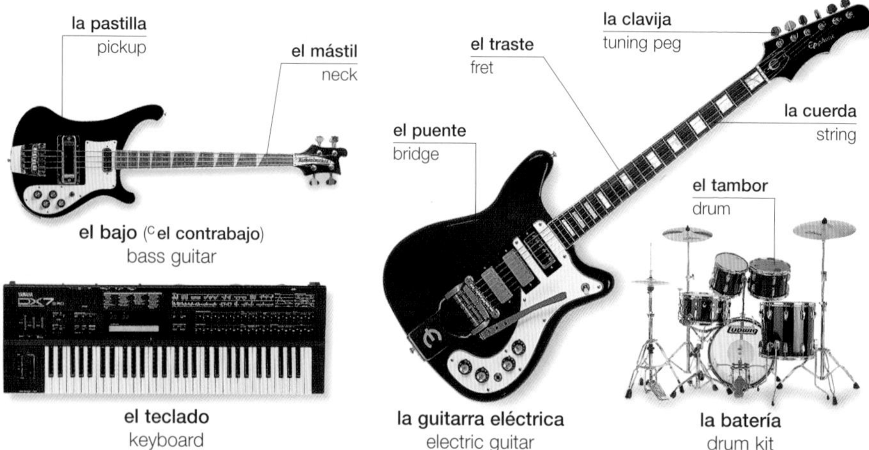

el bajo ([C]**el contrabajo**)
bass guitar

la clavija
tuning peg
el traste
fret
la cuerda
string
el puente
bridge
el tambor
drum

la guitarra eléctrica
electric guitar

el teclado
keyboard

la batería
drum kit

los estilos musicales • musical styles

el jazz
jazz

el blues
blues

el punk
punk

la música folklórica ([c]**folk**)
folk music

el pop
pop

la música de baile
dance

el rap
rap

el heavy metal
heavy metal

la música clásica
classical music

vocabulario • vocabulary

la canción	**la letra**	**la melodía**	**el ritmo**	**el reggae**	**la música country**	**el reflector** ([c]**el foco**)
song	lyrics	melody	beat	reggae	country	spotlight

el turismo • sightseeing

la atracción turística | tourist attraction

el autobús turístico | tour bus

la visita guiada
(C la visita con guía)
guided tour

los recuerdos
souvenirs

vocabulario • vocabulary

el precio de entrada
admission charge

abierto
open

cerrado
closed

la guía del viajero
guidebook

la cámara de vídeo
camcorder

las pilas
batteries

la película
film

la cámara (C la máquina) fotográfica
camera

las indicaciones
directions

la izquierda
left

la derecha
right

recto
straight ahead

¿Dónde está...?
Where is...?

Estoy perdido. (C Me he perdido.)
I'm lost.

¿Podría decirme cómo se va a...?
Can you tell me the way to....?

los lugares de interés • attractions

el cuadro
painting

la muestra
exhibit

la galería de arte
(ᶜel museo de arte)
art gallery

el monumento
monument

la exposición
exhibition

el museo
museum

la ruina famosa
famous ruin

el edificio histórico
historic building

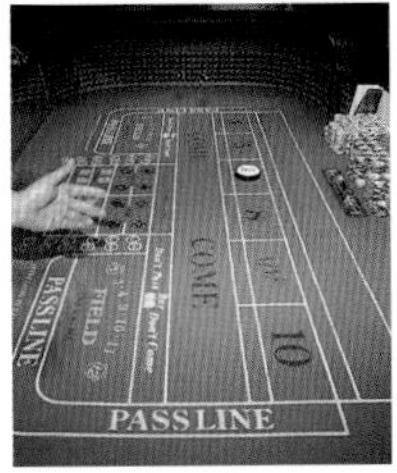

el casino
casino

los jardines
garden

el parque nacional
national park

la información • information

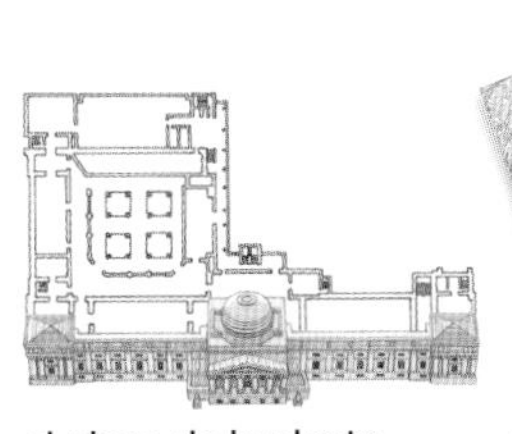

el plano de la planta
floor plan

el mapa (ᶜel plano)
map

las horas
times

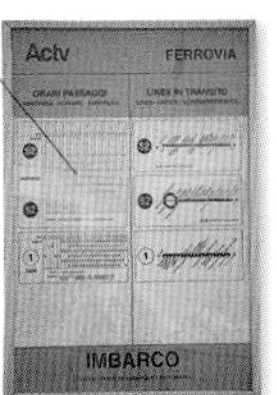

el horario
timetable

la oficina de
información
tourist information

las actividades al aire libre • outdoor activities

el sendero
footpath

el reloj de sol
sundial

la cafetería
café

el parque | park

el pasto ([C]la hierba)
grass

la banca ([C]el banco)
bench

los jardines clásicos
formal gardens

la montaña rusa
roller coaster

la feria
fair

el parque de diversiones ([C]el parque de atracciones)
amusement park

el safari park
wildlife park

el zoológico ([C]el zoo)
zoo

las actividades • activities

el ciclismo
cycling

el jogging
jogging

la patineta
(^c **montar en patinete**)
skateboarding

el patinaje
rollerblading

el sendero para caballos
riding trail

la ornitología
bird watching

la equitación
horseback riding

la caminata
(^c **el senderismo**)
hiking

la canasta
(^c **la cesta**)
hamper

el picnic
picnic

el área de juegos • playground

el cajón de arena
sandbox

la alberca (^c **la piscina**)
de plástico
wading pool

los columpios
swing

el changuero
(^c **la estructura para escalar**)
climber

la resbaladilla (^c **el tobogán**)
slide

el subibaja | seesaw

la playa • beach

asolear (ᶜ**tomar el sol**) | sunbathe (v)

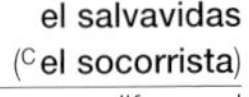

el salvavidas ([C]el socorrista)
lifeguard

la torre de vigilancia
lifeguard tower

la barrera contra el viento
windbreak

el paseo marítimo
promenade

el asoleadero ([C]la hamaca)
deck chair

los lentes obscuros ([C]las gafas de sol)
sunglasses

el sombrero para el sol
sunhat

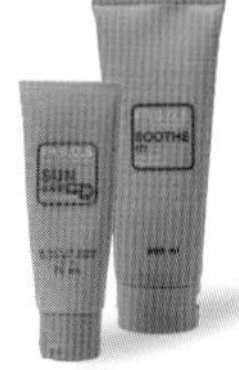

el bronceador ([C]la crema bronceadora)
suntan lotion

la crema protector ([C]la crema protectora)
sunblock

la pelota de playa
beach ball

la llanta ([C]el flotador)
rubber ring

el traje de baño ([C]el bañador)
swimsuit

la pala
shovel

la cubeta ([C]el cubo)
pail

el castillo de arena
sandcastle

la concha
shell

la toalla de playa
beach towel

el camping • camping

vocabulario • vocabulary

acampar
camp (v)

la oficina del director
manager's office

hay lugares (C **plazas**) **libres**
sites available

lleno (C **completo**)
full

el lugar (C **la plaza**)
site

el catre de campaña
cot

poner (C **montar**) **una tienda**
pitch a tent (v)

el tubo (C **el palo**) **de la tienda**
tent pole

la mesa de picnic
picnic bench

la hamaca
hammock

el cámper
camper van

el remolque
trailer

el carbón vegetal
charcoal

la hoguera
campfire

la pastilla para fogatas
firelighter

encender una fogata
light a fire (v)

la estructura
frame
el suelo aislante
ground cloth
la mochila
backpack
el termo
thermos
la cantimplora
water bottle
la tienda de campaña
tent
el mosquitero
mosquito net
el repelente de insectos
insect repellent
la linterna
flashlight
la ropa térmica
(C termoaislante)
thermal underwear
las botas de trekking
hiking boots
la manga
(C la ropa impermeable)
rain clothes
el saco de dormir
sleeping bag
la esterilla
sleeping mat
la estufilla (C el hornillo)
camp stove
la parrilla (C la barbacoa)
grill
la colchoneta | air mattress

el entretenimiento (ᶜel ocio) en el hogar • home entertainment

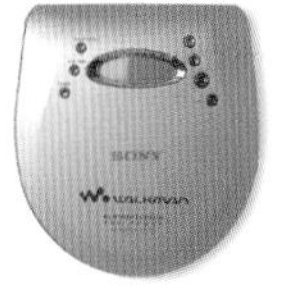

el discman
personal CD player

la grabadora de minidisks
mini disc recorder

el lector de MP3
MP3 player

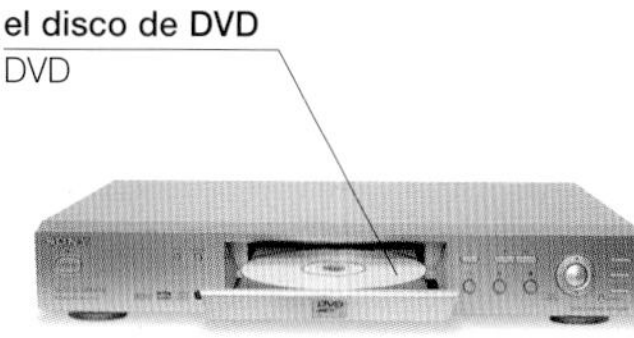

el disco de DVD
DVD

el reproductor de DVD
DVD player

el tocadiscos
record player

el lector de discos compactos
CD player

la radio
radio

el amplificador
amplifier

los audífonos (ᶜlos auriculares)
headphones

el mueble
stereo rack

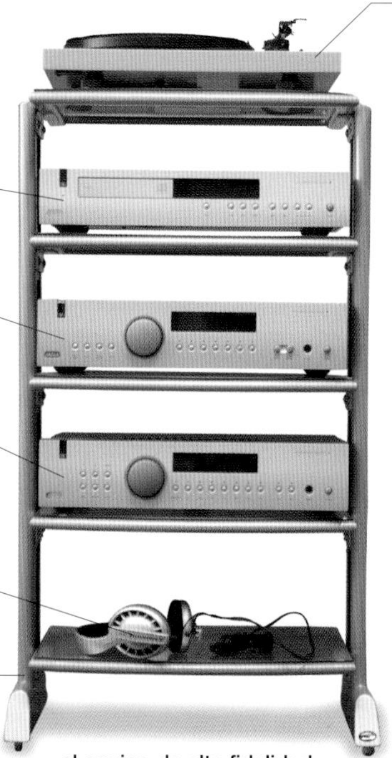

la bocina (ᶜel altavoz)
speaker

el pie de la bocina (ᶜel pie del altavoz)
speaker stand

el equipo de alta fidelidad
stereo system

vocabulario • vocabulary

el disco compacto CD	**la película** (C **el largometraje**) feature film	**la televisión por cable** cable television	**el canal de pago por evento** pay-per-view channel	**apagar la televisión** turn off the television (v)
el casete cassette tape	**el anuncio** advertisement	**el programa** programme	**ver la televisión** watch television (v)	**sintonizar la radio** tune the radio (v)
la casetera (C **el magnetofón**) cassette player	**digital** digital	**cambiar de canal** change channels (v)	**encender la televisión** turn on the television (v)	**estéreo** stereo

la fotografía • photography

el indicador de fotos
frame counter

el flash
flash

el obturador (C la rueda del diafragma)
aperture dial

el filtro
filter

el disparador
shutter release

la tapa del lente (C objetivo)
lens cap

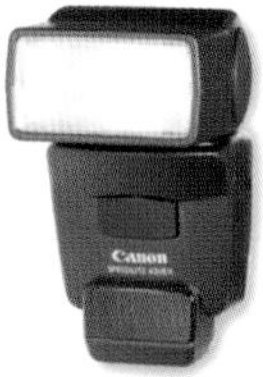

la rueda de la velocidad
shutter-speed dial

el lente (C el objetivo)
lens

la cámara réflex | SLR camera

el flash electrónico
flash gun

el fotómetro
light meter

el zoom (C el teleobjetivo)
zoom lens

el tripié (C el trípode)
tripod

los tipos de cámara • types of camera

la cámara digital
digital camera

la cámara APS
APS camera

la cámara Polaroid
instant camera

la cámara desechable
disposable camera

fotografiar • photograph (v)

el carrete
film spool

la pellicola
(**[c]la película**)
film

enfocar
focus (v)

revelar
develop (v)

el negativo
negative

apaisado
landscape

en formato vertical
portrait

la fotografía | photograph

el álbum de fotos
photo album

el portarretratos
picture frame

los problemas • problems

subexpuesto
underexposed

sobreexpuesto
overexposed

desenfocado
out of focus

los ojos rojos
red eye

vocabulario • vocabulary

el visor
viewfinder

la funda de la cámara
camera case

la exposición
exposure

el cuarto oscuro
darkroom

la foto (revelada)
print

mate
mat

con brillo
gloss

la ampliación
enlargement

Me gustaría revelar este rollo.
I'd like this film processed.

los juegos • games

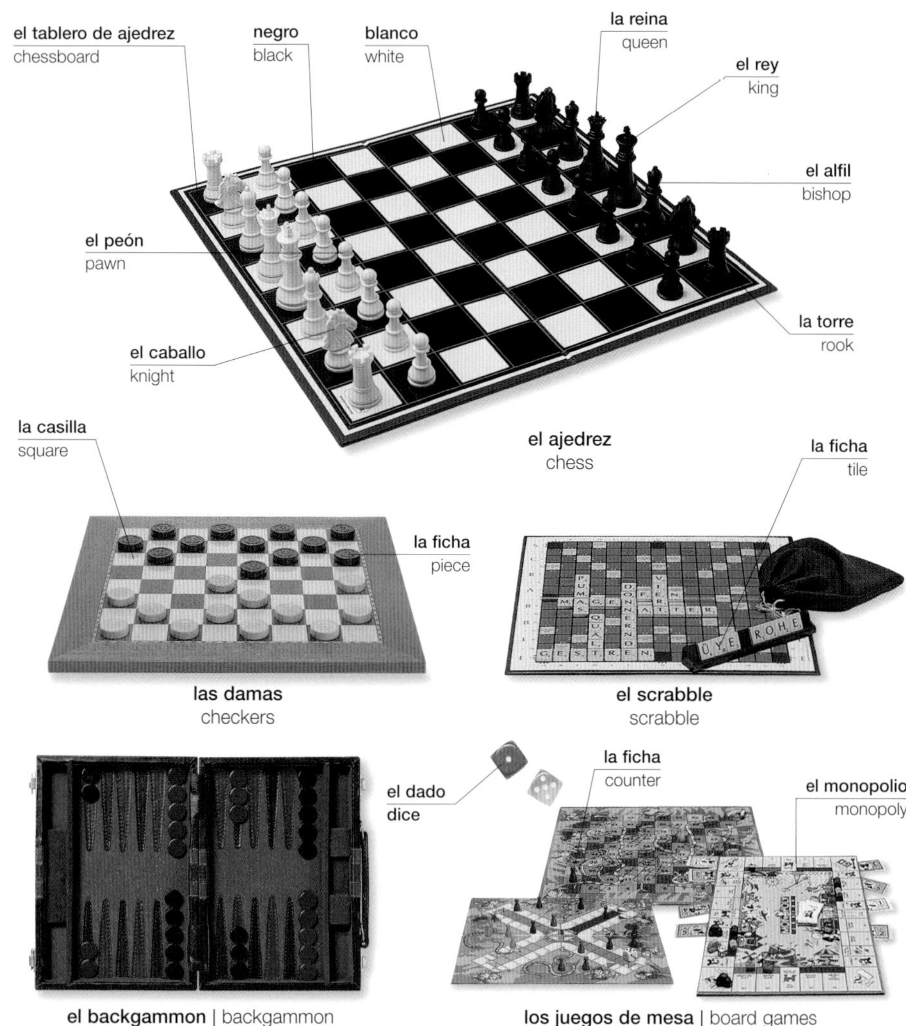

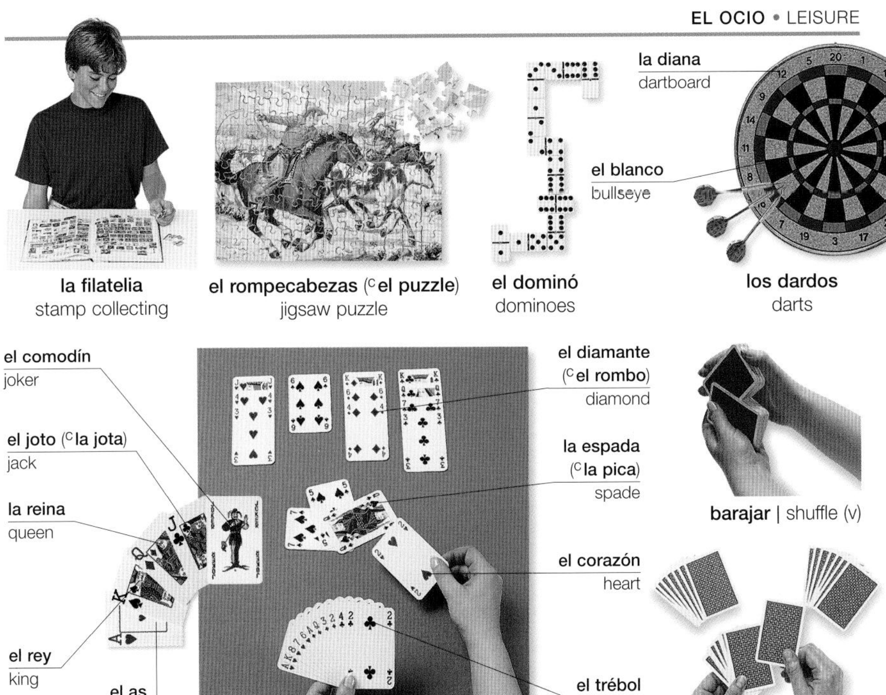

la filatelia
stamp collecting

el rompecabezas (C **el puzzle**)
jigsaw puzzle

el dominó
dominoes

los dardos
darts

las cartas
cards

barajar | shuffle (v)

repartir (C **dar**) | deal (v)

vocabulario • vocabulary

el turno move	**ganar** win (v)	**el perdedor** loser	**el punto** point	**el bridge** bridge
jugar play (v)	**el ganador** winner	**la partida** game	**la puntuación** score	**la baraja** deck of cards
el jugador player	**perder** lose (v)	**la apuesta** bet	**el póquer** poker	**el palo** suit

¿A quién le toca?
Whose turn is it?

Te toca a ti.
It's your move.

Tira los dados.
Roll the dice.

las manualidades 1 • arts and crafts 1

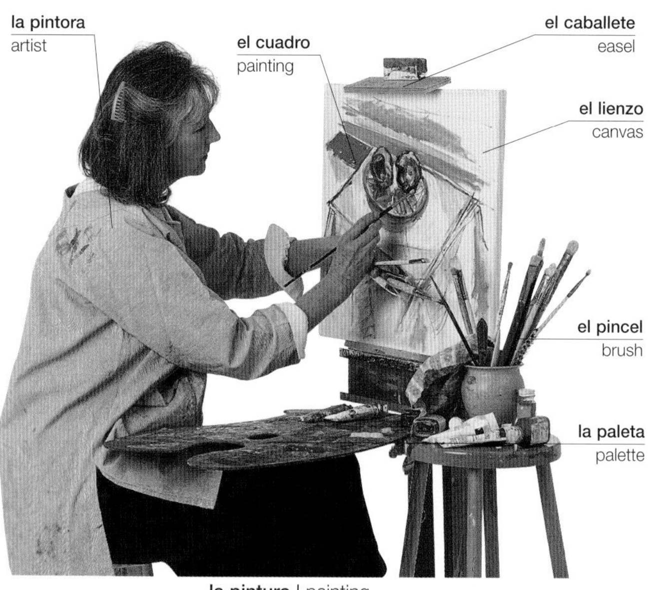

la pintura | painting

los colores • colors

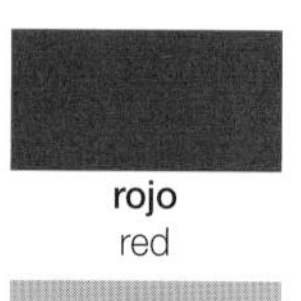

rojo
red

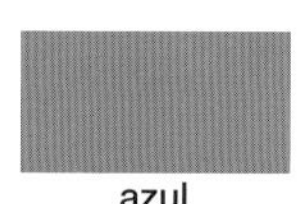

azul
blue

amarillo
yellow

verde
green

naranja
orange

morado
purple

blanco
white

negro
black

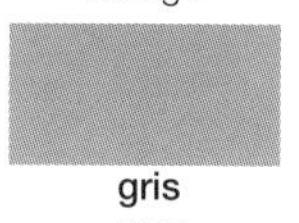

gris
gray

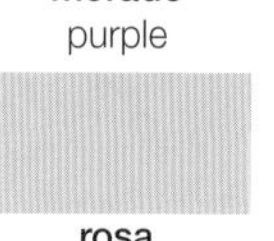

rosa
pink

marrón
brown

azul añil
indigo

las pinturas • paints

las pinturas al óleo
oil paints

las acuarelas
watercolors

los pasteles
pastels

la pintura acrílica
acrylic paint

la témpera
poster paint

las otras manualidades • other crafts

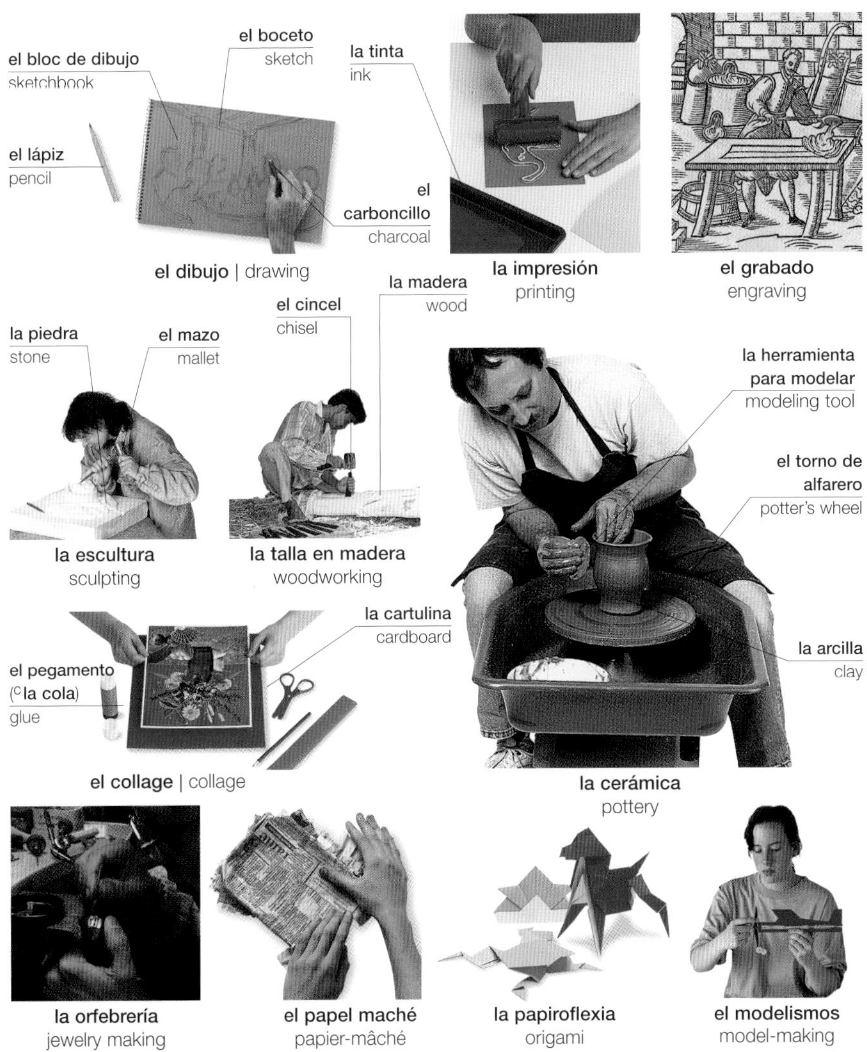

el dibujo | drawing

la impresión
printing

el grabado
engraving

la escultura
sculpting

la talla en madera
woodworking

el collage | collage

la cerámica
pottery

la orfebrería
jewelry making

el papel maché
papier-mâché

la papiroflexia
origami

el modelismos
model-making

las manualidades 2 • arts and crafts 2

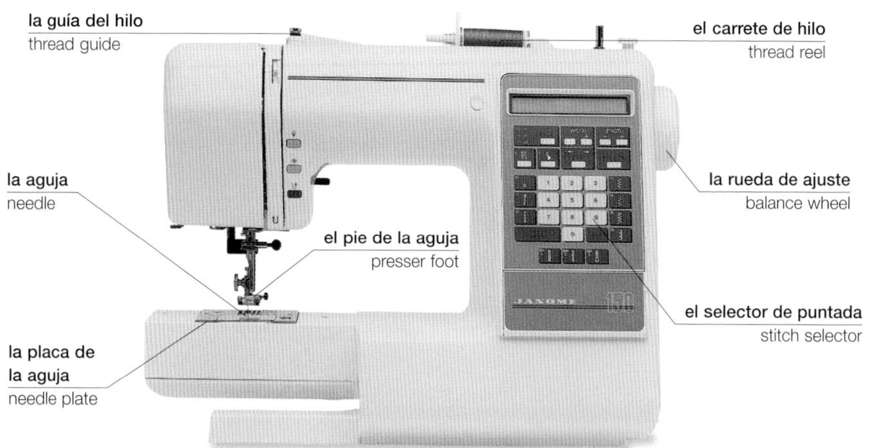

la máquina de coser | sewing machine

las tijeras
scissors

el patrón
pattern

la cinta métrica
tape measure

la tela
material

el alfiletero
pincushion

el alfiler
pin

el costurero | sewing basket

el hilo
thread

la hembra (**[C]el ojo**)
eye

la bobina
bobbin

el macho (**[C]el corchete**)
hook

el dedal
thimble

el jaboncillo
tailor's chalk

el maniquí
tailor's dummy

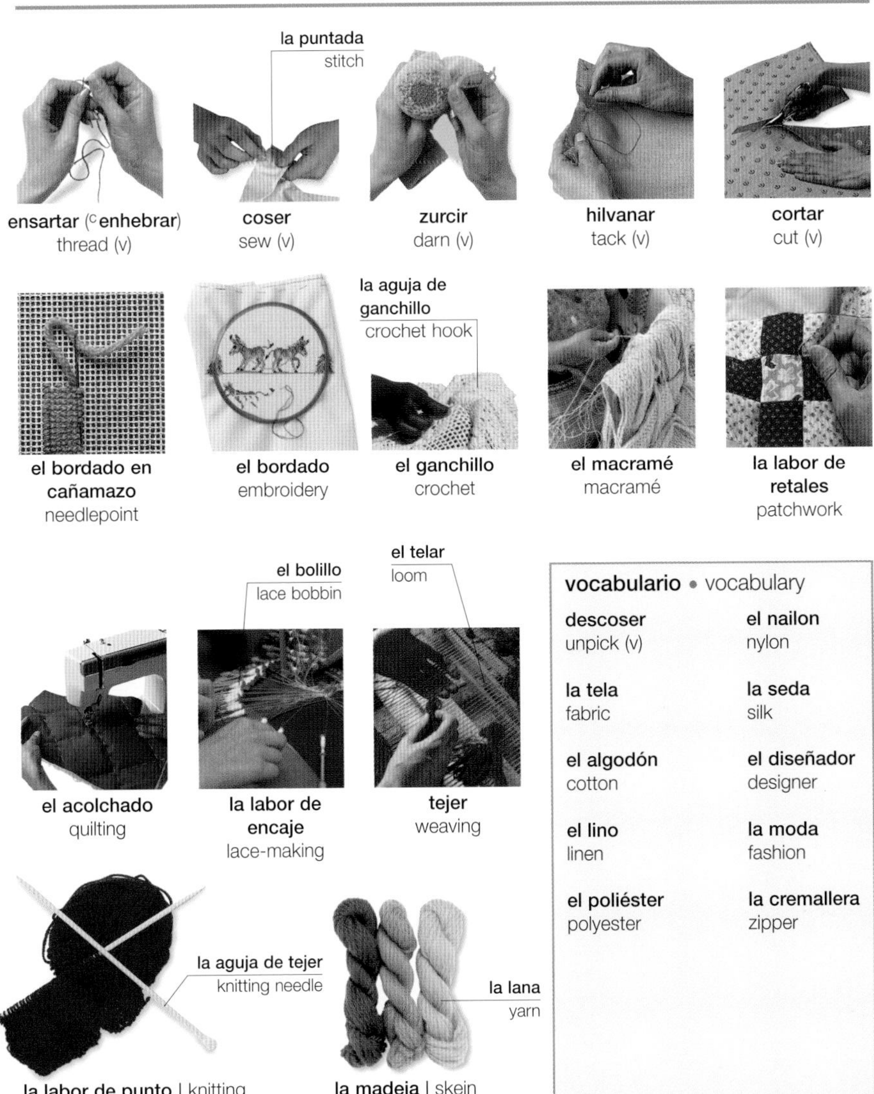

vocabulario • vocabulary

descoser unpick (v)	**el nailon** nylon
la tela fabric	**la seda** silk
el algodón cotton	**el diseñador** designer
el lino linen	**la moda** fashion
el poliéster polyester	**la cremallera** zipper

el medio ambiente
environment

el espacio • space

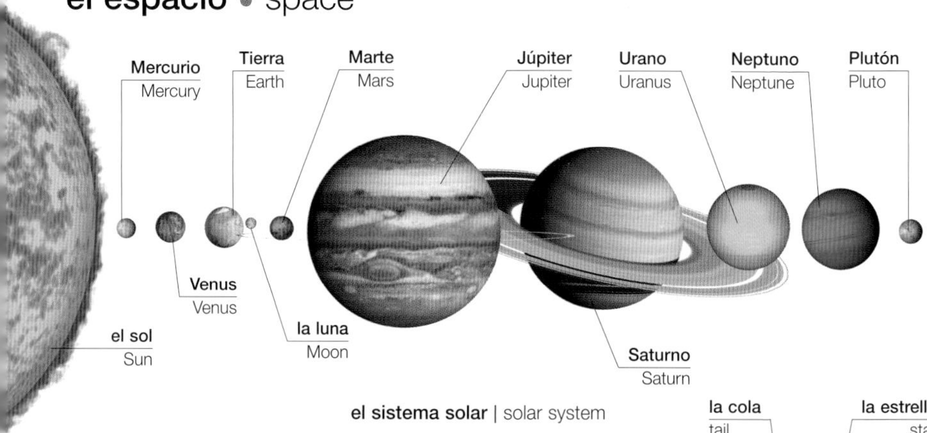

el sol
Sun

Mercurio
Mercury

Venus
Venus

Tierra
Earth

la luna
Moon

Marte
Mars

Júpiter
Jupiter

Saturno
Saturn

Urano
Uranus

Neptuno
Neptune

Plutón
Pluto

el sistema solar | solar system

la galaxia
galaxy

la nebulosa
nebula

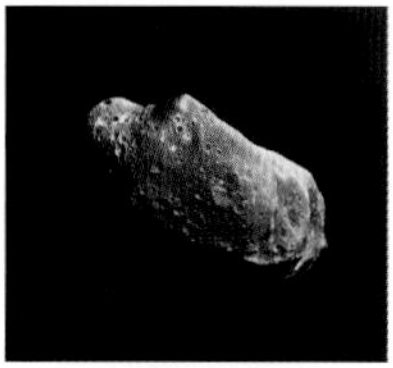

el asteroide
asteroid

la cola
tail

la estrella
star

el cometa
comet

vocabulario • vocabulary

el universo
universe

la órbita
orbit

la gravedad
gravity

el agujero negro
black hole

el planeta
planet

el meteorito
meteor

la luna llena
full moon

la luna nueva
new moon

la media luna
crescent moon

el eclipse | eclipse

la exploración espacial • space exploration

el radar
radar

el propulsor
thruster

la escotilla
crew hatch

el transbordador espacial
space shuttle

el traje espacial
space suit

el lanzacohetes
booster

el astronauta | astronaut

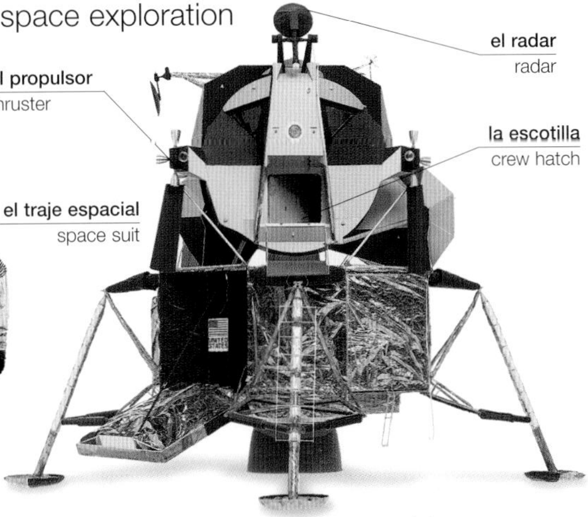

el módulo lunar | lunar module

la rampa de lanzamiento
launch pad

el lanzamiento
launch

el satélite
satellite

la estación espacial
space station

la astronomía • astronomy

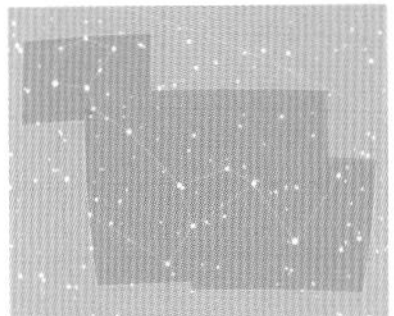

la constelación
constellation

los prismáticos
binoculars

el telescopio
telescope

el trípode
tripod

la Tierra • Earth

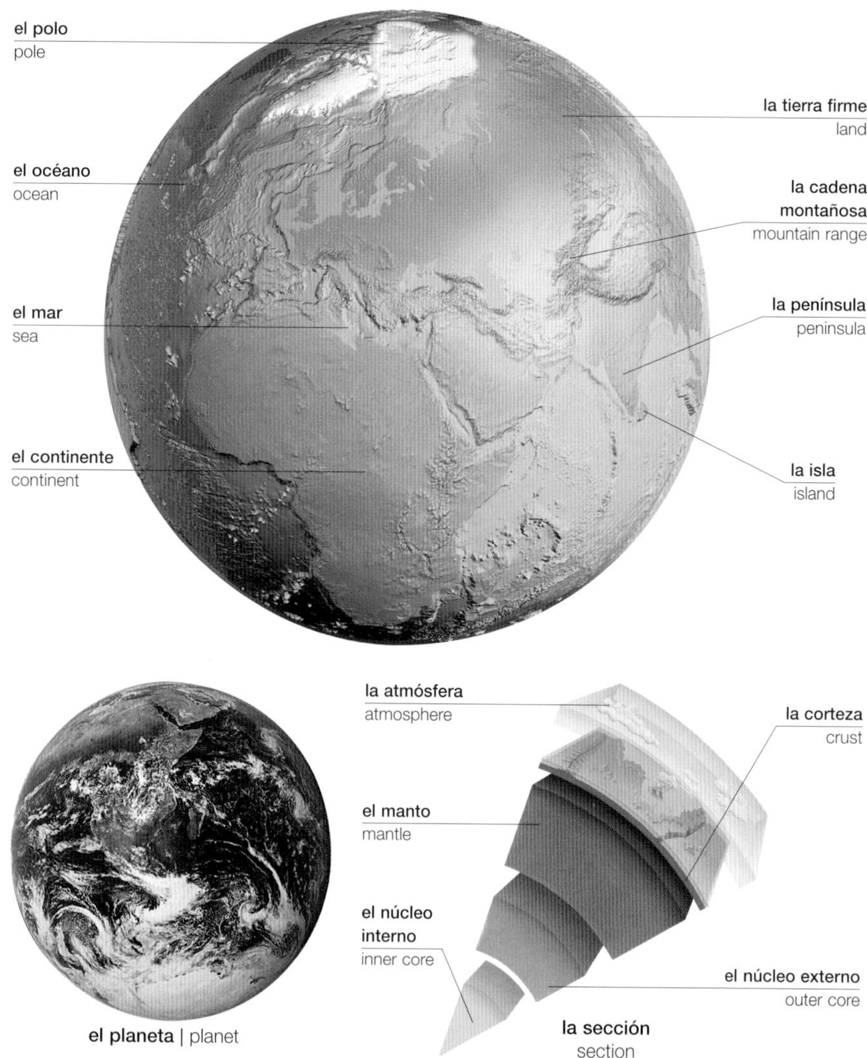

el planeta | planet

la sección
section

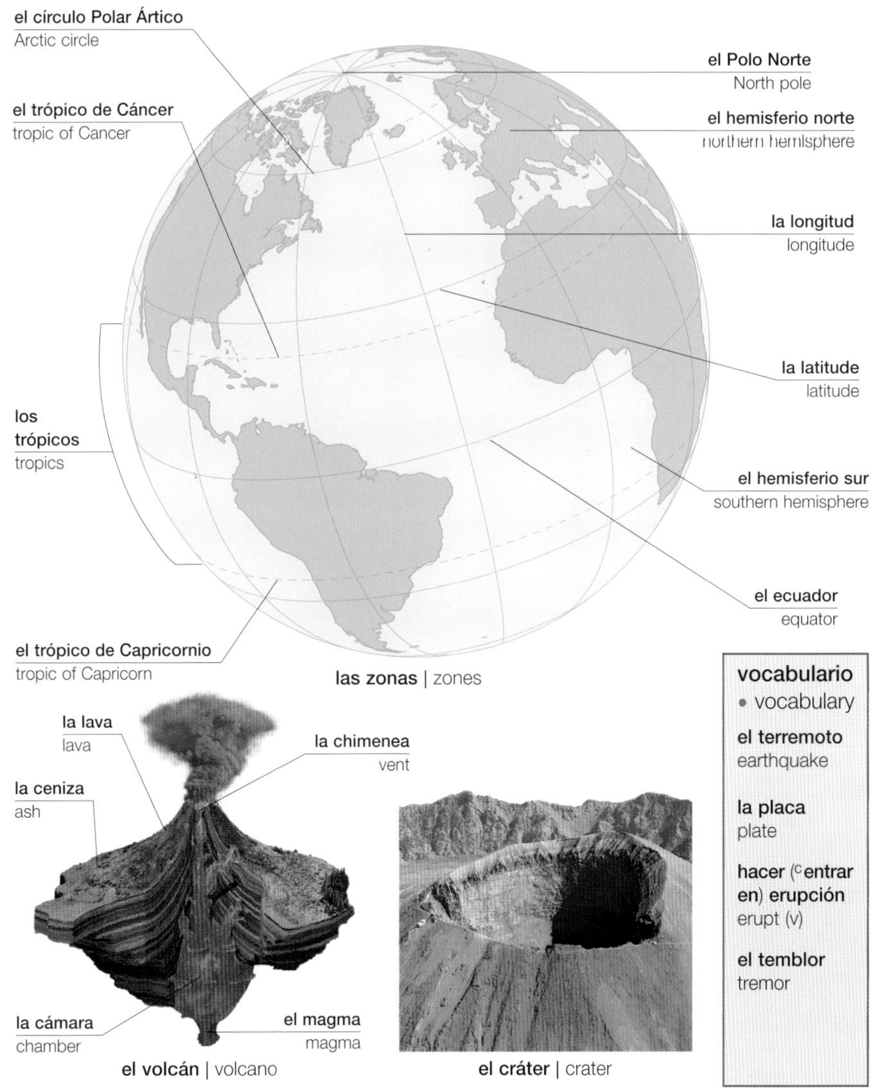

las zonas | zones

el volcán | volcano

el cráter | crater

vocabulario • vocabulary

el terremoto
earthquake

la placa
plate

hacer ([c]**entrar en) erupción**
erupt (v)

el temblor
tremor

el paisaje • landscape

la llanura | plain

el desierto | desert

el bosque | forest

el bosque | wood

la selva tropical
rain forest

el pantano
swamp

el prado
meadow

la pradera
grassland

la cascada
waterfall

el arroyo
stream

el lago
lake

el géiser
geyser

la costa
coast

el acantilado
cliff

el arrecife de coral
coral reef

el estuario
estuary

el tiempo • weather

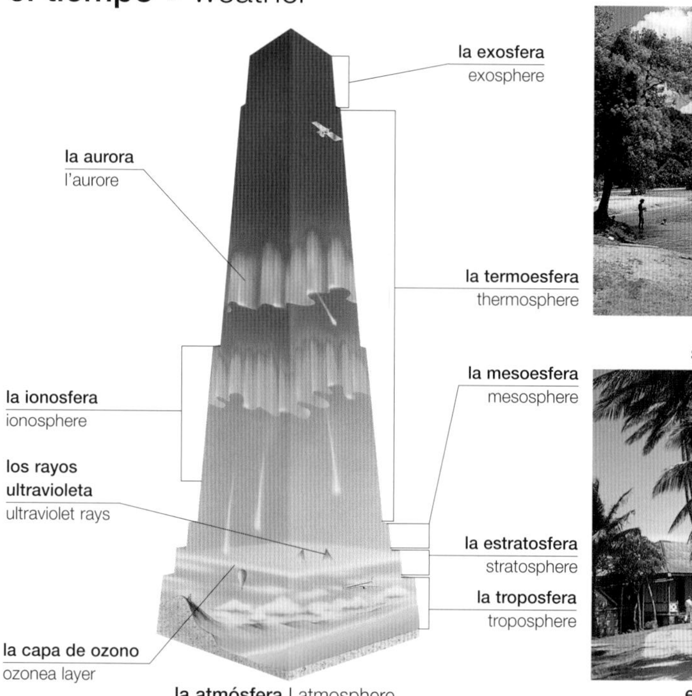

la atmósfera | atmosphere

el sol
sunshine

el viento
wind

vocabulario • vocabulary

el aguanieve sleet	**el chubasco** shower	**caluroso** hot	**seco** dry	**ventoso** windy	**Tengo calor/frío.** I'm hot/cold.
el granizo hail	**soleado** sunny	**frío** cold	**lluvioso** wet	**el temporal** gale	**Está lloviendo.** It's raining.
el trueno thunder	**nublado** cloudy	**cálido** warm	**húmedo** humid	**la température** temperature	**Estamos a … grados.** It's … degrees.

la nube
cloud

la lluvia
rain

la tormenta
storm

la neblina
mist

la niebla
fog

el arcoiris
rainbow

la nieve
snow

la escarcha
frost

el hielo
ice

la helada
freeze

el huracán
hurricane

el tornado
tornado

el monzón
monsoon

la inundación
flood

las rocas • rocks

ígneo • igneous

el granito
granite

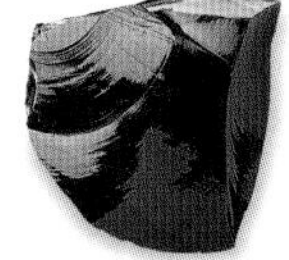

la obsidiana
obsidian

el basalto
basalt

la piedra pómez
pumice

sedimentario • sedimentary

la piedra arenisca
sandstone

la piedra caliza
limestone

la tiza
chalk

el pedernal
flint

el conglomerado
conglomerate

el carbón
coal

metamórfico • metamorphic

la pizarra
slate

el esquisto
schist

el gneis
gneiss

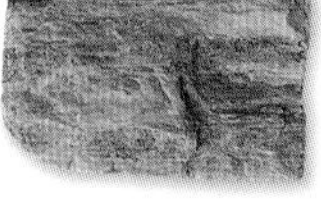

el mármol
marble

las gemas • gems

el rubí
ruby

la aguamarina
aquamarine

la amatista
amethyst

el diamante
diamond

el jade
jade

el azabache
jet

la esmeralda
emerald

el ópalo
opal

el zafiro
sapphire

la adularia (C **la piedra lunar**)
moonstone

el granate
garnet

el topacio
topaz

la turmalina
tourmaline

los minerales • minerals

el cuarzo
quartz

la mica
mica

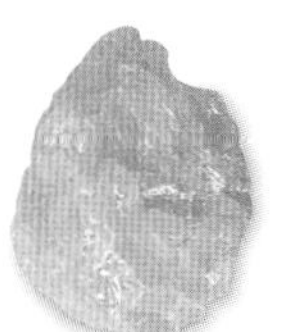
el azufre
sulfur

la hematita
(ᶜ**el hematites**)
hematite

la calcita
calcite

la malaquita
malachite

la turquesa
turquoise

el ónix (ᶜ**el ónice**)
onyx

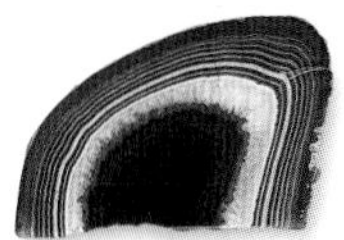
el ágata
agate

el grafito
graphite

los metales • metals

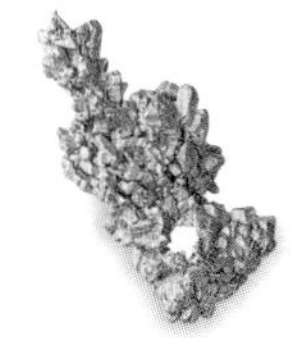
el oro
gold

la plata
silver

el platino
platinum

el níquel
nickel

el hierro
iron

el cobre
copper

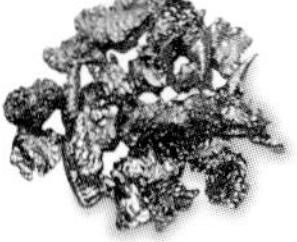
el estaño
tin

el aluminio
aluminum

el mercurio
mercury

el zinc
zinc

los animales 1 • animals 1

los mamíferos • mammals

los bigotes
whiskers

la cola
tail

el conejo
rabbit

el hámster
hamster

el ratón
mouse

la rata
rat

el erizo
hedgehog

la ardilla
squirrel

el murciélago
bat

el mapache
raccoon

el zorro
fox

el lobo
wolf

el cachorro
puppy

el gatito
kitten

la cría
pup

el perro
dog

el gato
cat

la nutria
otter

la foca
seal

la aleta
flipper

el orificio nasal
blowhole

el león marino
sea lion

la morsa
walrus

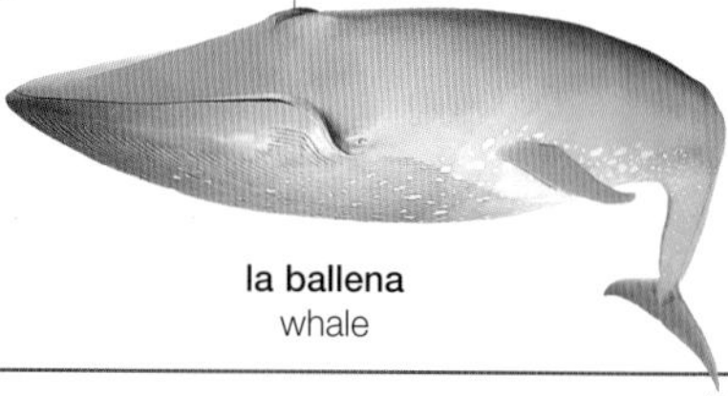

la ballena
whale

el delfín
dolphin

el asta
antler
la crin
mane
la pezuña
hoof
la joroba
(C la giba)
hump
el ciervo
deer
la cebra
zebra
la jirafa
giraffe
el camello
camel
la trompa
trunk
el colmillo
tusk
el cuerno
horn
el hipopótamo
hippopotamus
el elefante
elephant
el rinoceronte
rhinoceros
el tigre
tiger
la melena
mane
el león
lion
el chango (C el mono)
monkey
el gorila
gorilla
el koala
koala
la bolsa
pouch
el oso panda
panda
la zarpa
claw
el canguro
kangaroo
el oso
bear
el oso polar
polar bear

los animales 2 • animals 2

las aves • birds

el canario
canary

el gorrión
sparrow

el colibrí
hummingbird

la golondrina
swallow

el cuervo
crow

la paloma
pigeon

el pájaro carpintero
woodpecker

el halcón
falcon

el búho
owl

la gaviota
gull

el águila
eagle

el pelícano
pelican

el flamenco
flamingo

la cigüeña
stork

la grulla
crane

el pingüino
penguin

el avestruz
ostrich

los reptiles • reptiles

los animales 3 • animals 3

los anfibios • amphibians

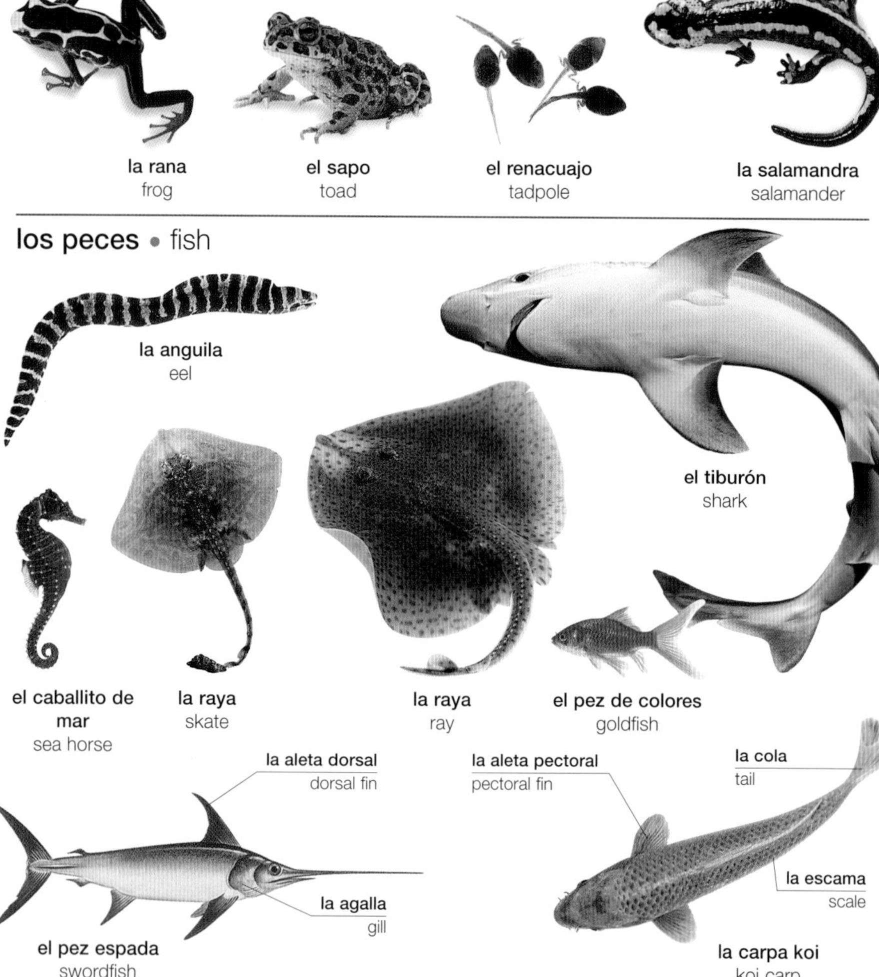

los invertebrados • invertebrates

la hormiga
ant

la termita
termite

la abeja
bee

la avispa
wasp

el escarabajo
beetle

la cucaracha
cockroach

la polilla
moth

la mariposa
butterfly

el capullo
cocoon

la oruga
caterpillar

el grillo
cricket

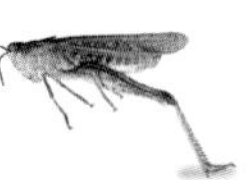
el saltamontes
grasshopper

la mantis religiosa
praying mantis

el alacrán
([C]**el escorpión**)
scorpion

el ciempiés
centipede

la libélula
dragonfly

la mosca
fly

el mosquito
mosquito

la catarina
([C]**la mariquita**)
ladybug

la araña
spider

la babosa
slug

el caracol
snail

el gusano
worm

la estrella de mar
starfish

el mejillón
mussel

el cangrejo
crab

la langosta
lobster

el pulpo
octopus

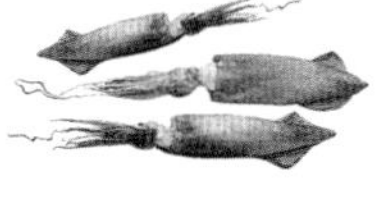
el calamar
squid

la medusa
jellyfish

las plantas • plants

el árbol • tree

la planta de flor • flowering plant

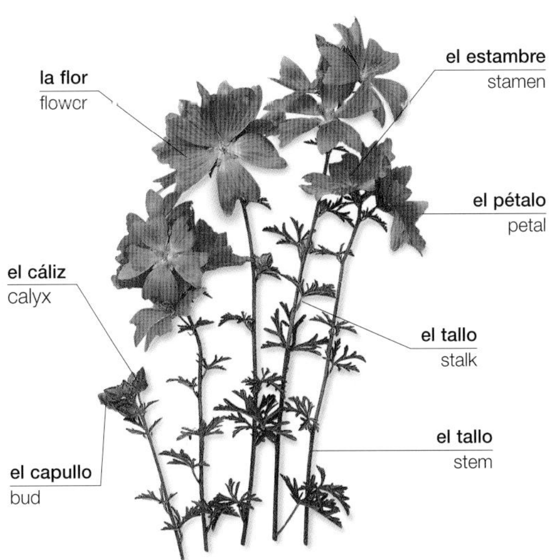

el ranúnculo
buttercup

la margarita
daisy

el cardo
thistle

el diente de león
dandelion

el brezo
heather

la amapola
poppy

la dedalera
foxglove

la madreselva
honeysuckle

el girasol
sunflower

el trébol
clover

los narcisos silvestres
bluebells

la prímula
primrose

el lupino
lupins

la ortiga
nettle

la ciudad • town

los edificios • buildings

el palacio municipal
town hall

la biblioteca
library

el cine
movie theater

el teatro
theater

la universidad
university

el rascacielos
skyscraper

la escuela
school

las zonas • areas

la zona industrial
industrial park

la ciudad
city

el suburbio
([c]**la periferia**)
suburb

el pueblo
village

vocabulario • vocabulary

la zona peatonal
pedestrian zone

la avenida
avenue

la calle lateral
side street

la plaza
square

la parada de autobús
bus stop

la coladera ([c]**la boca de alcantarilla**)
manhole

la alcantarilla
gutter

la fábrica
factory

la iglesia
church

el drenaje
([c]**el sumidero**)
drain

la arquitectura • architecture

los edificios y las estructuras • buildings and structures

el rascacielos
skyscraper

el castillo
castle

la iglesia
church

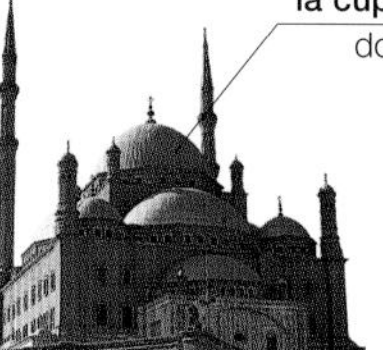

la mezquita
mosque

el templo
temple

la sinagoga
synagogue

el embalse
dam

el puente
bridge

la catedral | cathedral

los estilos • styles

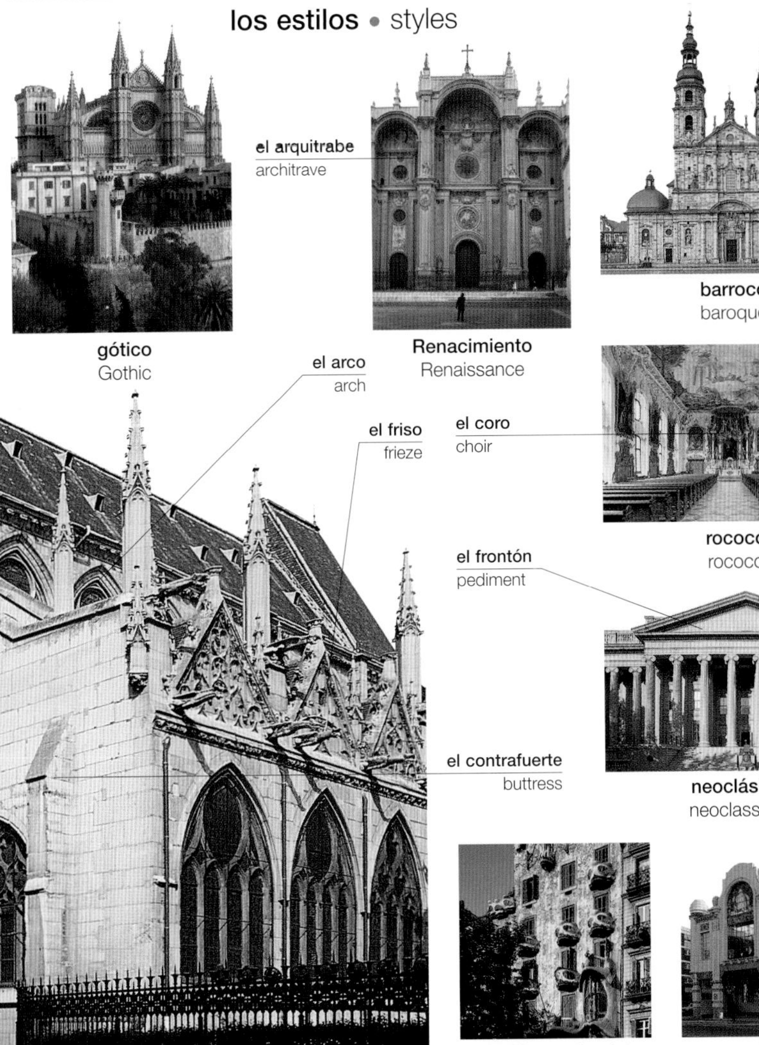

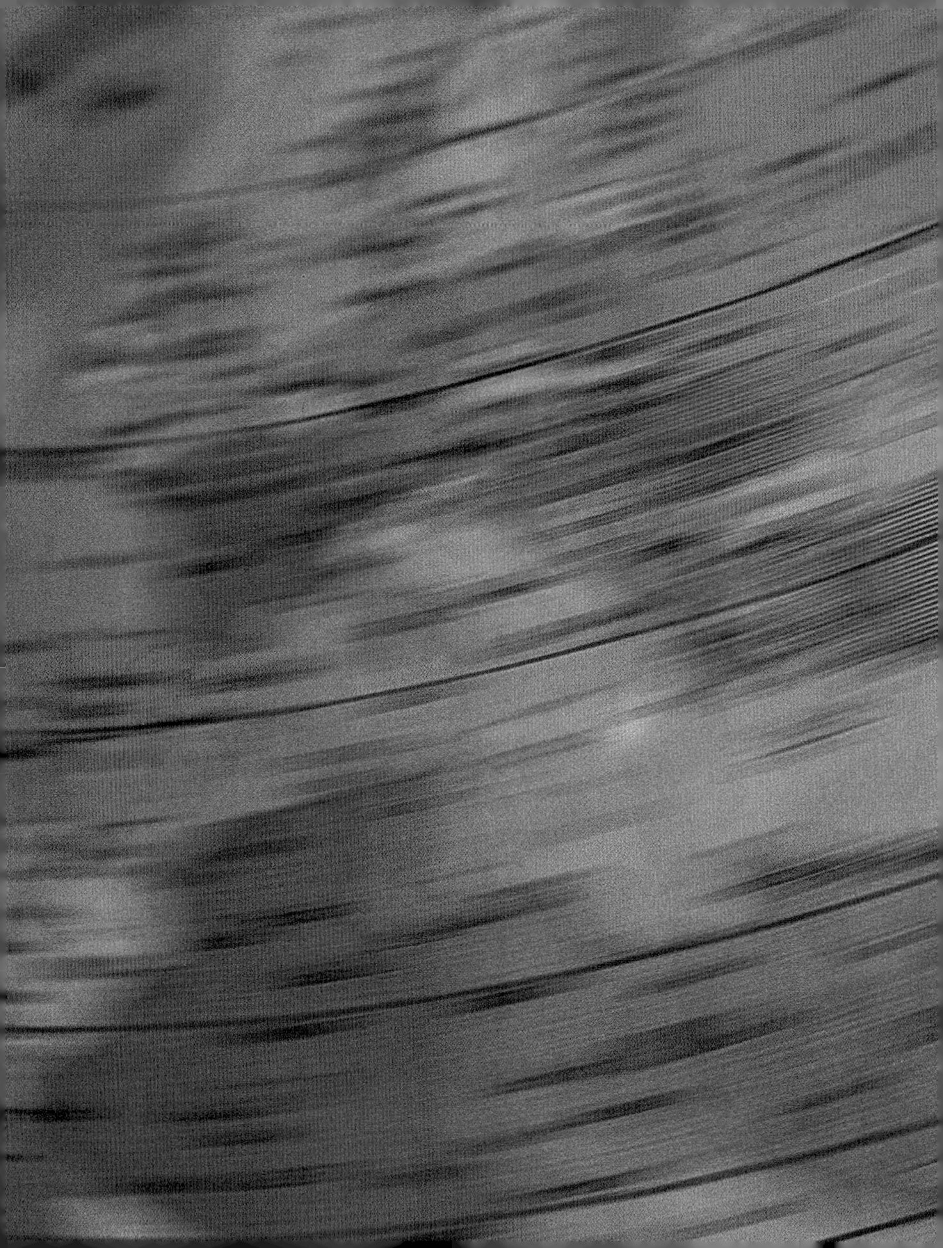

los datos
reference

el tiempo • time

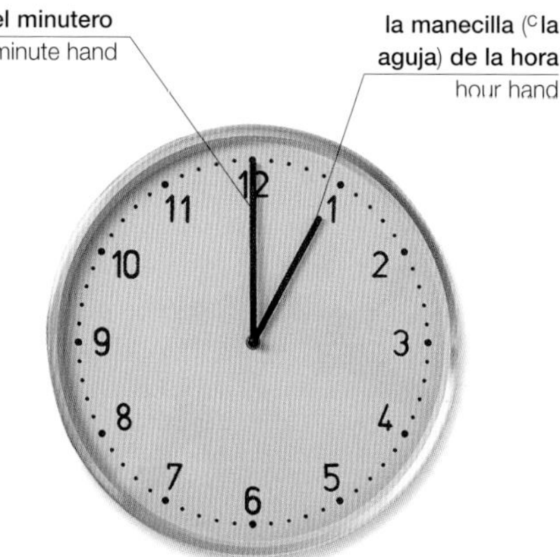

el reloj
clock

vocabulario • vocabulary

el segundo
second

el minuto
minute

la hora
hour

ahora
now

más tarde
later

media hora
half an hour

un cuarto de hora
a quarter of an hour

veinte minutos
twenty minutes

cuarenta minutos
forty minutes

¿Qué hora es?
What time is it?

Son las tres en punto.
It's three o'clock.

la una y cinco
five after one

la una y diez
ten after one

la una y cuarto
quarter after one

la una y veinte
twenty after one

la una y veinticinco
twenty-five after one

la una y media
one-thirty

las veinticinco para las dos (ᶜ**las dos menos veinticinco**)
twenty-five to two

las veinte para las dos (ᶜ**las dos menos veinte**)
twenty to two

el cuarto para las dos (ᶜ**las dos menos cuarto**)
quarter to two

las diez para las dos (ᶜ**las dos menos diez**)
ten to two

las cinco para las dos (ᶜ**las dos menos cinco**)
five to two

las dos en punto
two o'clock

la noche y el día • night and day

la medianoche
midnight

el amanecer
sunrise

el alba
dawn

la mañana
morning

el atardecer
(C**la puesta de sol**)
sunset

el mediodía
noon

el anochecer
dusk

la noche
evening

la tarde
afternoon

vocabulario • vocabulary

temprano
early

puntual
on time

tarde
late

Llegas temprano.
You're early.

Llegas tarde.
You're late.

Llegaré dentro de poco.
I'll be there soon.

Por favor, sé puntual.
Please be on time.

Hasta luego.
I'll see you later.

¿A qué hora comienza?
What time does it start?

¿A qué hora termina?
What time does it end?

¿Cuánto dura?
How long will it last?

Se está haciendo tarde.
It's getting late.

el calendario (ᶜel almanaque) • calendar

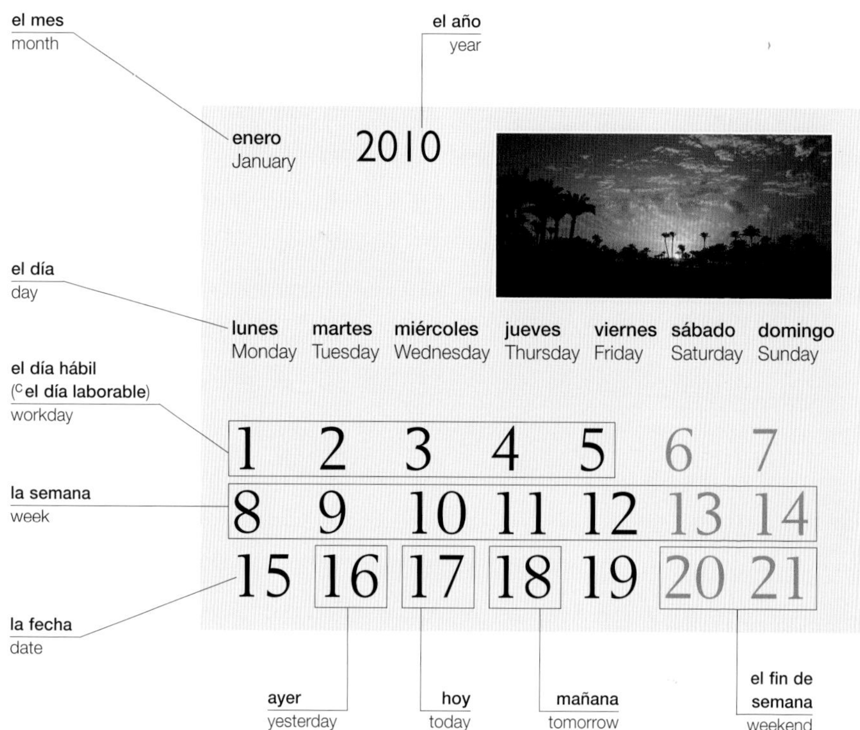

vocabulario • vocabulary

enero January	**marzo** March	**mayo** May	**julio** July	**septiembre** September	**noviembre** November
febrero February	**abril** April	**junio** June	**agosto** August	**octubre** October	**diciembre** December

los años • years

1900 **mil novecientos** • nineteen hundred

1901 **mil novecientos uno** • nineteen hundred and one

1910 **mil novecientos diez** • nineteen ten

2000 **dos mil** • two thousand

2001 **dos mil uno** • two thousand and one

las estaciones • seasons

la primavera
spring

el verano
summer

el otoño
fall

el invierno
winter

vocabulario • vocabulary

el siglo
century

la década
decade

el milenio
millennium

quince días
two weeks

esta semana
this week

la semana pasada
last week

la semana que viene
next week

anteayer (c**antes de ayer**)
the day before yesterday

pasado mañana
the day after tomorrow

semanalmente
weekly

mensual
monthly

anual
annual

¿Qué día es hoy?
What's the date today?

Es el siete de febrero del dos mil dos.
It's February seventh, two thousand and two.

los números • numbers

0 **cero** • zero
1 **uno** • one
2 **dos** • two
3 **tres** • three
4 **cuatro** • four
5 **cinco** • five
6 **seis** • six
7 **siete** • seven
8 **ocho** • eight
9 **nueve** • nine
10 **diez** • ten
11 **once** • eleven
12 **doce** • twelve
13 **trece** • thirteen
14 **catorce** • fourteen
15 **quince** • fifteen
16 **dieciséis** • sixteen
17 **diecisiete** • seventeen
18 **dieciocho** • eighteen
19 **diecinueve** • nineteen
20 **veinte** • twenty
21 **veintiuno** • twenty-one
22 **veintidós** • twenty-two
30 **treinta** • thirty
40 **cuarenta** • forty
50 **cincuenta** • fifty
60 **sesenta** • sixty
70 **setenta** • seventy
80 **ochenta** • eighty
90 **noventa** • ninety
100 **cien** • one hundred
110 **ciento diez** • one hundred and ten
200 **doscientos** • two hundred
300 **trescientos** • three hundred
400 **cuatrocientos** • four hundred
500 **quinientos** • five hundred
600 **seiscientos** • six hundred
700 **setecientos** • seven hundred
800 **ochocientos** • eight hundred
900 **novecientos** • nine hundred

1,000	**mil** • one thousand
10,000	**diez mil** • ten thousand
20,000	**veinte mil** • twenty thousand
50,000	**cincuenta mil** • fifty thousand
55,500	**cincuenta y cinco mil quinientos** • fifty-five thousand five hundred
100,000	**cien mil** • one hundred thousand
1,000,000	**un millón** • one million
1,000,000,000	**mil millones** • one billion

primero first

segundo second

tercero third

cuarto • fourth

quinto • fifth

sexto • sixth

séptimo • seventh

octavo • eighth

noveno • ninth

décimo • tenth

undécimo • eleventh

duodécimo • twelfth

decimotercero • thirteenth

decimocuarto • fourteenth

decimoquinto • fifteenth

decimosexto • sixteenth

decimoséptimo • seventeenth

décimo octavo • eighteenth

décimo noveno • nineteenth

vigésimo • twentieth

vigésimo primero • twenty-first

vigésimo segundo • twenty-second

vigésimo tercero • twenty-third

trigésimo • thirtieth

cuadragésimo • fortieth

quincuagésimo • fiftieth

sexagésimo • sixtieth

septuagésimo • seventieth

octogésimo • eightieth

nonagésimo • ninetieth

centésimo • one hundredth

los pesos y las medidas • weights and measures

el área • area

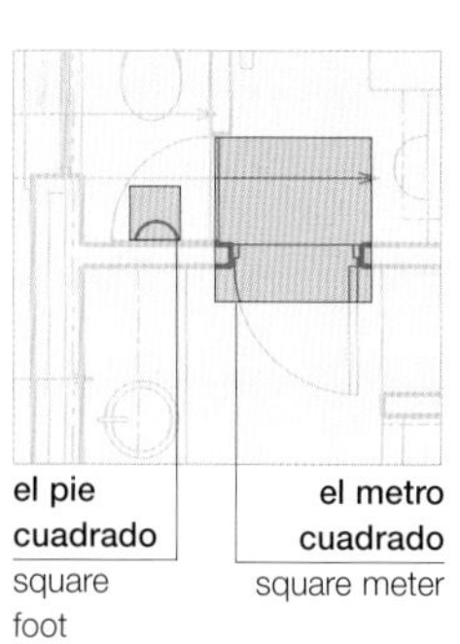

la distancia • distance

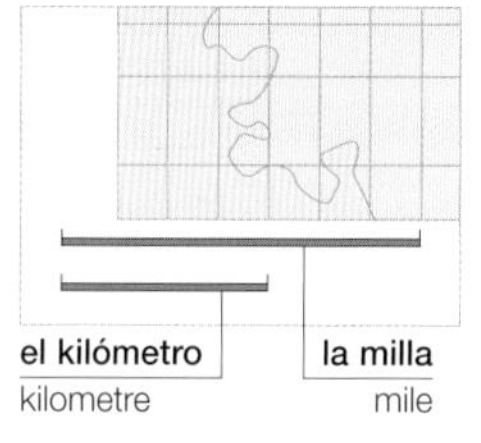

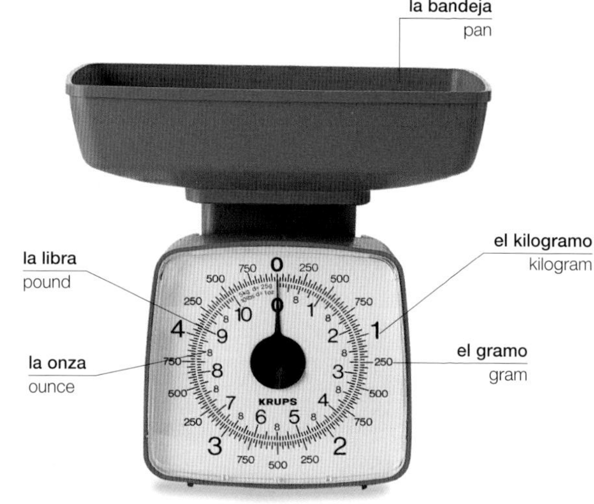

la báscula (^c la balanza) | scale

vocabulario • vocabulary

la yarda
yard

el metro
metre

la tonelada
tonne

el miligramo
milligram

medir
measure (v)

pesar
weigh (v)

la longitud • length

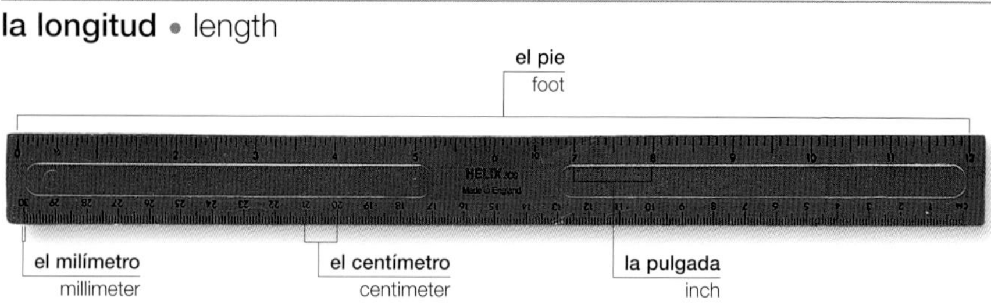

la capacidad • capacity

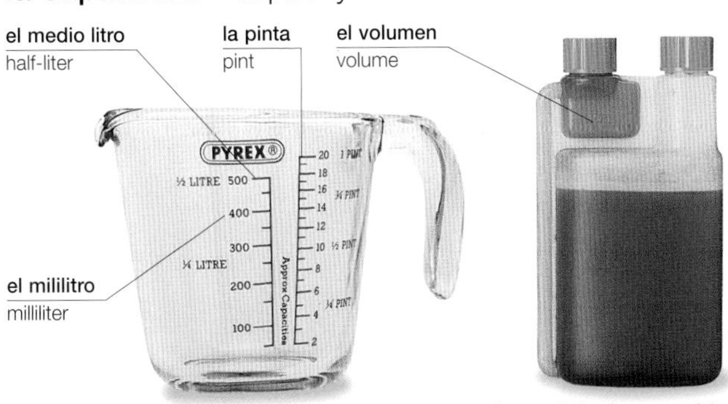

la jarra graduada
measuring cup

la medida de capacidad
liquid measure

vocabulario • vocabulary

el galón	gallon
el cuarto de galón	quart
el litro	liter

el recipiente • container

el tetrabrik
carton

el paquete
bag

la botella
bottle

la bolsa
sack

la tarrina | tub

el tarro | jar

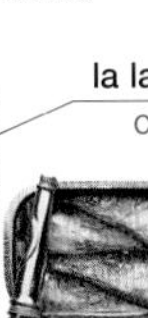

la lata | tin

el pulverizador
spray bottle

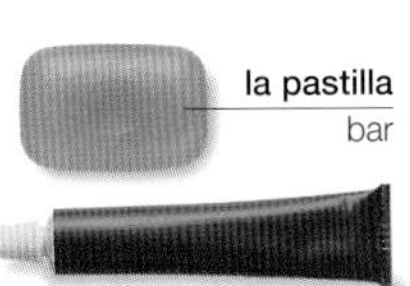

el tubo
tube

el rollo
roll

la cajetilla (ᶜ**el paquete**)
pack

el spray
spray can

el mapamundi • world map

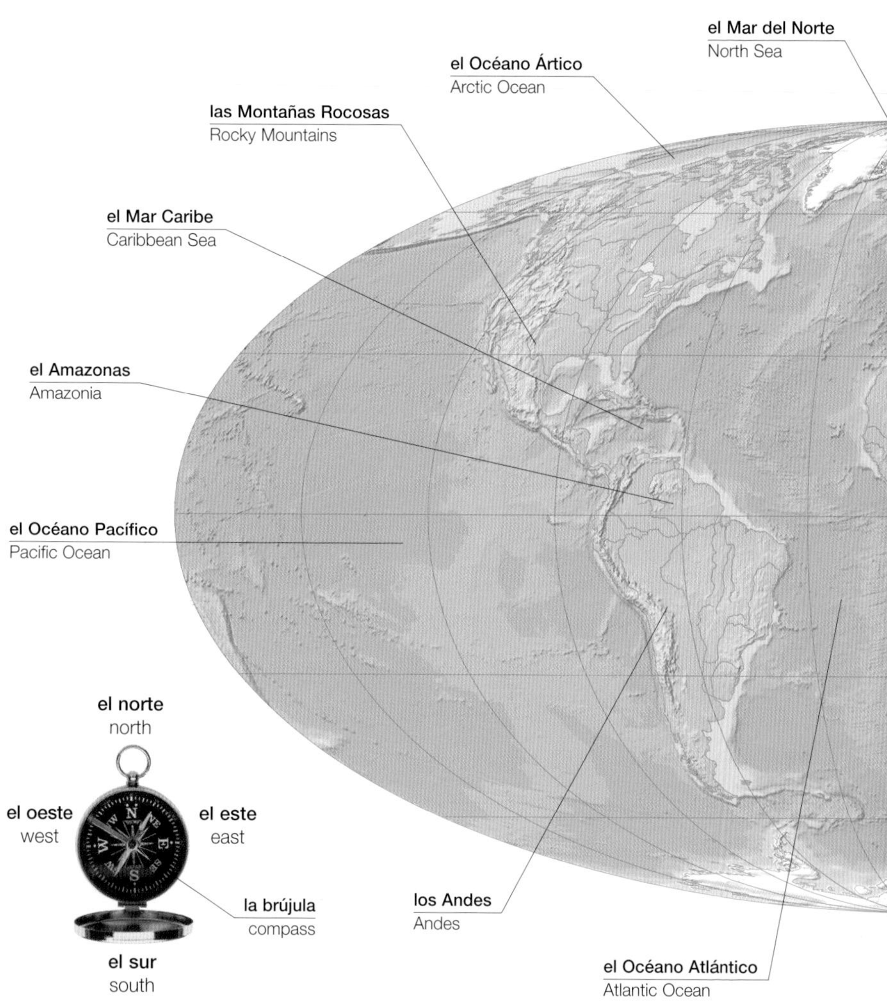

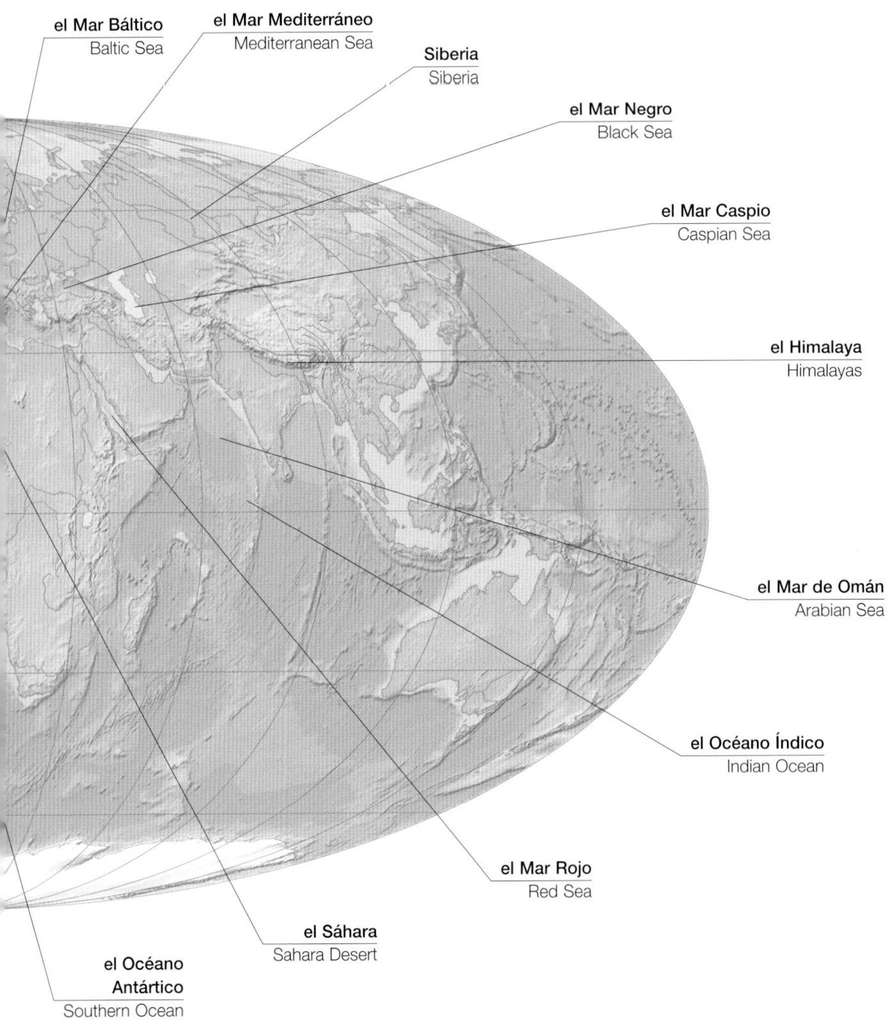
el Mar Báltico
Baltic Sea
el Mar Mediterráneo
Mediterranean Sea
Siberia
Siberia
el Mar Negro
Black Sea
el Mar Caspio
Caspian Sea
el Himalaya
Himalayas
el Mar de Omán
Arabian Sea
el Océano Índico
Indian Ocean
el Mar Rojo
Red Sea
el Sáhara
Sahara Desert
el Océano Antártico
Southern Ocean

América del Norte y Central • North and Central America

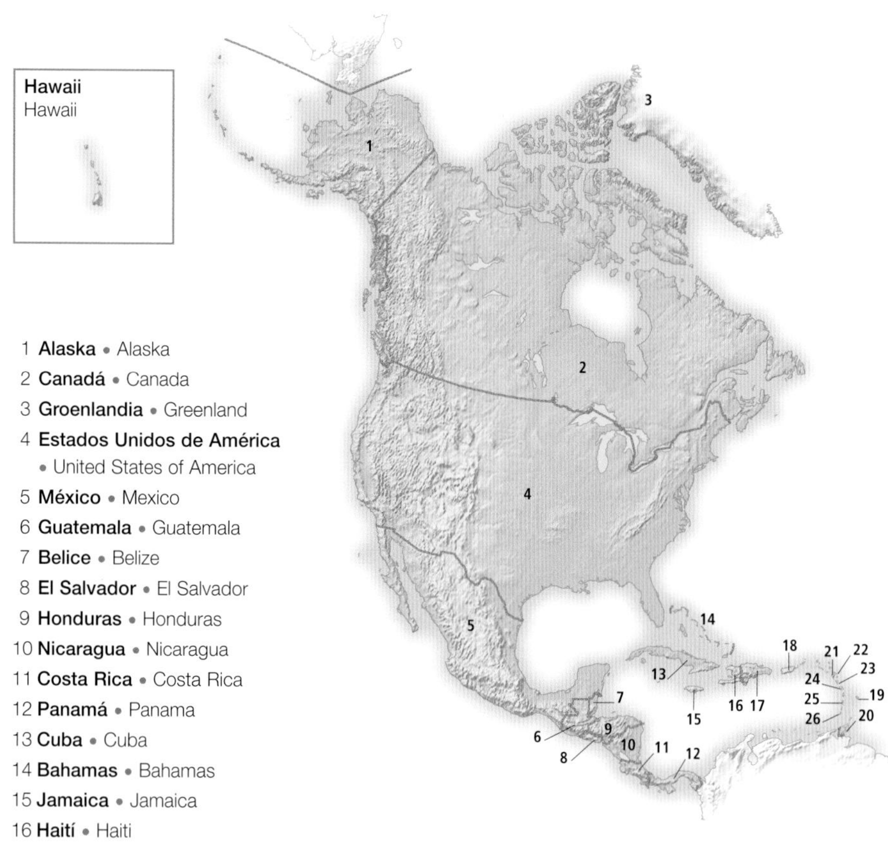

1 **Alaska** • Alaska

2 **Canadá** • Canada

3 **Groenlandia** • Greenland

4 **Estados Unidos de América** • United States of America

5 **México** • Mexico

6 **Guatemala** • Guatemala

7 **Belice** • Belize

8 **El Salvador** • El Salvador

9 **Honduras** • Honduras

10 **Nicaragua** • Nicaragua

11 **Costa Rica** • Costa Rica

12 **Panamá** • Panama

13 **Cuba** • Cuba

14 **Bahamas** • Bahamas

15 **Jamaica** • Jamaica

16 **Haití** • Haiti

17 **República Dominicana** • Dominican Republic

18 **Puerto Rico** • Puerto Rico

19 **Barbados** • Barbados

20 **Trinidad y Tobago** • Trinidad and Tobago

21 **Saint Kitts y Nevis** • St. Kitts and Nevis

22 **Antigua y Barbuda** • Antigua and Barbuda

23 **Dominica** • Dominica

24 **Santa Lucía** • St. Lucia

25 **San Vicente y las Granadinas** • St. Vincent and the Grenadines

26 **Granada** • Grenada

América del Sur • South America

1 **Venezuela** • Venezuela

2 **Colombia** • Colombia

3 **Ecuador** • Ecuador

4 **Perú** • Peru

5 **las Islas Galápagos** • Galápagos Islands

6 **Guyana** • Guyana

7 **Suriname** • Suriname

8 **la Guayana Francesa** • French Guiana

9 **Brasil** • Brazil

10 **Bolivia** • Bolivia

11 **Chile** • Chile

12 **Argentina** • Argentina

13 **Paraguay** • Paraguay

14 **Uruguay** • Uruguay

15 **las Malvinas** • Falkland Islands

vocabulario • vocabulary

el continente continent	**el principado** principality	**la provincia** province
el país country	**el territorio** territory	**el distrito** district
la nación nation	**la colonia** colony	**la región** region
el estado state	**la zona** zone	**la capital** capital

Europa • Europe

1 **Irlanda** • Ireland
2 **Reino Unido** • United Kingdom
3 **Portugal** • Portugal
4 **España** • Spain
5 **las Islas Baleares** • Balearic Islands
6 **Andorra** • Andorra
7 **Francia** • France
8 **Bélgica** • Belgium
9 **los Países Bajos** • Netherlands
10 **Luxemburgo** • Luxembourg
11 **Alemania** • Germany
12 **Dinamarca** • Denmark
13 **Noruega** • Norway
14 **Suecia** • Sweden
15 **Finlandia** • Finland
16 **Estonia** • Estonia
17 **Letonia** • Latvia
18 **Lituania** • Lithuania
19 **Kaliningrado** • Kaliningrad
20 **Polonia** • Poland
21 **República Checa** • Czech Republic
22 **Austria** • Austria
23 **Liechtenstein** • Liechtenstein
24 **Suiza** • Switzerland
25 **Italia** • Italy
26 **Mónaco** • Monaco
27 **Córcega** • Corsica
28 **Cerdeña** • Sardinia
29 **San Marino** • San Marino
30 **la Ciudad del Vaticano** • Vatican City
31 **Sicilia** • Sicily
32 **Malta** • Malta
33 **Eslovenia** • Slovenia
34 **Croacia** • Croatia
35 **Hungría** • Hungary
36 **Eslovaquia** • Slovakia
37 **Ucrania** • Ukraine
38 **Belarús** • Belarus
39 **Moldavia** • Moldova
40 **Rumanía** • Romania
41 **Serbia** • Serbia
42 **Bosnia y Herzegovina** • Bosnia and Herzogovina
43 **Albania** • Albania
44 **Macedonia** • Macedonia
45 **Bulgaria** • Bulgaria
46 **Grecia** • Greece
47 **Kosovo** • Kosovo (disputed)
48 **Montenegro** • Montenegro

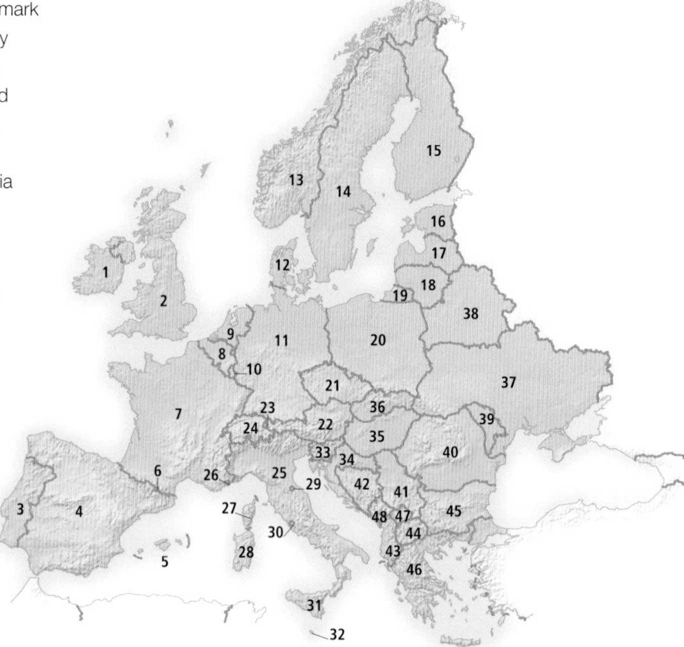

África • Africa

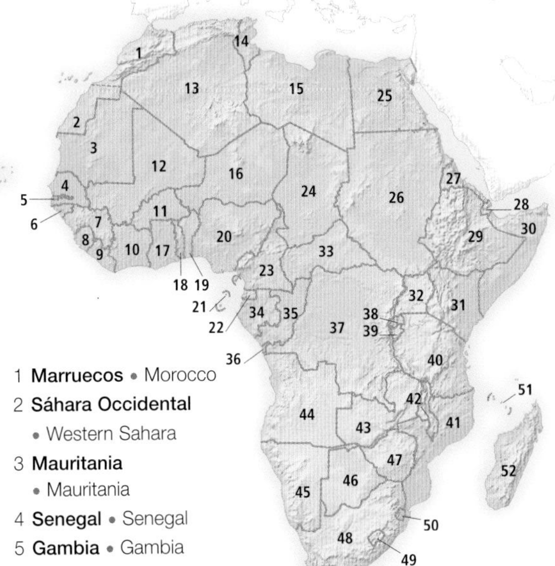

1 **Marruecos** • Morocco

2 **Sáhara Occidental** • Western Sahara

3 **Mauritania** • Mauritania

4 **Senegal** • Senegal

5 **Gambia** • Gambia

6 **Guinea-Bissau** • Guinea-Bissau

7 **Guinea** • Guinea

8 **Sierra Leona** • Sierra Leone

9 **Liberia** • Liberia

10 **Costa de Marfil** • Ivory Coast

11 **Burquina Faso** • Burkina Faso

12 **Malí** • Mali

13 **Argelia** • Algeria

14 **Túnez** • Tunisia

15 **Libia** • Libya

16 **Níger** • Niger

17 **Ghana** • Ghana

18 **Togo** • Togo

19 **Benin** • Benin

20 **Nigeria** • Nigeria

21 **Santo Tomé y Príncipe** • São Tomé and Principe

22 **Guinea Ecuatorial** • Equatorial Guinea

23 **Camerún** • Cameroon

24 **Chad** • Chad

25 **Egipto** • Egypt

26 **Sudán** • Sudan

27 **Eritrea** • Eritrea

28 **Djibouti** • Djibouti

29 **Etiopía** • Ethiopia

30 **Somalia** • Somalia

31 **Kenya** • Kenya

32 **Uganda** • Uganda

33 **República Centroafricana** • Central African Republic

34 **Gabón** • Gabon

35 **Congo** • Congo

36 **Cabinda (Angola)** • Cabinda (Angola)

37 **República Democrática del Congo** • Democratic Republic of the Congo

38 **Rwanda** • Rwanda

39 **Burundi** • Burundi

40 **Tanzania** • Tanzania

41 **Mozambique** • Mozambique

42 **Malawi** • Malawi

43 **Zambia** • Zambia

44 **Angola** • Angola

45 **Namibia** • Namibia

46 **Botswana** • Botswana

47 **Zimbabwe** • Zimbabwe

48 **Sudáfrica** • South Africa

49 **Lesotho** • Lesotho

50 **Swazilandia** • Swaziland

51 **Comoros** • Comoros

52 **Madagascar** • Madagascar

53 **Mauricio** • Mauritius

Asia • Asia

1 **Turquía** • Turkey
2 **Chipre** • Cyprus
3 **Federación Rusa** • Russian Federation
4 **Georgia** • Georgia
5 **Armenia** • Armenia
6 **Azerbaiyán** • Azerbaijan
7 **Irán** • Iran
8 **Iraq** • Iraq
9 **Siria** • Syria
10 **Líbano** • Lebanon
11 **Israel** • Israel
12 **Jordania** • Jordan
13 **Arabia Saudita** • Saudi Arabia
14 **Kuwait** • Kuwait
15 **Bahrein** • Bahrain
16 **Qatar** • Qatar
17 **Emiratos Árabes Unidos** • United Arab Emirates
18 **Omán** • Oman
19 **Yemen** • Yemen
20 **Kazajstán** • Kazakhstan
21 **Uzbekistán** • Uzbekistan
22 **Turkmenistán** • Turkmenistan
23 **Afganistán** • Afghanistan
24 **Tayikistán** • Tajikistan
25 **Kirguistán** • Kyrgyzstan
26 **Pakistán**• Pakistan
27 **India** • India
28 **Maldivas** • Maldives
29 **Sri Lanka** • Sri Lanka
30 **China** • China
31 **Mongolia** • Mongolia
32 **Corea del Norte** • North Korea
33 **Corea del Sur** • South Korea
34 **Japón** • Japan

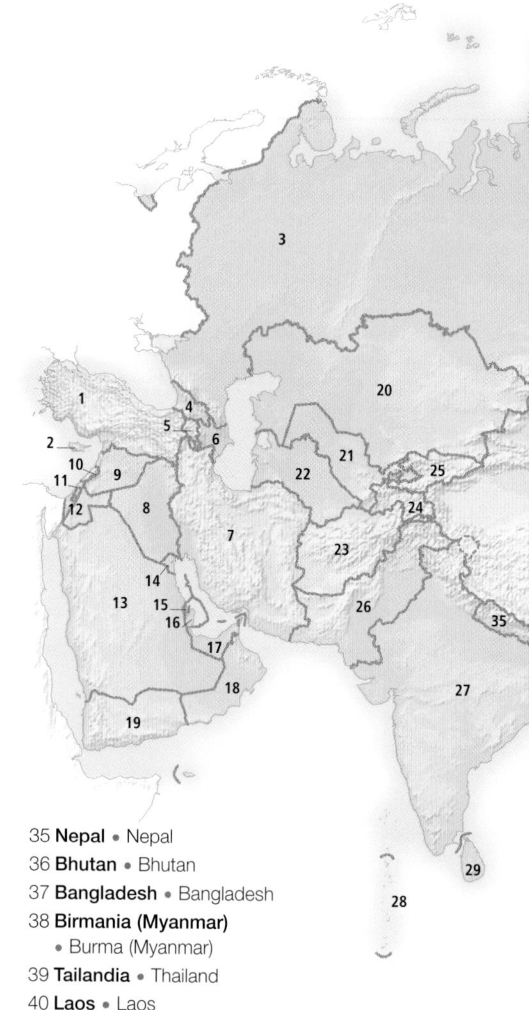

35 **Nepal** • Nepal
36 **Bhutan** • Bhutan
37 **Bangladesh** • Bangladesh
38 **Birmania (Myanmar)** • Burma (Myanmar)
39 **Tailandia** • Thailand
40 **Laos** • Laos
41 **Viet Nam** • Vietnam
42 **Camboya** • Cambodia

Australasia • Australasia

1 **Australia** • Australia
2 **Tasmania** • Tasmania
3 **Nueva Zelandia** • New Zealand

43 **Malasia** • Malaysia
44 **Singapur** • Singapore
45 **Indonesia** • Indonesia
46 **Brunei** • Brunei
47 **Filipinas** • Philippines
48 **Timor Oriental** • East Timor
49 **Papua Nueva Guinea**• Papua New Guinea
50 **Islas Salomón** • Solomon Islands
51 **Vanuatu** • Vanuatu
52 **Fiji** • Fiji

partículas y antónimos • particles and antonyms

a, hacia
to

de, desde
from

encima de
over

debajo de
under

delante de
in front of

detrás de
behind

sobre
onto

dentro de
into

en
in

fuera
out

sobre
above

bajo
below

dentro
inside

fuera
outside

arriba
up

abajo
down

en
at

más allá de
beyond

a través de
through

alrededor de
around

encima de
on top of

al lado de
beside

entre
between

en frente de
opposite

cerca
near

lejos
far

aquí
here

allí
there

para
for

hacia
toward

por
along

al otro lado de
across

con
with

sin
without

antes
before

después
after

antes de
by

hasta
until

temprano
early

tarde
late

ahora
now

más tarde
later

siempre
always

nunca
never

con frecuencia
(C **a menudo**) | often

rara vez
rarely

ayer
yesterday

mañana
tomorrow

primer
first

último
last

cada
every

algunos
some

unos
about

exactamente
exactly

un poco
a little

mucho
a lot

grande large	**pequeño** small
ancho wide	**estrecho** narrow
alto tall	**bajo** short
alto high	**bajo** low
grueso thick	**delgado** thin
ligero light	**pesado** heavy
duro hard	**blando** soft
húmedo wet	**seco** dry
bueno good	**malo** bad
rápido fast	**lento** slow
correcto correct	**incorrecto** wrong
limpio clean	**sucio** dirty
hermoso ([C] **bonito**) beautiful	**feo** ugly
caro expensive	**barato** cheap
silencioso quiet	**ruidoso** noisy

caliente hot	**frío** cold
abierto open	**cerrado** closed
lleno full	**vacío** empty
nuevo new	**viejo** old
claro light	**oscuro** dark
fácil easy	**difícil** difficult
libre free	**ocupado** occupied
fuerte strong	**débil** weak
gordo fat	**delgado** thin
joven young	**viejo** old
mejor better	**peor** worse
negro black	**blanco** white
interesante interesting	**aburrido** boring
enfermo sick	**bien** well
el principio beginning	**el final** end

frases útiles • useful phrases

frases esenciales • essential phrases

Sí
Yes

No
No

Quizás
Maybe

Por favor
Please

Gracias
Thank you

De nada
You're welcome

Perdone
Excuse me

Lo siento
I'm sorry

No
Don't

Vale
OK

Así vale
That's fine

Está bien
That's correct

Está mal
That's wrong

saludos • greetings

Hola
Hello

Adiós
Goodbye

Buenos días
Good morning

Buenas tardes
Good afternoon

Buenas tardes
Good evening

Buenas noches
Good night

¿Cómo está?
How are you?

Me llamo…
My name is…

¿Cómo se llama?
What is your name?

¿Cómo se llama?
What is his/her name?

Le presento a…
May I introduce…

Este es…
This is…

Encantado de conocerle
Pleased to meet you

Hasta luego
See you later

letreros • signs

Información
Tourist information

Entrada
Entrance

Salida
Exit

Salida de emergencia
Emergency exit

Empuje
Push

Peligro
Danger

Prohibido fumar
No smoking

Fuera de servicio
Out of order

Horario de apertura
Opening times

Entrada libre
Free admission

Llame antes de entrar
Knock before entering

Rebajado
Reduced

Saldos
Sale

Prohibido pisar el césped
Keep off the grass

ayuda • help

¿Me puede ayudar?
Can you help me?

No entiendo
I don't understand

No lo sé
I don't know

¿Habla inglés, francés…?
Do you speak English, French…?

Hablo inglés, español…
I speak English, Spanish…

Hable más lento ([C]despacio), por favor
Please speak more slowly

¿Me lo puede escribir?
Please write it down for me

He perdido…
I have lost…

indicaciones • directions

Me perdí (C**Me he perdido**) | I am lost

¿Dónde está el/la...?
Where is the...?

¿Dónde está el/la... más cercano/a?
Where is the nearest...?

¿Dónde están los servicios?
Where are the restrooms?

¿Cómo voy a...?
How do I get to...?

A la derecha
To the right

A la izquierda
To the left

Todo recto
Straight ahead

¿A qué distancia está...?
How far is...?

las señales de tránsito (C las señales de tráfico) • road signs

Todas las direcciones
All directions

Precaución | Caution

Prohibido el paso
No entry

Disminuir velocidad
Slow down

Desvío | Detour

Circular por la derecha
Keep right

Autopista | Freeway

Prohibido estacionar (C**Prohibido aparcar**)
No parking

Callejón sin salida
No through road

Sentido único
One-way

Ceda el paso
Yield

Carretera cortada
Road closed

Obras
Road construction

Curva peligrosa
Dangerous curve

alojamiento • accommodation

Tengo una reservación (C **Tengo una reserva**)
I have a reservation

¿A qué hora es el desayuno?
What time is breakfast?

El número de mi habitación es el ...
My room number is ...

Volveré a las ...
I'll be back at ... o'clock

¿Dónde está el comedor?
Where is the dining room?

Me marcho mañana
I'm leaving tomorrow

comida y bebida • eating and drinking

¡Salud!
Cheers!

Está buenísimo/malísimo
It's delicious/awful

Yo no bebo/fumo
I don't drink/smoke

Yo no como carne
I don't eat meat

Ya no más, gracias
No more for me, thank you

¿Puedo repetir?
May I have some more?

¿Me trae la cuenta?
Check, please.

¿Me da un recibo?
Can I have a receipt?

Zona de no fumadores
No-smoking area

la salud • health

No me encuentro bien
I don't feel well

Tengo náuseas
I feel sick

¿Cuál es el número del médico más cercano?
What is the telephone number of the nearest doctor?

Me duele aquí
It hurts here

Tengo fiebre
I have a fever

Estoy embarrazada de ... meses
I'm ... months pregnant

Necesito una receta para ...
I need a prescription for ...

Normalmente tomo ...
I normally take ...

Soy alérgico a ...
I'm allergic to ...

¿Estará bien?
Will he/she be all right?

índice español • Spanish index

A

a 320; a la carta 152; a la plancha 159; a través de 320
abadejo *m* 120
abajo 320
abarrotes *m* 105, 114
abdomen *m* 12
abdominal *m* 16, 251
abedul *m* 296
abeja *f* 295
abierta *f* 221
abierto 260, 321
abogado *m* 180, 190
abonar 91; abonar en la superficie 90
abono *m* 91; abono compuesto *m* 88
aborto espontáneo *m* 52
abrazadera *f* 78
abrebotellas *m* 68, 150
abrelatas *m* 68
abrigo *m* 31, 32
abril 306
absuelto 181
abuela/o *f/m* 22; abuelos *m* 23
aburrido 25
acacia *f* 110
academia de danza *f* 169
acampar 266
acantilado *m* 285
accesorios *m* 36, 38
accidente *m* 46; accidente de carro *m* 203
acciones *f* 77, 97, 227, 229, 233
acebo *m* 296
acedera *f* 123
aceite *m* 142, 199; aceite aromatizado *m* 134; aceite de almendra *m* 134; aceite de avellanas *m* 134; aceite de cacahuete *m* 135; aceite de colza *m* 13; aceite de girasol *m* 134; aceite de maiz *m* 135; aceite de nueces *m* 134; aceite de oliva *m* 134; aceite de presión en frío *m* 135; aceite de semillas de uva *m* 134; aceite de sésamo *m* 134; aceite vegetal *m* 135
aceites *m* 134; aceites esenciales *m* 55
aceituna *f* 151; aceituna negra *f* 143; aceituna rellena *f* 143; aceituna verde *f* 143
acelerador *m* 200, 204
acelga *f* 123; acelga china *f* 123
acera *f* 298
acero inoxidable *m* 79
aclarar 76
acolchado *m* 277
acomodador *m* 255
acompañamiento *m* 153
acondicionador *m* 38
acostarse 71
acotamiento *m* 194
acta *f* 174; acta de nacimiento *f* 26
actividades *f* 162, 183, 245, 263; actividades al aire libre *f* 262
actor *m* 191, 254
actores *m* 179
actriz *f* 254
acuarelas *f* 274
acupresión *f* 55
acupuntura *f* 55
acusación *f* 180
acusado *m* 180, 181
adelantar 195
aderezo *m* 158
adiós 322
adobado 143, 159
adolescente *f* 23
adornos para el jardín *m* 84
aduana *f* 212
aduanas del puerto *f* 216
adularia *f* 288
adulto *m* 23
adversario *m* 236
aerobic(s) *m* 251
aerodeslizador *m* 215
aeropuerto *m* 212
afeitado *m* 73
afilador *m* 68, 118
aftershave *m* 73
agalla *f* 294
agarradera *f* 166
agarre *m* 237
ágata *f* 289
agencia de viajes *f* 114
agencia inmobiliaria *f* 115
agenda *f* 173, 175
agente de bolsa *m* 97
agente de policía *m* 94
agente de viajes *f* 190
agente inmobiliario *f* 189
agitador *m* 150
aglomerado *m* 79
agosto 306
agresión *f* 94
agricultor *m* 189
agua *m* 144, 238; agua de colonia *m* 41; agua de la llave (del grifo) *m* 144; agua embotellada *m* 144; agua mineral *m* 144
aguacate *m* 128
aguamarina *f* 288
aguanieve *f* 286
aguarrás *m* 83
águila *f* 292
aguja *f* 109, 276, 300; aguja de ganchillo *f* 277; aguja de la hora *f* 304; aguja de tejer *f* 277
agujero negro *m* 280
agujeta *f* 37
ahogarse 47, 239
ahora 304
ahorros *m* 96
ahumado 118, 121, 143, 159
aikido *m* 236
airbag *m* 201
aire acondicionado *m* 200
airear 91
aislamiento *m* 61
ajedrez *m* 272
ajo *m* 125, 132
al horno 159
al lado de 320
al otro lado de 320
al vapor 159
ala *f* 210, 293; ala *m* 119; ala delta *m* 248
alacrán *m* 295
alambre *m* 79, 89, 155
álamo *m* 296
alargador *m* 78
alarma antirrobo *f* 58
alarma contra incendios *f* 95
alba *m* 305
albahaca *f* 133
albañil *m* 186, 188
albaricoque *m* 126
alberca *f* 238, 250; alberca de plástico *f* 263
albóndigas *f* 158
albornoz *m* 73
álbum de fotos *m* 271
alcachofa *f* 89, 124; alcachofa de la ducha *f* 72
alcantarilla *f* 299
alcaparras *f* 143
alcázar *m* 214
alcorza *f* 141
aldaba *f* 59
alerce *m* 296
alergia *f* 44
alero *m* 58
alerón *m* 210
aleta *f* 210, 239, 290; aleta dorsal *f* 294; aleta pectoral *f* 294
aletas de raya *f* 120
alfalfa *f* 184
alfil *m* 272
alfiler *m* 276; alfiler de corbata *m* 36
alfiletero *m* 276
alfombra 63
alfombrilla de baño *f* 72
algodón *m* 184, 277
alguacil *m* 180
alhelí *m* 110
alicatar 82
alicates *m* 80
aliciar 39
alimentar 183
alimentos *m* 118, 130; alimentos embotellados *m* 134
aliñado 159
aliño *m* 158
alisar 39, 79
almacén *m* 216
almanaque *m* 306
almeja *f* 121
almendra *f* 122, 129
almendras *f* 151
almohada *f* 70
alquilar 58
alquiler *m* 58; alquiler de coches *m* 213
alrededor de 320
altavoz *m* 176, 209, 258, 268
alternador *m* 203
altitud *f* 211
alto 321
altura *f* 165
alubia *f* 131; alubia blanca *f* 131; alubia de ojo negro *f* 131; alubia flageolet *f* 131; alubia morada *f* 131; alubia mung *f* 131; alubia pinta *f* 131; alubia roja *f* 131
alubias *f* 131
aluminio *m* 289
alumno *m* 162
amamantar 53
amanecer *m*
amapola *f* 297
amargo 124, 127
amarillo 274
amarrar 217
amasar 138
amasar con el rodillo 67
amatista *f* 288
ambulancero *m* 94
ambulancia *f* 94
americana *f* 33; americana sport *f* 33
amigo *m* 24; amigo por correspondencia *m* 24
amniocentesis *f* 52
amperio *m* 60
ampliación *f* 58, 271
ampliar 172
amplificador *m* 268
ampolla *f* 46
anacardo *m* 129, 151
analgésico *m* 109
analgésicos *m* 47
análisis *m* 49; análisis de sangre *m* 48
ancho 321
anchura *f* 165
ancla *f* 214, 240
anclar 217
andamio *m* 186
andar en bicicleta 207
andar en patineta 249
andén *m* 208
anestesista *m* 48
anfibios *m* 294
anfiteatro *m* 169
anfitrión/-a *m/f* 64
anguila *f* 294
ángulo *m* 164
anillas *f* 89, 235
anillo *m* 36
animadora 220
animales *m* 290, 292, 294
anís estrellado *m* 133
aniversario *m* 26
anochecer *m* 305
anteayer 307
antebrazo *m* 12
antecedentes *m* 181
antena *f* 295; antena de radio *f* 214; antena parabólica *f* 269
antes 320; antes de 320; antes de ayer 307
antiadherente 69
antiarrugas 41
anticoncepción *f* 21, 52
anticongelante *m* 199, 203
antiinflamatorio *m* 109
anual 86, 307
anular *m* 15
anuncio *m* 269
anzuelo *m* 244
año *m* 163, 306; Año Nuevo *m* 27

apagado 99
apagar 141; apagar la televisión 269
apaisado 271
aparato corrector *m* 50
aparatos eléctricos *m* 105
aparcamiento *m* 298; aparcamiento para minusválidos *m* 195
aparcar 195
aparejos *m* 245
apariencia *f* 30
apelación *f* 181
apéndice *m* 18
aperitivo *m* 153
aperitivos *m* 151
ápice *m* 165
apio *m* 122
apio-nabo *m* 124
apisonadora *f* 187
aplanadora *f* 187
aplaudir 255
aplicación *f* 176
aplique *m* 62
apolpejía *f* 44
apoyabrazos *m* 210
aprender 163
apuesta *f* 273
apuntalar 91
apuntes *m* 175
aquijón *m* 295
arándano *m* 127; arándano rojo *m* 127
arandela *f* 80
araña *f* 295
arañazo *m* 46
arar 183
árbitro *m* 222, 225, 226, 229
árbol *m* 86, 296
arbotante *m* 62
arbusto de flor *m* 87
arce *m* 296
arcén *m* 194
archivador *m* 170; archivador suspendido *m* 173
archivero *m* 172
archivo *m* 177
arcilla *f* 85, 275
arco *m* 85, 164, 249, 301; arco del empeine *m* 15
arcoiris *m* 287
ardida *f* 46
ardilla *f* 290
área *f* 165, 310; área de fumar *f* 152; área de juegos *f* 263; área de meta *f* 223; área de no fumar *f* 152; área de penalty *f* 223
arena *f* 85, 264
arenques ahumados *m* 157
arete *m* 36
argamasa *f* 187
argollas *f* 235
aritmética *f* 165
armario *m* 62, 66, 70; armario de las medicinas *m* 72; armario empotrado *m* 71; armario para clasificar la basura *m* 61
armazón *m* 230
aro *m* 226
aromaterapia *f* 55
arquitecto *m* 190
arquitectura *f* 300
arquitrabe *m* 301
arrancar 82, 91
arrecife de coral *m* 285
arreglos *m* 111
arresto *m* 94
arriate de plantas herbáceas *m* 85
arriba 320
arroyo *m* 285
arroz *m* 130, 158, 184; arroz bomba *m* 130; arroz con leche *m* 140; arroz integral *m* 130; arroz largo *m* 130; arroz salvaje *m* 130
arruga *f* 15
art déco 301
arte *m* 162
arteria *f* 19
artes marciales *f* 237
articulación *f* 17
artículos de aseo *m* 107
artículos de cocina *m* 105
artículos de tocador *m* 41
artículos deportivos *m* 105
artículos para el bebé *m* 107
as *m* 230, 273
asa *f* 88, 106; asa *m* 36
asado *m* 119, 158
asalto *m* 237
asar 67; asar a la parrilla 67
asas *f* 37
ascensor *m* 59, 100, 104
aseos *m* 104, 266
asesora financiera *f* 97
asesoría jurídica *f* 180
asfalto *m* 187
asiento *m* 64, 204, 206, 209, 210; asiento del conductor *m* 196; asiento trasero *m* 200, 204
asistente *f* 24
asistir 174
asma *m* 44
asoleadero *f* 265
asolear 264
aspa *f* 60, 211
aspersor *m* 89
aspiradora *f* 77, 188
asta *f* 291
asteroide *m* 280
astigmatismo *m* 51
astilla *f* 46
astillero *m* 217
astronauta *m* 281
astronomía *f* 281
asustado 25
ataque *m* 220; ataque cardiaco *m* 44
atardecer *m* 305
atasco de tráfico *m* 195
aterrizar 211
ático *m* 58
atleta *f* 234
atletismo *m* 234
atmósfera *f* 282, 286
atracar 217
atracción turistica *f* 260
atrapar 220, 229, 245; atrapar con la red 245
atrio *m* 104
atún *m* 120
audífonos *m* 268
auditor *m* 180
auditorio *m* 169
auricular *m* 99
auriculares *m* 268
aurora *f* 286
auto clásico *m* 199
autobús *m* 196; autobús de dos pisos *m* 196; autobús de enlace *m* 197; autobús directo *m* 197; autobús escolar *m* 196; autobús turístico *m* 197, 260
autobuses *m* 196
autocar *m* 196
autocue *m* 179
auto-lavado *m* 198
automático 200
automovilismo *m* 249
autopista *f* 194
autovía *f* 195
avalancha *f* 247
avance rápido *m* 269
avellana *f* 129
avena *f* 130, 157
avenida *f* 299
avergonzado 25
avería *f* 203
aves *f* 292
avestruz *f* 292
avión *m* 210; avión de línea *m* 212; avión de pasajeros *m* 210; avión supersónico *m* 211
avioneta *f* 211
avispa *f* 295
axila *f* 13
ayer 306
ayudante *m/f* 24; ayudante del chef *m* 152
ayurveda *f* 55
azabache *m* 288
azada *f* 88
azadón *m* 88
azafata *f* 190, 210
azafrán *m* 132
azucena *f* 110
azufre *m* 289
azul 274; azul añil 274

B

babero *m* 30
babosa *f* 295
baca *f* 198; baca para bicicletas *f* 207
bacalao *m* 120
backgammon *m* 272
backswing *m* 233
bacon *m* 118, 157
bádminton *m* 231
baguette *f* 138
bailarina *f* 191
bajar 177
bajista *m* 258
bajo 258, 320, 321; bajo par *m* 233
balancín *m* 263
balanza *f* 310; balanza de muelle *f* 166
balcón *m* 59
baliza *f* 298
ballena *f* 290
ballet *m* 255
balón *m* 220, 221, 222, 226; balón perdido *m* 220
baloncesto *m* 226
balonvolea *m* 227
balsa salvavidas *f* 240
bambineto *m* 75
bambú *m* 86, 122
banca *f* 229, 262
banco *m* 96, 250, 262; banco de trabajo *m* 78
banda *f* 203; banda caminadora *f* 250; banda de rodadura *f* 207; banda del calzapié *f* 207; banda del ventilador *f* 203; banda sonora *f* 255; banda transportadora *f* 106, 212
bandeja *f* 310, 152, 154, 210; bandeja de entrada *f* 172, 177; bandeja de horno *f* 69; bandeja de salida *f* 172; bandeja del desayuno *f* 101; bandeja para el papel *f* 172; bandeja para la pintura *f* 83
bandera *f* 221; bandera de esquina *f* 223
banderola *f* 232
banqueta *f* 298
banquete de boda *m* 26
banquillo *m* 229
bañador *m* 238, 265
bañarse 72
bañora *f* 72
baño *m* 72; baño privado *m* 100
baños *m* 104, 266
bar *m* 148, 150, 152
bar mitzvah *m* 26
baraja de cartas *f* 273
barajar 273
barandal *m* 59
barandilla *f* 59, 196
barbacoa *f* 267
barbero *m* 39, 188
barbilla *f* 14
barca de remos *m* 214
barco *f* 214; barco carguero *m* 215; barco de guerra *m* 215; barco de pesca *m* 217; barco de vela *m* 215; barco pesquero *m* 217
barman *m* 150, 191
barniz *m* 79, 83
barra *f* 139, 150, 235, 250, 256; barra de desplazamiento *f* 177; barra de equilibrio *f* 235; barra de herramientas *f* 177; barra de pesas *f* 251; barra del menú *f* 177; barra fija *f* 235
barrar 229
barras asimétricas *f* 235
barras paralelas *f* 235
barrer 77
barrera *f* 209, 222; barrera contra el viento *f* 265; barrera de seguridad *f* 75, 195, 246;
barrita *f* 113
barroco 301
barrotes *m* 74
basalto *m* 288
báscula *f* 45, 53, 69, 98, 118, 166, 310
base *f* 40, 83, 99, 164, 229; base del bateador *f* 228
bastidor *m* 277
bastidores *m* 254
bastón *m* 246
basurero *m* 177, 266
bata *f* 31, 32, 38, 73
bate *m* 225, 228
bateador *m* 225, 228
batear 225, 229
batería *f* 78, 202, 258
baterista *m* 258
batido *m* 137, 149

batidor de varillas *m* 68
batir 67; batir un récord 234
batuta *f* 256
bautizo *m* 26
baya *m* 296
bazo *m* 18
bebé *m* 23, 30
bebida malteada *f* 144
bebidas *f* 144, 107, 156; bebidas alcohólicas *f* 145; bebidas calientes *f* 144
beca *f* 169
béisbol *m* 228
belleza *f* 40
bemol 256
bengala *f* 240
berberecho *m* 121
berenjena *f* 125
berro *m* 123
berza *f* 123
besugo *m* 120
betabel *m* 125
biatlón *m* 247
biberón *m* 75
biblioteca *f* 168, 299
bibliotecaria/o *f/m* 168, 190
bíceps *m* 16
bicicleta *f* 206, 250; bicicleta de carretera *f* 206; bicicleta de montaña *f* 206; bicicleta de paseo *f* 206; bicicleta de pista *f* 206
bidé *m* 72
bienal 86
bifocal 51
bigotes *m* 290
bikini *m* 264
billar *m* 249; billar americano *m* 249
billete *m* 97, 209, 213; billete de autobús *m* 197
billetes de lotería *m* 112
biología *f* 162
biológico 9, 118, 122
biombo *m* 63
biplano *m* 211
birlos *m* 203
bis *m* 255
biscote *m* 139
bisturí *m* 167
blanco 39, 145, 272, 273, 274
blancos *m* 105
blando 129, 321
bloc de apuntes *m* 173
bloc de dibujo *m* 275
bloque de hormigón *m* 187
bloquear 227
bloqueo *m* 237
blues *m* 259
blusa *f* 34
bobina *f* 276
bobsleigh *m* 247
boca *f* 14; boca de agua *f* 95; boca de alcantarilla *f* 299
bocadillo *m* 155
bocado *m* 242
boceto *m* 275
bocina *f* 176, 201, 258, 268
boda *f* 26, 35
bodega *f* 215, 216
body *m* 30
bol *m* 65
bola *f* 149, 228, 230; bola de boliche *f* 249; bola de bowling *f* 249; bola de golf *f* 233
bolas de algodón *f* 41
boleto *m* 209, 213; boleto de autobús *m* 197
boliche *m* 249
bolígrafo *m* 163
bolillo *m* 277
bollo *m* 139, 140, 155
bolo *m* 249
bolos *m* 249
bolsa *f* 106, 190, 291, 311; bolsa de agua caliente *f* 70; bolsa de aire *f* 201; bolsa de correo *f* 98; bolsa de golf *f* 233; bolsa de mano *f* 37; bolsa de plástico *f* 122; bolsa de playa *f* 264; bolsa de valores *f* 97; bolsa de viaje *f* 37; bolsa para la hierba *f* 88
bolsas *f* 37
bolsillo *m* 32
bolsita de té *f* 144
bolso *m* 37; bolso de mano *m* 37
bomba *f* 199, 207; bomba de agua *f* 95; bomba del aire *f* 199
bombardero *m* 211
bombero *m* 189
bomberos *m* 95
bombilla *f* 60
bombón *m* 113
bongos *m* 257
boniato *m* 125
boquilla *f* 89
bordado *m* 277; bordado en cañamazo *m* 277
borde de la banqueta *m* 298
borde del ocular *m* 269
bordillo *m* 298
borla *f* 40
borrén *m* 242
bosque *m* 285
bostezar 25
bota *f* 220; bota de esquí *f* 246; bota de montar *f* 242; bota de trekking *f* 37
botana *f* 151
botar 227
botas *f* 30; botas altas de goma *f* 244; botas de agua *f* 31; botas de goma *f* 89; botas de trekking *f* 267
botavara *f* 240
bote de basura *m* 67, 172, 177
bote salvavida *m* 214
botella *f* 61, 135, 311; botella de aire *f* 239; botella del agua *f* 206
botiquín *m* 47, 72
botón *m* 30, 32; botón de ajuste *m* 167; botón de parada *m* 197; botón para grabar *m* 269; botón para rebobinar *m* 269
botones *m* 100
boutique *f* 115
bóveda *f* 300
boxeo *m* 236
boxers *m* 33
boya *f* 217
bragas *f* 35
braguitas de plástico *f* 30
brandy *m* 145
brassiere *m* 35; brassiere deportivo *m* 35; brassiere para la lactancia *m* 53
braza *f* 239
brazada *f* 239
brazal *m* 45
brazo *m* 13, 95, 166
brezo *m* 297
brida *f* 242
bridge *m* 273
brie *m* 142
brillo de labios *m* 40
brillo del sol *m* 286
broca *f* 78; broca de albañileriá *f* 80; broca de seguridad *f* 80; broca para madera *f* 80; broca para metal *f* 80
brocas *f* 80; brocas para madera *f* 80
brocha *f* 40, 83; brocha de cocina *f* 69; brocha de empapelador *f* 82; brocha de encolar *f* 82; brocha de tapicero *f* 82
broche *m* 31, 36
brocheta *f* 158
brócoli *m* 123
bronce *m* 235
bronceado *m* 41
bronceador *m* 265
brújula *f* 240, 312
buceo *m* 239
buenas noches 322
buenas tardes 322
buenísimo 64
bueno 321
buenos días 322
bufanda *f* 31
bufete *m* 180
buffet *m* 152; buffet de desayuno *m* 156
buggy *m* 232
búho *m* 292
bujía *f* 203
bulbo *m* 86
búnker *m* 232
buque porta-contenedores *m* 215
buque tanque *m* 215
buró *m* 70
burro *m* 185; burro de la plancha *m* 76
buscar 177
butaca *f* 254
butacas *f* 254; butacas generales *f* 254
buzo *m* 30
buzón *m* 58, 99
bytes *m* 176

C

caballa *f* 120
caballete *m* 174, 274
caballito de mar *m* 294
caballo *m* 185, 235, 242, 272; caballo con arcos *m* 235; caballo de carreras *m* 243
cabecear 222
cabecera *f* 70
cabecero *m* 70
cabello *m* 14, 38
cabestrillo *m* 46
cabestro *m* 243
cabeza *f* 12, 19, 81, 230
cabezal *m* 78
cabezales de destornillador *m* 80
cabezuela *f* 122
cabina *f* 95, 210; cabina de pilotaje *f* 210; cabina del conductor *f* 208; cabina telefónica *f* 99
cable *m* 79, 207; cable de alimentación *m* 176
cables *m* 60
cabra *f* 185
cabrestante *m* 214
cabrito *m* 185
cacahuete *m* 129
cacahuetes *m* 151
cacao *m* 156; cacao en polvo *m* 148
cacatúa *f* 293
cachar 227
cachorro *m* 290
cactus *m* 87
caddy *m* 233
cadena *f* 36, 59, 206; cadena montañosa *f* 282
cadera *f* 12
café *m* 144, 148, 153, 156, 184; café con hielo *m* 148; café con leche *m* 148; café de cafetera eléctrica *m* 148; café molido *m* 144; café solo *m* 148
cafetera *f* 150; cafetera de émbolo *f* 65
cafetería *f* 148, 262; cafetería con mesas fuera *f* 148
caída *f* 237
caimán *m* 293
caja *f* 106, 150; caja archivador *f* 173; caja de aparejos *f* 244; caja de cambios *f* 202, 204; caja de chocolates *f* 113; caja de fusibles *f* 203; caja de herramientas *f* 80; caja de los fusibles *f* 60; caja de pañuelos desechables 70; caja de velocidades *f* 204; caja para cortar en inglete *f* 81; caja torácica *m* 17
cajero *m* 96, 106; cajero automático *m* 97
cajetilla *f* 311; cajetilla de cigarros *f* 112
cajón *m* 66, 70, 172; cajón de las verduras *m* 67; cajón de salida *m* 234, 238
cajonera *f* 172
cajuela *f* 198
calabacín *m* 124, 125
calabacita *f* 125; calabacita gigante *f* 124
calabaza *f* 125; calabaza bellota *f* 125
calamar *m* 121, 295
calambre *m* 239
calambres *m* 44
calcetines *m* 33
calcio *m* 109
calcita *f* 289
calculadora *f* 165
caldera *f* 61
caldo *m* 158
calefacción *f* 201
calendario *m* 306
calentador *m* 60; calentador de convección *m* 60

cálido 286
caliente 321
calificación *f* 163
cáliz *m* 297
calle *f* 232, 234, 238, 298; calle de sentido único *f* 298; calle lateral *f* 299
callejón *m* 298
calmante *m* 109
caluroso 286
calvo 39
calzapié *m* 207
calzón de plástico *m* 30
calzoncillos de pata *m* 33
cama *f* 70; cama de matrimonio *f* 71; cama de rayos ultravioletas *f* 41; cama individual *f* 71; cama matrimonial *f* 71
cámara *f* 178, 207, 283; cámara APS *f* 270; cámara de video *f* 260, 269; cámara desechable *f* 270; cámara digital *f* 270; cámara fotográfica *f* 260; cámara Polaroid *f* 270; cámara réflex *f* 270
camarera/o *f/m* 191, 148, 150, 152
camarógrafo *m* 178
camarón *m* 121
camarones peladas *m* 120
camarote *f* 214
cambiador *m* 74
cambiar 209; cambiar de canal 269; cambiar de velocidad 207; cambiar una llanta 203
cambio *m* 223
cambios *m* 206
camello *m* 291
camembert *m* 142
camilla *f* 48, 94
caminata *f* 263
camino *m* 58, 85
camión *m* 194; camión de volteo *m* 187; camión volquete 187
camionero *m* 190
camioneta *f* 199
camisa *f* 32
camiseta *f* 30, 33, 251; camiseta de tirantes *f* 35; camiseta interior *f* 33
camisola *f* 35
camisón *m* 31, 35
camote *m* 125
campari *m* 145
campeonato *m* 230
cámper *m* 266
camping *m* 266
campo *m* 182, 220, 222, 225, 228, 234; campo de críquet *m* 225; campo de golf *m* 232; campo de rugby *m* 221; campo deportivo *m* 168
campus *m* 168
canal *m* 178, 269; canal de pago por evento *m* 269
canalón *m* 58
canario *m* 292
canasta *f* 106, 226, 263
canastilla *f* 207
cancha *f* 226
canción *f* 259
candado *m* 207
canela *f* 133
cangrejo *m* 121, 295; cangrejo de río *m* 121
cangurera *f* 75
canguro *m* 291
canoa *f* 214
canotaje *m* 241
cantante *m/f* 191, 258
cantidad *f* 96
cantimplora *f* 267
canto *m* 246
caña *f* 91; caña de azúcar *f* 184; caña de pescar *f* 244; caña del timón *f* 240
cañas *f* 89
capa de ozono *f* 286
capa superior de la tierra *f* 85
capacidad *f* 311
caparazón *m* 293
capital *f* 315
capitán *m* 214; capitán del puerto *m* 217
capó *m* 198
capoeira *f* 237
capota *f* 75
cápsula *f* 109; cápsula de Petri *f* 166
captafaros *m* 204, 207
capuccino *m* 148
capucha *f* 31
capulín *f* 127, 128
capullo *m* 111, 295, 297
caqui *m* 128
cara *f* 14
caracol *m* 295
carámbano *m* 287
carambola *f* 128
caramelo *m* 113; caramelo blando *m* 113
caramelos *m* 113; caramelos duros *m* 113
carbón *m* 288; carbón vegetal *m* 266
carboncillo *m* 275
carcaj *m* 249
cárcel *f* 181
cardamono *m* 132
cardigan *m* 32
cardiología *f* 49
cardiovascular 19
cardo *m* 297
careta *f* 228, 236
carga *f* 216
cargar 76
cargo *m* 94, 180
caricaturas *f* 178
caries *f* 50
carnaval *m* 27
carne *f* 119; carne blanca *f* 118; carne de caza *f* 119; carne de vaca *f* 118; carne fresca *f* 142; carne magra *f* 118; carne molida *f* 119; carne picada *m* 119; carne roja *f* 118
carnicería *f* 114
carnicero *m* 118, 188
carpa koi *f* 294
carpeta *f* 172, 177; carpeta de anillas *f* 173; carpeta de argollas *f* 173
carpintero *m* 188
carrera *f* 169, 228, 234; carrera al trote *f* 243; carrera de caballos *f* 243; carrera de carrozas *f* 243; carrera de lanchas *f* 241; carrera de motoras *f* 241; carrera de obstáculos *f* 243; carrera de relevos *f* 235; carrera de vallas *f* 235; carrera sin obstáculos *f* 243
carrete *m* 244, 245, 271; carrete de hilo *m* 276
carreteras *f* 194
carretilla *f* 88; carretilla elevadora *f* 186, 216
carril *m* 234, 238; carril central *m* 194; carril de adelantamiento *m* 194; carril de baja *m* 194; carril de bicicletas *m* 206; carril izquierdo *m* 194; carril para el tráfico lento *m* 194
carriola *f* 75
carrito *m* 100, 106, 208, 213, 232; carrito de golf *m* 233; carrito de los postres *m* 152
carro *m* 106, 198, 200, 213; carro de bomberos *m* 95; carro de cinco puertas *m* 199; carro deportivo *m* 199; carro familiar *m* 199
carta *f* 98, 148, 153; carta por avión *f* 98
cartas *f* 273
cartera *f* 37, 97, 162
cartero *m* 98, 190
cartílago *m* 17
cartón de leche *m* 136
cartón madera *m* 79
cartulina *f* 275
carvi *m* 131
casa *f* 58; casa club *f* 232; casa de juguete *f* 75; casa de la ciudad *f* 58; casa de labranza *f* 182; casa de muñecas *f* 75
casarse 26
cascada *f* 285
cáscara *f* 126, 127, 129, 130, 137
casco *m* 95, 186, 204, 206, 214, 220, 224, 228, 240, 242
caserola *f* 69
caseta *f* 264; caseta de cobro *f* 194; caseta de peaje *f* 194
casete *m* 269
casilla *f* 100, 272
casino *m* 261
caspa *f* 39
castaña *f* 129; castaña de agua *f* 124
castaño 39
castillo *m* 300; castillo de arena *m* 265
casual 34
catálogo *m* 168
catamarán *m* 215
catarata *f* 51
catarina *f* 295
catcher *m* 229
catedral *f* 300
catéter *m* 53
catorce 308
catre de campaña *m* 268
catsup *f* 135, 154
cavar 90
caza *m* 211
cazadora *f* 33
cazo *m* 69
cazoleta *f* 112
cazuela *f* 69; cazuela de barro *f* 69
cebada *f* 130, 184
cebar 245
cebo *m* 244
cebolla *f* 124
cebolleta *f* 125
cebollín *m* 125
cebollinos *m* 133
cebra *f* 291
cedro *m* 296
ceja *f* 14, 51
celador *m* 181
celda *f* 94, 181
celebración *f* 140
celebraciones *f* 27
celular *m* 99
cemento *m* 186; cemento blanco *m* 83
cena *f* 64
cenicero *m* 150
ceniza *f* 283
centésimo 309
centímetro *m* 310
centrífuga *f* 76
centrifugadora *f* 76
centrifugar 76
centro *m* 122, 164; centro comercial *m* 104; centro de salud *m* 168; centro del campo *m* 228
ceño fruncido *m* 25
cepillar 38, 79
cepillarse los dientes 50
cepillo *m* 38, 77, 81; cepillo de dientes *m* 72; cepillo del escusado *m* 72; cepillo para la espalda *m* 73; cepillo para las cejas *m* 40
cera *f* 77
cerámica *f* 275
cerca 320; cerca *f* 182
cercado *m* 242
cerdito *m* 185
cerdo *m* 118, 185
cereales *m* 107, 130, 156
cerebro *m* 19
ceremonia de graduación *f* 169
cereza *f* 126
cerillas *f* 112
cerillos *m* 112
cernir 138
cero 308
cerrada *f* 221
cerrado 260, 321
cerradura *f* 59
cerrojo *m* 59
cerveza *f* 145, 151; cerveza amarga *f* 145; cerveza negra *f* 145
cesárea *f* 52
césped *m* 87, 90
cesta *f* 95, 106, 207, 263; cesta colgante *f* 84; cesta de fruta *f* 126; cesta de jardinero *f* 88
cesto de la colada *m* 76
cesto de la ropa para planchar *m* 76
cesto de la ropa sucia *m* 76
cesto de los juguetes *m* 75
ceta *f* 85

chaleco *m* 33; chaleco salvavidas *m* 240
chalote *m* 125
chamarra *f* 31, 33
champán *m* 145
champanera *f* 150
champiñón *m* 125
champú *m* 38
chanchito *m* 185
chancla *f* 37
chándal *m* 31
chango *m* 291
changuero *m* 263
chapa *f* 202
chaqueta *f* 33, 34
chaquetón *m* 31
charcutería *f* 107, 142
charola *f* 67, 152, 154; charola de horno *f* 69; charola del desayuno *f* 101
chasis *m* 203
checador *m* 209
cheddar *m* 142
chef *m* 152, 190
cheque *m* 96; cheque de viaje *m* 97; cheque de viajero *m* 97
chica *f* 23
chícharo *m* 122
chícharos *m* 131; chícharos secos *m* 131
chichonera *f* 74
chicle *m* 113
chico *m* 23
chilaca *f* 124
chile piquín *m* 132, 143
chimenea *f* 58, 63, 214, 283
chinche *f* 173
chincheta *f* 173
chips de chocolate *m* 141
chiquero *m* 185
chirivía *f* 125
chocolate *m* 113; chocolate blanco *m* 113; chocolate caliente *m* 144, 156; chocolate de leche *m* 113; chocolate para untar *m* 135
chófer *m* 190, 196
chongo *m* 39; chongo francés *m* 39
chorizo *m* 143
chorro de agua *m* 95
chubasco *m* 286
chuleta *f* 119
chupón *m* 75
chutar 221, 223
chutney *m* 134
ciclismo *m* 263
ciempiés *m* 295
cien 308
cien mil 308
ciencia *f* 162
ciencias *f* 166; ciencias económicas *f* 169
cieno *m* 85
científico *m* 190
ciento diez 308
cierre *m* 36, 37; cierre de seguridad *m* 75
ciervo *m* 291
cigarrillos *m* 112
cigarros *m* 112
cigüeña *f* 292
cilantro *m* 133
cilindro *m* 164
cincel *m* 81, 275
cincha *f* 242
cinco 308
cincuenta 308
cincuenta mil 309
cincuenta y cinco mil quinientos 309
cine *m* 255, 299
cinta *f* 27, 111, 141, 235; cinta adhesiva protectora *f* 83; cinta aislante *f* 81; cinta de vídeo *f* 269; cinta métrica *f* 80, 276; cinta para el pie *f* 241; cinta reflectante *f* 205; cinta scotch *f* 173; cinta transportadora *f* 106, 212
cintura *f* 12
cinturilla *f* 35
cinturón *m* 32, 36, 236; cinturón de las herramientas *m* 186; cinturón de pesas *m* 239; cinturón de seguridad *m* 198, 211; cinturón negro *m* 237
círculo *m* 165; círculo central *m* 222, 224, 226; círculo de face-off *m* 224
circunferencia *f* 164
ciruela *f* 126; ciruela pasa *f* 129
cirugía *f* 48; cirugía plástica *f* 49
cirujano *m* 48
cisne *m* 293
cisterna *f* 61
cita *f* 45, 175
citación *f* 180
cítricos *m* 126
citronela *f* 133
ciudad *f* 298, 299
cizalla *f* 89
claqueta *f* 179
clara *f* 137
clarinete *m* 257; clarinete bajo *m* 257
claro 41, 321
clase preferente *f* 211
clase turista *f* 211
clavadista *m* 238
clavado *m* 239; clavado alto *m* 239; clavado de salida *m* 239
clavar 79
clave de fa *f* 256
clave de sol *f* 256
clavel *m* 110
clavícula *f* 17
clavija *f* 60, 259, 266
clavo *m* 80
clavos *m* 133, 233
claxon *m* 201, 204
cliente *f* 38; cliente *m* 96, 104, 106, 152, 175, 180
clínica *f* 48
clip *m* 173
clítoris *m* 20
club *m* 232; club sandwich *m* 155
cobertizo *m* 84, 182
cobija *f* 71, 74; cobija eléctrica *f* 71
cobrar 97
cobre *m* 289
cocer a fuego lento 67
cocer al horno 67
cocer al vapor 67
coche *m* 198; coche de bomberos *m* 95; coche de época *m* 199; coche de policía *m* 94; coche descapotable *m* 199; coche ranchera *m* 199
cochecama *m* 209
cochecito de niños *m* 75
cochera *f* 58
cocido en el horno 159
cocina *f* 66, 152, 214
cocinar 67
coco *m* 129
cocoa *f* 148
cocodrilo *m* 293
cóctel *m* 151
coctelera *f* 150
código de barras *m* 106
código postal *m* 98
codo *m* 13
codorniz *f* 119
cofre *m* 198
coger 220, 227, 229, 245; coger prestado 168
coito *m* 20
cojín *m* 62; cojín de la tinta *f* 173
col *f* 123; col rizada *f* 123
cola *f* 35, 121, 144, 210, 242, 275, 280, 290, 294; cola de caballo *f* 39; cola de carpintero *f* 78; cola para empapelar *f* 82
colada *f* 76
coladera *f* 72, 299
colador *m* 68
colcha *f* 70, 71
colchón *m* 70, 74
colchoneta *f* 54, 267
colegial/-a *m/f* 162
colegio *m* 162; colegio mayor *m* 168
coles de bruselas *f* 122
coletas *f* 39
colgante *m* 36, 173
colguije *m* 36
colibrí *m* 292
coliflor *f* 124
colina *f* 284
colinabo *m* 123
collage *m* 275
collar *m* 36; collar de perlas *m* 36
collarín *m* 46
colmillo *m* 50, 291
colonia *f* 315
color *m* 163
colores *m* 39, 274
colorete *m* 40
columna *f* 300
columpios *m* 263
colza *f* 184
comadrona *f* 53
combate *m* 237
combinación *f* 35
comedero *m* 183
comedia *f* 255
comedor *m* 64
comer 64
cometa *m* 280
comida *f* 64, 75, 149; comida de negocios *f* 175; comida para animales *f* 107; comida principal *f* 158; comida rápida *f* 154
comino *m* 132
comisión *f* 97; comisión del banco *f* 96
cómoda *f* 70
comodín *m* 273
compacto *m* 199
compañero/-a *m/f* 24, 23
compartimento *m* 209; compartimento del carrete *m* 270; compartimento portaequipajes *m* 210
compás *m* 165
complejo vitamínico *m* 109
completo 266
composta *f* 85, 88
compra *f* 106
compras *f* 104
compresa *f* 108
computadora *f* 172, 176
comunicaciones *f* 98
comunicando 99
con 320
con aros 35
con brillo 83, 271
con corriente 60
con gas 144
con hielo y limón 151
con los hombros al aire 35
con plomo 199
con varillas 35
concebir 20
concepción *f* 52
concha *f* 265
concierto *m* 255, 258; concierto de rock *m* 258
concurso *m* 178; concurso de saltos *m* 243
condón *m* 21
conducir 195
conducto seminal *m* 21
conductor *m* 196
conectar 177
conejo *m* 118, 290
conexión *f* 212
confitería *f* 107, 114
confuso 25
congelado 121, 124
congelador *m* 67
congelados *m* 107
congelar 67
conglomerado *m* 288
conífera *f* 86
conmoción *f* 46
conmutador de luces *m* 201
cono *m* 164, 187
conocido *m* 24
conseguir un trabajo 26
conservante *m* 83
conservas *f* 107; conservas dulces *f* 134
conservatorio *m* 169
consola *f* 179, 269
constelación *f* 281
construcción *f* 186
construir 186
consulta *f* 45
contable *m/f* 97, 190
contador *m* 97, 190; contador de la luz *m* 60
contar 165
contenedor *m* 216; contenedor de la basura *m* 266
contento 25
contestador automático *m* 99
contestadora *f* 99
contestar 99, 163
continente *m* 282, 315
contrabajo *m* 256, 258
contracción *f* 52
contrachapado *m* 79
contrafagote *m* 257
contrafuerte *m* 301
contraventana *f* 58
control de pasaportes *m* 213

control remoto m 269
controles m 201, 204, 269
convertible m 199
coñac m 145
copa f 152; copa de vino m 65
copas f 150
copiloto m 211
corazón m 18, 119, 122, 127, 273
corbata f 32
corchete m 30, 276
corcho m 134, 173
cordero m 118, 185
cordón umbilical m 52
cordonera f 37
córnea f 51
córner m 223
cornisa 300
corno de caza m 257
corno inglés m 257
coro m 301
corona f 50, 111
corral m 75, 182
correa f 37; correa del calzapié f 207; correa del disco 203; correa del ventilador 203
correo certificado m 98
correo electrónico m 98, 177
correr 228
correr en parada 251
corriente alterna f 60
corriente continua m 60
corriente eléctrica f 60
corsé m 35; corsé con liguero m 35
cortaalambres m 81
cortacésped m 88, 90
cortada m 46
cortadora f 88
cortar 38, 67, 79, 277; cortar el césped 90; cortar las puntas 39
cortatuberías m 81
cortaúñas m 41
corte m 46; corte de luz m 60
cortes m 119
corteza f 126, 127, 136, 139, 142, 282, 296
cortina f 63; cortina de ducha f 72; cortina de la regadera f 72
corto 33, 131, 151
cosecha f 183
cosechadora f 182
cosechar 91
coser 277
cosméticos m 105
costa f 285
costilla f 17, 119
costillas f 155
costura f 34
costurera f 277
costurero m 276
coxis m 17
CPU f 176
cráneo m 17
cráter m 283
credencial f 168
crema f 109, 137, 140, 157; crema ácida f 137; crema autobronceadora f 41; crema batida f 137; crema bronceadora f 41, 265; crema de cacahuetes f 135; crema de limón f 134; crema hidratante f 41; crema limpiadora f 41; crema líquida f 137; crema para después del sol f 108; crema para el cuerpo f 73; crema para la cara f 73; crema para las escoceduras f 74; crema para las rozaduras f 74; crema para montar f 137; crema pastelera 140; crema protectora f 108, 265; crema protectora total f 108
cremallera f 277
crepas f 157
crêpe f 155
cría f 290
criadero de peces m 183
criba f 89
cribar 91, 138
crimen m 94
criminal m 181
crin f 242
críquet m 225
crisantemo m 110
crisol m 166
cristal m 51
cristalería f 64
cristaloterapia m 55
croissant m 156
crol m 239
cronómetro m 166, 234
cruce m 298
crucero m 194, 298
crudo 124, 129
cuaderno m 163, 172
cuadra f 243
cuadrado m 164
cuadragésimo 309
cuadríceps m 16
cuadro m 62, 206, 261, 274
cuarenta 308
cuarenta iguales m 230
cuarenta minutos 304
cuarto 309
cuarto de estar m 62
cuarto de galón m 311
cuarto oscuro m 271
cuarto para cambiar a los bebés m 104
cuarzo m 289
cuatro 308
cuatrocientos 308
cuba libre f 151
cubeta f 82, 265
cubierta f 206, 214, 240
cubierto de chocolate 140
cubiertos m 64
cubito de hielo m 151
cúbito m 17
cubo m 77, 82, 164, 265; cubo de la basura m 61; cubo para reciclar m 61
cubrecanapé m 71
cucaracha f 295
cuchara f 65; cuchara de madera f 68; cuchara de servir f 68; cuchara medidora f 109; cuchara para helado f 68; cuchara sopera f 65
cucharilla de café f 65, 153
cucharón m 68
cuchilla f 66, 78
cuchillo m 65; cuchillo de cocina m 68; cuchillo de sierra m 68
cuello m 12, 32; cuello de pico m 33; cuello del útero m 20; cuello en V m 33; cuello redondo m 33; cuello uterino m 52
cuenco m 69; cuenco mezclador m 66
cuenta f 152; cuenta corriente f 96; cuenta de ahorros f 97; cuenta de correo f 177
cuentagotas m 167
cuentakilómetros m 201
cuentarrevoluciones m 201, 204
cuerda f 230, 248, 256, 258, 266; cuerda de plomada f 82; cuerda para tender la ropa f 76
cuerdas vocales f 19
cuerno m 291
cuero cabelludo m 39
cuerpo m 12
cuerpos geométricos m 164
cuervo m 292
cueva f 284
cuidado de la piel m 108
cuidado del bebé m 74
cuidado dental m 108
cuidar 91
culata f 202
culpable 181
cultivador m 182
cultivar 91
cultivos m 184
cumpleaños m 27
cuna f 74
cuñada f 23
cuñado m 23
cúpula f 300
curado 118, 143, 159
cúrcuma f 132
curling m 247
curry m 158; curry en polvo m 132
curso m 163
curvo 165
cuscús m 130
cúter m 80, 82
cutícula f 15
cutis m 41

D

dado de alta 48
dados m 272
damas f 272
dar 273; dar de comer 183; dar el pecho 53; dar marcha atrás 195
dardos m 273
darse un baño 72
darse una ducha 72
dársena f 216
dátil m 129
de 320; de cristal 69; de cuatro puertas 200; de fácil cocción 130; de granja 118; de hoja caduca 86; de hoja perenne 86; de mucho viento 286; de nada 322; de nalgas 52; de preparación al parto 52; de sentido único 194; de temporada 129; de tres puertas 200; de vestir 34
debajo de 320
deberes m 163
débil 321
débito directo m 96
década f 307
décimo 309
décimo noveno 309
décimo octavo 309
decimocuarto 309
decimoquinto 309
decimoséptimo 309
decimosexto 309
decimotercero 309
declaración f 180
decoración f 82, 141
decorado m 254
dedal m 276
dedalera f 297
dedo corazón m 15
dedo del pie m 15
dedo gordo del pie m 15
dedo pequeño del pie m 15
defender 229
defensa f 181, 198, 220
defensa m 223; defensa personal f 237
dejada f 230
delantal m 30, 50, 69
delante de 320
delantero m 222
deletrear 162
delfín m 290
delgado 321
delineador m 40
deltoides m 16
denominación m 97
denominador m 165
dentadura postiza f 50
dentista m 50, f 189
dentro 320; dentro de 320
denuncia f 94
departamento m 59, 169; departamento de atención al cliente m 175; departamento de contabilidad m 175; departamento de equipajes m 104; departamento de márketing m 175; departamento de niños m 104; departamento de recursos humanos m 175; departamento de ventas m 175; departamento de zapatería m 104; departamento legal m 175
dependiente m/f 104
depilación a la cera f 41
deportes m 220, 236, 248; deportes acuáticos m 241; deportes de combate m 236; deportes de invierno m 247
deportista m 191
depositar 96
depósito m 61; depósito del aceite m 204; depósito del limpiaparabrisas m 202; depósito del líquido de frenos m 202; depósito del líquido refrigerante m 202
derecha f 260
derecho m 169, 180, 231
dermatología f 49
derrame cerebral m 44
derribo m 237
desagüe m 61
desarmador m 151

desatapancaños *m* 81
desatascador *m* 81
desayuno *m* 64, 156; desayuno inglés *m* 157
descansabrazos *m* 210
descansillo *m* 59
descanso *m* 59, 223, 254
descarga eléctrica *f* 46
descenso *m* 247
desconectado 99
descongelar 67
descorazonador *m* 68
descoser 277
descubierto *m* 96, 260
desde 320
desecado 129
desechable 109
desembarcar 217
desenfocado 271
desfiladero *m* 284
desfile *m* 27
desierto *m* 285
desinfectante *m* 47
desmayarse 25, 44
desnatada 136
desodorante *m* 73
desodorantes *m* 108
despacho *m* 63
despegar 82, 211
desperdicios orgánicos *m* 61
despertarse 71
después 320
despuntar 39
destapador *m* 68, 150
destino *m* 213
destornillador *m* 80; destornillador de estrella *m* 80; destornillador de cruz *m* 81
desuiación *m* 195
desvío *m* 195
detective *m* 94
detector de humo *m* 95
detergente *m* 77
detrás de 320
día *m* 305, 306; día de Acción de Gracias *m* 27; día de Halloween *m* 27; día hábil 304; día laborable *m* 306
diabetes *f* 44
diablito *m* 100
diadema *f* 38
diafragma *m* 19, 21
diagonal *f* 164
diamante *m* 273, 288
diámetro *m* 164
diana *f* 249, 273
diarrea *f* 44, 109
dibujar 162
dibujo *m* 275
diccionario *m* 163
diciembre 306
diecinueve 308
dieciocho 308
dieciséis 308
diecisiete 308
diente *m* 50, 125
diente de león *m* 123, 297
diesel *m* 199
diez 308
diez mil 309
difícil 321
digestivo 19
digital 269
dilatación *f* 52
dinamo *f* 207
dinero *m* 97
dintel *m* 186
dioptría *f* 51
diploma *m* 169
dique seco *m* 217
dirección *f* 98; dirección de correo electrónico *f* 177
direccional *m* 198, 204
director *m* 163, 174, 254; director de banco *m* 96; director de orquesta *m* 256; director general *m* 175
directorio *m* 104
discman *m* 269
disco *m* 224; disco compacto *m* 269; disco de DVD *m* 269; disco duro *m* 176
discos protectores *m* 53
discutir 163
diseñador *m* 277
diseñadora *f* 191
diseñar 91
disolvente *m* 83
disparador *m* 270
dispensario *m* 108
dispositivo intrauterino DIU *m* 21
disquete *m* 176
distancia *f* 310
distribuidor *m* 203
distrito *m* 315
dividendos *m* 97
dividido entre 165
dividir 165
divisas *f* 97
divisor *m* 173
divorcio *m* 26
Diwali *m* 27
DJ *m* 179
dobladillo *m* 34
doble tracción *f* 199
doce 308
doctor *m* 45
doctorado *m* 169
documental *m* 178
documento adjunto *m* 177
dolor de cabeza *m* 44
dolor de estómago *m* 44
dolor de muelas *m* 50
doma y monta *f* 243
domiciliación bancaria *f* 96
domingo 306
dominó *m* 273
dona *f* 139
dormirse 71
dorsal *m* 16
dorso *m* 239
dos 308
dos en punto 304
dos mil 307
dos mil uno 307
dos puertas 200
doscientos 308
dosis *f* 109
drenaje *m* 91, 299
ducha *f* 72, 266
dulce 124, 127, 155
dulcería *f* 107, 113
dulces *m* 113; dulces a granel *m* 113
dulla *f* 69
duodécimo 309
duodeno *m* 18
dúplex 58
duro 129, 321
duty-free *m* 213

E

eccema *m* 44
echar 67
eclipse *m* 280
ecografía *f* 48, 52
ecuación *f* 165
ecuador *m* 283
edificio *m* 59; edificio de departamentos *m* 298; edificio de oficinas *m* 298; edificio de pisos *m* 298; edificio histórico *m* 261
edificios *m* 299
edredón *m* 71
educación física *f* 162
efecto *m* 230
efectos secundarios *m* 109
eje *m* 205, 206; eje de la transmisión *m* 202
ejecutivo *m* 174
ejercicio de bíceps *m* 251
ejercicios *f* 251; ejercicios de piernas *m* 251; ejercicios de piso *m* 235; ejercicios de suelo *m* 235; ejercicios pectorales *f* 251
ejote *m* 122
electricidad *f* 60
electricista *m* 188
electrodo negativo *m* 167
electrodo positivo *m* 167
electrodomésticos *m* 66, 107
elefante *m* 291
elevador *m* 59, 100, 104
eliminación de desechos *f* 61
embalse *m* 300
embarazada 52
embarazo *m* 52
embarcaciones *f* 215
embarcadero *m* 217
embarcar 217
embrague *m* 200, 204
embrión *m* 52
embudo *m* 166
emergencia *f* 46
emigrar 26
emisión *f* 179
emitir 178
emociones *f* 25
empanada *m* 158
empapelar 82
empaste *m* 50
empate *m* 223
empeine *m* 15
empezar el colegio 26
empleado *m* 24; empleado de correos *m* 98; empleado de la limpieza *m* 188
empresa *f* 175
empresaria *f* 24
en 320; en aceite 143; en almíbar 159; en diferido 178; en directo 178; en filetes 121; en formato vertical 271; en frente de 320; en línea 177; en polvo 77; en salmuera 143; en salsa 159; en vinagre 159
enamorarse 26
encaje *m* 35, 80
encendedor *m* 112
encender la televisión 269
encender una fogata 266
encendido *m* 200
enchufe *m* 60; enchufe macho *m* 60
encía *f* 50
enciclopedia *f* 163
encima de 320
encimera *f* 66
encinta 52
endibia *f* 122
endocrino 19
endocrinología *f* 49
eneldo *m* 133
enero 306
enfadado 25
enfermedad *f* 44; enfermedad de transmisión sexual *f* 20
enfermera *f* 45, 48, 52, 189
enfocar 271
engrane *m* 207
engrapadora *f* 173
enhebrar 277
enjuagar 38
enjuague bucal *m* 72
enredadera *f* 84
enrollador de manguera *m* 89
ensalada *f* 149; ensalada mixta *f* 158; ensalada verde *f* 158
ensaladera *f* 69
ensartar 277
ensayo *m* 221
enseñanza superior *f* 168
entallado 35
entarimado *m* 85
entero 129, 132
entrada *f* 59, 153, 194
entrante *m* 153
entrar en el sistema 177
entrar en erupción 283
entre 320
entreacto *m* 254
entrega a domicilio *f* 154
entrenadora personal *f* 250
entrenamiento *m* 237
entrenar 251
entretenimiento en el hogar *m* 268
entrevistador *m* 179
entusiasmado 25
envenenamiento *m* 46
enviar 177
envoltora *f* 111
enyesar 82
epidural *f* 52
epiglotis *f* 19
epilepsia *f* 44
episiotomía *f* 52
equipaje de mano *m* 211, 213
equipaje *m* 100, 198, 213
equipo *m* 205, 220, 229, 233, 238; equipo de alta fidelidad *m* 268; equipo de limpieza *m* 77; equipo de oficina *m* 172
equitación *f* 242, 263
erizo *m* 290
escala *f* 256
escalada *f* 248; escalada en hielo *f* 247
escalera *f* 59, 95, 186; escalera de emergencia *f* 210; escalera de mano *f* 82; escalera eléctrica *f* 104
escalfado 159
escalfar 67

escalpelo *f* 81
escama *f* 121, 294
escamas *f* 293
escáner *m* 106
escarabajo *m* 295
escarcha *f* 287
escardar 91
escariador *m* 80
escarola *f* 123
escenario *m* 254
escenografía *f* 254
escoba *f* 77
escorpión *m* 295
escota *f* 241
escote *m* 34
escotera *f* 240
escotilla *f* 281
escribir 162
escritorio *m* 172, 177
escroto *m* 21
escuadra *f* 165
escuchabebés *m* 75
escuela *f* 299; escuela de Bellas Artes *f* 169
escuelas *f* 169
escultor *m* 191
escultura *f* 275
escurridor *m* 67, 68
escusado *m* 72
esfera *f* 164
esgrima *f* 249
eslabón *m* 36
esmalte *m* 50; esmalte de uñas *m* 41
esmeralda *f* 288
esófago *m* 19
espacio *m* 280
espada *f* 236, 273
espalda *f* 13, 239
espaldera *f* 84
espantapájaros *m* 184
esparadrapo *m* 47
espátula *f* 68, 82, 167
especialista *m* 49
especias *f* 132
espectadores *m* 233
espejo *m* 40, 63, 71, 167; espejo lateral *m* 198; espejo retrovisor *m* 198
esperma *m* 20
espigón *m* 217
espina *f* 121; espina dorsal *f* 17
espinaca *f* 123
espinilla *f* 12
esponja *f* 73, 74, 83; esponja de luffa *f* 73
esposa *f* 22
esposas *f* 94
esposo *m* 22
esprinter *m* 234
espuma *f* 148
espumadera *f* 68
esqueje *m* 91
esqueleto *m* 17
esquí *m* 241, 246; esquí acuático *m* 241; esquí alpino *m* 247; esquí de fondo *m* 247
esquiador acuático *m* 241
esquiadora *f* 246
esquina *f* 298
esquisto *m* 288
esta semana 307
estabilizador horizontal *m* 210
establo *m* 185
estaca *f* 90, 266
estación de autobuses *f* 197
estación de bomberos *f* 95
estación de policía *f* 94
estación de radio *f* 179
estación de tren *f* 208
estación espacial *f* 281
estacionamiento *m* 298
estacionamiento para minusválidos *m* 195
estacionar 195
estaciones *f* 306
estado *m* 315
estambre *m* 297
estanque *m* 67, 85, 106, 232
estante *m* 67
estantería *f* 63, 168
estantes *m* 66
estaño *m* 289
estatuilla *f* 260
este *m* 312
estéreo 269
estéril 20, 47
esterilla *f* 267
esternón *m* 17
estética *f* 115
estetoscopio *m* 45
estilista *f* 38, 188
estilo modernista *m* 301
estilos *m* 39, 239, 301; estilos de jardín *m* 84; estilos musicales *m* 259
estiramiento *m* 251
estirar 251
estómago *m* 18
estor *m* 63
estor de láminas *m* 63
estornudo *m* 44
estragón *m* 133
estratosfera *f* 286
estrecho 321
estrella *f* 206, 280; estrella de mar *f* 295
estreno *m* 254
estrés *m* 55
estribo *m* 71, 242
estructura *f* 267
estructura para escalar *f* 263
estuario *m* 285
estuche *m* 51, 163; estuche para los pupilentes *m* 51
estudiante *m* 169
estudio *m* 63, 162; estudio de grabación *m* 179; estudio de televisión *m* 178
estufa *f* 60
estufilla *f* 267
etapas *f* 23
etiqueta *f* 172
etiquetas *f* 89
eucalipto *m* 296
evidencia *f* 181
examen *m* 163; examen de ojos *m* 51; examen médico *m* 45
excavadora mecánica *f* 187
exceso de equipaje *m* 212
exfoliar 41
exósfera *f* 286
experimento *m* 166
exploración espacial *f* 281
exposición *f* 261, 271
expreso *m* 148
expulsión *f* 223
extender con el rodillo 67
extensión *m* 78
exterior *m* 198, 229; exterior derecho *m* 229; exterior izquierdo *m* 228
extintor *m* 95
extracción *f* 50
extractor *m* 66

F

fábrica *f* 299
fácil 321
facturar 212
fagote *m* 257
faisán *m* 119, 293
falda *f* 30, 34
fallo *m* 228
falsa torre *f* 215
falta *f* 222, 226, 230
familia *f* 22
fans *m* 258
faringe *f* 19
farmacéutica/-o *f* /*m* 189, 108
farmacia *f* 108
faro *m* 198, 205, 207, 217; faro trasero *m* 207
farol *m* 298
farola *f* 298
fax *m* 98, 172
febrero 306
fecha *f* 306; fecha de caducidad *f* 109; fecha de devolución *f* 168; fecha del juicio *f* 180
feijoa *f* 128
felpudo *m* 59
femenino 20
fémur *m* 17
feng shui *m* 55
feria *f* 262
ferretería *f* 114
ferry *m* 215, 216
fertilización *f* 20
festivales *m* 27
feto *m* 52
fiambre *m* 118, 142, 143
fianza *f* 181
fibra *f* 127; fibra natural *f* 31
ficha *f* 272; ficha de retiro *f* 96
fichas de depósito *f* 96
fichero *m* 177
fideos *m* 158
fiebre *f* 44; fiebre del heno *f* 44
fierro *m* 233
fiesta de cumpleaños *f* 27
fila *f* 210, 254
filamento *m* 60
filatelia *f* 273
filete *m* 119, 121; filete de lomo *m* 119; filete de solomillo *m* 119
filetes de mero *m* 120
filosofía *f* 169
filtro *m* 270; filtro de papel *m* 167; filtro del aire *m* 202, 204
fin de semana *m* 306
final *m* 321
finanzas *f* 97
firma *f* 96, 98
firme 124
física *f* 162, 169
fisioterapia *f* 49
flamenco *m* 292
flan *m* 141
flanera *f* 69
flash *m* 270
flash electrónico *m* 270
flauta *f* 257
flautín *m* 257
flecha *f* 249
flexión *f* 251; flexión con estiramiento *f* 251
flexionar 251
flor *f* 297
florentina *f* 141
florería *f* 110
florero *m* 111
flores *f* 110; flores secas *f* 111
florete *m* 249
florista *f* 188
floristería *f* 110
florón 300
flotador *m* 61, 238, 244, 265; flotador de brazo *m* 238
foca *f* 290
foco *m* 50, 60, 178
fogata *f* 266
folículo *m* 20
follaje *m* 110
folleto *m* 175
folleto de viajes *m* 212
folletos *m* 96
fondear 217
fondo *m* 35, 177
fontanería *f* 61
fontanero *m* 188
footing *m* 251
foque *m* 240
fórceps *m* 53, 167
forma física *f* 250
formas *f* 164
forro *m* 32
foso *m* 300; foso de la orquesta *m* 254
foto *f* 271; foto (revelada) *f* 271; foto final *f* 234
fotocopiar 172
fotofinish *f* 234
fotografía *f* 270
fotografiar 271
fotógrafo *m* 191
fotómetro *m* 270
foul *m* 228
fracción *f* 165
fractura *f* 46
frágil 98
frambuesa *f* 127; frambuesa Logan *f* 127
franqueo *m* 98
frasco de cristal *m* 166
frecuencia *f* 179
fregadero *m* 66
fregador *m* 61
fregar 77
fregona *f* 77
freír 67
frenar 207
freno *m* 200, 204, 206, 242; freno de mano *m* 203
frenos *m* 50, 207
frente *f* 14; frente de la cocina *m* 66
fresa *f* 127
fresco 121, 127, 130
fresia *f* 110
friegaplatos *m* 66
frigorífico *m* 67; frigorífico congelador *m* 67
frijol blanco *m* 131
frijol blanco chico *m* 131
frijol de ojo negro *m* 131
frijol flageolet *m* 131
frijol morado *m* 131
frijol mung *m* 131
frijol pinto *m* 131
frijol rojo *m* 131
frío 286, 321
friso *m* 301
frito 159; frito con mucho aceite 159

frito con poco aceite 159
frontal m 16
frontalera f 242
frontón m 300, 301
fruta f 107, 126, 128; fruta con hueso f 126; fruta desecada f 156; fruta en conserva f 134; fruta escarchada f 129; fruta fresca f 157; fruta seca f 156
frutas tropicales f 128
frutero m 126, 188
fruto del pan m 124
frutos secos m 129, 151
fuente f 85, 177; fuente para gratinar f 69
fuera 225, 228, 320; fuera de banda 226; fuera de juego m 223; fuera de pista 247
fuerte 321
full contact m 236
fumar 112
funcionario de prisiones m 181
funda f 51; funda de la almohada f 71; funda de la cámara f 271
funeral m 26
fuselaje m 210
fusible m 60
fusta f 242
fútbol m 222; fútbol Americano m 220
futbolista m 222

G

gabardina f 32
gachas de avena f 157
gafas f 51, 239, 247; gafas de natación f 238; gafas de seguridad f 81; gafas de sol f 51, 265; gafas protectoras f 167
gajo m 126
galápago m 293
galaxia f 280
galería f 254; galería de arte f 115, 261
galleta f 113; galleta de centeno f 156
galletas f 141
gallina f 185
gallinero m 185
gallo m 185, 231
galón m 311
galope m 243
galvanizado 79
gambas peladas f 120
ganado m 183, 185
ganador m 273
ganar 273
ganchillo m 277
gancho m 70, 118, 187
ganso m 119
garaje m 58
garbanzos m 131
garganta f 19
garra f 291
gasa f 47
gasolina f 199
gasolinera f 199
gatito m 290
gato m 290
gaveta f 66
gaviota f 292
géiser m 285
gel m 38, 109; gel de baño m 73; gel de ducha m 73
gemas f 288
gemelo m 36
gemelos m 23
generación f 23
generador m 60
genitales m 12
gente f 12, 16
geografía f 162
geometría f 165
gerbera f 110
gerente m 174; gerente del banco m 96
germinado de soja m 122
giba f 291
gimnasia f 235; gimnasia prepugilística f 251; gimnasia rítmica f 235
gimnasio m 101, 250
gimnasta f 235
gin tonic m 151
ginebra f 145
ginecología f 49
ginecólogo m 52
girasol m 184, 297
giro m 238; giro postal m 98
gis m 162
glaciar m 284
gladiola f 110
glándula f 19; glándula del tiroides f 18
glasear 139
globo m 230; globo aerostático m 211; globo para batir m 68
glorieta f 195
glúteo m 16
gneis m 288
gofres m 157
goggles m 239, 247
golf m 232
golfista m 232
golondrina f 292
golpe m 233, 237
golpear 224
golpes m 231
goma f 163; goma del freno f 207; goma del pelo f 39; goma elástica f 173
gominola f 113
gomita f 113
góndola m 246
gong m 257
gordo 321
gorila m 291
gorra f 36, 238; gorra de montar f 242
gorrión m 292
gorro de baño m 238
gorro de cocinero m 190
gorro para el sol m 30
gotas f 109
gotero m 53, 109, 167
gótico 301
grabado m 275
grabadora de minidisks f 268
gracias 322
graduarse 26
gráfica del paciente f 48
grafito m 289
gramo m 310
granada f 128
granate m 288
grande 321
granero m 182
granito m 288
granizo m 286
granja f 182, 184; granja avícola f 183; granja de frutales f 183; granja de ganado ovino f 183; granja de ganado porcino f 183; granja de tierras cultivables f 183
granjero m 182
grano m 130
granos m 130, 144; granos procesados m 130
grapadora f 173
grapas f 173
grasa f 119
graso 39, 41
grava f 88
gravedad f 280
green m 232
grifo m 61, 66, 72; grifo de cerveza m 150
grillo m 295
gripe f 44
gris 39, 274
gritar 25
grosella blanca f 127
grosella espinosa f 127
grosella negra f 127
grúa de la cámara f 178
grúa f 187, 203, 216
grueso 321
grulla f 292
guajolote m 185, 293
guante m 224, 228, 233, 236, 246
guante de cocina m 69
guantes m 30, 36; guantes de boxeo m 237
guantes de jardín m 89
guardabarros m 205
guardacostas m 217
guardar 177
guardia m 180; guardia de seguridad m 189
guardián del rastrillo m 225
guarnecedor m 88
guayaba f 128
güero 39
guía f 172; guía del hilo f 276; guía del viajero f 260; guía turístico m 260
guiar 91
guimbarda f 78
guindilla f 124, 132, 143
guión m 254
guirnalda f 111
guisante m 122, 131
guisantes secos m 131
guisantes tiernos m 131
guiso m 158
guitarra eléctrica f 258
guitarrista m 258
gusano m 295
gypsofila f 110

H

haba f 122
habas f 131
habitación f 58; habitación con desayuno incluido f 101; habitación con dos camas individuales f 100; habitación de los niños f 74; habitación doble f 100; habitación individual f 100; habitación privada f 48; habitación sencilla f 100
habitaciones f 100
hacer agua 239
hacer agujeros con el trinche 90
hacer check-in 212
hacer ejercicios de calentamiento 251
hacer erupción 283
hacer la cama 71
hacer migos 26
hacer testamento 26
hacer un chip 233
hacer un drive 233
hacer un pase 223
hacer un swing 232
hacer una entrada 223
hacer una parada 223
hacha f 95; hacha de cocina f 68
hacia 320; hacia arriba 98
haciendo pan 138
halcón m 292
hamaca f 265, 268
hambriento 64
hamburguesa f 154; hamburguesa con patatas fritas f 154; hamburguesa de pollo f 155; hamburguesa vegetariana f 155
hamburguesería f 154
hámster m 290
handicap m 233
hardware m 176
harina blanca f 138, 139
harina con levadura f 139
harina de huesos f 88
harina integral f 138
harina morena f 138
harina para pan f 139
harinas f 138
harpa f 256
hasta 320; hasta la rodilla 34
haya f 296
heavy metal m 259
hebilla f 36
hecho puré 159
helada f 287
helado m 137, 149
helecho m 86
hélice f 211, 214
helicóptero m 211
hematita f 289
hematites m 289
hematoma m 46
hembra f 276
hemisferio norte m 283
hemisferio sur m 283
hemorragia f 46; hemorragia nasal f 44
heno m 184; heno griego m 132
herbicida m 91, 183
herbolario m 55
herboristería f 115
herida f 46
hermana/-o f/m 22
herradura f 242
herramienta para modelar f 275
herramientas f 187; herramientas de jardinería f 88
hervidor m 66
hervir a fuego lento 67
hexágono m 164
hidroavión m 211
hidrodeslizador m 215
hidroterapia f 55
hielo m 120, 287
hierba f 55, 86, 262
hierbas f 133, 134
hierro m 109, 289
hígado m 18, 118

higiene dental *f* 72
higiene femenina *f* 108
higo *m* 129; higo chumbo *m* 128
hija *f* 22
hijastra/-o *f/m* 23
hijo *m* 22
hilo *m* 276; hilo de bramante *m* 89; hilo de estaño *m* 79; hilo dental *m* 50, 72
hilvanar 277
hinojo *m* 122, 133
hipermetropía *f* 51
hipnoterapia *f* 55
hipoalergénico 41
hipódromo *m* 243
hipopótamo *m* 291
hipoteca *f* 96
hipotenusa *f* 164
historia *f* 162; historia del arte *f* 169
historieta *f* 112
hocico *m* 293
hockey *m* 224; hockey sobre hielo *m* 224; hockey sobre pasto *m* 224
hogaza *f* 139
hoja *f* 89, 122, 296
hojaldre *m* 140
hojas de ingreso *f* 96
hojuelas 132
hola 322
hombre *m* 12, 23; hombre de negocios *m* 175
hombrera *f* 35, 225
hombro *m* 13
home *m* 228
homeopatía *f* 55
homogeneizado 137
hora *f* 304; hora de dormir *f* 74; hora pico *f* 209; hora punta *f* 209
horario *m* 197, 209, 261
horas *f* 261; horas de visita *f* 48
horca *f* 88
horizontal 58
hormiga *f* 295
hormigonera *f* 186
hormona *f* 20
hornear 67, 138
hornilla *f* 67
hornillo *m* 267
horno *m* 66
horquilla *f* 38, 89, 207
horrorizado 25
hospital *m* 48
hot dog *m* 155
hotel *m* 100, 264
hoy 306
hoyo *m* 232; hoyo en uno *m* 233
hoyuelo *m* 15
huaraches *f* 31
huella dactilar *f* 94
huella digital *f* 94
huerto *m* 85, 182
hueso *m* 17, 119
huésped *m* 100
huevera *f* 65, 137
huevo de codorniz *m* 137
huevo de gallina *m* 137
huevo de ganso *m* 137
huevo de oca *m* 137
huevo de pato *m* 137
huevo frito *m* 156, 157
huevo tibio *m* 137, 157
huevos *m* 137; huevos revueltos *m* 157
húmedo 286, 321
húmero *m* 17
humo *m* 95
huracán *m* 287

I

icono *m* 177
idiomas *m* 162
iglesia *f* 298, 300
ígneo 288
igual a 165
iguana *f* 293
iluminación *f* 105
imán *m* 167
imperdible *m* 47
impermeable *m* 31, 32
impotente 20
impresión *f* 275
impresora *f* 172, 176
imprimación *f* 83
imprimir 172
impuestos *m* 96
incendio *m* 95
incisivo *m* 50
inconsciente 47
incubadora *f* 53
indicaciones *f* 260
indicador de fotos *m* 270
indicador de la gasolina *m* 201
indicador de temperatura *m* 201
indicador de velocidad *m* 201
indicador para medir la presión *m* 45
índice *m* 15
individual *m* 230
inducir el parto 53
infarto de miocardio *m* 44
infección *f* 44
información *f* 168, 261; información telefónica *f* 99
informe *m* 174
infusión *f* 149
ingeniería *f* 169
ingle *f* 12
ingredientes *m* 155
ingresado 48
inhalador *m* 44, 109
injertar 91
inmovilización *f* 237
inocente 181
inoculación *f* 45
inquilino *m* 58
insomnio *m* 71
inspector *m* 94
instalar 177
instrumentos *m* 256, 258
insulina *f* 109
integral 131
intento *m* 220, 221
interceptar y devolver 225
intercomunicador *m* 75
intercostal *m* 16
interfono *m* 59
interior *m* 200, 228
intermitente *m* 198, 204
internado 48
internet *m* 177
interruptor *m* 60
intestino delgado *m* 18
intestino grueso *m* 18
inundación *f* 287
invernadero *m* 85
inversión *f* 97
invertebrados *m* 295
investigación *f* 94, 169
invierno *m* 31, 307
invitado *m* 64
inyección *f* 48
ionosfera *f* 286
ir en bicicleta 207
iris *m* 51, 110
isla *f* 282
itinerario *m* 260
izquierda 260

J

jabón *m* 73
jaboncillo *m* 276
jabonera *f* 73
jade *m* 288
jamón *m* 119, 143, 156; jamón serrano *m* 143
jaqueca *f* 44
jarabe *m* 109; jarabe de arce *m* 134; jarabe para la tos *m* 108
jarcias *f* 215, 240
jardín *m* 84; jardín acuático *m* 84; jardín campestre *m* 84; jardín clásico *m* 84; jardín de plantas herbáceas *m* 84; jardín en la azotea *m* 84
jardinería *f* 90
jardinero *m* 188
jardines *m* 261; jardines clásicos *m* 262
jarra *f* 65, 151; jarra graduada *f* 69, 311; jarra para hervir *f* 66
jarrón *m* 63, 111
jazz *m* 259
jeans *m* 31
jefe *m* 24
jengibre *m* 125, 133
jeringa *f* 109, 167
jeringuilla *f* 109
jersey *m* 33
jet privado *m* 211
jinete *m* 242
jirafa *f* 179, 291
jitomate *m* 125, 157; jitomate cherry *m* 124
joggin *m* 251, 263
joroba *f* 291
jota *f* 273
joto *m* 273
joyas *f* 36
joyería *f* 114
joyero *m* 36, 188
judía verde *f* 122
judo *m* 236
juego *m* 230; juego de dobles *m* 230
juegos *m* 75, 272; juegos de mesa *m* 272; juegos de raqueta *m* 231
jueves 306
juez *m* 180; juez de línea *m* 220, 223, 230; juez de silla *m* 230
jugador *m* 220, 221, 231, 273; jugador de baloncesto *m* 226; jugador de críquet *m* 225; jugador de hockey sobre hielo *m* 224
jugadora de golf *f* 232
jugar 229, 273
jugo *m* 127; jugo de frutas *m* 156; jugo de manzana *m* 149; jugo de naranja *m* 148; jugo de piña *m* 149; jugo de tomate *m* 144, 149; jugo de uva *m* 144
jugos *m* 149
jugoso 127
juguete *m* 75
juguetería *f* 105
juicio *m* 180
julio 306
junco *m* 86
junio 306
junta *f* 61, 174
jurado *m* 180

K

K. O. *m* 237
karate *m* 236
kayak *m* 241
kendo *m* 236
ketchup *m* 135, 154
kilogramo *m* 310
kilómetro *m* 310
kit de reparaciones *m* 207
kiwi *m* 128
koala *m* 291
kumquat *m* 126
kung fu *m* 236

L

lá
labio *m* 14
labios *m* 20
labor de encaje *f* 277
labor de punto *f* 277
labor de retales *f* 277
laboratorio *m* 166
laca *f* 38
lacio 39
lacrosse *f* 249
lactancia *m* 53
lácteos *m* 107
lactosa *f* 137
ladera *f* 284
lado *m* 164
ladrillo *m* 187
lagarto *m* 293
lago *m* 285
lágrima *f* 51
laminado 132
lámpara *f* 50, 62, 217; lampara de la mesilla *f* 70; lámpara del buró *f* 70
lana *f* 277; lana de acero *f* 81
lancha de motor *f* 214
langosta *f* 121, 295
langostino *m* 121
lanzacohetes *m* 281
lanzador *m* 225
lanzamiento *m* 281; lanzamiento de bala *m* 234; lanzamiento de disco *m* 234; lanzamiento de jabalina *m* 234
lanzar 221, 225, 227, 229, 245
lápiz *m* 163, 275; lápiz corrector *m* 40; lápiz de cejas *m* 40; lápiz de colores *m* 163; lápiz de labios *m* 40; lápiz de ojos *m* 40; lápiz labial *m* 40
laptop *m* 175, 176
largo 32, 34, 131, 151
largometraje *m* 269
larguero *m* 222
laringe *f* 19
las golosinas *f* 113
lata *f* 145, 311; lata de bebida *f* 154; lata de pintura *f* 83
latitud *f* 283
laurel *m* 133
lava *f* 283
lavabo *m* 38, 50, 72
lavadería *f* 76

lavadero *m* 76; lavadero de coches *m* 199
lavadora *f* 76; lavadora secadora *f* 76
lavandería *f* 115
lavar 38
lavavajilla *f* 66
laxante *m* 109
lazo *m* 39
lección *f* 163
leche *f* 136, 156; leche condensada *f* 136; leche de cabra *f* 136; leche de oveja *f* 137; leche de vaca *f* 136; leche del cuerpo *f* 73; leche descremada *f* 136; leche en polvo *f* 137; leche entera *f* 136; leche semi-descremada *f* 136
lechuga *f* 123
lector de discos compactos *m* 268
lector de MP3 *m* 268
lector de rayos x *m* 45
leer 162
legumbres *f* 130
lejía *f* 77
lejos 320
lencería *f* 35, 105
lengua *f* 19, 118
lenguado *m* 120
lengüeta *f* 37, 244
lente *m* 270; lente del objetivo *f* 167
lenteja castellana *f* 131
lenteja roja *f* 131
lentes de contacto *f* 51
lentes obscuros *m* 51, 265
lentilla *f* 51
lento 321
león *m* 291; león marino *m* 290
leotardos *m* 251
lesión *f* 46; lesión en la cabeza *f* 46
letra *f* 259
letrero *m* 104
levadura *f* 138
levantamiento de pesas *m* 251
levantar 251
levantarse 71
levar 139
libélula *f* 295
libertad condicional *f* 181
libra *f* 310
libre 321
librería *f* 115
librero *m* 63, 168
libreta *f* 173
libro *m* 168; libro de texto *m* 163
licencia de pesca *f* 245
licenciada *f* 169
licenciarse 26
lichi *m* 128
licor *m* 145
licuadora *f* 66
lienzo *m* 274
liga *f* 35, 173, 223
ligamento *m* 17
ligas *f* 35
ligero 321
lijadora *f* 78
lijar 82
lima *f* 81, 126; lima de uñas *f* 41
límite de velocidad *m* 195
limón *m* 126
limonada *f* 144
limousine *f* 199
limpiaparabrisas *m* 198
limpiar 77; limpiar el polvo 77
limpieza de cutis *f* 41
limpio 121
línea central *f* 226
línea de banda *f* 220, 221, 226, 230
línea de falta *f* 229
línea de flotación *f* 214
línea de fondo *f* 221, 225, 226, 230
línea de gol *f* 220
línea de juego *f* 233
línea de meta *f* 223, 224, 234
línea de salida *f* 234
línea de servicio *f* 230
línea de tiro libre *f* 226
línea de tres *f* 226
línea del bateador *f* 225
línea divisoria *f* 194
líneas *f* 165
linfático 19
lino *m* 184, 277
linterna *f* 267
líquido 77; líquido amniótico *m* 52; líquido limpiador *m* 51; líquido limpiaparabrisas *m* 199
lista de lecturas *f* 168
lista de precios *f* 154
lista de vinos *f* 152
listón *m* 39, 141, 235
literatura *f* 162, 169
litro *m* 311
llamada a cobro revertido *f* 99
llamada por cobrar *f* 99
llanta *f* 198, 205, 206, 207, 265; llanta de refacción *f* 203
llanura *f* 285
llave *f* 59, 80, 203, 207; llave de agua caliente *f* 72; llave de agua fría *f* 72; llave de boca *f* 80; llave de la cerveza *m* 150; llave de la habitación *f* 100; llave de paso *f* 61; llave de tubo *f* 80; llave del desagüe *f* 61; llave inglesa *f* 80
llegadas *f* 213
lleno 64, 266, 321
llorar 25
lluvia *f* 287
lo siento 322
lobby *m* 100
lobo *m* 290
loción *f* 109
locomotora *f* 208
logotipo *m* 31
lomo *m* 121
loncha *f* 119
longitud *f* 165, 283, 310; longitud de onda *f* 179
loro *m* 293
lubina *f* 120
luces *f* 39, 94; luces de emergencia *f* 201
lucha libre *f* 236
lugar *m* 266; lugar en la mesa *m* 65
lugares de interés *m* 261
luge *m* 247
luna *f* 280; luna de miel *f* 26; luna llena *f* 280; luna nueva *f* 280
lunar *m* 14
lunes 306
lupino *m* 297
luz de lectura *f* 210
luz del porche *f* 58
luz trasera *f* 204

M

macadamia *f* 129
maceta *f* 89, 110
machacado 132
machacador *m* 68
macho *m* 276
macis *f* 132
macramé *m* 277
madeja *f* 277
madera *f* 79, 187, 233, 275; madera de pino *f* 79; madera noble *f* 79
madrastra *f* 23
madre *f* 22
madreselva *f* 297
maduro 129
maestra *f* 162, 190
maestría *m* 169
magdalena *f* 140
magma *m* 283
magnesio *m* 109
magnetofón *m* 269
maíz *m* 130, 184; maíz dulce *m* 122
malaquita *f* 288
malas hierbas *f* 86
maletero *m* 198
maletín *m* 37
mallas *f* 31
malo 321
malteada *m* 137; malteada al café *m* 149; malteada de chocolate *m* 149; malteada de fresa *m* 149
malteados *m* 149
malvarisco *m* 113
mameluco *m* 30; mameluco sin pies *m* 30
mamíferos *m* 290
mamila *f* 75
manada *f* 183
mancana *f* 94
manchego *m* 142
mancuernillas *f* 36
mandar un pase 223
mandarina *f* 126; mandarina clementina *f* 126; mandarina satsuma *f* 126
mandíbula *f* 14, 17
mandioca *f* 124
mando a distancia *m* 269
manecilla de la hora *f* 304
manga *f* 34, 267; manga pastelera *f* 69
mango *m* 36, 128, 187, 230
mangostán *m* 128
manguera *f* 89, 95
manicura *f* 41
manija *f* 200
manillar *m* 207
maniquí *m* 276
mano *f* 13, 15; mano de mortero *f* 68, 167
manopla *f* 228; manopla de cocina *f* 69
manoplas *f* 30
manta *f* 71, 74; manta eléctrica *f* 71
mantel *m* 64; mantel individual *m* 64
mantequilla *f* 137, 156
mantis religiosa *f* 295
manto *m* 282
manual 200
manualidades *f* 274, 275, 276
manubrio *m* 207
manzana *f* 126; manzana de Adán *f* 19
manzanilla *f* 149
mañana *f* 305, mañana 306
mapa *m* 195, 261
mapache *m* 290
mapamundi *m* 312
maqueta *f* 190
maquillaje *m* 40; maquillaje de fondo *m* 40
máquina de coser *f* 276
máquina de cross *f* 250
máquina de ejercicios *f* 250
máquina de los hielos *f* 67
máquina de rayos x *f* 212
máquina de remos *f* 250
máquina de step *f* 250
máquina del café *f* 148, 150
máquina fotográfica *f* 260
maquinaria *f* 187
mar *m* 264, 282
maracas *f* 257
maracuyá *m* 128
maratón *f* 234
marca personal *f* 234
marcador *m* 225
marcar 38, 99, 227; marcar un gol 223
marchas *f* 206
marco *m* 62
margarina *f* 137
margarita *f* 110, 297
marido *m* 22
marimba *f* 257
marinado 143
marino *m* 189
mariposa *f* 239, 295
mariquita *f* 295
marisco *m* 121
mármol *m* 288
marquesina *f* 197
marrón 274
Marte 280
martes 306
martillo *m* 80; martillo neumático *m* 187
martini *m* 151
marzo 306
más 165; más allá de 320; más tarde
masa *f* 138, 140; masa brisa *f* 140; masa de profiteroles *f* 140
masaje *m* 54
mascada *m* 36
máscara *f* 228, 249
mascarilla *f* 41, 189
masculino 21
masilla *f* 83
masking tape *m* 83
máster *m* 169
mástil *m* 240, 258
mastique *m* 83
matasellos *m* 98
mate *m* 83, 231, 271
matemáticas *f* 162, 164
materiales *m* 79, 165, 187
maternidad *f* 49
matraz *m* 166
matrícula *f* 198
matriz *f* 52, 96

mayo 306
mayonesa *f* 135
mazapán *m* 141
mazo *m* 187, 275; mazo de cocina *m* 68; mazo para puré de patatas *m* 68
mecánica/-o *f/m* 202, 188, 203
mechero *m* 112; mechero Bunsen *m* 166
medallas *f* 235
media luna *f* 280
media pensión *f* 101
mediana *f* 194
medianoche *f* 305
medias *f* 34, 35; medias de liguero *f* 35
medicación *f* 109
medicamento *m* 109
medicina *f* 169
médico *m* 45, 189
medida *f* 151; medida de capacidad *f* 311
medidas *f* 165
medidor *m* 150; medidor de altura *m* 45; medidor óptico *m* 150
medio galope *m* 243
medio litro *m* 311
medio ambiente *m* 280
mediodía *m* 305
medios de comunicación *m* 178
medir 310
meditación *f* 54
médula *f* 126
medusa *f* 295
mejilla *f* 14
mejillón *m* 121, 295
mejorana *f* 133
melée *f* 221
melena *f* 39
melocotón *m* 126, 128
melodía *f* 259
melón *m* 127
membrete *m* 173
membrillo *m* 128
memoria *f* 176
menaje de hogar *m* 105
menos 165, 304
mensaje de texto *m* 99
mensaje de voz *m* 99
mensajería *f* 99
mensajes *m* 100
menstruación *f* 20
mensualmente 307
menta *f* 133; menta poleo *f* 149
menú *m* 154; menú de la cena *m* 152; menú de la comida *m* 152; menú para niños *m* 153
menudillos *m* 118
meñique *m* 15
mercado *m* 115
mercería *f* 105
mercurio *m* 289
merengue *m* 140
mermelada *f* 134, 156; mermelada de frambuesa *f* 134; mermelada de naranja *f* 134, 156
mes *m* 306
mesa *f* 64, 148; mesa de café *f* 62; mesa de centro *f* 62; mesa de encolar *f* 82; mesa de mezclas *f* 179; mesa de picnic *f* 268; mesa del desayuno *f* 156; mesa plegable *f* 210
mesera/-o *f/m* 191, 148, 152
meseta *f* 284
mesilla de noche *f* 70
mesoesfera *f* 286
metacarpo *m* 17
metal *m* 79
metales *m* 289
metamórfico 288
metatarso *m* 17
meteorito *m* 280
meter reversa 195
metralleta *f* 189
metro *m* 45, 209, 310; metro cuadrado *m* 310
mezcladora de cemento *f* 186
mezclar 67, 138
mezquita *f* 300
mica *f* 289
microbús *m* 197
micrófono *m* 179, 258; micrófono de aire *m* 179
microondas *m* 66
microscopio *m* 167
miel compacta *f* 134
miel cristalizada *f* 134
miel de maple *f* 134
miel líquida *f* 134
miércoles 306
migración 212
migraña *f* 44
mijo *m* 130
mil 309
mil millones 309
mil novecientos 307
mil novecientos diez 307
mil novecientos uno 307
milenio *m* 307
miligramo *m* 310
mililitro *m* 311
milímetro *m* 310
milla *f* 310
millón *m* 309
minerales *m* 289
mini bar *m* 101
minivan *f* 199
minuta *f* 174
minutero *m* 304
minuto *m* 304
miopía *f* 51
mirilla *f* 59
misil *m* 211
mobiliario para el hogar *m* 105
mocasín *m* 37
mochila *f* 31, 37, 162, 267; mochila de bebé *f* 75
moda *f* 277
modalidades *f* 243
modelismo *m* 275
modelo *f* 169
modelos *m* 199
módem *m* 176
modista *f* 191
modo de empleo *m* 109
módulo lunar *m* 281
moisés *m* 74
molde individual *m* 69
molde para bizcocho *m* 69
molde para magdalenas *m* 69
molde para panqués *m* 69
molde para pastel *m* 69
molde para suflé *m* 69
molde redondo *m* 69
moldura *f* 63
molido 132
mondador *m* 68
moneda *f* 97
monedas devueltas *f* 99
monedero *m* 37
monitor *f* 176, monitor *m* 53
mono *m* 36, 39, 83, 291
moño francés *m* 39
monopatín *m* 249
monopolio *m* 272
monorraíl *m* 208
monorriel *m* 208
monovolumen *m* 199
montacargas *m* 186
montaña *f* 284; montaña rusa *f* 262
montar en monopatín 249
montar en patinete 263
montar una tienda 266
montículo del pitcher *f* 228
montura *f* 51
monumento *m* 261
monzón *m* 287
moqueta *f* 71
mora *f* 127
morado 274
morcilla *f* 157
mordisco *m* 46
moreno 41
moretón *m* 46
morir 26
morro *m* 210
morsa *f* 290
mortero *m* 68, 167
mosca *f* 244, 295
mosquitero *m* 267
mosquito *m* 295
mostaza *f* 155; mostaza en grano *f* 131, 135; mostaza francesa *f* 135; mostaza inglesa *f* 135
mostrador *m* 96, 98, 100, 142; mostrador de bocadillos *m* 143; mostrador de check-in *m* 213; mostrador de préstamos *m* 168
moto acuática *f* 241
moto de carreras *f* 205
moto de carretera *f* 205
moto de nieve *f* 247
motocicleta *f* 204
motociclismo *m* 249
motocross *f* 205, motocross *m* 249
motor *m* 88, 202, 204, 210; motor fueraborda *m* 215
mousse *m* 141
móvil *m* 74
movimientos *m* 237
mozo de cuadra *m* 243
mozzarella *f* 142
mueble *m* 268
mueblería *f* 115
muela *f* 50
muelle *m* 71, 214, 216; muelle comercial *m* 216; muelle de pasajeros 216
muerte súbita *f* 230
muestra *f* 261
muffin *m* 140
mujer *f* 12, 22, 23; mujer de negocios *f* 175
muletilla *f* 31
multimezclador *m* 66
multiplicado por 165
multiplicar 165
muñeca *f* 13, 15, 75
muñeco de peluche *m* 75
muñequera *f* 230
murciélago *m* 290
muro de contención *m* 195
muro de división *m* 194
músculos *m* 16
museo de arte *m* 261
muserola *f* 242
música *f* 162; música clásica *f* 255, 259; música country *f* 259; música de baile *f* 259; música folklórica *f* 259
musical *m* 255
músico *m* 191
muslo *m* 12, 119

N, Ñ

naan *m* 139
nabo *m* 124; nabo sueco *m* 125
nacer 26
nacimiento *m* 52
nación *f* 315
nada *f* 200
nadador *m* 238
nadar 238
nado sincronizado *m* 239
nailon *m* 277
nalga *f* 13, 16
naranja 274, naranja *f* 126
naranja China *f* 126
naranjada *f* 144
narciso *m* 111
narcisos silvestres *m* 297
nariz *f* 14, 210
nasa *f* 245
nata *f* 137, 140, 157; nata agria *f* 137; nata líquida *f* 137; nata montada *f* 137; nata para montar *f* 137
natación *f* 238
natillas *f* 140
natural 256
naturopatía *f* 55
náusea *f* 44
navaja *f* 121; navaja de afeitar desechable *f* 73
navegación por satélite *f* 201
navegador *m* 177
navegar 177, 240
Navidad *f* 27
neblina *f* 287
nebulosa *f* 280
nectarina *f* 126
negativo *m* 271
negligé *m* 35
negocios *m* 175
negro 39, 272, 274
neoclásico 301
Neptuno *m* 280
nervio *m* 19, 50; nervio óptico *m* 51
nervioso 19, 25
neumático *m* 198, 205
neurología *f* 49
neutro 60
niebla *f* 287
nieta/-o *f/m* 22
nietos *m* 23
nieve *f* 287
niña/-o *f/m* 23, 31; niño pequeño *m* 30
niños *m* 23
níquel *m* 289
nivel *m* 80, 187
no 322
noche *f* 305
nómina *f* 175
nonagésimo 309

noray *m* 214
normal 39
norte *m* 312
nota *f* 163, 156; nota con saludos *f* 173
notación *f* 256
notas *f* 175, 191
noticiario *m* 178
novecientos 308
noveno 309
noventa 308
novia *f* 24
noviembre 306
novio *m* 24
nube *f* 110, 113, 287
nublado 286
nuca *f* 13
núcleo externo *m* 282
núcleo interno *m* 282
nudillo *m* 15
nueces de la India *f* 151
nuera *f* 22
nueve 308
nuevo 321
nuez *f* 19, 129; nuez de Castilla *f* 129; nuez de la India *f* 129; nuez del Brasil *f* 129; nuez moscada *f* 132
nuggets de pollo *m* 155
numerador *m* 165
número *m* 226; número de andén *m* 208; número de cuenta *m* 96; número de la habitación *m* 100; número de puerta de embarque *m* 213; número de ruta *m* 196; número de vuelo *m* 213
números *m* 308
nutria *f* 290
ñame *m* 125

O

obertura *f* 256
objetivo *m* 270
oboe *m* 257
obra *f* 186, 254
obras *f* 187, 195; obras viales *f* 187
obsidiana *f* 288
obstetra *m* 52
obturador *m* 270
oca *f* 119; oca *m* 293
océano *m* 282
ochenta 308
ocho 308
ochocientos 308
ocio *m* 254, 258, 264; ocio en el hogar *m* 268
octágono *m* 164
octavo 309
octogésimo 309
octubre 306
ocular *m* 167
ocupado 99, 321
odómetro *m* 201
oeste *m* 312
ofertas *f* 106
oficina central *f* 175
oficina de cambio *f* 97
oficina de correos *f* 98
oficina de información *f* 261
oficina del director *f* 266
oficina *f* 24, 172, 174
oftalmología *f* 49
ojal *m* 32, 37
ojo *m* 14, 51, 244, 276; ojo de buey *m* 214
ojos rojos *m* 271
ola *f* 241, 264
olla de barro *f* 69
olmo *m* 296
ombligo *m* 12
omoplato *m* 17
once 308
oncología *f* 49
onda corta *f* 179
onda larga *f* 179
onda media *f* 179
ónice *m* 289
ónix *m* 289
onza *f* 310
ópera *m* 255
operación *f* 48
operador *m* 99
óptico *m* 51, 189
optometrista *m* 189
orador *m* 174
órbita *f* 280
orden del día *m* 174
orden judicial *f* 180, 180
ordenador *m* 170, 176; ordenador portátil *m* 175, 176
ordenar 153
ordeñar 183
orégano *m* 133
oreja *f* 14
orfebrería *f* 275
orgánico 91, 118
organizador de las herramientas *m* 78
órganos reproductores *m* 20
orgulloso 25
orificio nasal *m* 290
orilla *f* 284
orinal *m* 74
ornamental 87
ornitología *f* 263
oro *m* 235, 289
orquesta *f* 254, 256
orquídea *f* 111
ortiga *f* 297
ortopedia *f* 49
oruga *f* 295
orza *v* 241
orzuela *f* 39
oscuro 321
oso *m* 291; oso de peluche *m* 75; oso panda *m* 291; oso polar *m* 291
osteopatía *f* 54
ostra *f* 121
otoño *m* 31, 307
otorrinolaringología *f* 49
óvalo *m* 164
ovario *m* 20
oveja *f* 185
overol *m* 82
ovulación *f* 20, 52
óvulo *m* 20

P

paca *f* 184
pacana *f* 129
paciente *f* 45; paciente externo *m* 48
paddle *m* 231
padrastro *m* 23
padre *m* 22
padres *m* 23
pagar 153
pago *m* 96
país *m* 315
paisaje *m* 284
pajarería *f* 115
pajarita *f* 36
pájaro carpintero *m* 292
pajita *f* 144, 154
pala *f* 68, 88, 187, 231, 265; pala mecánica *f* 187; pala pequeña *f* 89
palacio municipal *m* 299
paladar *m* 19
palanca *f* 61, 150; palanca de cambios *f* 201; palanca de emergencia *f* 209; palanca de la llanta *f* 207; palanca de luces *f* 201; palanca de velocidades *f* 201, 207
palco *m* 254
paleta *f* 113, 186, 187, 274
palma de la mano *f* 15
palmera *f* 86, 296
palmitos *m* 122
palmtop *m* 175
palo *m* 224, 225, 249, 273; palo de hockey *m* 224; palo de la tienda *m* 266
paloma *f* 292
palomitas *f* 255
palos de golf *m* 233
pan *m* 138, 157; pan al bicarbonato sódico *m* 139; pan blanco *m* 139; pan con grano *m* 139; pan con semillas *m* 139; pan danés *m* 139; pan de caja *m* 138; pan de centeno *m* 138; pan de frutas *m* 139; pan de maíz *m* 139; pan de molde *m* 138; pan dulce *m* 157; pan fermentado *m* 139; pan francés *m* 157; pan integral *m* 139, 149; pan molido *m* 139; pan negro *m* 139; pan negro *m* 139; pan rallado *m* 139; pan sin levadura *m* 139; pan tostado *m* 156
panadería *f* 107, 114, 138
panadero *m* 139
panal *m* 135
páncreas *m* 18
pandereta *f* 257
pandero *m* 257
panecillo *m* 139, 143
pantaletas *f* 35
pantalla *f* 97, 172, 176, 255, 269; pantalla informativa *f* 213
pantalón de montar *m* 242
pantalones *m* 32, 34; pantalones con peto *m* 30; pantalones cortos *m* 30, 33; pantalones de chándal *m* 33; pantalones de chándal *m* 33; pantalones vaqueros *m* 31
pantano *m* 285
pantimedias *f* 34, 35
pantiprotector *m* 108
pantorrilla *f* 13, 16
pants *m* 31, 32
pantuflas *f* 31
pañal *m* 75; pañal de felpa *m* 30; pañal desechable *m* 30
pañalera *f* 75
pañuelo *m* 36; pañuelo de papel *m* 108; pañuelo desechable *m* 108
papa *f* 124; papa nueva *f* 124
papas fritas *f* 113, 151, 154
papaya *f* 128
papel celo *m* 173
papel de apresto *m* 83
papel de lija *m* 81, 83
papel estampado en relieve *m* 83
papel maché *m* 275
papel pintado *m* 82
papel tapiz *m* 82
papelera *f* 170
papelería *f* 105, 173
paperas *f* 44
papiroflexia *f* 275
paquete *m* 99, 311; paquete de tabaco *m* 112
par *m* 233
para 320; para comer en el local 154; para llevar 154
parabrisas *m* 198, 205
paracaídas *m* 248
paracaidismo 248; paracaidismo en caída libre *m* 248
parachoques *m* 198
parada *f* 237; parada de autobús *f* 197, 299; parada de taxis *f* 213
paraguas *m* 36, 233
paragüero *m* 59
paralelas *f* 235
paralelo 165
paralelogramo *m* 164
paramédico *m* 94
parapente *m* 248
parar 223
parche *m* 207
pared *f* 58, 186
pareja *f* 24
parientes *m* 23
parmesano *m* 142
párpado *m* 51
parque *m* 75, 262; parque de atracciones *m* 262; parque de bomberos *m* 95; parque de diversiones *m* 262; parque nacional *m* 261
parquímetro *m* 195
parrilla *f* 69, 267
parte interna del pie *f* 15
partera *f* 53
parterre *m* 85, 90
partida *f* 273; partida de nacimiento *f* 26
partido *m* 230
partitura *f* 255, 256
parto *m* 52, 53; parto asistido *m* 53; parto de espaldas *m* 52
pasa *f* 129; pasa de Corinto *f* 129; pasa sultana *f* 129
pasado mañana 307
pasador *m* 38
pasajero *m* 216
pasamanos *m* 59
pasaporte *m* 213
pasar 220; pasar la bayeta 77
pasarela *f* 212, 214
Pascua judía *f* 27
pase *m* 226
paseo *m* 75, 243; paseo marítimo *m* 265
pasillo *m* 106, 168, 210, 254

paso *m* 243; paso a desnivel *m* 194; paso de peatones *m* 195; paso elevado *m* 194; paso subterráneo *m* 194
pasta *f* 158; pasta de dientes *f* 72
pastel *m* 149, 158; pastel de bodas *f* 141; pastel de chocolate *f* 140; pastel de crema *m* 141; pastel de cumpleaños *f* 141
pasteles *m* 140, 274; pasteles de carne *m* 143; pasteles para celebraciones *f* 141
pasteurizado 137
pastilla *f* 21, 258, 311; pastilla de menta *f* 113; pastilla para fogatas *f* 266; pastilla para la garganta *f* 109
pasto *m* 87, 90, 182, 262
pata *f* 64, 119
patata *f* 124, 237, 239
patatas fritas *f* 113, 151, 154
paté *m* 142, 156
patear 221, 223
patín *m* 247; patín de cuchilla *m* 224; patín de ruedas *m* 249
patinaje *m* 249, 263; patinaje artístico *m* 247; patinaje de velocidad *m* 247; patinaje sobre hielo *m* 247
patinar 224
patineta *f* 249, 263
patio *m* 58, 84; patio con jardín *m* 85; patio de butacas *m* 254
patito *m* 185
pato *m* 119, 185
patología *f* 49
patrimonio neto *m* 97
patrón *m* 276
patrulla *f* 94
patucos *m* 30
pausa *f* 256, 269
pavo *m* 119, 185, 293; pavo real *m* 293
PDA *m* 175
peca *f* 15
peces *m* 294
pecho *m* 12, 239
pechuga *f* 119
pectoral *m* 16
pedal *m* 61, 206; pedal de los frenos *m* 205
pedalear 207
pedernal *m* 288
pediatría *f* 49
pedicura *f* 41
pedir 153
pegamento *m* 275; pegamento de carpintero *m* 78; pegamento para tapizar *m* 82
peinar 38
peine *m* 38
pelacables *m* 81
pelado 129
pelador *m* 68
pelar 67
pelele *m* 30
pelícano *m* 292
película *f* 260, 269, 270; película de aventuras *f* 255; película de ciencia ficción *f* 255; película de dibujos animados *f* 255; película de miedo *f* 255; película de suspenso *f* 255; película de vaqueros *f* 255; película del oeste *f* 255; película romántica *f* 255
peligro *m* 195
pelirrojo 39
pelo *m* 14; pelo corto *m* 39
pelota *f* 75, 224, 228, 230; pelota de críquet *f* 225; pelota de golf *f* 233; pelota de playa *f* 265
peloteo *m* 230
peluca *f* 39
peluquera *f* 38
peluquería *f* 115
peluquero *m* 39, 188
pelvis *f* 17
penalti *m* 222
pendiente *m* 36
pene *m* 21
península *f* 282
pensión completa *f* 101
pentágono *m* 164
pentagrama *f* 256
peón *m* 272
peonía *f* 111
pepino *m* 125
pepita *f* 127
pequeño 321
pera *f* 127
percha *f* 70
percusión *f* 257
perdedor *m* 273
perder 273
perdone 322
perejil *m* 133
perenne 86
perforadora *f* 173
perfumado 130
perfume *m* 41
perfumería *f* 105
pérgola *f* 84
periferia *f* 299
perilla de ajuste *f* 167
periódico *m* 112, 168
periodista *m* 190
periquera *f* 75
permanente *f* 39
peroné *m* 17
perpendicular 165
perrito caliente *m* 155
perro *m* 290
perseguir 229
persiana *f* 63
personal *m* 175
pértiga *f* 245
pesa *f* 166, 251
pesado 321
pesar 310
pesas *f* 250
pesca *f* 244; pesca con arpón *f* 245; pesca con mosca *f* 245; pesca de altura *f* 245; pesca deportiva *f* 245; pesca en agua dulce *f* 245; pesca en alta mar *f* 245; pesca en la orilla *f* 245
pescadera *f* 188
pescadería *f* 114, 120
pescadilla *f* 120
pescado *m* 107, 120; pescado ahumado *m* 143; pescado con papas fritas *m* 155
pescador *m* 189; pescador de caña *m* 244
peso *m* 118; peso al nacer *m* 53
pestaña *f* 14, 51
pesticida *m* 89, 183
pestillo *m* 200
pétalo *m* 297
petrolero *m* 215
pez de colores *m* 294
pez espada *m* 120, 294
pezón *m* 12
pezuña *f* 291
phisicallis *m* 128
piano *m* 256
pica *f* 273
picadura *f* 46
picante 124
picar 245
picnic *m* 263
pico *m* 187, 293
pie *m* 12, 15, 310; pie cuadrado *m* 310; pie de apoyo *m* 207; pie de la aguja *m* 276; pie de la bocina *m* 268; pie de la cama *m* 71; pie del altavoz *m* 268
piedra *f* 36, 275; piedra arenisca *f* 288; piedra caliza *f* 288; piedra afiladora *f* 81; piedra lunar *f* 288; piedra pómez *f* 73, 288
piel *f* 14, 119, 128
pierna *f* 12, 119
pijama *m* 33; pijama enterizo *m* 30
pila *f* 167
pilas *f* 260
pilates *m* 251
píldora *f* 21, 109
píldoras para el mareo *f* 109
piloto *m* 190, 211; piloto de carreras *m* 249
pimentón *m* 132
pimienta *f* 64, 152; pimienta de Jamaica *f* 132; pimienta en grano *f* 132
pimiento *m* 124
pin *m* 96
pincel *m* 274; pincel de labios *m* 40
pinchadiscos *m* 179
pinchazo *m* 203, 207
pincho *m* 68, 158; pincho moruno *m* 155
ping-pong *m* 231
pingüino *m* 292
pino *m* 249, 296
pinta *f* 311
pintar 83
pintor *m* 82
pintora *f* 191, 274
pintura *f* 83, 274; pintura acrílica *f* 274; pintura al agua *f* 83
pinturas *f* 274; pinturas al óleo *f* 274
pinza *f* 167, 173; pinza para la nariz *f* 238; pinza para la ropa *f* 76
pinzas *f* 40, 47, 150, 167; pinzas de alambre *f* 80
piña *f* 89, 128; piña de la regadera *f* 72
piñón *m* 129, 207
pipa *f* 112; pipa de calabaza *f* 131
pipeta *f* 167
pipita de calabaza *f* 131
piragüismo *m* 241
pirámide *f* 164
piruleta *f* 113
piscifactoría *f* 183
piscina *f* 101, 238, 250; piscina de plástico *f* 263
piso *m* 58, 59, 62
pista *f* 212, 234, 246; pista de esquí *f* 246; pista de estacionamiento *f* 212; pista de hockey sobre hielo *f* 224; pista de tenis *f* 230
pistache *m* 129
pistacho *m* 129
pistola *f* 94; pistola para encolar *f* 78
pita *f* 139
pitcher *m* 229
pivote *m* 207
piyama *f* 33
pizarra *f* 162, 174, 179, 288
pizarrón *m* 162, 174
pizza *f* 154
placa *f* 67, 94, 283; placa bacteriana *f* 50; placa de identificación *f* 189; placa de la aguja *f* 276; placa vitrocerámica *f* 66
placar 220, 221
placenta *f* 52
plancha *f* 66, 76
planchar 76
planeador *m* 211, 248
planeta *m* 280, 282
plano *m* 261; plano de la planta *m* 261; plano del metro *m* 209
planta *f* 48; planta acuática *f* 86; planta alpestre *f* 87; planta baja *f* 104; planta de flor *f* 297; planta de maceta *f* 87; planta de sombra *f* 87; planta del pie *f* 15; planta para cubrir suelo *f* 87; planta suculenta *f* 87; planta trepadora *f* 87
plantar 183; plantar en tiesto 91
plantas *f* 296; plantas de jardín *f* 86; plantas podadas con formas *f* 87
plantilla *f* 83
plantón *m* 91
plata *f* 235, 289
plátano *m* 128
platea *f* 254; platea alta *f* 254
platija *f* 120
platillos *m* 257; platillos del día *m* 152
platina portaobjeto *f* 167
platino *m* 289
platito *m* 65
plato *m* 65, 178, plato llano *m* 65, plato principal *m* 153; plato sopero *m* 65
plató de rodaje *m* 179
platos *m* 153; platos del día *m* 152; platos preparados *m* 107
play *m* 269
playa *f* 264
playera *f* 30
plaza *f* 266, 299

pletina f 268
plomada f 82
plomero m 188
plomo m 244
pluma f 163, 293
plumcake m 139, 140
pocilga f 185
podadora f 88, 90; podadora de mango largo f 88
podadoras f 89
podar 90, 91
podio m 235, 256
podrido 127
póker m 273
policía f 94, 189; policía de tráfico m 195; policía de tránsito m 195
poliéster m 277
polilla f 295
política f 169
pollito m 185
pollo m 119; pollo frito m 155; pollo preparado m 119
polluelo m 185
polo m 243, 282
polvera f 40
polvos m 109; polvos compactos m 40; polvos de talco m 73
pomada f 47, 109
pomelo m 126
pomo de la puerta m 59
ponchadura m 203, 207
poner azulejos 82
poner césped 90
poner el despertador 71
poner en remojo 130
poner la mesa 64
poner una tienda 266
pool m 249
pop m 259
popa f 240
popote m 144, 154
popurrí m 111
por 320; por avión 98; por favor 322
porcentaje m 165
porche m 58
poro m 15
porra f 94
porrista f 220
portaaviones m 215
portabolígrafos m 170
portacinta m 173
portaequipaje m 196, 204, 209
portalámparas de bayoneta m 60
portaobjetos m 167
portaplumas m 172
portarretratos m 271
portatubos m 166
portería f 221, 223, 224
portero m 222, 224
portón m 85
posavasos m 150
posgrado 169
poste m 166, 222, 247; poste de la portería m 220; poste del asiento m 206
póster m 255
postigo m 58
postre m 153; postre de soletillas, gelatina de frutas y crema m 141
postura f 232
potro m 185
pradera f 285
prado m 285
precio m 152, 199, 209; precio de entrada m 260
pregrabado 178
pregunta f 163
preguntar 163
prematuro 52
premolar m 50
prendedor m 36
prensa f 178
prensaajos m 68
preocupado 25
prepucio m 21
presentación f 174
presentador m 178, 191
presentadora de las noticias f 179
presidir 174
presión arterial f 44
presión del neumático f 203
préstamo m 96, 168
primavera f 307
primer piso m 104, 141
primera mano f 83
primero 309
primeros auxilios m 47
primo m 22
prímula f 297
principado m 315
príncipe valiente m 39
principio m 321
prismáticos m 281
proa f 215, 240
probadores m 104
problemas m 271
procesador m 176
productor m 254
productos de belleza m 105
productos de limpieza m 107
productos lácteos m 136
profesiones f 188, 190
profesor m 54, 169
profesora f 162, 190
profiterol m 140
profundidad f 165
programa m 176, 254, 269
programación f 178
prohibido el paso m 195
prohibido parar 195
prometida/-o f/m 24
propagar 91
propietario m 58
propuesta f 174
propulsor m 281
prórroga f 223
próstata f 21
protector m 74, 83, 88, 236
protector de la cara m 225
protector de la pierna m 225
protegedientes m 237
proveedor de servicios m 177
provincia f 315
proyector de acetatos m 163
proyector m 174
prueba f 181; prueba del embarazo f 52
pruebas f 247
psicoterapia f 55
psiquiatría f 49
público m 254
pueblo m 299
puente m 15, 194, 214, 258, 300
puenting m 248
puerco m 185
puerro m 125
puerta f 85, 182, 196, 198, 209; puerta abatible f 198; puerta automática f 196; puerta de la regadera f 72; puerta del maletero f 198; puerta exterior f 59; puerta principal f 58
puerto m 176, 214, 216, 217; puerto de pesca m 217; puerto deportivo m 217; puerto pesquero m 217
puesta de sol f 305
puesto m 154
pulgada f 310
pulgar m 15
pulir 77
pulmón m 18
pulpa f 124, 127, 129
pulpejo m 15
pulpo m 121, 295
pulsera f 36; pulsera de identificación f 53
pulso m 47
pulverizador m 89, 311
punta f 36, 122, 163, 244, 246
puntada f 277
puntas abiertas f 39
punto m 273; punto de amarre m 217
puntos m 52
puntuación f 220, 273
puntual 305
puñetazo m 237
puño m 15, 32, 237
pupila f 51
pupilentes m 51
pupitre m 162
puro m 112
putter m 233
puzzle m 273

Q

quebrado m 165
quemacocos m 202
quemador m 61, 67
quemadura f 46; quemadura de sol f 46
queso m 136, 156; queso azul m 136; queso cremoso m 136; queso cremoso semicurado m 136; queso curado m 136; queso de bola m 142; queso de cabra m 142; queso fresco m 136; queso rallado m 136; queso semicurado m 136
quiche f 142
quilla f 214
química f 162
quince 308; quince días 307
quincuagésimo 309
quingombó m 122
quinientos 308
quinoa f 130
quinto 309
quirófano m 48
quiropráctica f 54
quitaesmalte m 41
quitar las flores muertas 91
quizá 322

R

rábano m 124; rábano picante m 125
ración f 64
rack para bicicletas m 207
radar 281, radar m 214
radiador m 60, 202
radicchio m 123
radio f 179, 207, 268, radio m 17, 164; radio del coche f 201; radio despertador f 70
radiografía f 48, 50
radiología f 49
rafting m 241
raices f 39
raíz f 50, 124, 296; raíz del taro f 124
rajas f 133
ralentí m 203
rallador m 68
rallar 67
rally m 249
RAM m 176
rama f 296
ramadán m 26
ramas f 133
ramillete aromático m 132
ramita f 296
ramo m 111; ramo de flores m 35
rampa de lanzamiento f 281
rampa de salida f 194
rampa para sillas de ruedas f 197
rana f 294
ranúnculo m 297
ranura de la tarjeta f 97
rap m 259
rape m 120
rápido 321
rápidos m 240, 284
rappel m 248
raqueta f 230, 231
rascacielos m 299, 300
raspada m 46
raspador m 82
raspar 77
rastrillar 90
rastrillo m 88, 225; rastrillo para el pasto m 88
rasuradora f 73
rata f 290
ratón m 176, 290
raya f 120, 294
rayo m 207
rayos ultravioleta m 286
rayos x dentales m 50
reanimación f 47
rebanada f 119, 139
rebanador m 139
rebaño m 183
rebasar 195
recalentar 154
recámara f 70
recepción f 100
recepcionista f 100, 190
receta f 45
recibir 177, 227
recibo m 152
recién nacido m 53
recipiente m 66, 311
recogebolas m 231
recogedor m 77
recogepelotas m 231
recoger 245
recogida f 98; recogida de equipajes f 213
recolectar 183
récord m 234
rectángulo m 164
recto 165, 260, recto m 21
recuerdos m 260

red f 176, 217, 222, 226, 227, 231; red ferroviaria f 209; red para las capturas f 244; red para recoger f 244
redacción f 163
redactora f 191
redil m 185
reducir 172
refectorio m 168
referencia f 49
reflector m 178, 204, 207, 259
reflejos m 39
reflexología f 54
refresco m 154; refresco en lata m 154
refrescos m 144
refrigerador m 67; refrigerador congelador m 67
regadera f 72, 89
regaderas f 266
regaliz m 113
regalo m 27
regar 90, 183
regatear 223
reggae m 259
región f 315; región plantar f 15
registro m 100
regla f 163, 165
regulador m 239
reiki m 55
reina f 272, 273
reír 25
rejilla f 69
relaciones f 24
relajación f 55
relámpago m 287
relevo m 235
rellenar 82
relleno 159, relleno m 140, 155
reloj m 36, 62, 304; reloj de sol m 262; reloj despertador m 70
remar 241
remate 231
remedios de herbolario m 108
remedios naturistas m 108
remero m 241
remite m 98
remitente m 98
remo m 241
remolacha f 125
remolcador m 215
remolcar 195
remolque m 266; remolque del equipaje m 212
remover 67
Renacimiento 301
renacuajo m 294
renovar 168
renta f 58; renta de carros f 213
rentar 58
repartir 273
reparto m 98, 254
repelente de insectos m 108
repelente de insectos m 267
repisa de la chimenea f 63
reporte m 174
reportera f 179
reposabrazos m 200
reposacabezas m 200
repostería f 69, 140
reproducción f 20
reproductor 19
reproductor de DVD m 268
reptiles m 293
requesón m 136
resbaladilla f 263
resbalar 229
reserva m 223
reservar 168; reservar un vuelo 212
resfriado m 44
residencias de estudiantes f 168
resistencia f 61
resistente al horno 69
resorte m 71
respaldo m 64, 210
respiración f 47
respiratorio 19
respuesta f 163
restar 165
restaurante m 101, 152
restaurant de hamburguesas m 154
resto m 231
restregar 77
resultado m 49
retina f 51
retirarse 26
retraso m 209
retrato hablado m 181
retrato robot m 181
retrete m 61
retrovisor exterior m 198
reunión f 174
revelar 271
revés m 231
revestimiento m 187
revisión f 50
revisor m 209
revista f 112, 168
revistas f 107
revuelto m 158
rey m 272, 273
riego f 89
riel m 208; riel electrificado m 209
riendas f 242
rímel m 40
rin m 206
ring m 237
rinoceronte m 291
riñon m 18, 119
río m 284
ritmo m 259
rizado 39
roble m 296
robo m 94
robot de cocina m 66
rocalla f 84
rocas f 284, 288
rociar 91
rococó 301
rodaja f 121
rodeo m 243
rodilla f 12
rodillera f 205, 227
rodilleras f 220
rodillo m 83; rodillo de cocina m 69
rojizo 39
rojo 274
rollo m 271, 311; rollo de papel higiénico m 72
rombo m 164, 273
romero m 133
rompecabezas f 273
romper aguas 52
rompiente f 241
ron m 145; ron con cola m 150
roncar 71
rondana f 80
ropa casual f 33
ropa de caballero f 32, 105
ropa de cama f 71, 74
ropa de dama f 34, 105
ropa de hogar f 105
ropa de niño f 30
ropa de señora f 105
ropa impermeable f 245, 267
ropa interior f 32
ropa interior térmica f 35
ropa limpia f 76
ropa para dormir f 31
ropa sport f 33
ropa sucia f 76
ropa térmica f 267
ropa termoaislante f 267
roqueta f 123
rosa 274, rosa f 110
rosado 145
rosquilla f 139
rótula f 17
rótulo m 173
rough m 232
roulotte f 266
round m 237
rubí m 288
rubio 39
rubor m 40
rueda f 198, 207; rueda de ajuste f 276; rueda de repuesto f 203
rueda del diafragma f 270; rueda del diafragma f 270; rueda delantera f 196; rueda trasera f 197
ruedas de apoyo f 207
ruedo m 243
rugby m 221
ruibarbo m 127
ruina famosa f 261
rulo m 38

S

sábado 306
sábana f 71, 74
saca postal f 98
sacacorchos m 150
sacaleches m 53
sacapuntas m 163
sacar 231
sacar brillo 77
saco m 32, 33, 34; saco de arena m 237; saco de dormir m 267; saco sport m 33
sacudidor m 77
sacudir 77
safari park m 262
safe 228
sal f 64, 152
sala f 62; sala de embarque f 213; sala de espera f 45; sala de juntas f 174; sala de lecturas f 168; sala de máquinas f 214; sala de maternidad f 48; sala de pediatría f 48; sala de reuniones f 174; sala de urgencias f 48; sala del tribunal f 180
salado 121, 129, 137, 143, 155
salamandra f 294
salami m 142
salchicha f 155, 157
salchichas f 118
salchichón m 142
salida f 61,194, 210, 232; salida de incendios f 95
salidas f 213
salir 233
salmón m 120
salmonete m 120
salón m 162
salpicadera f 205
salpicadero m 201
salsa f 134, 143, 155
saltamontes m 295
saltar 227; saltar a la comba 251
saltear 67
salto m 235, 237, 239, 243, 247; salto bungee m 248; salto con pértiga m 234
salto de altura m 235; salto de cama m 35; salto de longitud m 235; salto entre dos m 226; salto mortal m 235
salud f 44
salvado m 130
salvaslip m 108
salvavidas m 239, 240, 265
salvia f 133
sandalia f 37
sandalias f 31
sandía f 127
sandwich abierto m 155
sandwich tostado m 149
sapo m 294
saque de banda m 223, 226
sarampión m 44
sardina f 120
sarpullido m 44
sartén f 69
sastre m 191
sastrería f 115
satélite m 281
Saturno m 280
sauce m 296
sauna m 250
saxofón m 257
sazonado 159
scanner m 176
scrabble m 272
secador m 38
secadora f 38, 76
secar 76; secar con la secadora 38
sección f 104, 282
seco 39, 41, 130, 145, 286, 321
secretaría f 168
seda f 277
sedal m 244
sedimentario 288
segundero m 304
segundo 309, segundo m 304; segundo piso m 104
seguridad f 75,212, 240
seguro m 47, 200, 203; seguro de sí mismo 25
seis 308
seiscientos 308
selector de puntada m 276
sellador m 83
sellante m 83
sello m 98, 112, 173
selva tropical f 285
semáforo m 194
semana f 306; semana pasada f 307; semana que viene f 306
semanalmente 307
sembrar 90, 183

semidesnatada 136
semilla *f* 122, 127, 128, 130; semilla de girasol *f* 131; semilla de mostaza *f* 131; semilla de sésamo *f* 131; semilla de soja *f* 131
semillas *f* 88, 131; semillas de hinojo *f* 133; semillas de mapola *f* 138
semillero *m* 89
sémola *f* 130
senderismo 263
sendero *m* 262; sendero para caballos *m* 263
seno *m* 19
sensible 41
sentarse en cuclillas 251
sentencia *f* 181
señal *m* 209; señal de tráfico *f* 298
señales de piso *f* 194
señales de tránsito *f* 195
señales horizontales *f* 194
Señor *m* 23
Señora *f* 23
Señorita *f* 23
señuelo *m* 244
sepia *f* 121
septiembre 306
séptimo 309
septuagésimo 309
serie *f* 179
serie televisiva *f* 178
serpiente *f* 293
serrar 79
serrucho *m* 80; serrucho de costilla *m* 81
servicio *m* 231; servicio al cliente *m* 104; servicio de habitaciones *m* 101; servicio de lavandería *m* 101; servicio de limpieza *m* 101; servicio incluido 152; servicio no incluido 152
servicios *m* 49; servicios de emergencia *m* 94
servidor *m* 176
servilleta *f* 65, 152; servilleta de papel *f* 154
servilletero *m* 65
servir 64
sesenta 308
set *m* 230
setecientos 308
setenta 308
seto *m* 85, 90, 182
sexagésimo 309
sexto 309
shampoo para el cuerpo *m* 73
shiatsu *m* 54
shock *m* 47
shock eléctrico *m* 46
shorts *m* 30, 33
sí 322
sidra *f* 145
sien *f* 14
sierra circular *f* 78
sierra de calar *f* 81
sierra de mano *f* 89
sierra de vaivén *f* 78
sierra para metales *f* 81
siete 308
siglo *m* 307
silenciador *m* 203, 204
silla *f* 64, 150, 242; silla de montar de escaramuza *f* 242; silla de montar *f* 242; silla de ruedas *f* 48; silla giratoria *f* 172; silla para el niño *f* 207; silla para niños *f* 198
silleta de paseo *f* 75
sillín *m* 206, 242
sillón *m* 63; sillón del dentista *m* 50
silo *m* 183
sin 320; sin escamas 121; sin espinas 121; sin gas 144; sin grasa 137; sin mangas 34; sin pasteurizar 137; sin piel 121; sin plomo 199; sin sal 137; sin semillas 127; sin tirantes 34
sinagoga *f* 300
sinfonía *f* 256
singles *m* 230
sintético 31
sintonizar 179; sintonizar la radio 269
sirena *f* 94
sistema *m* 176; sistema de megafonía *m* 209; sistema solar *m* 280
sistemas *m* 19
sitio de taxis *m* 213
sitio web *m* 177
slálom *m* 247; slálom gigante *m* 247
snowboard *m* 247
sobre *m* 98, 173, sobre 320; sobre par *m* 233
sobrecargo *f* 190, 210
sobreexpuesto 271
sobregiro *m* 96
sobrina/-o *f/m* 23
socia *f* 24
socorrista *m* 239, 265
soda *f* 144
sofá *m* 62
sofá-cama *m* 63
software *m* 176
sol *m* 280
sola (casa) 58
solapa *m* 32
soldado *m* 189
soldador *m* 81
soldadura *m* 79, 81
soldar 79
soleado 286
soletillas *f* 141
soltar 245
soluble 109
solución desinfectante *f* 51
solvente *m* 83
sombra de ojos *f* 40
sombrero *m* 36; sombrero para el sol *m* 265
sombrilla *f* 264
somnífero *m* 109
sonaja *f* 74
sonajero *m* 74
sonata *f* 256
sonda *f* 50
sonrisa *f* 25
sopa *f* 153, 158
soporte del sillín *m* 206
soporte *m* 88, 166, 187, 205
sorbete *m* 141
sorprendido 25
sospechoso *m* 94, 181
sostenido 256
sótano *m* 58
soufflé *m* 158
spikes *m* 233
sport 34
spray *m* 109, 311
squash *m* 231
stop *m* 269
strike *m* 228
suavizante *m* 38, 76
subexpuesto 271
subibaja *m* 263
subir 139
submarino *m* 215
subsuelo *m* 91
suburbio *m* 299
sucursal *f* 175
sudadera *f* 33
suegra/-o *f/m* 23
suela *f* 37
sueldo *m* 175
suelo *m* 62, 71; suelo aislante *m* 267
suero *m* 53; suero de la leche *m* 137
suéter *m* 33
sujetador *m* 35; sujetador deportivo 35; sujetador para la lactancia *m* 53
sujetapapeles *m* 173
sumar 165
sumidero *m* 299
suministro de electricidad *m* 60
sumo *m* 237
supermercado *m* 105, 106
suplemento *m* 55
supositorio *m* 109
sur *m* 312
surco *m* 183
surfing *m* 241
surfista *m* 241
surtidor *m* 199
suspensión *f* 203, 205
suspirar 25
swing de práctica *m* 233

T

tabaco *m* 112, 184
tabacos y revistas 112
tabla *f* 238, 241; tabla con portapapeles *f* 173; tabla de gimnasia *m* 251; tabla de la plancha *f* 76; tabla de surf *f* 241; tabla para cortar *f* 68
tablero *m* 201, 226; tablero de ajedrez *m* 272; tablero de densidad media *m* 79
tableta de chocolate *f* 113
tablilla *f* 47; tablilla con sujetapapeles *f* 173; tablilla de chocolate *f* 113
taburete *m* 150
taclear 220, 221
taco *m* 155; taco del freno *m* 207
tacómetro *m* 201
tacón *m* 37
tacos *m* 223
taekwondo *m* 236
tai-chi *m* 236
taladrar 79
taladro eléctrico *m* 78
taladro inalámbrico *m* 78
taladro manual *m* 78, 81
talco *m* 73
talla en madera *f* 275
tallar 79
taller *m* 78, 199, 203
tallo *m* 111, 122, 297
talón *m* 13,15
talonario de cheques *m* 96
tambor pequeño *m* 257
tampón *m* 108
tándem *m* 206
tanque *m* 61; tanque de aire *m* 239; tanque de la gasolina *m* 203, 204; tanque del agua *m* 61
tapa *f* 61, 66, 72; tapa del escusado *f* 72; tapa del lente *f* 270; tapa del objetivo *f* 270
tapacubo *m* 202
tapadera *f* 69
tapete *m* 59, 63, 71; tapete de baño *m* 72
tapizar 82
tapón *m* 72, 166, 202
taquígrafa *f* 181
taquilla *f* 209, 255
taquillas *f* 239
tarde 305, *f* 305
tarea *m* 163
tarifa *f* 197
tarima *f* 186
tarjeta *f* 27; tarjeta de crédito *f* 96; tarjeta de débito *f* 96; tarjeta de embarque *f* 213; tarjeta de la biblioteca *f* 168; tarjeta marilla *f* 223; tarjeta membretada *f* 173; tarjeta postal *f* 112; tarjeta roja *f* 223
tarrina *f* 311
tarro *m* 134, 311; tarro hermético *m* 135
tarta de cumpleaños *f* 141
tarta nupcial *f* 141
tartaleta de fruta *f* 140
tasa de interés *f* 96
tatuaje *m* 41
taxista *m* 190
taza *f* 61, 65, 75; taza de café *f* 65; taza de té *f* 65; taza medidora *f* 69; taza para el huevo *f* 65, 137
té *m* 144, 149, 184; té con hielo *m* 149; té con leche *m* 149; té con limón *m* 149; té de hierbas *m* 149; té en hoja *m* 144; té solo *m* 149; té verde *m* 149
teatro *m* 254, 299
tebeo *m* 112
techo *m* 62, 203; techo solar *m* 202
tecla *f* 176
teclado *m* 97, 99, 172, 176, 258
técnicas *f* 79, 159
técnico de sonido *m* 179
tee *m* 233
teja *f* 58, 187
tejado *m* 58
tejer 277
tela *f* 276, 277; tela adhesiva *f* 47; tela metálica *f* 167
telar *m* 277
teleférico *m* 246
teléfono *m* 99, 172; teléfono de

emergencia *m* 195; teléfono de monedas *m* 99; teléfono de tarjeta *m* 99; teléfono inalámbrico *m* 99
telegrama *m* 98
telenovela *f* 178
teleobjetivo *m* 270
telepizzería *f* 154
telepompter *m* 179
telescopio *m* 281
telesilla *f* 246
televisión *f* 268; televisión de pantalla panorámica *f* 269; televisión por cable *f* 269
telón *m* 254; telón de fondo *m* 254
temblor *m* 283
témpera *f* 274
temperatura *f* 286
templo *m* 300
temprano 305
tenacillas *f* 38
tenazas *f* 38, 81, 167; tenazas de alambre *f* 80
tendedero *m* 76
tendón *m* 17; tendón de Aquiles *m* 16; tendón de la corva *m* 16; tendón porplíteo *m* 16
tenedor *m* 65, 153; tenedor para trinchar *m* 68
tener un hijo 26
tenis *m* 31, 37, 220, 230, 231, 251
tensión arterial *f* 44
teñido 39
tequila *m* 145
terapeuta *m/f* 55
terapia de grupo *f* 55
terapias alternativas *f* 54
tercero 309
terminal *f* 212; terminal del ferry *f* 216
termita *f* 295
termo *m* 267
termoesfera *f* 286
termómetro *m* 45, 167
termostato *m* 61
ternera *f* 118
ternero *m* 185
terraza *f* 85, 148; terraza ajardinada *f* 84
terremoto *m* 283
territorio *m* 315
tesina *f* 169
tesis *f* 169
testículo *m* 21
testigo *m* 180, 235
tetera *f* 65
tetina *f* 75
tetrabrik *m* 311
tía *f* 22
tibia *f* 17
tiburón *m* 294
tiempo *m* 234, 286, 304; tiempo extra *m* 223; tiempo fuera *m* 220
tienda *f* 298; tienda de antigüedades *f* 114; tienda de artículos usados *f* 115; tienda de campaña *f* 269; tienda de discos *f* 115; tienda de fotografía *f* 115; tienda de golosinas *f* 113; tienda de licores *f* 115; tienda de mascotas *f* 115; tienda de materiales de arte *f* 115; tienda de muebles *f* 115; tienda de ragalos *f* 114; tienda libre de impuestos *f* 213; tienda naturista *f* 115
tiendas *f* 114; tiendas departamentales *f* 105
tierra *f* 85; Tierra *f* 280, 282; tierra firme *f* 282
tierras de labranza *f* 182
tigre *m* 291
tijeras *f* 38, 47, 82, 89, 188, 207, 276; tijeras de podar *f* 89; tijeras de uñas *f* 41
tilo *m* 296
timbal *m* 257
timbre *m* 48, 59, 98, 197
timbres *m* 112
tímido 25
timón *m* 210, 241
tina de plástico *f* 74
tinta *f* 275
tinte para el pelo *m* 40
tinte para madera *m* 79
tinto 145
tintorería *f* 115
tío *m* 22
tipo de cambio *m* 97
tipo de interés *m* 96
tipos *m* 205; tipos de autobuses *m* 196
tipos de cámara *m* 270
tipos de granja *m* 183
tipos de pesca *m* 245
tipos de plantas *m* 86
tipos de tren *m* 208
tirador *m* 200
tiraleches *m* 53
tirante *m* 35
tirar 223, 227; tirar al hoyo con un putter *m* 233; tirar de cabeza 222
tirarse en trineo 247
tirarse un clavado 238
tirita *f* 47
tiro *m* 249; tiro con arco *m* 249; tiro con efecto *m* 230; tiro de esquina *m* 223; tiro libre *m* 222
tirón *m* 239; tirón en el cuello *m* 46
título *m* 168
tiza *f* 162, 188
toalla de ducha *f* 73
toalla de lavabo *f* 73
toalla de mano *f* 73
toalla de playa *f* 265
toallas *f* 73; toallas femeninas *f* 108
toallero *m* 72
toallita antiséptica *f* 47
toallita húmeda *f* 108
toallitas húmedas *f* 75
tobillo *m* 13, 15
tobogán *m* 263
tocadiscos *m* 268
tocador *m* 71
tocino *m* 118, 156
tocólogo *m* 52
todoterreno *m* 199
toffee *m* 113
toga *f* 169
toldo *m* 148, 266
toma *f* 61; toma de tierra *f* 60; toma del agua *f* 61
tomar apuntes 163
tomar el sol 264
tomate *m* 125, 157; tomate cherry *m* 124
tomillo *m* 133
tonelada *f* 310
tónica *f* 144
tónico *m* 41
tono *m* 41, 256
topacio *m* 288
topinambur *m* 125
torcedura *f* 46
tormenta *f* 287
tornado *m* 287
tornear 79
torneo *m* 233
tornillo *m* 80; tornillo de banco *m* 78
tornillos *m* 203
torno de alfarero *m* 275
torno de banco *m* 78
torno de dentista *m* 50
toro *m* 185
toronja *m* 126
torre *f* 272, 300
torre de control *f* 212
torre de vigilancia *f* 265
torreón *m* 300
torrija *f* 157
tortilla *f* 158
tortuga *f* 293
tos *f* 44
tostado 129
tostador *m* 66
trabajo *m* 172
tractor *m* 182
tráfico *m* 194, 195
trago *m* 151
traje *m* 32, 255; traje de baño *m* 238, 265; traje de buzo *m* 239; traje de chaqueta *m* 32; traje de cuero *m* 205; traje de esquí *m* 246; traje de invierno *m* 30; traje de noche *m* 34; traje espacial *m* 281; traje minifaldero *m* 34
trampa de arena *f* 232
trampolín *m* 235, 238
transatlántico *m* 215
transbordador espacial *f* 281
transferencia bancaria *f* 96
transformador *m* 60
tránsito *m* 194
transmisión *f* 179, 202
transmitir 178
transplantar 91
transportador *m* 165
transporte *m* 194
tranvía *m* 196, 208
trapeador *m* 77
trapear 77
trapecio *m* 16, 164
trapo del polvo *m* 77
tráquea *f* 18
traspaso *m* 223
traste *f* 258
tratamientos *m* 23; tratamientos de belleza *m* 41
trébol *m* 273, 297
trece 308
treinta 308
trementina *f* 83
tren *m* 208; tren de alta velocidad *m* 208; tren de aterrizaje *m* 210; tren de carga *m* 208; tren de mercancías *m* 208; tren de vapor *m* 208; tren delantero *m* 210; tren diesel *m* 208; tren eléctrico *m* 208; tren intercity *m* 209
trenca *f* 31
trenza *f* 39
tres 308
trescientos 308
triángulo *m* 164, 257
tribuna del jurado *f* 180
tríceps *m* 16
trigésimo 309
trigo *m* 130, 184; trigo partido *m* 130
trimestre *m* 52
trinche *m* 68, 88, 89
trineo con perros *m* 247
tripié *m* 270
trípode *m* 166, 270, 281
tripulación *f* 241
triste 25
triturador de basuras *m* 61
trocitos de chocolate *m* 141
trolebús *m* 196
trombón de varas *m* 257
trompa *f* 291; trompa de Falopio *f* 20
trompeta *f* 257
trona *f* 75
tronco *m* 296
trópico de Cáncer *m* 283
trópico de Capricornio *m* 283
trópicos *m* 283
troposfera *f* 286
trote *m* 243
trozo *m* 140
trucha *f* 120; trucha arco iris *f* 120
trueno *m* 286
trufa *f* 113, 125
tuba *f* 257
tubo *m* 112, 202, 239, 311; tubo de desagüe *m* 61; tubo de ensayo *m* 166; tubo de escape *m* 203, 204; tubo de la aspiradora *m* 77; tubo de la tienda *m* 266; tubo superior *m* 207
tuerca *f* 80
tulipán *m* 111
tuna *f* 128
turbo *m* 203
turismo *m* 199, 260
turista *m* 260
turmalina *f* 288
turno *m* 228, 273
turquesa *f* 289
turrón *m* 113
tutú *m* 191

U

ugli *m* 126
última mano *f* 83
último piso *m* 141
ultraligero *m* 211
ultramarinos *m* 114
ultrasonido *f* 48, 52, *m* 52
umpire *m* 229
un cuarto de hora 304
undécimo 309
unidad de cuidados intensivos *f* 48
uniforme *m* 94, 162, 189, 222; uniforme de rugby *m* 221; uniforme del equipo *m* 31
universidad *f* 299
universo *m* 280
uno 308

uña *f* 15; uña del pie *f* 15
Urano *m* 280
uréter *m* 21
uretra *f* 20
urgencia *f* 46
urinario 19
urología *f* 49
usar el hilo dental 50
utensilios de cocina *m* 68
útero *m* 20, 52

V

vaca *f* 185
vacaciones *f* 212
vaciar 67
vacío 321
vagina *f* 20
vagón *m* 208; vagón restaurante *m* 209
vaina *f* 122
vainilla *f* 132
vajilla *f* 64; vajilla y los cubiertos *f*, *m* 65
vajillas *f* 105
vale 322
valla *f* 85, 243
valle *m* 284
valor de las acciones *m* 97
valor nominal *m* 97
válvula de la presión *f* 61
vaquería *f* 183
varicela *f* 44
varilla de cristal *f* 167
varilla del nivel del aceite *f* 202
vaso *m* 65; vaso de precipitados *m* 167
vasos *m* 150
vecino *m* 24
vehículo de servicio *m* 212
veinte 308
veinte mil 309
veinte minutos 304
veintidós 308
veintiuno 308
vejiga *f* 20
vela *f* 63, 240, 241; vela mayor *f* 240
velas de cumpleanos *f* 141
vellón *m* 74
velo 35
velocímetro *m* 201, 204
vena *f* 19
venado *m* 118
venda *f* 47
vendaje *m* 47
vendedor *m* 104
vendedor de golosinas *m* 113
vendedor de periódicos *m* 112
vendedora *f* 188
ventaja *f* 230
ventana *f* 58, 177, 186, 197; ventana de la buhardilla *f* 58; ventana de la nariz *f* 14
ventanilla *f* 96, 98, 197, 209, 210; ventanilla de boletos *f* 216; ventanilla de pasajes *f* 216
ventarrón 286
ventilador *m* 60, 202, 210
ventosa *f* 53
Venus 280
ver la televisiòn 269
verano *m* 31, 307
verde 129, 274
verdulería *f* 114
verdura *f* 107
verduras *f* 122, 124
veredicto *m* 181
vértebras cervicales *f* 17
vértebras dorsales *f* 17
vértebras lumbares *f* 17
vesícula seminal *f* 21
vespa *f* 205
vestido *m* 31, 34
vestíbulo *m* 59, 100, 209, 255
vestido de novia *m* 35
vestuario *m* 255
veterinaria *f* 189
vía *f* 208; vía de acceso *f* 194, 216; vía de salida *f* 194
viaje de negocios *m* 175
viajero de cercanías *m* 208
vibráfono *m* 257
vídeocasete *f* 269
videocasetera *m* 269
videojuego *m* 269
videoteléfono *m* 99
vieira *f* 121
viejo 321
viento *m* 241, 286
viento-madera *m* 257
viento-metal *m* 256
viernes 306
viga de acero *f* 186
viga de equilibrio *f* 235
viga de madera *f* 186
viga del tejado *f* 186
vigésimo 309, vigésimo primero 309; vigésimo segundo 309; vigésimo tercero 309
vinagre *m* 135, 142; vinagre balsámico *m* 135; vinagre de malta *m* 135; vinagre de sidra *m* 135; vinagre de vino *m* 135
vino *m* 145, 151; vino de jerez *m* 145; vino de oporto *m* 145
viña *f* 183
viñedo *m* 183
viola *f* 256
violín *m* 256
violoncelo *m* 256
virar 241
virus *m* 44
virutas de madera *f* 78
visa *f* 213
visado *m* 213
visera *f* 205
visillo *m* 63
visita guiada *f* 260
visor *m* 239, 271
vista *f* 51
vitaminas *f* 108
vitrina *f* 66
vivero *m* 115
vivienda de una planta *f* 58
vocalista *m* 258
vodka *m* 145; vodka con naranja *m* 150
volante *m* 49, 201, 231; volante a la derecha *m* 201; volante a la izquierda *m* 201
volar 211
volcán *m* 283
volcar 241
volea *f* 231
vóleibol *m* 227
voltaje *m* 60
voltereta lateral *f* 235
volumen *m* 165, 179, 269, 311
vomitar 44
vuelo con ala delta *m* 248
vuelo internacional *m* 212
vuelo nacional *m* 212
vuelo sin motor *m* 248

W

waffles *m* 157
wáter *m* 72
waterpolo *m* 239
wedge *m* 233
whisky *m* 145
whisky escocés con agua *m* 151
windsurfing *m* 241
windsurfista *m* 241
wok *m* 69

Y

yarda *f* 310
yate *m* 215, 240
yema *f* 137, 157
yerno *m* 22
yeso *m* 83
yoga *m* 54
yogurt *m* 137; yogurt de frutas *m* 157; yogurt helado *m* 137

Z

zacate *m* 73
zafiro *m* 288
zanahoria *f* 124
zapapico *m* 292
zapatería *f* 114
zapatilla deportiva *f* 37
zapatillas de deporte *f* 31
zapato de agujetas *m* 37
zapato de caballero *m* 37
zapato de cordoneras *m* 37
zapato de golf *m* 233
zapato de piel *m* 37
zapato de plataforma *m* 37
zapato de tacón *m* 37
zapatos *m* 34, 37; zapatos de piel *m* 32
zarpa *f* 291
zarpar 217
zarzamora *f* 127
zinc *m* 289
zodiac *m* 215
zona *f* 315; zona de abastecimiento *f* 199; zona de ataque *f* 224; zona de defensa *f* 224; zona de fumadores *f* 152; zona de marca *f* 221; zona de no fumadores *f* 152; zona final *f* 220; zona industrial *f* 299; zona lumbar *f* 13; zona neutral *f* 224; zona peatonal *f* 299; zona poco profunda *f* 239; zona profunda *f* 239
zonas *f* 283, 299
zoo *m* 262
zoología *f* 169
zoológico *m* 262
zoom *m* 270
zorro *m* 290
zumo *m* 127, 149; zumo de frutas *m* 156; zumo de tomate *m* 144; zumo de uva *m* 144
zurcir 277

índice inglés • English index

A

à la carte 152
abdomen 12
abdominals 16
above 320
acacia 110
accelerator 200
accessories 36, 38
accident 46
account number 96
accountant 97, 190
accounts department 175
accused 180
ace 230, 273
Achilles tendon 16
acorn squash 125
acquaintance 24
acquitted 181
across 320
acrylic paints 274
actions 237, 229, 227, 233, 183
activities 263, 245, 162, 77
actor 254, 191
actors 179
actress 254
acupressure 55
acupuncture 55
Adam's apple 19
add *v* 165
address 98
adhesive tape 47
adjustable wrench 80
admission charge 260
admissions office 168
admitted 48
aduki beans 131
adult 23
advantage 230
adventure 255
advertisement 269
aerate *v* 91
aerobics 251
after 320
afternoon 305
aftershave 73
aftersun 108
agate 289
agenda 174
aikido 236
aileron 210
air bag 201
air conditioning 200
air cylinder 239
air filter 202, 204
air mattress 267
air supply 199
air vent 210
aircraft 210; aircraft carrier 215
airliner 210, 212
airport 212
aisle 106, 168, 210, 254
alarm clock 70
alcoholic drinks 145
alfalfa 184
allergy 44
alley 298
alligator 293; alligator clip 167
all-purpose flour 139
allspice 132
almond 129; almond oil 134
almonds 151
along 320
alpine 87; alpine skiing 247
alternating current 60
alternative therapy 54
alternator 203
altitude 211
aluminum 289
ambulance 94
amethyst 288
amniocentesis 52
amniotic fluid 52
amount 96
amp 60
amphibians 294
amplifier 268
anchor 214, 240
anesthetist 48
angle 164
angler 244
angry 25
animals 292, 294
animated film 255
ankle 13, 15
ankle-length 34
anniversary 26
annual 86, 307
answer 163; answer *v* 99, 163
answering machine 99
ant 295
antenna 295
antifreeze 199, 203
anti-inflammatory 109
antique shop 114
antiseptic 47; antiseptic wipe 47
anti-wrinkle 41
antler 291
apartment building 298
apéritif 153
aperture dial 270
apex 165
appeal 181
appearance 30
appendix 18
applaud *v* 255
apple 126; apple corer 68; apple juice 149
appliances 66
application 176
appointment 45, 175
apricot 126
apron 30, 50, 69, 212
APS camera 270
aquamarine 288
arc 164
arch 15, 85, 301
archery 249
architect 190
architecture 300
architrave 301
area 165, 310
areas 299
arena 243
arithmetic 165
arm 13
armband 238
armchair 63
armpit 13
armrest 200, 210
aromatherapy 55
around 320
arrangements 111
arrest 94
arrivals 213
arrow 249
art 162; art college 169; Art Deco 301; art gallery 261; art history 169; Art Nouveau 301; art shop 115
artery 19
artichoke 124
artist 274
arts and crafts 274, 276
ash 283
ashtray 150
asphalt 187
assault 94
assistant 24
assisted delivery 53
asteroid 280
asthma 44
astigmatism 51
astronaut 281
astronomy 281
asymmetric bars 235
at 320
athlete 234
athletic shoes 31, 251
ATM 97
atmosphere 282, 286
atrium 104
attachment 177
attack 220; attack zone 224
attend *v* 174
attic 58
attractions 261
auburn 39
audience 254
August 306
aunt 22
aurora 286
automatic 200; automatic door 196; automatic payment 96
avalanche 247
avenue 299
avocado 128
awning 148
ax 95
axle 205
ayurveda 55

B

baby 23, 30; baby bath 74; baby care 74; baby changing facilities 104; baby monitor 75; baby products 107; baby sling 75
back 13; back brush 73; back seat 200; back up v 195
backboard 226
backdrop 254
backgammon 272
backhand 231
backpack 31, 37, 267
backsplash 66
backstroke 239
backswing 233
bacon 118, 119, 157
bad 321
badge 94, 189
badminton 231
bag 311
bagel 139
baggage claim 213
baggage trailer 212
bags 37
baguette 138
bail 181
bailiff 180
bait 244; bait *v* 245
bake *v* 67, 138
baked 159
baker 139
baker's 114
bakery 107, 114, 138
baking 69; baking sheet 69
balance wheel 276
balcony 59, 254
bald 39
bale 184
ball 15, 75, 221,224, 226, 228, 230; ball boy 231
ballet 255
balsamic vinegar 135
bamboo 86,122
banana 128
bandage 47
banister 59
bank 96, 284; bank charge 96; bank manager 96; bank transfer 96
bar 150, 152, 250, 256, 311; bar code 106; bar counter 150; bar mitzvah 26; bar snacks 151; bar stool 150
barb 244
barbecue 267
barber 39, 188
bark 296
barley 130, 184
barn 182
baroque 301
bars 74
bartender 150, 191
basalt 288
base 164, 229; base station 99
baseball 228
baseline 230
baseman 228
basement 58
basil 133
basket 106, 207, 226; basket of fruit 126
basketball 226; basketball player 226
basque 35

english

bass clarinet 257
bass clef 256
bass guitar 258
bass guitarist 258
bassinet 74
bassoon 257
bat 225, 228, 231, 290; bat *v* 225, 229
bath mat 72
bath towel 73
bathrobe 31, 32, 73
bathroom 72
bathtub 72
baton 235, 256
batsman 225
batter 228
batteries 260
battery 167, 202; battery pack 78
battleship 215
bay leaf 133
be born *v* 26
beach 264; beach bag 264; beach ball 265; beach hut 264; beach towel 265; beach umbrella 264
beaker 167
beam 186, 235
bean sprout 122
beans 131, 144
bear 291
beat 259
beauty 40, 105; beauty treatments 41
bed 70; bed and breakfast 101; bed linen 71
bedding 74
bedroom 70
bedside lamp 70
bedspread 70
bee 295
beech 296
beef 118
beer 145,151; beer tap 150
beetle 295
beet 125
before 320
beginning 321
behind 320
bell 197
below 320
belt 32, 36, 236
bench 250, 262
berry 296
beside 320
bet 273
between 320
beyond 320
biathlon 247
bib 30
biceps 16; biceps curl 251
bicycle 206
bidet 72
biennial 86
bifocal 51
big toe 15
bike rack 207
bikini 264
bill 152, 293
binoculars 281
biology 162
biplane 211
birch 296
birds 292
bird-watching 263
birth 52; birth weight 53; birth certificate 26
birthday 27; birthday cake 141; birthday candles 141; birthday party 27
bishop 272
bit 242; bit brace 78
bite 46; bite *v* 245
bitter 124, 145
black 39, 272, 274; black belt 237; black coffee 148; black currant 127; black hole 280; black olive 143; black pudding 157; black tea 149
blackberry 127
blackboard 162
black-eyed beans 131
bladder 20
blade 60, 66, 78, 89
blanket 71, 74
blazer 33
bleach 77
blender 66
blister 46
block 237; block *v* 227
blonde 39
blood pressure 44; blood pressure gauge 45
blood test 48
blouse 34
blow-dry *v* 38
blow out *v* 141
blowhole 290
blue 274; blue cheese 136
bluebells 297
blueberry 127
blues 259
blusher 40
board 241; board *v* 217; board games 272
boarding pass 213
boardwalk 265
bob 39
bobbin 276
bobsled 247
body 12; body lotion 73; body systems 19
bodywork 202
boil *v* 67
boiled egg 137, 157
bollard 214, 298
bolt 59
bomber 211
bone 17, 119, 121; bone meal 88
boned 121
bongos 257
book 168
bookstore 115
bookshelf 63, 168
boom 95, 240
booster 281
booties 30
bored 25
borrow *v* 168
bottle 61, 75, 135, 311; bottle opener 68, 150
bottled foods 134
bottled water 144
bottom tier 141
boundary line 225
bouquet 35, 111; bouquet garni 132
bout 237
boutique 115
bow 240, 249; bow tie 36
bowl 61, 65, 112; bowl *v* 225
bowler 225
bowling 249; bowling ball 249
box 254; box file 173; box of chocolates 113; box of tissues 70; box office 255
boxer shorts 33
boxercise 251
boxing 236; boxing gloves 237; boxing ring 237
boy 23
boyfriend 24
bra 35
braces 50
bracelet 36
braid 39
brain 19
brake 200, 204, 206
brake *v* 207; brake block 207; brake fluid reservoir 202; brake lever 207; brake pedal 205
bran 130
branch 296
brandy 145
brass 256
Brazil nut 129
bread 157; bread flour 139; bread knife 68; bread roll 143
breadcrumbs 139
breadfruit 124
breads 138
break a record *v* 234
break water *v* 52
breakdown 203
breakfast 64, 156; breakfast buffet 156; breakfast cereals 107; breakfast table 156; breakfast tray 101
breast 12, 119; breast pump 53
breastbone 17
breastfeed *v* 53
breaststroke 239
breathing 47
breech 52
brick 187
bridge 15, 214, 258, 273, 300
bridle 242; bridle path 263
brie 142
briefcase 37
briefs 33, 35
brioche 157
broadcast 179; broadcast *v* 178
broccoli 123
brochure 96, 175
brogue 37
broil *v* 67
bronze 235
brooch 36
broom 77
broth 158
brother 22
brother-in-law 23
browband 242
brown 274; brown bread 139, 149; brown flour 138; brown lentils 131; brown rice 130
browse *v* 177
browser 177
bruise 46
brunette 39
brush 38, 40, 77, 83, 274; brush *v* 38, 50
Brussels sprout 122
bubble bath 73
buckle 36
bud 111, 297
buffet 152
build *v* 186
building site 186
buildings 299
built-in wardrobe 71
bulb 86
bull 185
bulldog clip 173
bullnose pliers 80
bullseye 273
bumper 74, 198
bun 39, 140, 139, 155
bunch 111
bungalow 58
bungee jumping 248
bunker 232
bunsen burner 166
buoy 217
bureau de change 97
burger 154; burger bar 154; burger meal 154
burglar alarm 58
burglary 94
burn 46
burner 67
bus 196; bus driver 190; bus stop 197; bus station 197; bus stop 197, 299; bus ticket 197
buses 196
business 175; business class 211; business deal 175; business lunch 175; business partner 24; business suit 32; business trip 175
businessman 175
businesswoman 175
busy 99
butcher 118, 188; butcher shop 114
butter 137, 156; butter beans 131
buttercup 297
butterfly 239, 295
buttermilk 137
butternut squash 125
buttock 13, 16
button 32
buttonhole 32
buttress 301
by 320; by airmail 98
bytes 176

english

C

cab 95; cab driver 190
cabbage 123
cabin 210, 214
cabinet 66
cable 79, 207; cable car 246; cable television 269
cactus 87
caddy 233
cesarean section 52
café 148, 262
cafeteria 168
cafetière 65
cake pan 69
cakes 140
calcite 289
calcium 109
calculator 165
calendar 306
calf 13, 16, 185
call button 48
calyx 297
cam belt 203
camcorder 260, 269
camel 291
camembert 142
camera 178, 260, 270; camera case 271; camera crane 178; camera shop 115
cameraman 178
camisole 35
camp *v* 266; camp bed 266
campari 145
camper van 266
campfire 266
camping 266; camping stove 267
campground 266
campus 168
can 145, 289, 311; can opener 68
canary 292
candied fruit 129
candle 63
candy 113; candy store 113
cane 91
canes 89
canine 50
canned drink 154
canned food 107
canoe 214
canoeing 241
canola oil 135
canter 243
canvas 274
cap 21, 36, 238
capacity 311
cape gooseberry 128
capers 143
capital 315
capoeira 237
cappuccino 148
capsize *v* 241
capsule 109
captain 214
car 198, 200; car accident 203; car rental 213; car seat 198, 207; car stereo 201; car wash 198
caramel 113
caraway 131
card 27; card phone 99; card slot 97
cardamom 132
cardboard 275
cardigan 32
cardiology 49
cardiovascular 19
cards 273
cargo 216
carnation 110
carnival 27
carousel 212
carpenter 188
carpentry bits 80
carpet 71
carriage race 243
carrier 75, 204
carrot 124
carry-on luggage 211, 213
cart 48, 100, 106, 208, 213
cartilage 17
carton 311
cartoon 178
carve *v* 79
carving fork 68
case 51
cash *v* 97
cashew 129
cashews 151
cashier 96, 106
casino 261
cassava 124
casserole dish 69
cassette player 269
cassette tape 269
cast 254; cast *v* 245
castle 300
casual 34; casual wear 33
cat 290
catalog 168
catamaran 215
cataract 51
catch *v* 220, 227, 229, 245
catcher 229
caterpillar 295
cathedral 300
catheter 53
cauliflower 124
cave 284
CD 269; CD player 268
cedar 296
ceiling 62
celebration 140; celebration cakes 141
celebrations 27
celeriac 124
celery 122
cell 94, 181; cell phone 99
cello 256
cement 186; cement mixer 186
centimeter 310
centipede 295
central reservation 194
center 164; center circle 222, 224, 226; center field 228; center line 226
centerboard 241
century 307
CEO 175
ceramic range 66
cereal 130, 156
cervical vertebrae 17
cervix 20, 52
chain 36, 206
chair 64; chair *v* 174
chairlift 246
chalk 85, 162, 288
chamber 283
chamomile tea 149
champagne 145
championship 230
change *v* 209; change a tire *v* 203; change channels *v* 269; change gears *v* 207
changing mat 74
changing room 104
channel 178
charcoal 266, 275
charge 94, 180
chart 48
chassis 203
check 96
checkbook 96
checkers 272
check-in *v* 212; check-in desk 213
checking account 96
checkout 106
checkup 50
cheddar 142
cheek 14
cheerleader 220
cheese 136, 156
chef 152, 190
chef's hat 190
chemistry 162
cherry 126; cherry tomato 124
chess 272
chessboard 272
chest 12; chest of drawers 70; chest press 251
chestnut 129
chewing gum 113
chick 185
chicken 119, 185; chicken burger 155; chicken coop 185; chicken nuggets 155; chicken pox 44
chicory 122
child 23, 31; child lock 75
childbirth 53
children 23
children's clothing 30
children's department 104
children's meal 153
children's ward 48
chili pepper 124, 132, 143
chill 44
chimney 58
chin 14
china 105
chip *v* 233
chips 113, 151
chipboard 79
chiropractic 54
chisel 81, 275
chives 133
chocolate 113; chocolate bar 113; chocolate cake 140; chocolate chip 141; chocolate milkshake 149; chocolate spread 135
chocolate-coated 140
choir 301
choke *v* 47
chop 119, 237
chorizo 143
choux pastry 140
christening 26
Christmas 27
chrysanthemum 110
chuck 78
church 298, 300
chutney 134
cider 145; cider vinegar 135
cigar 112
cigarettes 112
cilantro 133
cinnamon 133
circle 165, 254
circular saw 78
circuit training 251
circulation desk 168
circumference 164
citrus fruit 126
city 299
clam 121
clamp 78, 166; clamp stand 166
clapper board 179
clarinet 257
clasp 36
classical music 255, 259
classroom 162
claw 291
clay 85, 275
clean *v* 77; clean clothes 76
cleaned 121
cleaner 188
cleaning equipment 77
cleaning fluid 51
cleanser 41
clear honey 134
cleat 240
cleaver 68
clementine 126
client 38, 175, 180
cliff 285
climber 87
climbing frame 263
clinic 48, 168
clipboard 173
clitoris 20
clock 62; clock radio 70
closed 260, 321
cloth diaper 30
clothesline 76
clothespin 76
clothing 205
cloud 287
cloudy 286
clove 125
clover 297
cloves 133
club 273; club sandwich 155
clubhouse 232
clutch 200, 204
coach 196
coal 288
coast 285
coaster 150
coastguard 217

english

coat 32; coat hanger 70
cockatoo 293
cockle 121
cockpit 210
cockroach 295
cocktail 151; cocktail shaker 150
cocoa powder 148
coconut 129
cocoon 295
cod 120
coffee 144, 148, 153, 156, 184; coffee cup 65; coffee machine 148, 150; coffee milkshake 149; coffee spoon 153; coffee table 62
cog 206
coin 97; coin phone 99; coin return 99
cola 144
colander 68
cold 44, 286, 321; cold faucet 72
cold-pressed oil 135
collage 275
collar 32
collarbone 17
colleague 24
collect call 99
collection 98
college 168
cologne 41
colony 315
colored pencil 163
colors 39, 274
comb 38; comb *v* 38
combat sports 236
combine 182
comedy 255
comforter 71
comet 280
comic 112
commis chef 152
commission 97
communications 98
commuter 208
compact 40; compact car 199
company 175
compartment 209
compass 165, 312, 240
complaint 94
complexion 41
composite 181
compost 88; compost pile 85
computer 172, 176
concealer 40
conceive *v* 20
conception 52
concert 255, 258
concourse 209
concrete block 187
concussion 46
condensed milk 136
conditioner 38
condom 21
conductor 256
cone 164, 187
confectionery 107, 113
confident 25
confused 25
conglomerate 288
conifer 86
connect *v* 177
connection 212
conning tower 215
console 269
constellation 281
construction 186; construction worker 186, 188
consultant 49
consultation 45
contact lenses 51
container 216, 311; container port 216; container ship 215
continent 282, 315
contraception 21, 52
contraction 52
control tower 212
controller 269
controls 201, 204
convenience food 107
convertible 199
conveyer belt 106
cooked meat 118, 143
cookies 113, 141
cooking 67
coolant reservoir 202
cooling rack 69
co-pilot 211
copper 289
copy *v* 172
cor anglais 257
coral reef 285
cordless drill 78
cordless phone 99
core 127
cork 134
corkscrew 150
corn 122, 130, 184; corn bread 139; corn oil 135
cornea 51
corner 223; corner flag 223
cornice 300
corset 35
costume 255
cottage cheese 136
cottage garden 84
cotton 184, 277; cotton balls 41
cough 44; cough drop 109; cough medicine 108
counselor 55
count *v* 165
counter 96, 98, 100, 142, 272
countertop 66
country 259, 315
couple 24
courier 99
courses 153
court 226; court case 180; court clerk 180; court date 180
courtroom 180
courtyard 58, 84
couscous 130
cousin 22
coverall 30
cow 185
cow's milk 136
CPU 176
crab 121, 295
cracked wheat 130
cradle 95
craft knife 82
crafts 275
cramp 239
cramps 44
cranberry 127
crane 187, 216, 292
crater 283
crayfish 121
cream 109, 137, 140, 157; cream cheese 136; cream pie 141
crease 225
credit card 96
creel 245
creeper 87
crème caramel 141
crème patisserie 140
crêpe 155, 157
crescent moon 280
crew 241; crew hatch 281
crib 74
cricket 225, 295; cricket ball 225
cricketer 225
crime 94
criminal 181; criminal record 181
crisp 127
crispbread 139, 156
crisper 67
crochet 277; crochet hook 277
crockery 64; crockery and cutlery 65
crocodile 293
croissant 156
crop 39, 183; crop farm 183
crops 184
crossbar 207, 222, 235
cross-country skiing 247
cross-trainer 250
crosswalk 195
crow 292
crown 50
crucible 166
crushed 132
crust 139, 282
cry *v* 25
crystal healing 55
cube 164
cucumber 125
cuff 32, 45
cufflink 36
cultivate *v* 91
cultivator 182
cumin 132
curb 298
cured 118, 159, 143
curler 38
curling 247; curling iron 38
curly 39
currant 129
curry 158; curry powder 132
curtain 63, 254
curved 165
cushion 62
custard 140
customer 96, 104, 106, 152; customer service department 175; customer services 104
customs 212; customs house 216
cut 46; cut *v* 38, 79, 277
cuticle 15
cutlery 64
cuts 119
cutting 91; cutting board 68
cuttlefish 121
cycle *v* 207; cycle lane 206
cycling 263
cylinder 164; cylinder head 202
cymbals 257

D

daffodil 111
dairy 107; dairy farm 183; dairy produce 136
daisy 110, 297
dam 300
dance 259; dance academy 169
dancer 191
dandelion 123, 297
dandruff 39
dark 41, 321
darkroom 271
darn *v* 277
dartboard 273
darts 273
dashboard 201
date 129, 306
daughter 22
daughter-in-law 22
dawn 305
day 305, 306; day after tomorrow 307; day before yesterday 307
dead ball line 221
deadhead *v* 91
deal *v* 273
debit card 96
decade 307
decay 50
December 306
deciduous 86
decimal 165
deck 214; deck chair 265; deck of cards 273
decking 85
decorating 82
decoration 141
decorator 82
deep end 239
deep-fried 159
deep-sea fishing 245
deer 291
defense 181, 220
defendant 181
defender 223
defending zone 224
defrost *v* 67
degree 169
delay 209
deli 107
delicatessen 142
delivery 52, 98
deltoid 16
denomination 97
denominator 165
dental care 108
dental floss 50, 72
dental hygiene 72
dental X-ray 50

dentist 50, 189
dentist's chair 50
dentures 50
deodorant 73, 108
department 169; department store 105
departments 49
departure lounge 213
departures 213
deposit v 96; deposit slips 96
depth 165
dermatology 49
descaled 121
desert 285
desiccated 129
designer 191, 277
desk 162, 172
desktop 177
dessert 153; dessert cart 152
desserts 140
destination 213
detached 58
detective 94
detergent 77
detour 195
deuce 230
develop *v* 271
diabetes 44
diagonal 164
dial *v* 99
diameter 164
diamond 273, 288
diaper 75; diaper bag 75; diaper rash cream 74
diaphragm 19, 21
diarrhea 44, 109
dice 272
dictionary 163
die *v* 26
diesel 199; diesel train 208
difficult 321
dig *v* 90, 227
digestive 19
digital 269; digital camera 270
dilation 52
dill 133
dimensions 165
dimple 15
dining car 209
dining room 64
dinner 64, 158; dinner plate 65
diopter 51
diploma 169
dipstick 202
direct current 60
directions 260
director 254
directory assistance 99
dirt bike 205
dirty laundry 76
disabled parking 195
discharged 48
disconnected 99
discus 234
discuss *v* 163
disembark *v* 217
dishwasher 66
disinfectant solution 51
disk 176
disposable 109; disposable camera 270; disposable diaper 30; disposable razor 73
dissertation 169
distance 310
distributor 203
district 315
dive 239; dive *v* 238
diver 238
divide *v* 165
divided by 165
divided highway 195
dividends 97
divider 173, 194
divorce 26
Diwali 27
DJ 179
do not bend *v* 98
dock 214, 216; dock *v* 217
doctor 45, 189
doctorate 169
documentary 178
dog 290
dog-sledding 247
doll 75
dollhouse 75
dolphin 290
dome 300
domestic flight 212
dominoes 273
donkey 185
door 196, 198, 209; door chain 59; door knob 59; door knocker 59; door lock 200
doorbell 59
doormat 59
dormer 58
dorsal fin 294
dosage 109
double 151; double bass 256; double bassoon 257; double bed 71; double room 100
double-decker bus 196
doubles 230
dough 138
Dover sole 120
down 320
downhill skiing 247
download *v* 177
dragonfly 295
drain 61, 72, 299; drain cock 61
drainage 91
draining board 67
draw 223; draw *v* 162
drawer 66, 70, 172; drawer unit 172
drawing 275
dress 31, 34
dressage 243
dressed 159; dressed chicken 119
dressing 47, 158; dressing table 71
dribble *v* 223, 227
dried flowers 111
dried fruit 156
drill 50; drill *v* 79
drill bit 78
drill bits 80
drinking cup 75
drinking fountain 262
drinks 107, 144, 156
drip 53
drive *v* 195, 233
driver 196
driver's seat 196
driveshaft 202
drop anchor *v* 217
dropper 109, 167
drops 109
dropshot 230
drown *v* 239
drum 258; drum kit 258
drummer 258
dry 39, 41, 130, 145, 286, 321; dry *v* 76; dry dock 217
dry-cleaner 115
duck 119, 185; duck egg 137
duckling 185
duffle bag 37
duffle coat 31
dugout 229
dumb bell 251
dumper truck 187
dunk *v* 227
duodenum 18
duplex 58
dusk 305
dust *v* 77
dustpan 77
duster 77
dust sheet 83
duty-free shop 213
DVD 269; DVD player 268
dyed 39
dynamo 207

E

eagle 292
ear 14
early
earring 36
Earth 280, 282
earthenware dish 69
earthquake 283
easel 174, 274
east 312
Easter 27
easy 321; easy cook 130
eat *v* 64
eat-in 154
eating 75
eaves 58
éclair 140
eclipse 280
economics 169
economy class 211
eczema 44
edam 142
edge 246
editor 191
eel 294
egg 20; egg cup 65, 137; egg white 137
eggplant 125
eggs 137
eight 308; eight hundred 308
eighteen 308
eighteenth 309
eighth 309
eightieth 309
eighty 308
ejaculatory duct 21
elbow 13
electric blanket 71
electric drill 78
electric guitar 258
electric meter 60
electric razor 73
electric shock 46
electric train 208
electrical goods 105, 107
electrician 188
electricity 60
elephant 291
elevator 59, 100, 104
eleven 308
eleventh 309
elm 296
email 98, 177
email account 177; email address 177
embarrassed 25
embossed paper 83
embroidery 277
embryo 52
emerald 288
emergency 46; emergency exit 210; emergency lever 209; emergency phone 195; emergency room 48; emergency services 94
emigrate *v* 26
emotions 25
employee 24
employer 24
empty 321
enamel 50
encore 255
encyclopedia 163
end 321; end zone 220
endive 123
endline 226
endocrine 19
endocrinology 49
engaged couple 24
engine 202, 204, 208, 210; engine room 214
engineering 169
English breakfast 157
English mustard 135
engraving 275
enlarge *v* 172
enlargement 271
ENT (otolaryngology) 49
entrance 59
entrée 153
envelope 98, 173
environment 280
epidural 52
epiglottis 19
epilepsy 44
episiotomy 52
equals 165
equation 165
equator 283
equipment 165, 233, 238
equity 97
eraser 163
erupt *v* 283
escalator 104
esophagus 19
espresso 148
essay 163
essential oils 55
estate 199
estuary 285
eucalyptus 296
evening 305

english

evening dress 34; evening menu 152
events 243, 247
evergreen 86
evidence 181
excavator 187
excess baggage 212
exchange rate 97
excited 25
excuse me 322
executive 174
exercise bike 250
exercises 251
exfoliate *v* 41
exhaust pipe 203, 204
exhibit *v* 261
exhibition 261
exit 210; exit ramp 194
exosphere 286
expanding file 173
expectant 52
experiment 166
expiration date 109
exposure 271
express train 209
extend *v* 251
extension 58; extension cord 78
exterior 198
extra time 223
extraction 50
extractor 66
eye 14, 51, 244, 276; eye shadow 40; eye test 51
eyebrow 14, 51; eyebrow brush 40; eyebrow pencil 40
eyecup 269
eyelash 14, 51
eyelet 37
eyelid 51
eyeliner 40
eyepiece 167

F

fabric 277; fabric conditioner 76
face 14; face cream 73; face mask 225; face pack 41; face powder 40
faceoff circle 224
facial 41
factory 299
faint *v* 25, 44
fair 41
fairground 262
fairway 232
falcon 292
fall 237; fall (autumn) 31, 307; fall in love *v* 26
fallopian tube 20
family 22
famous ruin 261
fan 60, 202; fan belt 203
fans 258
far 320
fare 197, 209
farm 182, 183, 184
farmer 182, 189
farmhouse 182
farmland 182
farmyard 182
farsightedness 51
fashion 277
fast 321; fast food 154
fastening 37
fast-forward 269
fat 119, 321; fat-free 137
father 22
father-in-law 23
fault 230
fava beans 122, 131
fax 98, 172; fax machine 172
feather 293
feature film 269
February 306
feed *v* 183
feijoa 128
female 12, 20
feminine hygiene 108
femur 17
fence 85, 182, 243
fencing 249
feng shui 55
fennel 122, 133; fennel seeds 133
fenugreek 132
fern 86
ferry 215, 216; ferry terminal 216
fertilization 20
fertilize *v* 91
fertilizer 91
festivals 27
fetus 52
fever 44
fiancé 24
fiancée 24
fiber 127
fibula 17
field 182, 222, 225, 228, 234, 258, 266; field *v* 225, 229; field hockey 224
fifteen 308
fifteenth 309
fifth 309
fiftieth 309
fifty 308
fifty five thousand five hundred 309
fifty thousand 309
fig 129
fighter plane 211
figure skating 247
figurine 260
filament 60
file 81, 172, 177
filing cabinet 172
fill *v* 82
filler 83
fillet 119, 121
filleted 121
filling 50, 140, 155
film chamber 270
film spool 271
filter 270; filter coffee 148; filter paper 167
fin 210
finance 97
financial advisor 97
fingerprint 94
finial 300
finish line 234
fire 95; fire alarm 95; fire department 95; fire engine 95; fire escape 95; fire extinguisher 95; fire station 95
firefighter 95, 189
firelighter 266
fireplace 63
firm 124
first 309; first aid 47; first-aid box 47; first night 254
fish 107, 120, 294; fish and chips 155; fish farm 183
fisherman 189
fishhook 244
fishing 244, 245; fishing boat 217; fishing permit 245; fishing port 217; fishing rod 244
fish-seller 114, 120, 188
fist 15, 237
fitness 250
five 308; five hundred 308
flag 221, 232
flageolet beans 131
flakes 132
flamingo 292
flan 142
flare 240
flash 270; flash gun 270
flashlight 267
flask 166
flat 59, 256; flat race 243; flat tire 203, 207; flat wood bit 80
flatbread 139
flavored oil 134
flax 184
fleece 74
flesh 124, 127, 129
flex *v* 251
flight attendant 190, 210
flight number 213
flint 288
flipchart 174
flip-flop 37
flipper 239, 290
float 238, 244; float ball 61
flock 183
flood 287
floor 58, 62, 71; floor exercises 235; floor plan 261
florentine 141
floret 122
florist 110, 188
floss *v* 50
flours 138
flower 297
flowerbed 85, 90
flowering plant 297
flowering shrub 87
flowers 110
flu 44
flute 139, 257
fly 244, 295; fly *v* 211
fly-fishing 245
flysheet 266
foal 185
focus *v* 271
focusing knob 167
fog 287
foil 249
folder 177
foliage 110
folk music 259
follicle 20
font 177
food 118, 130, 149; food hall 105; food processor 66
foot 12, 15, 310
football 220
footboard 71
footpath 262
footstrap 241
for 320
forceps 53, 167
forearm 12
forecourt 199
forehand 231
forehead 14
foreign currency 97
foreskin 21
forest 285
fork 65, 88, 153, 207
forklift truck 186, 216
formal 34
formal garden 84, 262
fortieth 309
forty 308; forty minutes
forward 222
foul 222, 226
foul ball 228
foul line 229
foundation 40
fountain 85
four 308; four hundred 308
four-door 200
fourteen 308
fourteenth 309
fourth 309
four-wheel drive 199
fox 290
foxglove 297
foyer 59
fraction 165
fracture 46
fragile 98
fragranced 130
frame 51, 62, 206, 230, 269; frame counter 270
freckle 15
free 321; free kick 222; free weights 250
free-range 118
freesia 110
free-throw line 226
freeway 194
freeze 287; freeze *v* 67
freezer 67
freight train 208
freighter 215
French bean 122
French braid 39
french fries 154
French horn 257
French mustard 135
French toast 157
frequency 179
fresh 121, 127, 130; fresh cheese 136; fresh fruit 157
freshwater fishing 245
fret 258
fretsaw 81
Friday 306
fried 159; fried chicken 155; fried egg 157
friend 24
frieze 301
frog 294
from 320

english

front crawl 239
front door 58
front wheel 196
frontage road 194, 216
frontal 16
frost 287
froth 148
frown 25
frozen 121, 124; frozen food 107; frozen yogurt 137
fruit 107, 126, 128; fruit bread 139; fruit cake 140; fruit farm 183; fruit juice 127, 156; fruit tart 140; fruit yogurt 157
fry *v* 67
frying pan 69
fuel gauge 201
fuel tank 204
full 64, 266, 321; full board 101; full moon 280
fumble 220
funeral 26
funnel 166, 214
furniture store 115
furrow 183
fuse 60; fuse box 60, 203
fuselage 210

G

gable 300
galaxy 280
gale 286
galley 214
gallon 311
gallop 243
galvanized 79
game 119, 230, 273; game show 178
games 272
gangway 214
garage 58, 199, 203
garbage can 61, 67
garbanzos 131
garden 84; garden center 115; garden features 84; garden pea 122; garden plants 86; garden styles 84; garden tools 88
gardener 188
gardening 90; gardening gloves 89
gardens 261
garland 111
garlic 125, 132; garlic press 68
garnet 288
garter 35; garter belt 35
gas burner 61
gas pump 199
gas station 199
gas tank 203
gasket 61
gasoline 199
gate 85, 182, 247; gate number 213
gauze 47, 167
gear lever 207
gearbox 202, 204
gears 206
gearshift 201
gel 38, 109
gems 288
generation 23
generator 60
genitals 12
geography 162
geometry 165
gerbera 110
get a job *v* 26
get married *v* 26
get up *v* 71
geyser 285
giant slalom 247
gift shop 114
gill 294
gin 145; gin and tonic 151
ginger 125, 133
giraffe 291
girder 186
girl 23
girlfriend 24
girth 242
glacier 284
gladiolus 110
gland 19
glass 69, 152; glass bottle 166; glass stirrer 167
glasses 51, 150
glassware 64
glaze *v* 139
glider 211, 248
gliding 248
gloss 83, 271
glove 224, 233, 236, 246
gloves 36
glue 275; glue gun 78
gneiss 288
go to bed *v* 71
go to sleep *v* 71
goal 221, 223, 224; goal area 223; goal line 220, 223, 224
goalkeeper 222, 224
goalpost 220, 222
goat 185
goat's cheese 142
goat's milk 136
goggles 238, 247
going out 75
gold 235, 289
goldfish 294
golf 232; golf bag 233; golf ball 233; golf cart 232, 233; golf clubs 233; golf course 232; golf shoe 233
golfer 232
gong 257
good 321; good afternoon 322; good evening 322; good morning 322; good night 322
goodbye 322
goose 119, 293; goose egg 137
gooseberry 127
gorge 284
gorilla 291
gothic 301
grade 163
graduate 169; graduate *v* 26
graduation ceremony 169
graft *v* 91
grains 130
gram 310
grandchildren 23
granddaughter 22
grandfather 22
grandmother 22
grandparents 23
grandson 22
granite 288
grape juice 144
grapefruit 126
grapeseed oil 134
graphite 289
grass 86, 262; grass bag 88
grasshopper 295
grassland 285
grate *v* 67
grated cheese 136
grater 68
gratin dish 69
gravel 88
gravity 280
gray 39, 274
graze 46
greasy 39
green 129, 232, 274; green olive 143; green onion 125; green peas 131; green salad 158; green tea 149
greenhouse 85
grill pan 69
grilled 159
grip 78
groceries 106
grocery store 114
groin 12
groom 243
ground 60, 132; ground coffee 144; ground cover 87; ground floor 104; ground meat 119; ground sheet 267
groundnut oil 135
group therapy 55
grout 83
guard 236; guard rail 195, 246
guava 128
guest 64, 100
guidebook 260
guided tour 260
guilty 181
guitarist 258
gull 292
gum 50
gumdrop 113
gun 94
gutter 58, 299
guy rope 266
gym 101, 250; gym machine 250
gymnast 235
gymnastics 235
gynecologist 52
gynecology 49
gypsophila 110

H

hacksaw 81
haddock 120
hail 286
hair 14, 38; hair dye 40
hairband 38
hairdresser 38, 115, 188
hair-dryer 38
hairpin 38
hairspray 38
half an hour 304
half-board 101
half-time 223
half-liter 311
halibut fillets 120
Halloween 27
hallway 59
halter 243; halter neck 35
ham 119, 143, 156
hammer 80; hammer *v* 79
hammock 266
hamper 263
hamster 290
hamstring 16
hand 13, 15; hand drill 81; hand fork 89; hand rail 59; hand saw 89; hand towel 73
handbag 37
handcuffs 94
handicap 233
handkerchief 36
handle 36, 88, 106, 187, 200, 230
handlebar 207
handles 37
handrail 196
handsaw 80
handset 99
hang *v* 82
hang-glider 248
hang-gliding 248
hanging basket 84
hanging file 173
happy 25
harbor 217; harbor master 217
hard 129, 321; hard candy 113; hard cheese 136; hard drive 176; hard hat 186; hard shoulder 194
hardboard 79
hardware 176
hardware store 114
hardwood 79
haricot beans 131
harness race 243
harp 256
harvest *v* 91, 183
hat 36
hatchback 199
have a baby *v* 26
hay 184
hayfever 44
hazard 195
hazard lights 201
hazelnut 129; hazelnut oil 134
head 12, 19, 81, 230; head *v* 222; head injury 46
headache 44
headboard 70
headlight 198, 205
headphones 268
headquarters 175
headrest 200
headsail 240
health 44; health food store 115
heart 18, 119, 122, 273; heart attack 44

english

heater 60
heather 297
heating element 61
heavy 321; heavy metal 259
hedge 85, 90, 182
hedgehog 290
heel 13, 15, 37
height 165; height bar 45
helicopter 211
hello 322
helmet 95, 204, 206, 220, 224, 228
helpdesk 168
hem 34
hematite 289
hemorrhage 46
hen's egg 137
herb 55, 86; herb garden 84
herbaceous border 85
herbal remedies 108
herbal tea 149
herbalism 55
herbicide 183
herbs 132, 133, 134
herd 183
hexagon 164
high 321; high chair 75; high dive 239; high jump 235; high speed train 208
high-heeled shoe 37
highlights 39
hiking 263
hill 284
hip 12
hippopotamus 291
historic building 261
history 162
hit *v* 224
hockey 224; hockey stick 224
hoe 88
hold 215, 237
hole 232; hole in one 233; hole punch 173
holly 296
home 58; home delivery 154; home entertainment 268; home furnishings 105; home plate 228
homeopathy 55
homework 163
homogenized 137
honeycomb 135
honeymoon 26
honeysuckle 297
hood 31, 75, 198
hoof 242, 291
hook 187, 276
hoop 226, 277
horizontal bar 235
hormone 20
horn 201, 204, 291
horror movie 255
horse 185, 235, 242; horse race 243
horseback riding 242, 263
horseradish 125
horseshoe 242
hose 89, 95; hose reel 89
hospital 48
host 64
hostess 64
hot 124, 286, 321; hot chocolate 144, 156; hot dog 155; hot drinks 144; hot faucet 72
hot-air balloon 211
hot-dog vendor 154
hot-water bottle 70
hotel 100, 264
hour 304; hour hand 304
house 58
household products 107
hovercraft 215
hub 206
hubcap 202
hull 214, 240
human resources 175
humerus 17
humid 286
hummingbird 292
hump 291
hundred 308; hundred and ten 308; hundred thousand 308
hundredth 309
hungry 64
hurdles 235
hurricane 287
husband 22
husk 130
hydrant 95
hydrofoil 215
hydrotherapy 55
hypnotherapy 55
hypoallergenic 41
hypotenuse 164

I

ice 120, 287; ice and lemon 151; ice bucket 150; ice climbing 247; ice cream 149; ice cube 151; ice hockey 224; ice hockey player 224; ice hockey rink 224; ice maker 67; ice cream 137
iced coffee 148
iced tea 149
ice-skate 224
ice-skating 247
icicle 287
icing 141
icon 177
identity tag 53
igneous 288
ignition 200
iguana 293
illness 44
immigration 212
impotent 20
in 320; in brine 143; in front of 320; in oil 143; in sauce 159; in syrup 159
inbox 177
inch 310
incisor 50
incubator 53
index finger 15
indigo 274
induce labor *v* 53
industrial park 299
infection 44
infertile 20
infield 228
inflatable dinghy 215
information 261; information screen 213
in-goal area 221
inhaler 44, 109
injection 48
injury 46
ink 275; ink pad 173
inlet 61
inner core 282
inner tube 207
inning 228
innocent 181
inoculation 45
insect repellent 108, 267
inside 320
insomnia 71
inspector 94
install *v* 177
instant camera 270
instep 15
instructions 109
instruments 256, 258
insulating tape 81
insulation 61
insulin 109
insurance 203
intensive care unit 48
interchange 194
intercom 59
intercostal 16
intercourse 20
interest rate 96
interior 200
international flight 212
internet 177
intersection 298
interval 254
interviewer 179
into 320
in-tray 172
invertebrates 295
investigation 94
investment 97
ionosphere 286
iris 51, 110
iron 76, 109, 233, 289; iron *v* 76
ironing board 76
island 282
itinerary 260
IUD 21

J

jack 203, 273
jacket 32, 34
jackhammer 187
jade 288
jam 134, 156
January 306
jar 134, 311
javelin 234
jaw 14, 17
jazz 259
jeans 31
jelly bean 113
jellyfish 295
Jerusalem artichoke 125
jet 288
jet-skiing 241
jetty 217
jeweler 188
jewelry 36; jewelry box 36; jewelry store 114
jewelry-making 275
jigsaw 78; jigsaw puzzle 273
jodhpurs 242
jog in place 251
jogging 251, 263; jogging suit 31, 32
joint 17, 119
joker 273
journal 168
journalist 190
judge 180
judo 236
jug 65
juices 149
juicy 127
July 306
jumbo shrimp 121
jump 237, 243; jump *v* 227; jump ball 226
jumping rope 251
June 306
Jupiter 280
jury 180; jury box 180

K

kale 123
kangaroo 291
karate 236
kayak 241
kebab 155, 158
keel 214
keep net 244
kendo 236
kernel 122, 129, 130
ketchup 135, 154
kettle 66
kettledrum 257
key 59, 80, 176, 207
keyboard 172, 176, 258
keypad 97, 99
kick 237, 239; kick *v* 221, 223
kickboxing 236
kickstand 207
kid 185
kidney 18, 119
kilogram 310
kilometer 310
king 272, 273
kippers 157
kitchen 66, 152; kitchen knife 68
kitchenware 68, 105
kitten 290
kiwifruit 128
knead *v* 138
knee 12; knee pad 205; knee support 227
knee-length 34
kneecap 17
knife 65, 80; knife sharpener 68, 118
knight 272
knitting 277; knitting needle 277
knock out 237
knuckle 15
koala 291
kohlrabi 123
koi carp 294
kumquat 126
kung fu 236

L

label 172
labels 89
labia 20

laboratory 166
lace 35, 37; lace bobbin 277
lace-making 277
lace-up 37
lacrosse 249
lactose 137
ladder 95, 180
ladle 68
lady fingers 141
ladybug 295
lake 285
lamb 118, 185
lamp 62, 207, 217
land 282; land *v* 211
landing 59; landing gear 210; landing net 244
landlord 58
landscape 271, 284; landscape *v* 91
lane 234, 238
languages 162
lapel 32
laptop 175
larch 296
large 321; large intestine 18
larynx 19
last week 307
late 305
later 304
latex paint 83
latitude 283
laugh *v* 25
launch 281; launch pad 281
laundromat 115
laundry 76; laundry basket 76; laundry service 101
lava 283
law 169, 180
lawn 85, 90; lawn rake 88
lawnmower 88, 90
lawyer 180, 190
lawyer's office 180
laxative 109
lead singer 258
leaded 199
leaf 122, 296
league 223
lean meat 118
learn *v* 163
leather shoe 37
leather shoes 32
leathers 205
lecture hall 169
leek 125
left 260; left field 228
left-hand drive 201
leg 12, 119; leg pad 225; leg press 251
legal advice 180
legal department 175
leggings 31
legumes 130
leisure 258, 254, 264
lemon 120; lemon curd 134; lemon grass 133; lemon sole 120
lemonade 144
length 165, 310
lens 270; lens (eye) 51; lens (glasses) 51; lens cap 270; lens case 51
lesson 163
let 231
letter 98; letter slot 58, 99
letterhead 173
lettuce 123
level 80, 187
lever 61, 150
librarian 168, 190
library 168, 299; library card 168
license plate 198
liquor store 115
licorice 113
lid 61, 66
life jacket 240
life preserver 240
life raft 240
lifeboat 214
lifeguard 239, 265; lifeguard tower 265
ligament 17
light 178, 321; light a fire *v* 266; light aircraft 211; light bulb 60
lighter 112
lighthouse 217
lighting 105
lightmeter 270
lightning 287
lights 94; lights switch 201
lily 110
lime 126, 296
limestone 288
limousine 199
line 244; line judge 220; line of play 233
linen 105, 277; linen basket 76
lines 165
linesman 223, 230
lingerie 35, 105
lining 32; lining paper 83
link 36
lintel 186
lion 291
lip 14; lip brush 40; lip gloss 40; lip liner 40
lipstick 40
liqueur 145
liquid 77; liquid dispenser 311; liquid measure 311
liter 311
literature 162, 169
little finger 15
little toe 15
live 60, 178; live rail 209
liver 18, 118
livestock 183, 185
living room 62
lizard 293
load *v* 76; load line 214
loaf 139
loan 96, 168
lob 230
lobby 100, 255
lobster 121, 295
lock 59, 207
lockers 239
log on *v* 177
loganberry 127
logo 31
loin 121
lollipop 113
long 32; long jump 235; long wave 179
long-grain 130
long-handled shears 88
longitude 283
loofah 73
loom 277
loose tea 144
lose *v* 273
loser 273
lotion 109
lottery tickets 112
love 230
low 321
luge 247
luggage 100, 198, 213; luggage department 104; luggage hold 196; luggage rack 209
lumbar vertebrae 17
lunar module 281
lunch 64; lunch menu 152
lung 18
lunge 251
lupins 297
lure 244
lychee 128
lymphatic 19
lyrics 259

M

macadamia 129
mace 132
machine gun 189
machinery 187
mackerel 120
macramé 277
magazine 112
magazines 107
magma 283
magnesium 109
magnet 167
maid service 101
mail carrier 98, 190
mailbag 98, 190
mailbox 99
mainsail 240
make a will *v* 26
make friends *v* 26
make the bed *v* 71
makeup 40
making bread 138
malachite 288
male 12, 21
mallet 78, 275
malt vinegar 135
malted drink 144
mammals 290
man 23
manager 24, 174
manchego 142
mane 242, 291
mango 128
mangosteen 128
manhole 299
manicure 41
mantelpiece 63
mantle 282
manual 200
map 195, 261
maple 296; maple syrup 134
maracas 257
marathon 234
marble 288
March 306
margarine 137
marina 217
marinated 143, 159
marine fishing 245
marjoram 133
mark *v* 227
market 115
marketing department 175
marmalade 134, 156
marrow 124
Mars 280
marshmallow 113
martial arts 237
martini 151
marzipan 141
mascara 40
mashed 159
masher 68
mask 189, 228, 236, 239, 249
masking tape 83
masonry bit 80
massage 54
mast 240
masters 169
mat 54, 83, 235, 271
match 230
matches 112
material 276
materials 79, 187
maternity 49; maternity ward 48
math 162, 164
mattress 70, 74
May 306
maybe 322
mayonnaise 135
MDF 79
meadow 285
meal 64
measles 44
measure 150, 151; measure *v* 310
measurements 165
measuring cup 69, 311
measuring spoon 109
meat 119; meat and poultry 106; meat tenderizer 68
meatballs 158
meathook 118
mechanic 188, 203
mechanics 202
medals 235
media 178
medical examination 45
medication 109
medicine 109, 169; medicine cabinet 72
meditation 54
medium wave 179
meeting 174; meeting room 174
melody 259
melon 127
memory 176
men's clothing 32
menswear 105
menstruation 20
menu 148, 153, 154; menu bar 177
mercury 289; Mercury 280
meringue 140
mesosphere 286

messages 100
metacarpal 17
metal 79; metal bit 80
metals 289
metamorphic 288
metatarsal 17
meteor 280
meter 310
mica 289
microphone 179, 258
microscope 167
microwave oven 66
midday 305
middle finger 15
midnight
midwife 53
migraine 44
mile 310
milk 136, 156; milk *v* 183; milk carton 136; milk chocolate 113
milkshake 137
millennium 307
millet 130
milligram 310
milliliter 311
millimeter 310
mineral 144; mineral spirits 83
minerals 289
mini bar 101
mini disc recorder 268
minibus 197
minivan 199
mini-dress 34
mint 113, 133; mint tea 149
minus 165
minute 304; minute hand 304
minutes 174
mirror 40, 63, 71, 167
miscarriage 52
Miss 23
missile 211
mist 287
miter block 81
mitt 228
mittens 30
mix *v* 67, 138
mixing bowl 66, 69
mixing desk 179
moat 300
mobile 74
model 169, 190
modeling tool 275
model-making 275
modem 176
moisturizer 41
molar 50
mole 14
Monday 306
money 97; money order 98
monitor 53, 172, 176
monkey 291
monkfish 120
monopoly 272
monorail 208
monsoon 287
month 306
monthly 307
monument 261
Moon 280
moonstone 288
moor *v* 217
mooring 217
mop 77
morning 305
mortar 68, 167, 187
mortgage 96
mosque 300
mosquito 295; mosquito net 267
moth 295
mother 22
mother-in-law 23
motocross 249
motor 88; motor racing 249
motorcycle 204; motorcycle racing 249
molding 63
mountain 284; mountain bike 206; mountain range 282
mouse 176, 290
mousse 141
mouth 14; mouth guard 237
mouthwash 72
move 273
movie 260, 271; movie set 179; movie theater 255, 299
mow *v* 90
mozzarella 142
MP3 player 268
Mr. 23
Mrs. 23
mudguard 205
muffin 140; muffin pan 69
muffler 203, 204
mug 65
mulch *v* 91
multigrain bread 139
multiply *v* 165
multivitamin tablets 109
mumps 44
mung beans 131
muscles 16
museum 261
mushroom 125
music 162; music school 169
musical 255; musical score 255; musical styles 259
musician 191
mussel 121, 295
mustard 155; mustard seed 131

N

naan bread 139
nail 15, 80; nail clippers 41; nail file 41; nail polish 41; nail polish remover 41; nail scissors 41
nape 13
napkin 65, 152; napkin ring 65
narrow 321
nation 315
national park 261
natural 256; natural fiber 31
naturopathy 55
nausea 44
navel 12
navigate *v* 240
near 320
nearsightedness 51
nebula 280
neck 12, 258; neck brace 46
necklace 36
neckline 34
nectarine 126
needle 109, 276; needle plate 276
needlenose pliers 80
needlepoint 277
negative 271; negative electrode 167
negligée 35
neighbor 24
neoclassical 301
nephew 23
Neptune 280
nerve 19, 50
nervous 19, 25
net 217, 222, 226, 227, 231; net *v* 245; net curtain 63
nettle 297
network 176
neurology 49
neutral 60; neutral zone 224
new 321; new moon 280; new potato 124
New Year 27
newborn baby 53
news 178
newscaster 179, 191
newspaper 112
newsstand 112
next week 306
nib 163
nickel 289
niece 23
night 305
nightgown 35
nightie 31
nightwear 31
nightstand 70
nightstick 94
nine 308; nine hundred 308
nineteen 308
nineteen hundred 307; nineteen hundred and one 307
nineteen ten 307
nineteenth 309
ninetieth 309
ninety 308
ninth 309
nipple 12
no 322; no entry 195; no right turn 195; no stopping 195
nonsmoking section 152
nonstick 69
noodles 158
normal 39
north 312
nose 14, 210; nose clip 238
noseband 242
nosebleed 44
nosewheel 210
nostril 14
notation 256
note 97, 256
notecard 173
notepad 173
notebook 163, 172
notes 175, 191
notice board 173
notions 105
nougat 113
November 306
now 304
nozzle 89
number 226
numbers 308
numerator 165
nurse 45, 48, 52, 189
nursery 74
nursing 53
nursing bra 53
nut 80
nutmeg 132
nuts 151; nuts and dried fruit 129
nylon 277

O

oak 296
oar 241
oatmeal 156
oats 130
objective lens 167
oboe 257
obsidian 288
obstetrician 52
occupations 188, 190
occupied 321
ocean 282; ocean liner 215
octagon 164
October 306
octopus 121, 295
odometer 201
offal 118
offers 106
office 24, 172, 174; office building 298; office equipment 172; office supplies 173
off-piste 247
off-side 223
oil 142, 199; oil paints 274; oil tank 204; oil tanker 215
oils 134
oily 41
ointment 47, 109
okra 122
old 321
olive oil 134
olives 151
omelet 158
on time 305
on top of 320
oncology 49
one 308; one billion 309; one million 309; one thousand 309
one-way 194; one-way system 298
onion 124
on-line 177
onto 320
onyx 289
opal 288
open 260, 321; open sandwich 155
open-top 260
opera 255
operating room 48

operation 48
operator 99
ophthalmology 49
opponent 236
opposite 320
optic 150; optic nerve 51
optician 51, 189
orange 126, 274; orange juice 148
orangeade 144
orbit 280
orchestra 254, 256; orchestra pit 254
orchid 111
order *v* 153
oregano 133
organic 91, 118, 122; organic waste 61
organizer 175
origami 275
ornamental 87
orthopedics 49
osteopathy 54
ostrich 292
otter 290
ounce 310
out 225, 228, 320; out of bounds 226; out of focus 271
outboard motor 215
outbuilding 182
outdoor activities 262
outer core 282
outfield 229
outlet 61
outpatient 48
outside 320
out-tray 172
oval 164
ovary 20
oven 66; oven mitt 69
ovenproof 69
over 320; over par 233
overalls 30, 82
overdraft 96
overexposed 271
overflow pipe 61
overhead bin 210
overhead projector 163
overpass 194
overture 256
ovulation 20, 52
owl 292
oyster 121
ozone layer 286

P

pack 311; pack of cigarettes 112
package 99, 311
pad 224
paddle 241
paddock 242
pads 53, 220
painkiller 109
painkillers 47
pail 77, 82, 265
paint 83l paint *v* 83; paint can 83; paint tray 83
painter 191
painting 62, 261, 274
paints 274
pajamas 33
pak-choi 123
palate 19
palette 274
pallet 186
palm 15, 86, 296; palm hearts 122
palmtop 175
pan 310
pan-fried 159
pancreas 18
panda 291
panties 35
pants 32, 34
panty liner 108
papaya 128
paper clip 173
paper guide 172
paper napkin 154
paper tray 172
papier-maché 275
paprika 132
par 233
parachute 248
parachuting 248
paragliding 248
parallel 165; parallel bars 235
parallelogram 164
paramedic 94
parents 23
park 262; park *v* 195
parka 31, 33
parking brake 203
parking meter 195
parking lot 298
parmesan 142
parole 181
parrot 293
parsley 133
parsnip 125
partner 23
pass 226; pass *v* 195, 220, 223
passenger 216; passenger port 216
passion fruit 128
Passover 27
passport 213; passport control 213
pasta 158
pastels 274
pasteurized 137
pasting brush 82
pasting table 82
pastry 140, 149; pastry brush 69
pasture 182
patch 207
patchwork 277
pâté 142, 156
path 58, 85
pathology 49
patient 45
patio garden 85
pattern 276
pause 269
paving 85
pawn 272
pay *v* 153
pay-per-view channel 269
payment 96
payroll 175
peach 126, 128
peacock 293
peanut 129; peanut butter 135
peanuts 151
pear 127
peas 131
pecan 129
pectoral 16; pectoral fin 294
pedal 61, 206; pedal *v* 207
pedestrian zone 299
pediatrics 49
pedicure 41
pediment 301
peel *v* 67
peeled shrimp 120
pelican 292
pelvis 17
pen 163, 185; pen holder 172; pen pal 24
penalty 222; penalty area 223
pencil 163, 275; pencil case 163; pencil sharpener 163
pendant 36
penguin 292
peninsula 282
penis 21
pentagon 164
peony 111
people 12, 16
pepper 64, 124, 152
peppercorn 132
pepperoni 142
percentage 165
percussion 257
perennial 86
perfume 41, 105
pergola 84
periodical 168
perm 39
perpendicular 165
persimmon 128
personal best 234
personal CD player 269
personal organizer 173, 175
personal trainer 250
pesticide 89, 183
pestle 68, 167
pet food 107
pet store 115
petal 297
petri dish 166
pharmacist 108, 189
pharmacy 108
pharynx 19
pheasant 119, 293
Phillips screwdriver 81
philosophy 169
photo album 271
photo finish 234
photographer 191
photograph 271; photograph *v* 271
photography 270
phyllo pastry 140
physical education 162
physics 162, 169
physiotherapy 49
piano 256
piccolo 257
pick *v* 91
pick-and-mix 113
pickax 187
pickled 159
pickup 258
picnic 263; picnic bench 266
picture frame 271
pie 158; pie pan 69
piece 272
pier 217
pies 143
pig 185; pig farm 183
pigeon 292
pigeonhole 100
piglet 185
pigsty 185
pigtails 39
Pilates 251
pill 21, 109
pillar 300
pillion 204
pillow 70
pillowcase 71
pilot 190, 211
pin 60, 237, 249, 276
PIN 96
pincushion 276
pine 296; pine nut 129
pineapple 128; pineapple juice 149
pink 274
pint 311
pinto beans 131
pipe 112, 202; pipe cutter 81
pipette 167
piping bag 69
pistachio 129
pita bread 139
pitch *v* 229; pitch a tent *v* 266
pitcher 151, 229
pitcher's mound 228
pitches available 266
pith 126
pizza 154
pizzeria 154
place mat 64
place setting 65
placenta 52
plain 285
plane 81; plane *v* 79
planet 280, 282
plant *v* 183
plant pot 89
plants 86, 296
plaque 50
plaster *v* 82
plastic bag 122
plastic pants 30
plastic surgery 49
plate 283
plateau 284
platform 208; platform number 208; platform shoe 37
platinum 289
play 254, 269; play *v* 229, 273
player 221, 231, 273
playground 263
playhouse 75
playing 75
playpen 75
plea 180
please 322
plow *v* 183
plug 60, 72
plum 126
plumb line 82
plumber 188
plumbing 61
plunger 81

english

english

plus 165
Pluto 280
plywood 79
poach v 67
poached 159
pocket 32
pod 122
podium 235, 256
point 273
poisoning 46
poker 273
polar bear 291
pole 245, 282; pole vault 234
police 94; police car 94; police officer 94, 189; police station 94
polish 77; polish v 77
politics 169
polo 243
polyester 277
pomegranate 128
pommel 242; pommel horse 235
pond 85
ponytail 39
pool 249
pop 259
popcorn 255
poplar 296
popper 30
poppy 297; poppy seeds 138
porch 58; porch light 58
pore 15
pork 118
port 145, 176, 214, 216
porter 100
portfolio 97
porthole 214
portion 64
portrait 271
positive electrode 167
post office 98
postage 98
postal worker 98
postcard 112
poster 255
poster paint 274
postgraduate 169
postmark 98
pot v 91
potato 124
potpourri 111
potted plant 87, 110
potter's wheel 275
pottery 275
potty 74
pouch 291
poultry 119; poultry farm 183
pound 310
pour v 67
powder 77, 109; powder puff 40
powdered milk 137
power 60; power cord 176; power outage 60
practice swing 233
pram 75
praying mantis 295
pregnancy 52; pregnancy test 52
pregnant 52
premature 52
premolar 50
prenatal 52
prerecorded 178
prescription 45
present 27
presentation 174
presenter 178
preservative 83
preserved fruit 134
press 178
presser foot 276
pressure valve 61
price 152, 199; price list 154
prickly pear 128
primer 83
primrose 297
principal 163
principality 315
print 271; print v 172
printer 172, 176
printing 275
prison 181; prison guard 181
private bathroom 100
private jet 211
private room 48
probe 50
problems 271
processed grains 130
procession 27
processor 176
produce stand 114, 188
producer 254
professor 169
program 176, 254, 269
programming 178
projector 174
propagate v 91
propeller 211, 214
proposal 174
prosciutto 143
prosecution 180
prostate 21
protractor 165
proud 25
prove v 139
province 315
prow 215
prune 129; prune v 91
pruners 89
psychiatry 49
psychotherapy 55
public address system 209
puck 224
pudding rice 130
puff pastry 140
pull up v 251
pulp 127
pulse 47
pumice 288; pumice stone 73
pump 207
pumpkin 125; pumpkin seed 131
punch 237
punching bag 237
pup 290
pupil 51, 162
puppy 290
purple 274
pushup 251
purse 37
putt v 233
putter 233
pyramid 164

Q

quadriceps 16
quail 119; quail egg 137
quart 311
quarter of an hour 304
quarterdeck 214
quartz 289
queen 272, 273
question 163; question v 163
quiche pan 69
quilt 71
quilting 277
quince 128
quinoa 130
quiver 249

R

rabbit 118, 290
raccoon 290
race 234
race-car driver 249
racecourse 243
racehorse 243
racing bike 205, 206
racing dive 239
rack 166
racket 230
racket games 231
racquetball 231
radar 214, 281
radiator 60, 202
radicchio 123
radio 179, 268; radio antenna 214; radio station 179
radiology 49
radish 124
radius 17, 164
rafter 186
rafting 241
rail 208
rail network 209
rain 287; rain gear 245, 267
rainbow 287; rainbow trout 120
raincoat 31, 32
rainforest 285
raisin 129
rake 88; rake v 90
rally 230; rally driving 249
RAM 176
ramekin 69
range 67
rap 259
rapeseed 184
rapids 240, 284
rappeling 248
rash 44
raspberry 127; raspberry jam 134
rat 290
rattle 74
raw 124, 129
ray 294
razor blade 73
razorshell clam 121
read v 162
reading light 210
reading list 168
reading room 168
reamer 80
rear light 207
rear wheel 197
rearview mirror 198
receipt 152
receive v 177
receiver 99
reception 100
receptionist 100, 190
record 234, 269; record player 268; record store 115
recording studio 179
rectangle 164
rectum 21
recycling bin 61
red 145, 274; red card 223; red kidney beans 131; red lentils 131; red meat 118; red mullet 120
red-eye 271
reduce v 172
reduced-fat milk 136
reel 244; reel in v 245
referee 222, 226
referral 49
reflector 50, 204, 207; reflector strap 205
reflexology 54
refrigerator 67
reggae 259
region 315
register 100
registered mail 98
regulator 239
reheat v 154
reiki 55
reins 242
relationships 24
relatives 23
relaxation 55
relay race 235
release v 245
remote control 269
Renaissance 301
renew v 168
rent 58; rent v 58
repair kit 207
report 174
reporter 179
reproduction 20
reproductive 19; reproductive organs 20
reptiles 293
research 169
reserve v 168
residence hall 168
respiratory 19
rest 256
restaurant 101, 152
result 49
resurfacing 187
resuscitation 47
retina 51
retire v 26
return 231; return address 98; return date 168
rewind 269
rhinoceros 291
rhombus 164
rhubarb 127
rhythmic gymnastics 235
rib 17, 119; rib cage 17
ribbon 27, 39, 111, 141, 235
ribs 155

rice 130, 158, 184; rice pudding 140
rider 242
riding boot 242
riding crop 242
riding hat 242
rigging 215, 240
right 260; right field 229
right-hand drive 201
rim 206
rind 119, 127, 136, 142
ring 36; ring binder 173; ring finger 15; ring ties 89
rings 235
rinse *v* 38, 76
ripe 129
rise *v* 139
river 284
road bike 206
road markings 194
road signs 195
road work 187, 195
roads 194
roast 158; roast *v* 67
roasted 129
roasting pan 69
robe 38, 169
rock climbing 248
rock concert 258
rock garden 84
rocket 123
rocks 284, 288
rococo 301
rodeo 243
roll 139, 311; roll *v* 67
roller 83, 187; roller coaster 262; roller shade 63; roller skating 249
rollerblading 263
rollerskate 249
rolling pin 69
romance 255
romper 30
roof 58, 203; roof garden 84; roof tile 187; roof rack 198
rook 272
room 58; room key 100; room number 100; room service 101
rooms 100
rooster 185
root 50, 124, 296
roots 39
rope 248
rose 89, 110, 145
rosé 145
rosemary 133
rotor blade 211
rotten 127
rough 232
round 237; round neck 33
roundabout 195
route number 196
router 78
row 210, 254; row *v* 241
rower 241
rowboat 214
rowing machine 250
rubber band 173
rubber boots 89
rubber ring 265
rubber stamp 173
ruby 288
ruck 221
rudder 210, 241
rug 63
rugby 221
ruler 163, 165
rum 145; rum and coke 151
rump steak 119
run 228; run *v* 228
runway 212
rush 86; rush hour 209
rutabaga 125
rye bread 138

S

sad 25
saddle 206, 242
safari park 262
safe 228
safety 75, 240; safety goggles 81, 167; safety pin 47
saffron 132
sage 133
sail 241
sailboat 215
sailing 240
sailor 189
salad 149
salamander 294
salami 142
salary 175
sales clerk 104, 188
sales department 175
salmon 120
salt 64, 152
salted 121, 129, 137, 143
sand 85, 264; sand *v* 82
sandal 37
sandals 31
sandbox 263
sandcastle 265
sander 78
sandpaper 81, 83
sandstone 288
sandwich 155; sandwich counter 143
sanitary napkin 108
sapphire 288
sardine 120
satellite 281; satellite dish 269; satellite navigation 201
satsuma 126
Saturday 306
Saturn 280
sauce 134, 143, 155
saucepan 69
sauna 250
sausage 155, 157
sausages 118
sauté *v* 67
save *v* 177, 223
savings 96; savings account 97
savory 155
saw *v* 79
saxophone 257
scaffolding 186
scale 121, 256, 294
scales 45, 53, 69, 98, 118, 166, 212, 293, 310
scallop 121
scalp 39
scalpel 167
scan 48, 52
scanner 106, 176
scarecrow 184
scared 25
scarf 31, 36
schedule 197, 209, 261
schist 288
scholarship 169
school 162, 299; school bus 196; school uniform 162
schoolbag 162
schoolboy 162
schoolgirl 162
schools 169
science 162, 166; science fiction movie 255
scientist 190
scissors 38, 47, 82,188, 276
scoop 68, 149
scooter 205
score 220, 256, 273; score a goal *v* 223
scoreboard 225
scorpion 295
scotch and water 151
scrabble 272
scrambled eggs 157
scrape *v* 77
scraper 82
screen 59, 63, 97, 176, 255, 269
screw 80
screwdriver 80, 151; screwdriver bits 80
script 254
scrollbar 177
scrotum 21
scrub *v* 77
scrum 221
scuba diving 239
sculpting 275
sculptor 191
sea 264, 282; sea bass 120; sea bream 120; sea horse 294; sea lion 290; sea plane 211
seafood 121
seal 290
sealant 83
sealed jar 135
seam 34
seamstress 191
search *v* 177
seasonal 129
seasons 306
seat 61, 204, 209, 210, 242, 254; seat back 210; seat belt 198, 211; seat post 206
seating 254
second 304, 309; second floor 104
second-hand 304; second-hand store 115
section 282
security 212; security bit 80
security guard 189
sedan 199
sedative 109
sedimentary 288
seed 122, 127, 128, 130; seed tray 89
seeded bread 139
seedless 127
seedling 91
seeds 88, 131
seesaw 263
segment 126
self-defense 237
self-rising flour 139
self-tanning cream 41
semi-hard cheese 136
seminal vesicle 21
semi-soft cheese 136
semisweet chocolate 113
semolina 130
send *v* 177
send off 223
sensitive 41
sentence 181
September 306
series 179
serve 231; serve *v* 64, 231
server 176
service included 152
service line 230
service not included 152
service provider 177
service vehicle 212
serving spoon 68
sesame seed 131
sesame oil 134
set 178, 230, 254; set *v* 38; set honey 134; set sail *v* 217; set the alarm *v* 71; set the table v 64
seven 308; seven hundred 308
seventeen 308
seventeenth 309
seventh 309
seventieth 309
seventy 308
sew *v* 277
sewing basket 276
sewing machine 276
sexually transmitted disease 20
shade 41; shade plant 87
shallot 125
shallow end 239
shampoo 38
shapes 164
share price 97
shares 97
shark 294
sharp 256
shaving 73
shaving foam 73
shears 89
shed 84
sheep 185; sheep farm 183
sheep's milk 137
sheet 71, 74, 241
shelf 67, 106
shell 129, 137, 265, 293
shelled 129
shelves 66
sherbet 141
sherry 145
shiatsu 54

english

shield 88
shin 12
ship 214
ships 215
shipyard 217
shirt 32
shock 47
shocked 25
shoe department 104
shoe store 114
shoes 34, 37
shoot *v* 223, 227
shop 298
shopping 104; shopping bag 106; shopping center 104
shops 114
short 32, 321; short wave 179
short-grain 130
shorts 30, 33
shot 151
shotput 234
shoulder 13; shoulder bag 37; shoulder blade 17; shoulder pad 35; shoulder strap 37
shout *v* 25
shovel 187
shower 72, 286; shower block 266; shower curtain 72; shower door 72; shower gel 73; shower head 72
showjumping 243
shuffle *v* 273
shutoff valve 61
shutter 58; shutter release 270
shutter-speed dial 270
shuttle bus 197
shuttlecock 231
shy 25
side 164; side effects 109; side mirror 198; side order 153; side plate 65; side street 299
sidedeck 240
sideline 220, 226, 230
side-saddle 242
sidewalk 298; sidewalk café 148
sieve 68, 89; sieve *v* 91
sift *v* 138
sigh *v* 25
sightseeing 260
sign 104
signal 209
signature 96, 98
silk 277
silo 183
silt 85
silver 235, 289
simmer *v* 67
singer 191
single 151; single room 100
singles 230
sink 38, 60, 61, 66, 72
sinus 19
siren 94
sirloin steak 119
sister 22
sister-in-law 23
site manager's office 266
situp 251
six 308; six hundred 308
sixteen 308
sixteenth 309
sixth 309
sixtieth 309
sixty 308
skate 120, 247, 294; skate *v* 224; skate wings 120
skateboard 249
skateboarding 249, 263
skein 277
skeleton 17
sketch 275; sketch pad 275
skewer 68
ski 241, 246; ski boot 246; ski jump 247; ski pole 246; ski run 246; ski slope 246; ski suit 246
skier 246
skiing 246
skim milk 136
skin 14, 119, 128; skin care 108
skinned 121
skirt 30, 34
skull 17
skydiving 248
skyscraper 299, 300
slalom 247
slate 288
sledding 247
sledgehammer 187
sleeper 30
sleeping 74; sleeping bag 267; sleeping compartment 209; sleeping mat 267; sleeping pill 109
sleet 286
sleeve 34
sleeveless 34
slice 119, 139, 140, 230
slice *v* 67
sliced bread 138
slicer 139
slide 167, 263; slide *v* 229
sling 46
slip 35
slip-on 37
slippers 31
slope 284
slotted spatula 68
slotted spoon 68
slow 321
slug 295
small 321; small intestine 18; small of back 13
smash 231
smile 25
smoke 95; smoke alarm 95
smoked 118, 121, 143, 159; smoked fish 143
smoking 112; smoking section 152
snack bar 113, 148
snail 295
snake 293
snare drum 257
sneeze 44
snore *v* 71
snorkel 239
snout 293
snow 287
snowboarding 247
snowmobile 247
snowsuit 30
soak *v* 130
soap 73, 178; soap dish 73
soccer 220, 222; soccer field 220; soccer player 220, 222; soccer uniform 31, 222
socket 60, 80; socket wrench 80
socks 33
soda bread 139
soda water 144
sofa 62
sofabed 63
soft 129, 321; soft cheese 136; soft drink 154; soft drinks 144; soft toy 75
software 176
softwood 79
soil 85
solar system 280
solder 79, 80; solder *v* 79
soldering iron 81
soldier 189
sole 15, 37
solids 164
soluble 109
solvent 83
somersault 235
son 22
sonata 256
song 259
son-in-law 22
sorrel 123
sorting unit 61
soufflé 158; soufflé dish 69
sound boom 179
sound technician 179
soundtrack 255
soup 153, 158; soup bowl 65; soup spoon 65
sour 127; sour cream 137
sourdough bread 139
south 312
souvenirs 260
sow *v* 90, 183
soybeans 131
space 280; space exploration 281; space heater 60; space shuttle 281; space station 281; space suit 281
spade 88, 265, 273
spare tire 203
spark plug 203
sparkling 144
sparring 237
sparrow 292
spatula 68, 167
speaker 174, 176, 258, 268; speaker stand 268
spearfishing 245
specials 152
spectators 233
speed limit 195
speed skating 247
speedboat 241
speedometer 201, 204
spell *v* 162
sperm 20
sphere 164
spices 132
spicy sausage 142
spider 295
spike *v* 90
spikes 233
spin 230; spin *v* 76
spinach 123
spin-dryer 76
spine 17
spire 300
spleen 18
splint 47
splinter 46
split ends 39
split peas 131
spoke 207
sponge 73, 74, 83; sponge cake 140
spool 245
spoon 65
sport fishing 245
sports 105, 220, 236, 248; sports car 198; sports field 168
sportcoat 33
sportsman 191
spotlight 259
sprain 46
spray 109; spray *v* 91; spray can 311; spray bottle 89
spring 71, 307; spring balance 166; spring greens 123
springboard 235, 238
sprinkler 89
sprinter 234
sprocket 207
spy hole 59
square 164, 165, 272, 299; square foot 310; square meter 310
squash 231
squat 251
squid 121, 295
squirrel 290
stable 185, 243
stadium 223
staff 175, 256
stage 167, 254
stages 23
stainless steel 79
stair gate 75
staircase 59
stake 90; stake *v* 91
stalk 122, 297
stalls 254
stamen 297
stamp 98; stamp collecting 273
stamps 112
stance 232
stand 88, 205, 268
stapler 173
staples 173
star 280; star anise 133
starfish 295
starfruit 128
start school *v* 26
starter 153

starting block 234, 238
starting line 234
state 315
statement 180
stationery 105
steak 121
steam v 67; steam train 208
steamed 159
steeplechase 243
steel wool 81
steering wheel 201
stem 111, 112, 297
stencil 83
stenographer 181
step machine 250
stepdaughter 23
stepfather 23
stepladder 82
stepmother 23
stepson 23
stereo 269; stereo system 268
sterile 47
stern 240
stethoscope 45
stew 158
stick 224, 249
sticks 133
still 144
sting 46, 295
stir v 67
stir-fry 158
stirrer 150
stirrup 242
stitch 277; stitch selector 276
stitches 52
stock broker 97
stock exchange 97
stockings 35
stocks 97, 110
stomach 18
stomachache 44
stone 36, 275; stone fruit 126
stop 269; stop button 197
stopper 166
stopwatch 234
store directory 104
stork 292
storm 287
stout 145
straight 39, 165; straight ahead 260
straighten v 39
strap 35
strapless 34
stratosphere 286
straw 144, 154
strawberry 127
strawberry milkshake 149
stream 285
street 298; street corner 298; street sign 298
streetlight 298
stress 55
stretch 251
stretcher 94
strike 228, 237
string 230, 258; string of pearls 36; string bean 122
strings 256
strip v 82
stroke 44, 233, 239
strokes 231
stroller 75
strong 321
stub 96
study 63, 162
stuffed 159; stuffed olive 143
stump 225
styles 39, 239, 301
submarine 215
subsoil 91
substitute 223
substitution 223
subtract v 165
suburb 299
subway map 209
subway train 209
succulent 87
suction hose 77
sugarcane 184
suit 273
sulfur 289
summer 31, 307
summons 180
sumo wrestling 237
Sun 280; sun hat 30, 265
sunbathe v 264
sunbed 41
sunblock 108, 265
sunburn 46
Sunday 306
sunflower 184, 297; sunflower oil 134; sunflower seed 131
sunglasses 51, 265
sunny 286
sunrise 305
sunroof 202
sunscreen 108
sunset 305
sunshine 286
suntan lotion 265
supermarket 106
supersonic jet 211
supplement 55
supply pipe 61
support 187
suppository 109
surf 241
surfboard 241
surfcasting 245
surfer 241
surfing 241
surgeon 48
surgery 45, 48
surprised 25
suspect 94, 181
suspension 203, 205
swallow 292
swamp 285
swan 293
sweater 33
sweatpants 33
sweatshirt 33
sweep v 77
sweet 124, 127, 155; sweet potato 125; sweet spreads 134
swim v 238
swimmer 238
swimming 238; swimming pool 101, 238, 250
swimsuit 238, 265
swing v 232
swings 263
swiss chard 123
switch 60
swivel chair 172
sword 236
swordfish 120, 294
symphony 256
synagogue 300
synchronized swimming 239
synthetic 31
syringe 109, 167
syrup 109
system 176

T

tab 173
table 64, 148; table tennis 231
tablecloth 64
tachometer 201
tack v 241, 277
tackle 245; tackle v 220, 223; tackle box 244
tadpole 294
tae kwon do 236
tag v 229
tai chi 236
tail 121, 210, 242, 280, 290, 294
tailbone 17
tailgate 198
taillight 204
tailor 191
tailored 35
tailor's 115; tailor's chalk 276; tailor's dummy 276
tailplane 210
take a bath v 72
take a shower v 72
take notes v 163
take off v 211
talcum powder 73
tall 321
tambourine 257
tampon 108
tan 41
tandem 206
tangerine 126
tank 61
tap 61, 66; tap water 144
tape deck 268
tape dispenser 173
tape measure 80, 276
target 249
target shooting 249
taro root 124
tarragon 133
tattoo 41
tax 96
taxi stand 213
tea 144, 149, 184; tea bag 144; tea with lemon 149; tea with milk 149
teacher 54, 162, 191
teacup 65
team 220, 229
teapot 65
tear 51
teaspoon 65
teat 75
techniques 79, 159
teddy bear 75
tee 233
teeing ground 232
teenager 23
tee off v 233
telegram 98
telephone 99, 172; telephone booth 99
teleprompter 179
telescope 281
television 268; television series 178; television studio 178
temperature 286; temperature gauge 201
temple 14, 300
ten 308; ten thousand 309
tenant 58
tend v 91
tendon 17
tennis 230; tennis court 230; tennis shoes 231
tenon saw 81
tent 267; tent peg 266; tent pole 266
tenth 309
tequila 145
terminal 212
termite 295
terrace café 148
territory 315
test 49, 163; test tube 166
testicle 21
text message 99
textbook 163
thank you 322
Thanksgiving 27
theater 254, 299
theme park 262
therapist 55
thermal underwear 35
thermals 267
thermometer 45, 167
thermosphere 286
thermostat 61
thesis 169
thick 321
thigh 12, 119
thimble 276
thin 321
third 309; third floor 104
thirteen 308
thirteenth 309
thirtieth 309
thirty 308
this way up 98
this week 307
thistle 297
thoracic vertebrae 17
thread 276; thread v 277; thread guide 276; thread reel 276
three 308; three hundred 308
three-point line 226
thriller 255
throat 19
throttle 204
through 320
throw 237; throw v 221, 227, 229
throw-in 223, 226
thruster 281
thumb 15
thumbtack 173
thunder 286
Thursday 306
thyme 133
thyroid gland 18

english

tibia 17
ticket 209, 213; ticket gate 209; ticket inspector 209; ticket office 209, 216
tie 32
tiebreaker 230
tie-pin 36
tiger 291
tights 35, 251
tile 58, 272
tile *v* 82
till 106, 150
tiller 240
timber 187
time 234, 304; time out 220
timer 166
times 165, 261
timing 203
tip 36, 122, 246
tissue 108
title 168
titles 23
to 320; to go 154
toad 294
toast 157
toasted sandwich 149
toaster 66
tobacco 112, 184
today 306
toddler 30
toe 15; toe clip 207; toe strap 207
toenail 15
toffee 113
toggle 31
toilet 61, 72; toilet brush 72; toilet paper 72; toilet seat 72
toiletries 41, 107
toilets 104, 266
toll booth 194
tomato 125, 157; tomato juice 144, 149
tomorrow 306
ton 310
toner 41
tongs 150, 167
tongue 19, 37, 118
tonic water 144
tool rack 78
toolbar 177
toolbelt 186
toolbox 80
tools 187
tooth 50
toothache 50
toothbrush 72
toothpaste 72
top coat 83
top tier 141
topaz 288
top-dress *v* 90
topiary 87
topping 155
topsoil 85
tornado 287
tortoise 293
tossed salad 158
touch line 221
touchdown 221
tour bus 197, 260
tour guide 260
tourer 205
touring bike 206
tourist 260; tourist attraction 260; tourist information 261
tourmaline 288
tournament 233
tow away *v* 195
tow truck 203
toward 320
towel bar 72
towels 73
tower 300
town 298; town hall 299
townhouse 58
toy 75; toy basket 75
toys 105
track 208, 234; track and field 234
tractor 182
traffic 194; traffic jam 195; traffic light 194; traffic police 195
trailer 266
train 35, 208; train *v* 91, 251; train station 208
trainer 37
training wheels 207
tram 196, 208
transfer 223
transformer 60
transmission 202
transplant *v* 91
transportation 194
trapezium 164
trapezius 16
trash 177
travel agent 190, 114
travel brochure 212
travel sickness pills 109
traveler's check 97
tray 152, 154
tray-table 210
tread 207; tread water *v* 239
treadmill 250
treble clef 256
tree 86, 296
trekking 243
trellis 84
tremor 283
triangle 164, 257
triceps 16
trifle 141
trim *v* 39, 90
trimester 52
trimmer 88
tripod 166, 270, 281
trolley bus 196
trombone 257
tropic of Cancer 283
tropic of Capricorn 283
tropical fruit 128
tropics 283
troposphere 286
trot 243
trough 183
trout 120
trowel 89, 187
truck 194; truck driver 190
truffle 113, 125
trumpet 257
trunk 198, 291, 296
trunks 238
try 221
T-shirt 30, 33
tub 311
tuba 257
tube 311
Tuesday 306
tugboat 215
tulip 111
tumble 235
tumble-dryer 76
tumbler 65
tuna 120
tune *v* 179; tune the radio *v* 269
tuning peg 258
turbocharger 203
turf *v* 90
turkey 119, 185, 293
turmeric 132
turn 238; turn *v* 79; turn off the television *v* 269; turn on the television *v* 269; turn signal 198, 204
turnip 124
turpentine 83
turquoise 289
turret 300
turtle 293
tusk 291
tutu 191
tweezers 40, 47, 167
twelfth 309
twelve 308
twentieth 309
twenty 308; twenty minutes 304; twenty thousand 309
twenty-first 309
twenty-one 308
twenty-second 309
twenty-third 309
twenty-two 308
twig 296
twin bed 71
twin room 100
twine 89
twins 23
twist ties 89
two 308; two hundred 308; two o'clock 304; two thousand 307; two thousand and one 307
two-door 200
types 199, 205; types of buses 196; types of cameras 270; types of farms 183; types of plants 86; types of fishing 245; types of trains 208
tire 198, 205, 206; tire iron 207; tire pressure 203

U

ugli fruit 126
ulna 17
ultralight 211
ultrasound 52
ultraviolet rays 286
umbilical cord 52
umbrella 36, 233; umbrella stand 59
umpire 225, 229, 230
uncle 22
unconscious 47
uncooked meat 142
under 320; under par 233
undercoat 83
underexposed 271
undergraduate 169
underpass 194
underwear 32, 35
underwired 35
uniform 94, 189
universe 280
university 299
unleaded 199
unpasteurized 137
unpick *v* 277
unsalted 137
until 320
up 320
upset 25
Uranus 280
ureter 21
urethra 20
urinary 19
urology 49
usher 255
uterus 20, 52
utility knife 81
utility room 76

V

vacation 212
vacuum cleaner 77, 188
vacuum cup 53
vacuum flask 267
vagina 20
valance 71
valley 284
valve 207
vanilla 132
varnish 79, 83
vas deferens 21
vase 63, 111
vault 235, 300
veal 118
vegetable garden 85, 182
vegetable oil 135
vegetable peeler 68
vegetables 107, 122, 124
veggie burger 155
veil 35
vein 19
venetian blind 63
venison 118
vent 283
Venus 280
verdict 181
vest 33, 35, 251
veterinarian 189
vibraphone 257
video game 269
video phone 99
video recorder 269
video tape 269
viewfinder 271
village 299
vine 183
vinegar 135, 142
vineyard 183
vintage 199
viola 256
violin 256
virus 44
visa 213
vise 78
vision 51
visiting hours 48

visor 205
vitamins 108
V-neck 33
vocal cords 19
vodka 145
voice message 99
volcano 283
volley 231
volleyball 227
voltage 60
volume 165, 179, 269, 311
vomit *v* 44

W

waders 244
wading pool 263
waffles 157
waist 12
waistband 35
waistcoat 33
waiter 148, 152
waiting room 45
waitress 191
wake up *v* 71
walk 243
walking boot 37, 267
walkway 212
wall 58, 186, 222; wall light 62
wallet 37
wallpaper 82, 177; wallpaper *v* 82; wallpaper brush 82; wallpaper paste 82
walnut 129; walnut oil 134
walrus 290
ward 48
wardrobe 70
warehouse 216
warm 286; warm up *v* 251
warrant 180
wash *v* 38, 77
washer 80; washer fluid 199; washer fluid reservoir 202
washing machine 76
wasp 295
waste disposal 61, 266; waste disposal unit 61
waste pipe 61
wastebasket 172
watch 36; watch television *v* 269
water 144, 238; water *v* 90, 183; water bottle 206, 267; water chamber 61; water chestnut 124; water garden 84; water hazard 232; water heater 61; water jet 95; water plant 86; water polo 239
watercolor paints 274
watercress 123
waterfall 285
watering 89; watering can 89
watermelon 127
waterskier 241
waterskiing 241
watersports 241
wave 241, 264
wavelength 179
wax 41
weak 321
weather 286
weaving 277
website 177
wedding 26. 35; wedding cake 141; wedding dress 35; wedding reception 26
wedge 233
Wednesday 306
weed *v* 91
weedkiller 91
weeds 86
week 306
weekend 306
weekly 307
weigh *v* 310
weight 166, 244
weight bar 251; weight belt 239; weight training 251
wellington boots 31
west 312
western 255
wet 286, 321; wet wipe 75, 108
wetsuit 239
whale 290
wheat 130, 184
wheel 198, 207; wheel nuts 203
wheelbarrow 88
wheelchair 48; wheelchair access 197
whetstone 81
whiplash 46
whipped cream 137
whisk 68; whisk *v* 67
whiskers 290
whiskey 145
white 39, 145, 272, 274; white bread 139; white chocolate 113; white coffee 148; white currant 127; white flour 138; white meat 118; white rice 130
whiting 120
whole 129, 132; whole milk 136
whole-grain 131; whole-grain mustard 135
whole-wheat bread 139
whole-wheat flour 138
wicket 225
wide 321
widescreen television 269
width 165
wife 22
wig 39
wild rice 130
willow 296
win *v* 273
wind 241, 286
windbreak 265
windbreaker 33
windlass 214
window 58, 96, 98, 177, 186, 197, 209, 210
windpipe 18
windshield 198, 205; windshield wiper 198
windsurfer 241
windsurfing 241
windy 286
wine 145, 151; wine glass 65; wine list 152; wine vinegar 135
wing 119, 210, 293
wings 254
winner 273
winter 31, 307
winter sports 247
wipe *v* 77
wire 79; wire cutter 80; wire strippers 81
wires 60
with 320
withdrawal slip 96
without 320
witness 180
wok 69
wolf 290
woman 23
womb 52
women's clothing 34, 105
wood 79, 233, 275, 285; wood glue 78; wood shavings 78; wood stain 79
wooden spoon 68
woodpecker 292
woodwind 257
woodworking 275
wool 277
work 172; work day 306
workbench 78
workshop 78
world map 312
worm 295
worried 25
wound 46
wrap 155
wrapping 111
wreath 111
wrench 80, 81, 203
wrestling 236
wrinkle 15
wrist 13, 15
wristband 230
writ 180
write *v* 162

X

X-ray 48; X-ray film 50; X-ray machine 212; X-ray viewer 45

Y

yacht 215, 240
yam 125
yard 310
yawn *v* 25
year 163, 306
yeast 138
yellow 274; yellow card 223
yes 322
yesterday 306
yoga 54
yogurt 137
yolk 137, 157
you're welcome 322

Z

zebra 291
zero 308
zest 126
zinc 289
zip 277
ZIP code 98
zone 315
zones 283
zoo 262
zoology 169
zoom lens 270
zucchini 125

agradecimientos • acknowledgments

DORLING KINDERSLEY would like to thank Tracey Miles and Christine Lacey for design assistance, Georgina Garner for editorial and administrative help, Sonia Gavira, Polly Boyd, and Cathy Meeus for editorial help, and Claire Bowers for compiling the DK picture credits.

The publisher would like to thank the following for their kind permission to reproduce their photographs:
Abbreviations key:
t=top, b=bottom, r=right, l=left, c=centre

Abode: 62; **Action Plus:** 224bc; **alamy.com:** 154t; A.T. Willett 287bcl; Michael Foyle 184bl; Stock Connection 287bcr; **Allsport/Getty Images:** 238cl; **Alvey and Towers:** 209 acr, 215bcl, 215bcr, 241cr; **Peter Anderson:** 188cbr, 271br. **Anthony Blake Photo Library:** Charlie Stebbings 114cl; John Sims 114tcl; **Andyalte:** 98tl; **apple mac computers:** 268tcr; **Arcaid:** John Edward Linden 301bl; Martine Hamilton Knight, Architects: Chapman Taylor Partners, 213cl; Richard Bryant 301br; **Argos:** 41tcl, 66cbl, 66cl, 66br, 66bcl, 69cl, 70bcl, 71t, 77tl, 269tc, 270tl; **Axiom:** Eitan Simanor 105bcr; Ian Cumming 104; Vicki Couchman 148cr; **Beken Of Cowes Ltd:** 215cbc; **Bosch:** 76tcr, 76tc, 76tcl; **Camera Press:** 27c, 38tr, 256t, 257cr; Barry J. Holmes 148tr; Jane Hanger 159cr; Mary Germanou 259bc; **Corbis:** 78b; Anna Clopet 247tr; Bettmann 181tl, 181tr; Bo Zauders 156t; Bob Rowan 152bl; Bob Winsett 247cbl; Brian Bailey 247br; Carl and Ann Purcell 162l; Chris Rainer 247ctl; ChromoSohm Inc. 179tr; Craig Aurness 215bl; David H.Wells 249cbr; Dennis Marsico 274bl; Dimitri Lundt 236bc; Duomo 211tl; Gail Mooney 277ctcr; George Lepp 248c; Gunter Marx 248cr; Jack Fields 210b; Jack Hollingsworth 231bl; Jacqui Hurst 277cbr; James L. Amos 247bl, 191ctr, 220bcr; Jan Butchofsky 277cbc; Johnathan Blair 243cr; Jon Feingersh 153tr; Jose F. Poblete 191br; Jose Luis Pelaez.Inc 153tc, 175tl; Karl Weatherly 220bl, 247tcr; Kelly Mooney Photography 259tl; Kevin Fleming 249bc; Kevin R. Morris 105tr, 243tl, 243tc; Kim Sayer 249tcr; Lynn Goldsmith 258t; Macduff Everton 231bcl; Mark Gibson 249bl; Mark L. Stephenson 249tcl; Michael Pole 115tr; Michael S. Yamashita 247ctcl; Mike King 247cbl; Neil Rabinowitz 214br; Owen Franken 112t; Pablo Corral 115bc; Paul A. Sounders 169br, 249ctcl; Paul J. Sutton 224c, 224br; Peter Turnley 105tcr; Phil Schermeister 227b, 248tr; R. W Jones 309; R.W. Jones 175tr; Richard Hutchings 168b; Rick Doyle 241ctr; Robert Holmes 97br, 277ctc; Roger Ressmeyer 169tr; Russ Schleipman 229; Steve Raymer 168cr; The Purcell Team 211ctr; Tim Wright 178; Vince Streano 194t; Wally McNamee 220br, 220bcl, 224bl; Yann Arhus-Bertrand 249tl; **Demetrio Carrasco / Dorling Kindersley (c) Herge / Les Editions Casterman:** 112ccl; **Dixons:** 270cl, 270cr, 270bl, 270bcl, 270bcr, 270ccr; **Education Photos:** John Walmsley 26tl; **Empics Ltd:** Adam Day 236br; Andy Heading 243c; Steve White 249cbc; **Getty Images:** 48bcl, 100t, 114bcr, 154bl, 287tr; 94tr; **Dennis Gilbert:** 106tc; **Hulsta:** 70t; **Ideal Standard Ltd:** 72r; **The Image Bank/Getty Images:** 58; **Impact Photos:** Eliza Armstrong 115cr; John Arthur 190tl; Philip Achache 246t; **The Interior Archive:** Henry Wilson, Alfie's Market 114bl; Luke White, Architect: David Mikhail, 59tl; Simon Upton, Architect: Phillippe Starck, St Martins Lane Hotel 100bcr, 100br; **Jason Hawkes Aerial Photography:** 216t; **Dan Johnson:** 26cbl, 35r; **Kos Pictures Source:** 215cbl, 240tc, 240tr; David Williams 216b; **Lebrecht Collection:** Kate Mount 169bc; **MP Visual.com:** Mark Swallow 202t; **NASA:** 280cr, 280ccl, 281tl; **P&O Princess Cruises:** 214bl; **P A Photos:** 181br; **The Photographers' Library:** 186bl, 186bc, 186t; **Plain and Simple Kitchens:** 66t; **Powerstock Photolibrary:** 169tl, 256t, 287tc; **Rail Images:** 208c, 208 cbl, 209br; **Red Consultancy:** Odeon cinemas 257br; **Redferns:** 259br; Nigel Crane 259c; **Rex Features:** 106br, 259tc, 259tr, 259bl, 280b; Charles Ommaney 114tcr; J.F.F Whitehead 243cl; Patrick Barth 101tl; Patrick Frilet 189cbl; Scott Wiseman 287bl; **Royalty Free Images:** Getty Images/Eyewire 154bl; **Science & Society Picture Library:** Science Museum 202b; **Skyscan:** 168t, 182c, 298; Quick UK Ltd 212; **Sony:** 268bc; **Robert Streeter:** 154br; **Neil Sutherland:** 82tr, 83tl, 90t, 118, 188ctr, 196tl, 196tr, 299cl, 299bl; **The Travel Library:** Stuart Black 264t; **Travelex:** 97cl; **Vauxhall:** Technik 198t, 199tl, 199tr, 199cl, 199cr, 199ctcl, 199ctcr, 199tcl, 199tcr, 200; **View Pictures:** Dennis Gilbert, Architects: ACDP Consulting, 106t; Dennis Gilbert, Chris Wilkinson Architects, 209tr; Peter Cook, Architects: Nicholas Crimshaw and partners, 208t; **Betty Walton:** 185br; **Colin Walton:** 2, 4, 7, 9, 10, 28, 42, 56, 92, 95c, 99tl, 99tcl, 102, 116, 120t, 138t, 146, 150t, 160, 170, 191ctcl, 192, 218, 252, 260br, 260l, 261tr, 261c, 261cr, 271cbl, 271cbr, 271ctl, 278, 287br, 302, 401.

DK PICTURE LIBRARY:
Akhil Bahkshi; Patrick Baldwin; Geoff Brightling; British Museum; John Bulmer; Andrew Butler; Joe Cornish; Brian Cosgrove; Andy Crawford and Kit Hougton; Philip Dowell; Alistair Duncan; Gables; Bob Gathany; Norman Hollands; Kew Gardens; Peter James Kindersley; Vladimir Kozlik; Sam Lloyd; London Northern Bus Company Ltd; Tracy Morgan; David Murray and Jules Selmes; Musée Vivant du Cheval, France; Museum of Broadcast Communications; Museum of Natural History; NASA; National History Museum; Norfolk Rural Life Museum; Stephen Oliver; RNLI; Royal Ballet School; Guy Ryecart; Science Museum; Neil Setchfield; Ross Simms and the Winchcombe Folk Police Museum; Singapore Symphony Orchestra; Smart Museum of Art; Tony Souter; Erik Svensson and Jeppe Wikstrom; Sam Tree of Keygrove Marketing Ltd; Barrie Watts; Alan Williams; Jerry Young.

Additional Photography by Colin Walton.

Colin Walton would like to thank:
A&A News, Uckfield; Abbey Music, Tunbridge Wells; Arena Mens Clothing, Tunbridge Wells; Burrells of Tunbridge Wells; Gary at Di Marco's; Jeremy's Home Store, Tunbridge Wells; Noakes of Tunbridge Wells; Ottakar's, Tunbridge Wells; Selby's of Uckfield; Sevenoaks Sound and Vision; Westfield, Royal Victoria Place, Tunbridge Wells.